Revelation
Pentecostal Commentary

Pentecostal Commentary Series

Editor

John Christopher Thomas

Deo Publishing

REVELATION

Pentecostal Commentary

Rebecca Skaggs
and
Priscilla Benham

BLANDFORD FORUM

Pentecostal Commentary Series

Published by Deo Publishing
P.O. Box 6284, Blandford Forum, Dorset DT11 1AQ, UK

Copyright © 2009 Deo Publishing

All rights reserved. No part of this publication may be reproduced, translated, stored in a retrieval system, or transmitted in any form or by any means, electronic, mechanical, photocopying, recording or otherwise, without prior written permission from the publisher.

The Odyssea Greek font used in the publication of this work is available from Linguist's Software, Inc., www.linguistsoftware.com, P.O. Box 580, Edmonds, WA 98020-0580 USA, tel. (425) 775-1130.

Printed in the United Kingdom by Henry Ling Limited, at the Dorset Press, Dorchester, DT1 1HD

British Library Cataloguing-in-Publication data
A catalogue record for this book is available from the British Library

ISBN 978-1-905679-05-8

Contents

Editor's Preface vii
Author's Preface xi

Introduction 1
Literary Genre 1
Authorship 5
Date 8
Place of Composition 10
Audience 10
Interpretation of Revelation 11
Testimony of Jesus 16
The Holy Spirit 18

Revelation 1:1-8 19
Commentary 19
Reflection and Response (Part 1) 24

Revelation 1:9–3:22 26
The Commission: 1:9-20 26
The Churches: 2:1–3:22 31
The Church of Ephesus: 2:1-7 32
The Church of Smyrna: 2:8-11 35
The Church of Pergamum: 2:12-17 37
The Church of Thyatira: 2:18-28 41
The Church of Sardis: 3:1-6 44
The Church of Philadelphia: 3.7-13 47
The Church of Laodicea: 3.14-22 51
Reflection and Response (Part 2) 56

Revelation 4:1–5:14 58
Chapter 4 58
The Throne-Room: 4.1-11 58
Chapter 5 66
The Scroll: 5.1-4 66

Reflection and Response (Part 3) 73

Revelation 6:1–9:21 75
Chapter 6 75
Chapter 7 83
The 144,000 and the Great Multitude 83
Chapter 8 92
Chapter 9 98
Reflection and Response (Part 4) 104

Revelation 10:1–11:9 106
Chapter 10 106
The Little Scroll 106
Chapter 11 111
Measuring the Temple 111
The Two Witnesses 114
Reflection and Response (Part 5) 121

Revelation 12:1–19:21 123
Chapter 12 123
The Sun-Clothed Woman 123
The Testimony of Jesus 132
Chapter 13 133
The Two Beasts 133
Chapter 14 142
Chapters 15 and 16 155
Chapter 17 168
Chapter 18 181
Chapter 19 190
Reflection and Response (Part 6) 203

Revelation 20:1–22:21 205
Chapter 20 205
Gog and Magog 209
Chapter 21 213
Chapter 22 227
The Epilogue 232
Reflection and Response (Part 7) 237

Conclusion 239

Bibliography 241
Index of Names 249
Index of Biblical and Other References 252

Editor's Preface

The purpose of this commentary series is to provide reasonably priced commentaries written from a distinctively Pentecostal perspective primarily for pastors, lay persons, and Bible students. Therefore, while the works are based upon the best of scholarship, they are written in popular language. The aim is to communicate the meaning of the text, with minimal technical distractions.

In order to explain the need for such an attempt to read the biblical text, it is necessary to understand something of the ethos of Pentecostalism.

Pentecostalism is a relatively recent phenomenon in comparison to its Christian siblings, given that its formal origins go back about a hundred years. By any means of calculation it continues to grow very rapidly in many places around the globe and accounts for a not insignificant percentage of the world's Christians. Current estimates of those who would identify themselves as part of the Pentecostal-Charismatic movements range from 380,000,000 to 600,000,000. According to David Barrett, the global profile of Pentecostalism is as follows:

> Some 29 percent of all members worldwide are white, 71 percent are nonwhite. Members are more urban than rural, more female than male, more children (under eighteen years) than adults, more third-world (66 per cent) than western world (32 per cent), more living in poverty (87 per cent) than affluence (13 per cent), more family-related than individualist.[1]

Yet, despite its demographic significance, Pentecostalism continues to be largely misunderstood by many outside the movement. For example, there are those who '... see Pentecostalism as essentially fundamentalist Christianity with a doctrine of Spirit baptism and gifts added on' and others who view it '... as an experience which fits equally well in any spirituality or theological system – perhaps adding some needed

---

[1] D. Barrett, 'Statistics, Global', *Dictionary of the Pentecostal and Charismatic Movements* (S.M. Burgess and G.B. McGee, eds.; Grand Rapids: Zondervan, 1988), pp. 811.

zest or interest.'[2] Yet, those who know the tradition well are aware how far from the truth such assessments are. As Donald W. Dayton[3] and Steven J. Land[4] have demonstrated, standing at the theological heart of Pentecostalism is the message of the five-fold Gospel: Jesus is Savior, Sanctifier, Holy Spirit Baptizer, Healer, and Coming King. This paradigm not only identifies the theological heart of the tradition, but also immediately reveals the ways in which Pentecostalism as a movement is both similar to and dissimilar from others within Christendom. When the five-fold gospel paradigm is used as the main point of reference Pentecostalism's near kinship to the holiness tradition is obvious, as is the fundamental difference with many of those within the more reformed evangelical tradition. It also reveals the surprising similarities between Pentecostalism and the Roman Catholic and Orthodox traditions.

Therefore, the production of a Pentecostal Commentary Series representative of the tradition's ethos requires more that simply selecting contributors who have had a glossolalic experience. Rather, the process of composition as well as the physical format of the commentary should be in keeping with the ethos and spirituality of the tradition.

In the attempt to insure a writing process representative of the tradition, each contributor has been urged to incorporate the following disciplines in the writing of the commentary on a particular biblical book.

Writers have been encouraged to engage in prayer for this project, both as individuals and as members of a community of believers. Specifically, the guidance of the Holy Spirit has been sought in these times of prayer, for the leadership of the Spirit in interpretation is essential. Specific times of prayer where the body intercedes on the writer's behalf and seeks to hear from the Lord have been encouraged.

Given the Pentecostal commitment to body ministry, where various members of the body have specific calls and responsibilities, writers have been asked to explore ways in which their scholarship might be contextualized within their own local church body and thereby be strengthened by the dynamic interaction between the Holy Spirit, the body of Christ, and the Word of God. Writers were encouraged to covenant with their churches concerning this writing project in order to seek out their spiritual support. Where possible, writers were asked to explore the possibility of leading a group Bible study on the given

---

[2] Steven J. Land, *Pentecostal Spirituality: A Passion for the Kingdom* (JPTS 1; Sheffield: Sheffield Academic Press, 1993), p. 29.

[3] Donald W. Dayton, *The Theological Roots of Pentecostalism* (Peabody, MA: Hendrickson, 1991).

[4] Land, *Pentecostal Spirituality*.

biblical book. Ideally, such groups included representatives from each group of the target readership.

Writers were also encouraged to seek out the advice and critique of gifted colleagues who would join with them in this project so as not to work in isolation. This endeavor was conceived as too difficult and far reaching to go alone. Rather it is conceived of as part of the ministry of the body of Christ, for the glory of God.

The commentary attempts to be in keeping with the ethos and spirituality of the tradition in its physical format as well. Specifically, the commentaries seek to reflect the dialogical way in which the tradition tends to approach the biblical text. Thus, each commentary begins with a series of questions designed to lift up corporate and individual issues that are illuminated in the biblical book under examination. This section identifies those key issues that are taken up in the commentary which follows. As a hermeneutical task, this section invites the reader to interpret his/her life context in a confessional-critical manner, revealing the need(s) to be addressed by the text. Such an opening serves to contextualize the commentary in the life of the church from the very beginning and serves to teach the reader how the Bible can legitimately be used in contemporary life.

Flowing out of this initial section, the introduction proper seeks to inform the reader as to the need, process, purpose, time, and place of composition. As a trajectory of the initial section, the introduction proper seeks be a necessity for the reader, and seeks to avoid the strange and irrelevant discussions that introductions often pursue. The introductions normally include topics of special interest to Pentecostals along with the normal introductory matters of authorship, place of composition, destination, audience, date, and theological emphases. A rather detailed discussion of the genre and structure of the book forms the basis of organization for the exposition that follows. In addition, a section devoted to the book's teaching about the Holy Spirit is included in the introduction.

The commentary proper provides a running exposition on the text, provides extended comments on texts of special significance for Pentecostals, and acknowledges and interacts with major options in interpreting individual passages. It also provides periodic opportunities for reflection upon and personal response to the biblical text. The reflection and response components normally occur at the end of a major section of the book. Here, a theme prominent in a specific passage is summarized in the light of the reading offered in the commentary. Next, the readers encounter a series of questions designed to lead them in corporate and personal reflection about this dimension of the text. Finally, the readers are encouraged to respond to the biblical text in specific ways. Such reflection and response is consistent with the tradition's practice of not simply hearing the words of Scripture but responding to them in concrete ways. It is the literary equivalent to the altar call.

In the attempt not to overtax the popular reader footnotes have been used *carefully and sparingly*. However, when additional, more technical discussions are deemed necessary, they are be placed in the footnotes. In addition, Greek and Hebrew words are found only within parentheses or in the footnotes.

Every attempt has been made to insure that the constituency of the movement are represented in some way among the contributors. It is my hope and prayer that the work of these women and men, from a variety of continents, races, and communities, will aid the Pentecostal community (and other interested individuals and communities) in hearing the biblical text in new and authentic ways.

The General Editor

Preface

I was first introduced to the book of Revelation by my mother, Dr. Bebe H. Patten (Founder of Patten University and Pastor of Christian Cathedral for over 60 years). As a lover of God and Scripture, she passed on her fascination with Revelation to both my twin sister and myself. In particular, we grew up hearing about the intrigue and mystery of Revelation. As we grew and completed our doctoral studies in New Testament, we never lost our awe of this text. Priscilla was the first of us to accept the challenge of teaching Revelation at Patten College in 1985. She had the benefit of her doctoral study of apocalypticism (her dissertation was 'The Gospel of Mark in Light of Apocalyptic Literature', Drew University, 1976). Priscilla continued to teach Eschatology until her death in 2000.

Priscilla was overjoyed yet awed at the prospect of working on Revelation for the commentary series and diligently wrote until the day before her death. Indeed, the study of Revelation sustained her seven-year struggle with cancer. During the last year, she seemed to sense that time was running out and she would often study through the night. Her husband, Don Benham, was thoroughly supportive of her endeavors and spent considerable time editing and refining the manuscript.

Fortunately, when Priscilla passed away, she had completed the entire introductory section and the text through ch. 13 (almost two-thirds of the text). She had also prepared her notes to begin on ch. 14.

Dr. John Christopher Thomas, editor of this series and Professor of New Testament at the Church of God Seminary in Cleveland, TN, discussed with me alternatives as to what should be done with the remainder of the text. With some trepidation (on the part of Dr. Thomas), and fear and trembling (on my part) we agreed that I could complete what Priscilla had begun. This was an awesome undertaking, yet one I felt compelled to try. In short, these last three and a half years, which I have spent completing this task, has shown me that the more I study Revelation, the more I stand in awe before the majesty, mystery, and grandeur of this text. Indeed, it has been almost an overwhelming task, but one which helped me through the darkest time of my life – the death of my twin.

Priscilla's section (Introduction, chs. 1-13) is as she wrote it except for a few 'touches' which refined or explicated a point. At these times, I could almost hear her saying to me, 'Rebec, fix that. Be sure it's as good as possible!' I want to express my appreciation to Dr. Thomas for allowing me the opportunity to complete Priscilla's work, and also for treating her work with such respect so that it could appear as close as possible to her original work. I also want to thank Esther Carlson who with loving devotion typed this manuscript from my rough drafts. Without her meticulous effort, this book would have been more overwhelming. I also want to thank my dear friend and colleague, Father Thomas Doyle, for his invaluable hours 'haranguing' through theories with me. Finally, I want to thank my husband, John, who inexhaustibly supported me through alternative theories, rewrites, frustrations and the final joy of completion.

Most of all, I thank God for allowing both Priscilla and me to have the opportunity to work on this text. I hope that the readers to come will find the joy and peace, encouragement and hope available in this text.

This manuscript does not seek to be the 'last word' on the interpretive challenges of Revelation. Hopefully, however, it will elucidate some of the more formidable issues and thereby encourage the reader to approach the text more readily.

I urge my readers to let the text challenge and perhaps change them. Most of all, I pray that as you study, may you, like all of us before you, hear the message of Revelation – God is in control, worship him!

Introduction

Where do we go after death? What happens to us physically and spiritually? Which factors influence our destiny? What will happen to the world in years to come? Is there a God, a controlling force in human destiny, or is life a product of random occurrences, of chance? Is there a divine plan to the universe? Should there be distinctions between the ethically, morally righteous who are persecuted and suffer while the wicked seem to prosper? Is there justice in the universe?

These questions and others like them have been addressed by people such as the ancient Sumerians, Babylonians, and Greeks to the present. Some have sought to explain the journeys of the soul after death by legendary folklore or philosophic logic, while others have attempted to abandon the idea of the afterlife altogether. The book of Revelation seeks to answer many of these questions. Since however it is one of the more difficult of the New Testament books to read and interpret, it is often overlooked and neglected by today's Christians. Yet it addresses many prophetic issues which are important for the one seeking to understand God's plan for the future. Filled with symbolism and visions of heaven, angels, beasts, earthly turmoil and destruction, this book can provide hope that God will overcome evil and that he does control human destiny.

Before looking at the text of Revelation itself it is important that one understands the context of the book: its genre, authorship, date, recognition by the early church, and purpose for its original readers. Some of the major methods of interpretation and their implications will also be discussed. Hopefully these discussions will form a background which will be helpful when one analyzes the text itself.

Literary Genre

The opening verses of Revelation suggest that the book falls into three literary genres: apocalyptic literature, prophecy, and a circular letter.[1]

---

[1] See Richard Bauckham, *The Theology of the Book of Revelation* (Cambridge–New York: Cambridge University Press, 1993), p. 1.

An understanding of some of the particular characteristics of each can help one understand the nature and content of this book.

The term 'apocalyptic' means 'revelatory' and generally refers to a body of Jewish and Christian literature written primarily between 250 BCE–100 CE.[2] These writers attempted to deal with important issues by recording their visionary experiences which had been communicated to them by God. The books of *4 Ezra*, *2 Baruch* and *2 Enoch* are examples of such apocalyptic literature. Old Testament books such as Daniel and parts of Isaiah, Ezekiel and Zechariah are also considered to be apocalyptic.

Christian apocalyptic literature was written in the first century CE, and Revelation is usually put into this category. Even the Synoptic Gospels reflect apocalyptic concerns. For example, the disciples ask Jesus when the end will come and about the signs leading to it (Mk 13:4). Also apocalyptic questions are raised in the Pauline and General Epistles (e.g. 1 Thess. 4:13; 2 Thess. 2; 2 Pet. 2:4; 3:4).

Apocalyptic writings, which include a wide variety of forms, incorporate symbolic utterances, visions, blessings, wisdom sayings, sacred sayings, and paraenetic teaching. The account is presented in the form of a vision or rapture experience and is usually pseudonymous, that is, written under the name of an ancient spiritual person (e.g. Enoch, Ezra, Baruch, or Moses).

The apocalyptic message involves such ideas as time and history, angels and demons, the messianic kingdom, and life after death. In this literature the secrets of the world beyond are disclosed to a prophet-like figure and interpreted by a divine agent. Answers are given to such issues as 'why do the righteous suffer?' (*4 Ezra*), 'when will the end time be?' (*2 Baruch*), and 'what is God's plan for his people?' (Daniel).[3]

The origin of apocalyptic concepts is difficult to determine. Some trace their roots to foreign ideas found in Babylonia and Persia. For example, when Israel experienced extreme persecution during the Seleucid oppression (200–100 BCE), the Jewish prophets were stimulated to look for answers with regard to God's justice, judgment and his vindication of the righteous in the future. There was also a need for

---

[2] D.S. Russell, *Prophecy and the Apocalyptic Dream: Protest and Promise* (Peabody, MA: Hendrickson, 1994), p. 2.

[3] For information on apocalyptic characteristics, see D.S. Russell, *The Method and Message of Jewish Apocalyptic, 200 BC–AD 100* (Philadelphia: Westminster, 1964), pp. 88-89; J.J. Collins, *The Apocalyptic Imagination: An Introduction to the Jewish Matrix of Christianity*, New York: Crossroad, 1984; idem, 'The Genre Apocalypse in Hellenistic Judaism', in *Apocalypticism*, ed. D. Hellholm, 531-48.

secrecy. Therefore, writers tended to cloak in symbolic code the message of divine retribution, perhaps because of fear.[4]

Apocalyptic literature can also be seen as a continuation of Jewish prophecy, an expression of folklore, esoteric rabbinic literature, or as a product of the wisdom tradition, where symbolic language was accepted as a divine means of communicating a message. The fact that it was difficult to interpret only heightened the idea that one cannot easily understand God.[5]

The second literary genre as suggested in Rev. 1:1–3 is prophecy. Prophecy was usually presented in two forms: (a) oracles given publicly, and (b) visions which were received by a prophet privately and then passed on to the people.[6] Traditional Jewish prophecy is usually concerned with ethical behavior and social justice, the lack of which brings God's judgments, and/or restoration of God's nation Israel. Prophecy invariably incorporates a call to repentance.

Apocalyptic literature and Jewish prophecy are widely thought to be related, and it is possible to view apocalyptic literature as an outgrowth of Jewish prophecy.[7] The apocalyptist expanded the scope of prophecy to encompass a broader concept of time and space than previously known, the belief in a future life, the expectation of a new heaven and earth, and the catastrophic end of the present world. These are eschatological themes which were no doubt developed to meet spiritual needs during times of persecution and social turmoil.[8] As people faced unbearable circumstances, which often included martyrdom, their

---

[4] Russell, *Prophecy and the Apocalyptic Dream*, pp. 11-16, describes three 'pressure points' which brought about the rise of apocalyptic literature: (1) a corrupt society; (2) the strong influence of Hellenism; and (3) the determined effort of the Jewish people to believe in visions of a better world in which God would bring deliverance and vindication of the righteous. (Some of the mystical code such as symbolism, and numerology, may have been borrowed from the eastern people.)

[5] See R. Sturm, 'Defining the Word Apocalyptic' in *Apocalyptic and the New Testament: Essays in Honor of J. Louis Martyn*, ed. Joel Marcus and Marion L. Soards (Sheffield: JSOT Press, 1989), pp. 25-26, for a historical survey of recent scholarship. Some scholars have shown the relationship between theological themes within Judaism while others stressed the connection to mythology. Some biblical scholars have begun to define apocalyptic in terms of theological content. This approach includes the fact that the concept 'the Kingdom of God' was an eschatological, apocalyptic one.

In addition, George Wesley Buchanan, *The Book of Revelation: Its Introduction and Prophecy* (MBCNT 22; Lewiston, NY: E. Mellen, 1993), pp. 4-14, shows that the Jewish thought forms and literary patterns found in Revelation are themes based on financial metaphors, cyclical patterns, sabbatical rules, and eschatological terminology common to first-century Judaism.

[6] Russell, *Prophecy and the Apocalyptic Dream*, pp. 19-30, outlines similarities and differences of prophecy and apocalypse.

[7] Paul D. Hanson, *The Dawn of Apocalyptic* (Philadelphia: Fortress Press, 1975), p. 12.

[8] Harold H. Rowley, *The Relevance of Apocalyptic* (London: Lutterworth, 1944), p. 15.

minds turned to hopes for God's vengeance and the emergence of a new social order where righteousness would reign.

It is most likely that many of the distinctions currently made between apocalyptic concepts and prophecy would not have been made by John, who saw himself as standing in the prophetic tradition and calls his book 'the Apocalypse'. He also calls his book a prophecy (1:3, 22:7), writes in his own name, emphasizes ethical and moral considerations, alludes to Hebrew scripture, insists on monotheism, and describes a coming Kingdom. One should therefore consider the book of Revelation to be a 'prophetic apocalypse' or an 'apocalyptic prophecy'.[9] As such, John's book stands in the apocalyptic tradition in two broad ways. First, it discloses a transcendent perspective of the world and helps his audience see the divine purpose in life's situations. The apocalyptic dimension is also seen in the fact that John is taken out of the world and given visions to see the heavenly secrets. The apocalyptic motifs of secrets, angels, visions, symbols, etc., help to reveal the transcendent world. Second, John's book shares with other apocalyptists the questions, 'Who is Lord over all the world?', 'Why do the righteous suffer?' and 'When will God bring judgment to the wicked?'

Revelation is, finally, a letter. Unlike most other apocalyptic or prophetic books, the Apocalypse is a letter written to specific destinations. The author's audience and purpose are all mentioned in the opening verses. Then seven specific letters are given to individual churches (chs. 2, 3). The letters to the churches form an introduction to the book, incorporating words of commendation and warning. The body of the book (chs. 4–22) may have been intended for many churches throughout Asia Minor. In fact, even the seven specifically named churches may be representative of the 'church universal'.[10]

In summary, the book of Revelation actually reflects traits of three literary genres:[11] apocalyptic literature, prophetic literature, and the letter. Readers in the late first century CE would be familiar with all of these types of literature and be able to respond to the message as one which God sent to fortify and encourage the church to endure in a time of political and social stress. The Jewish ethical demands of obedience are combined with the prophetic message of God's salvation and

---

[9] Bauckham, p. 6; cf. George E. Ladd, 'Why Not Prophetic-Apocalyptic?' *JBL* 76 (1957), pp. 192-200.

[10] See Bauckham, pp. 16-17, for the theory that the number seven means perfection. This number may be a symbolic suggestion that the book is to all churches and to these particularly as representatives. Also, note Rev. 2:7,11,17,29; 3:6,13,22, which are invitations to *all* readers.

[11] Buchanan, pp. 638-40, suggests that Revelation should fit into the category of 'redemption literature', a genre which 'includes many kinds of midrashic literary expression'. He distinguishes this genre from the general apocalyptic genre.

judgment. The apocalyptic symbolic motifs heighten an eschatological message which is presented in a form familiar to the church – the letter. In this letter form, it would be circulated and read among the churches of Asia Minor.

Authorship

As with any New Testament writing, one must consider both internal evidence (data given within the text) and external evidence (data given by early church tradition) with regard to the issue of authorship. This issue is particularly important for the book of Revelation since a dominant characteristic of apocalyptic literature is that the author writes under an assumed name.

In the Apocalypse the author writes under his own name, John (Rev. 1:1,4,9; 22:8), a significant difference from other apocalyptic books. The writer also classifies himself as a prophet (22:9) and refers to his work as prophecy (1:3; 22:7,10,18,19). This suggests that the author was well known in his circle as an authoritative figure who could deliver such a prophetic message in his own name. But who is this 'John'?

External evidence (the early Church fathers' writings) gives us some clues. Papias (120–130 CE) of Hierapolis, was one of the earliest writers to show an acquaintance with Revelation. According to Andreas, Bishop of Caesarea in Cappadocia, Papias referred to John the disciple as its author (Andreas, *Comm. in Apoc.*, quotes Papias). An equally significant attestation (Charles dates the writing about 135 CE)[12] is Justin Martyr (d. 165 CE). He held that John the Apostle was the author (*Dial. with Trypho*, 81.15); Eusebius (*Hist. Eccl.* IV 18) supports this by commenting on Justin's reference to the authorship of the apostle. Both Irenaeus, Rome (d. circa 202) and Tertullian, North Africa, (d. circa 220) quoted it often, referring to Revelation as Scripture and as the work of the Apostle John.[13] Also, the *Shepherd of Hermas*, 2nd century (Rome), shows a dependence on Rev. 7:14 using similar imagery (*Vision*, II 2,5,7; III 6). Later, the Muratorian Canon included it as a work of John the disciple. Hippolytus of Rome (d. circa 256; *Antichrist*, 36, 50), accepted it as Scripture and, in fact, defended its authorship against Dionysus. In Alexandria, Clement (d. circa 220), *Paed.* II 119, *Quis Div. Salv.* 42, *Strom.* VI 106-107; Origen (d. circa 254), *Comm. in Joh.*, 11.5; and Athanasius (d. circa 373), attested to the authorship of the Apostle John, as did Augustine (d. circa 430) and the

---

[12] Robert H. Charles, *The Apocrypha and Pseudepigrapha of the Old Testament in English*, I (Oxford: Clarendon, c1913, 1973), p. xxxvii, n. 2.

[13] Irenaeus, *Adv. haer.* IV, 14.1; 17.6; 18.6; 21.3; 28.2; 34.2; Tertullian, *Adv. Marc.* III, 14.24.

Council of Carthage (367 CE). One of the Gnostic documents found in Egypt in 1945 also lends valuable support to the authorship of John the Apostle: the *Apocryphon of John* (dated by some as early as 150 CE) cites Rev. 1:19 as written by 'John the brother of James, these who are the sons of Zebedee'. Hence, the authorship of Revelation was attributed to John the Apostle by an early date and was also acknowledged throughout a wide geographical region.

The Johannine authorship of Revelation was first seriously challenged by Marcion in the second century, followed by Dionysus from Alexandria (d. circa 264; cf. Eusebius, *Hist. Eccl.* V 2.25). Mostly for theological and linguistic reasons, the arguments put forward by Dionysus were significant enough to influence the renowned biblical scholar and historian Eusebius from Caesarea.[14] Dionysus's arguments are similar to those used by scholars today to refute apostolic authorship.

The major problem in the question of authorship involves internal concerns. These are particularly obvious when Revelation is compared with the Gospel of John: the Greek of the Apocalypse is rougher and less polished than that of the Gospel, and there are irregular uses of participles, broken sentence constructions, addition of unnecessary pronouns, confusion of genders, numbers and cases. Also, there is relatively little Johannine vocabulary and apostolic language.

There are a variety of solutions to the linguistic issue. First, the Apocalypse may have been written at an earlier date than the Gospel, which reflects an improvement of the author's use of Greek. Second, the influence of apocalyptic language taken from Old Testament models may account for the different uses of the Greek language in the Apocalypse. Finally, the Apostle John may have used an amanuensis (a secretary) for the writing of the Gospel. This latter suggestion is a good possibility. It would account for the polish of the Gospel's language in contrast to that of the Apocalypse, which may have been written in John's own hand.

It seems quite clear that the Greek of Revelation is closer to other Johannine books than to any other New Testament writings. This close affinity can be seen in common terminology: Christ is called 'logos' in the personal sense (Jn 1:1; Rev. 19:13), He is described as a

---

[14] Eusebius, *Hist. Eccl.* IV 18, lists the Apocalypse with both the acknowledged and spurious works. Ned Bernard Stonehouse, *The Apocalypse in the Ancient Church* (Goes, Netherlands: Oosterbann & Le Cointre, 1929), p. 133, comments on the significance of Eusebius's attitude: 'Now this hesitating attitude can only mean that Eusebius was at odds with the Church. Personally, he is quite ready to classify it with the spurious works, but in deference to its acceptance as canonic not only in the West, but also by the leading teachers of the East, including Origen, he places it also among the disputed books.'

lamb (28 times in Rev. and in Jn 1:29,36, although different Greek words are used), and as a shepherd (Jn 10:11,14). The author makes a symbolic allusion to manna (Jn 6:13f.; Rev. 2:17). The dualistic themes so common to the Gospel of John can also be seen in the Apocalypse: e.g. light and darkness, truth and falsehood, good and evil, God and Satan. Another significant common feature is the theme of the number seven.

Although the internal linguistic problems pose some evidence against Johannine authorship, and there are a variety of possible writers, there are no conclusive alternatives. Other possibilities of authorship include: (1) one of the Johannine group who wrote in the style of John, (2) John the Elder, as mentioned in 2 or 3 John,[15] (3) John the Baptist and his followers,[16] (4) another Jewish Christian, John, leader of the church in the late first century, who transcribed a prophetic book brought to him by the Angelos, a fellow servant of the Lord (Rev. 1:1),[17] and (5) John Mark, suggested by Dionysus, who later rejected the option himself.

In conclusion, it must be acknowledged that early external evidence favors Johannine authorship. Even internal evidence, although more dubious, shows the Apocalypse to have more affinity with the Gospel of John than with any other New Testament writing. Finally, there is no general consensus for another alternative.

For these reasons, I take the position of Johannine authorship. John, disciple of Jesus, was the son of Zebedee, brother of James, and a fisherman who lived near the Sea of Galilee (Mk 1:19,20). The family may have enjoyed some social status, for they had hired servants (Mk 1:20), and John was known to the high priest's house (Jn 18:15). He was a disciple of John the Baptist (Jn 1:35) and with Andrew was among the first to meet Jesus as their future leader. John is included with the Twelve throughout the Gospels and, as a member of the Inner Circle (Peter, James and John), witnessed the Transfiguration and the agony in the Garden (Mk 9:2; Mt. 26:36-37). John is mentioned in Acts: he is in the Upper Room (Acts 1:13); he is with Peter, who heals the lame man (Acts 3:1-10), and he is a member of the Church Council at Jerusalem (Gal. 2:9).

Tradition suggests that John later lived in Ephesus, ministering to the churches of Asia Minor. Eusebius says he was banished to Patmos by Domitian around 95 CE and was released by Nerva 18 months later

---

[15] For this option, see John Christopher Thomas, *1,2,3 John* (PCS; London: T&T Clark International, 2004), pp. 6-9.

[16] Argued by J. Massyngberde Ford, *Revelation* (Anchor Bible; New York: Doubleday, 1975), pp. 28-37.

[17] Buchanan, pp. 646-47.

(Eusebius, *Hist. Eccl.* III 20.8-9). He died a peaceful death in Ephesus, where there is a grave attributed to him.[18] The Gospel of John and three Epistles are attributed to this apostle (though some question the authenticity of 2 and 3 John).

John is presented in the Gospels as faithful to Jesus even during the Passion events, and he is described in his Gospel as 'the disciple whom Jesus loved'. His writings reflect a deep understanding of the divine/human nature of Jesus as well as a clear concept of Jesus' mission of salvation. Some suggest that this background would make John 'worthy' to fill the prophetic role of receiving the message of Revelation.

Date

Two of the more prominent options for the date of the Apocalypse's composition are, (a) during Domitian's reign 95-100 CE, and (b) during or just after Nero's reign, 64-70 CE. Again, internal and external evidence can provide some clues.

Domitian's Reign: 95–100 CE

Evidence for this position is as follows: First, the condition of the churches as described in Revelation 2 and 3 suggests this later date: (a) Ephesus had lost its 'first love', which is usually associated with the lapse of the original evangelistic fervor over a period of time. (b) The Nicolaitans are described as a well-established and influential sect, which would be possible by 95 CE. (c) Laodicea is described as a prosperous city. This city was devastated by an earthquake around 62 CE, and by 95 CE would have regained its stature. (d) Polycarp's letter to the Philippians suggests that the church at Smyrna, described in Rev. 2:8, may not have existed prior to 60-64 CE.[19]

Second, the description of persecution reflected in Revelation suggests the Emperor Domitian's reign.[20] Under Domitian, persecution of the Christians was sporadic but widespread throughout the Roman Empire and was for religious reasons. In contrast, persecution under Nero was primarily in the city of Rome, where the Christians were blamed for the burning of the city.

---

[18] There are actually two tombs attributed to John: cf. Everett F. Harrison, *Introduction to the New Testament* (Grand Rapids, MI: Eerdmans, 1964), p. 457.

[19] Cf. Charles, *Apocrypha*, I, p. xciv; David E. Aune, *Revelation 1-5* (Word Biblical Commentary 52a; Dallas, TX: Word, 1997), p. lvii.

[20] See Donald Guthrie, *New Testament Introduction. Hebrews to Revelation* (Downers Grove, IL: InterVarsity Press, 1970), p. 953; and Merrill C. Tenney, *New Testament Times* (Grand Rapids, MI: Eerdmans, 1957), pp. 949-63, for a description of persecution under each emperor.

Finally, allusions in the Church fathers to this later date suggest that Revelation was written around 95 CE. Irenaeus, writing about 180 CE, *Adv. haer* V 30.3 (d. circa 202) says of the Revelation, 'It was seen not very long ago, almost in our own generation, at the close of the reign of Domitian'. Eusebius follows Irenaeus and clearly states that 'under him [Domitian], the Apostle John is banished to Patmos and sees his Apocalypse, as Irenaeus mentions' (Eusebius, *Chronicle*, quoted by Aune, p. lix. Aune discusses the Church fathers' references at some length). Also, Victorinus refers to John on the island of Patmos, condemned by Domitian.[21]

Nero's Reign: 64-70 CE

Arguments for this date are as follows: First, Jerusalem is mentioned (ch. 11) as though it is still standing. Second, the description of the sequence of kings in 17:9-11 'one who was and is not' may refer to Nero, who, according to legend, did not die and was expected to return. (A slight variation is the rumor that Vespasian was Nero reincarnated.) Third, the number of the beast coincides with the numerical value of the Hebrew characters for Nero Caesar. (It should be observed, however, that Domitian's abbreviated title can also yield this numerical value.) Fourth, the early date would account for the rough Greek which the author improved by the time of the writing of the Gospel, assuming the Gospel was written *after* the Revelation.[22]

---

[21] Irenaeus, *Adv Haer.* V 30.3; II 22.5; III 4.4. These last two passages are quoted by Eusebius (*Hist. Eccl.* III 23.3-4); Victorinus in *Apoc.* X 11; XVII 10; see also Albert A. Bell, 'The Date of John's Apocalypse' *NTS* 25 (1978), pp. 93-102; Charles, *Apocrypha* I, p. xciv.

[22] Buchanan, p. 638. The question of sources for the book of Revelation is an area of disagreement between scholars and is related to the question of authorship and date. The traditional view held for many years was: one source, one author. Researchers emphasized the symmetry of the book, the plan which seems to pervade the writing, and the dramatic sequence, which suggests more than a mere collection of documents. Others, however, are quick to show the variations in descriptions of certain events or groups (e.g., the 144,000 are described differently in separate references), and certain details which seem to point to different dates (e.g. ch. 11 implies the Temple was still standing and the beast of ch. 13 may describe Domitian). The solutions are many and varied: some suggest two basic sources, both by the same author, but written at different times. These scholars show that the introduction and conclusion are different than the rest of the book and conclude they must have been written later and joined to the book. Buchanan argues that the Apocalypse is an anthology written by different authors at different times and was put together by an editor, the contents unified by the subject matter. He argues that as such, Revelation fits into redemptive literature, which includes many kinds of midrashic literary expression. Massyngberde Ford suggests that parts of the book reflect John the Baptist's perspective and were therefore written early and later joined to form Revelation.

In conclusion, the description of the churches, the character of the persecution, and the witness of the Fathers are key historical factors which play an important role in determining the date of the Apocalypse. These seem to suggest that the author, John the disciple, wrote the final form of Revelation around 95–100 CE. In his own hand he made use of Hebrew scripture, apocalyptic imagery, and visions of his own conveyed by the Spirit to construct a message of hope to persecuted Christians.

Place of Composition

The island of Patmos is located off the coast of Asia Minor in the Aegean Sea, about 28 miles south of Samos. It is approximately ten miles long, six miles wide, and was described by the Roman historian Pliny as about thirty miles in circumference.[23] The land is barren and rocky with an irregular coastline. It is made of volcanic hills, one of which rises to 800 feet, and is shaped like a horse's head. In the time of John, Patmos was a place to which political prisoners were sent by the Romans. Eusebius mentions that in the fourteenth year of Domitian's reign John was exiled there. According to tradition he was released during Nerva's reign.[24]

Audience

The book itself names its readers as the seven churches (Rev. 1:4; 2:1–3:14), so there is little debate as to the original intended audience. The seven churches of Asia (Ephesus, Smyrna, Pergamum, Thyatira, Sardis, Philadelphia and Laodicea) are located on an important circular postal route in Asia Minor and represent the most populous and influential part of the province.[25] The author probably wrote to these particular churches as centers of communications for the rest of Asia Minor.

Asia Minor was an important area for early church expansion. According to the Acts of the Apostles, it was evangelized by Priscilla and Aquilla (Acts 18:18,19), Apollos (18:24–28), and Paul, who is said to have ministered there for over two and one-half years (19:1–41). Tradition says that the Apostle John also lived and worked in Ephesus.

---

[23] Pliny, *Hist. Nat.* 4.69-70.
[24] Tacitus, *The Annals of Imperial Rome*, IV 30; Eusebius, *Hist. Eccl.* III 18-20. See also Irenaeus, *Adv. Haer.* V 30.3; *Dio Cassius*, 68.1.
[25] See W.M. Ramsay, *The Letters to the Seven Churches of Asia* (Grand Rapids, MI: Baker Book House, 1904, 1963). p. 132; Edwin M. Yamauchi, *The Archaeology of New Testament Cities in Western Asia Minor* (Grand Rapids, MI: Baker Book House, 1980), pp. 30-161, for details on the archaeology, geography and sociology of the cities.

The members of the seven churches were most likely Hellenistic Jews and Greeks (Acts 19:10,17). In the early days of their founding, these churches experienced salvation, baptism, outpouring of the Holy Spirit, miracles and exorcisms. Magicians gave up their practice and people abandoned worship of their ethnic goddess Artemis to embrace Christianity (Acts 19).

The Asian churches were active in ministry, for Paul in his letter to the Ephesians refers to the callings (offices) God gave: apostles, prophets, evangelists, pastors and teachers (Eph. 4:11). By the time Revelation was written these churches were faced with a variety of problems (Rev. 2; 3): persecution (e.g. Smyrna, Pergamum), false teaching (Pergamum, Thyatira) and loss of religious fervor (Ephesus, Sardis). Confronted by these conflicts, many church members persevered (2:3,24; 3:4), some were martyred (2:13), some compromised with heathen practices (2:14,20), and some lapsed into indifference (2:4).[26] To these churches the prophetic/apocalyptic message was sent to encourage perseverance and enhance hope for a future vindication of God's triumph over evil.

Interpretation of Revelation

There are several schools of interpretation of the Apocalypse, and within each view there are many variations. The following is a brief summary of the four prevailing views:

1. *The Preterist view.* In this view, the Apocalypse was written to the church of the first century only. Its message grew out of the Roman Empire's political scene and the conditions within the church of that day. Therefore, the book was exceedingly meaningful for its immediate audience. As W.G. Kümmel says: 'The apocalypse is a book of its time, written out of its time and for its time, not for the distant generations of the future or even of the end time.'[27]

2. *The Historical view.* The Historists propose that the Apocalypse is a prophecy of the entire human race. The symbols have meaning for human destiny until the second coming of Christ. Several problems emerge, however. Many who hold this position ignore the importance of the message for its original first century audience except to show God's control in history. They show that the churches of Rev. 2; 3 represent periods of church history, and they tend to equate scripture with particular historical events in Western Europe from 100 CE to the

---

[26] See Pliny's letter to Emperor Trajan describing this church era in Merrill C. Tenney, *New Testament Times*, p. 329.

[27] W.G. Kummel, *The New Testament: The History of the Investigation of Its Problems* (New York: Abingdon, 1972), p. 324.

present, to the exclusion of the rest of the world. Finally, most Historists disagree as to which specific historical events match the scriptural descriptions, and they tend to adjust the timeline to their own generation as the 'last times'.

3. *The Futurist view*. The Futurists argue that the book is concerned primarily with the future end times and that it has little relevance for the church in the first century, in fact for the church at large, until the end of the age.

4. *The Idealistic view*. The Idealists tend to interpret the Apocalypse allegorically, as primarily concerned with ideas and principles, rather than set in a particular historical framework. Proponents of this view tend to ignore the literal events of an 'end time'.[28]

It seems that one's understanding of Revelation is enhanced by using elements of each view. Because of the multifaceted nature of the text, one begins to grasp the book's complexity by considering as many perspectives as possible. It is essential to have an adequate knowledge of the religious, political, historical, and social conditions of John's time and recognize that the message was read and understood by the early church. An accurate understanding of the situation in John's day can help one interpret the content of the book. One must, however, see and hear the message for the future for Revelation to have meaning for the contemporary church.

One of the critical issues in these methods of interpretation has to do with the extent to which the text should be interpreted allegorically or literally. Therefore, it is important to understand these terms.

The allegorical method interprets a literary text in a more 'spiritual' sense. It looks for the deeper, more profound meaning of the text and is concerned primarily with the larger principles set forth rather than the exact meaning of specific words and historical details. For example, the allegorist looks for timeless symbols in Revelation, seeing the book as a theological, poetic expression of how God acts throughout history. If this method is used exclusively there is often no specific historical fulfillment anticipated. The narrated events function primarily as parables and metaphors to convey spiritual comfort to readers.

In the literal approach, scholars tend to look for the exact meaning of words and the historical–political context to interpret the text. Symbolic language does exist and must be interpreted as figurative speech. The danger of this method is that one can sometimes attempt to find literal historical meaning to the exclusion of the larger message.

---

[28] For more discussion on these positions, see Leon Morris, *The Book of Revelation* (rev. ed.; Tyndale New Testament Commentary series 20; Downers Grove, IL: InterVarsity Press, 1987), pp. 17-24, and Dwight J. Pentecost, *Things to Come* (Grand Rapids, MI: Zondervan, 1964), chs. 1 and 2.

In recent times the tendency has been to blend the allegorical and literal methods of interpretation. For example, Alan Johnson says that one must pay attention to the historical situation of early Christianity in order to understand the book of Revelation, but that the message should encourage all Christians of all ages. While John does describe the final judgment and the physical return of Christ to the world, he also describes the deeper realities of the conflict of Christ and Satan.

Johnson comments:

> Revelation may then be viewed, on the one hand, as an extended commentary on Paul's statement in Ephesians 6:12: 'For our struggle is not against flesh and blood, but against the rulers, against the authorities, against the powers of the world and against the spiritual forces of evil in the heavenly realms.' On the other hand, it also reveals the final judgment upon evil and the consummation of God's Kingdom in time and eternity.[29]

The present study will examine the words, context and historical background of the text in order to understand the message the author was conveying to his audience. At the same time, I recognize the abundance of symbolic material and figurative speech in the book. Therefore, I will attempt to determine the meaning of the symbols in their immediate context and their meaning for John's message as a whole. Taking a modified historical–grammatical approach, then, I will interpret the text literally unless it does not make sense to do so.

Once I have determined the meaning of John's message to his audience, I will attempt to determine the relevance of the book for contemporary church history. I recognize that John does describe events which will be fulfilled at the end of the age.[30] At the same time, Revelation is written to encourage Christians of all ages as they face times of persecution, for Christ will ultimately triumph over evil Satanic forces.

Symbol/Figurative Language

Figurative or symbolic language is used often in the book of Revelation. In fact, it is one of the major characteristics of apocalyptic literature. Heightening the intensity of the message, it adds nuances which

---

[29] Alan F. Johnson, *Revelation* (The Expositor's Bible Commentary Series with the New International Version of the Holy Bible 12; Grand Rapids, MI: Zondervan, 1981), pp. 410-11.

[30] Robert H. Mounce, *The Book of Revelation* (New International Commentary on the New Testament 17; Grand Rapids, MI: Eerdmans, 1977), pp. 44-45, holds a similar position. He says, 'It will be better to hold that the predictions of John, while expressed in terms reflecting his own culture, will find their final and complete fulfillment in the last days of history'. See also George R. Beasley-Murray, *The Book of Revelation* (New Century Bible Commentary 56; Grand Rapids, MI: Eerdmans, 1974).

embellish the text far beyond that which could be conveyed in normal speech.

Two major issues are to be considered in interpreting material figuratively. First, one must determine what material is to be interpreted figuratively. Second, one must determine how to interpret the symbols. A simple approach is to take everything literally unless it does not make sense to do so.[31] Metaphors, similes, 'signs', or animals are usually obvious as figurative speech and therefore would be interpreted as symbols.

The symbols/figures in Revelation generally fall into one of three categories.[32] First, some symbols are explained in the text's context. For example, the seven stars (1:20) are the angels of the churches, the seven lampstands (1:20) are the seven churches of Asia, the great dragon (12:9) is Satan, the Devil, and the seven heads of the beast (17:9) are seven mountains. Some symbols are taken from Old Testament imagery, for example, the Tree of Life (2:7, 22:2), the hidden manna (2:17), the living creatures (4:7) and the beast (ch. 13). An interpretation should therefore take into account their Old Testament meaning. Finally there are symbols which can be interpreted from a background knowledge of secular and apocalyptic literature. These include the white stone (2:17), the pillar (3:12), the winepress (14:20, 19:15), and the Lake of Fire (19:20).

As one seeks to interpret a symbol one must understand the context, the background of the image (similar uses in Old Testament, apocalyptic, or other literature) and the sense or meaning of the figure for the original reader. The sense of the figure should help develop and support the message of the book itself; a figure should not stand by itself.

Literary Structure

The book of Revelation opens with the phrase 'The Revelation of Jesus Christ'. This could mean the revelation of the person Jesus himself, or of the revelation which he gave. In either case, Jesus Christ is the central figure. The following outline helps to identify the book's literary structure based on the work of this central figure.[33]

> Prologue: Christ Communicating 1:1–8
> Vision I: Christ in the Church 1:9–3:22
> Vision II: Christ in the Cosmos 4:1–16:21
> Vision III: Christ in Conquest 17:1–21:8
> Vision IV: Christ in Consummation 21:9–22:5
> Epilogue: Christ Challenging 22:6-21

---

[31] Pentecost, p. 40.
[32] Merrill C. Tenney, *Interpreting Revelation* (Grand Rapids, MI: Eerdmans, 1980), p. 186.
[33] Tenney, p. 33.

These divisions are based on a recurring phrase 'in the Spirit', e.g. 'I was in the Spirit on the Lord's Day' (1:10), 'Straightway I was in the Spirit...' (4:2), 'And he carried me away in the Spirit...' (17:3; 21:10). The sections include a variety of materials and are of unequal length. They provide a progression and change of geographical location.

Significant Words and Phrases

Numbers are important in apocalyptic literature. In the book of Revelation the number seven predominates: there are seven of each of these: candlesticks, churches, spirits of God, seals, trumpets, bowls, persons and new things. Other numbers that appear are 24 elders (4:4), four living creatures (4:6), four horsemen (6:1–8), four angels (9:14), 144,000 (7:4; 14:1,3), twelve gates of the city of God (21:12), twelve foundations (21:14), twelve kinds of fruit in the tree of life (22:2).

Several phrases recur: one phrase is 'there were lightnings, voices, and thunders', found in 4:5, 8:5, 11:19, 16:18. All four incidents are in the second vision and may indicate progression of the disasters. Another phrase 'and I saw' occurs over forty times between chs. 1 and 21. In each case it introduces a new visual item or a new aspect of the vision.

The dualism of light/dark, good/evil, Christ/Satan, rewards/punishment is striking as the book of Revelation unfolds. In fact, the book sometimes seems to present its material on two screens: one that depicts heaven with God, light, worship, and joy abounding; the other that shows the earth influenced by evil, pain, sorrow, disaster, death and darkness.

Eleven songs in Revelation appear to affirm the righteous acts of God. These could be compared to the chorus in a Greek play. They are:

1. 'Holy, holy' sung by the four living creatures (4:8)
2. 'Worthy art thou' sung by the 24 elders (4:11)
3. 'Worthy art thou to take the Book' sung by the four living creatures and 24 elders (5:8-10)
4. 'Worthy is the Lamb that was slain' sung by thousands of angels, the four living creatures and 24 elders (5:11-12)
5. 'Praise and honor and glory and power be to God and the Lamb' sung by every created thing in heaven and earth (5:13)
6. 'Salvation to our God and to the Lamb' sung by an innumerable multitude (7:9,10)
7. 'Amen, blessing and glory' sung by angels, elders and four living creatures (7:11,12)
8. 'Kingdoms of the world' sung by voices in heaven (11:15)
9. 'We give thanks' sung by the 24 elders (11:16-18)

10. 'Song of Moses and of the Lamb' sung by those victorious over the beast (15:2-4)
11. 'Hallelujahs' sung by a great multitude, the elders and living creatures (19:1-8)

Testimony of Jesus

The word *marturia*, although associated today with death (our word martyr comes from it), at the time of Revelation meant 'witness'.[34] The word came from the legal sphere "where it denotes one who can and does speak from personal experience about actions" in which he participated. Hence, for John and the readers of the Apocalypse, 'witness' did not connote passive sacrifice but active engagement: John is not asking his readers to accept death passively, but is challenging them to witness actively, to bring testimony even though this witness might result in death.[35] With this understanding the testimony (or witness) of Jesus is apparently a significant concept for John because it is mentioned several times throughout Revelation:

1:2	'The Revelation of Jesus Christ which God gave ... to his bond-servant John ... who bore witness to the Word of God and to the *testimony of Jesus*'.
1:9	'I, John, was on the Isle of Patmos because of the Word of God and the *testimony of Jesus*'.
6:9	'I saw underneath the altar the souls of those who had been slain because of the Word of God and because of the testimony of Jesus which they had maintained'.
12:17	'The dragon makes war with the woman's offspring who keep the commandments of God and the testimony of Jesus'.
19:10	'... for the testimony of Jesus is the spirit of prophecy'.
20:4	'... and I saw the souls of those who had been beheaded because of the testimony of Jesus and because of the Word of God'.
22:16-20	'The words and content of Revelation are verified by John and Jesus himself'.

The word 'testimony' ($\mu\alpha\rho\tau\upsilon\rho\iota\alpha$) can be translated 'witness', 'attestation', 'validation', 'verification'.[36] John uses it in several of these ways: (1) as verification or validation of something, for example in 1:2, Jesus verifies the content of Revelation itself as prophecy; (2) other times, the word seems to refer to the reason for which people die (6:9;

---

[34] See Blount, *Witness*, p. 46.

[35] For discussion of this powerful and pivotal concept with its corresponding imagery of the lion/lamb metaphors, see Blount, *Witness*, pp. 47-49 and Bauckham, *Theology*, pp. 72-73.

[36] Johnson, p. 417.

20:4), or for which a particular action is taken: in 1:9 John is on Patmos because of it; in 6:9 the souls under the altar have been killed because of it. As mentioned above, the construction of the phrase 'testimony of Jesus' can be understood as the witness or testimony, (1) *to* or *about* Jesus, or (2) *from* or *by* Jesus. A consideration of the above passages suggests that the translation '*from*' or '*by*' is best. Revelation 1:2 and 19:10 especially suggest that the content of Jesus' witness is more than the message *about* Jesus' life and even death. Indeed, the content appears to be the essence of Jesus' own message. The question is, then, what is the essence of Jesus' witness?

Each reference (except 19:10, which identifies the testimony of Jesus with the spirit of prophecy) where the 'testimony of Jesus' is mentioned is directly associated with the 'Word of God': the 'Word of God and the Testimony of Jesus'. Particularly in 1:2, the Word of God is linked to the content of Revelation itself. John clearly states that Revelation is prophecy (1:1-3), is verified by Jesus (22:20), is witnessed to by the angel who communicates it to John (22:16), and is validated by John himself (1:2). Revelation 19:10 directly identifies 'the testimony of Jesus' as the spirit of prophecy. So there is a definite association between prophecy, the Word of God, and the testimony of Jesus.

A close consideration of Rev. 19:10 sheds more light on the meaning of the testimony of Jesus as the spirit of prophecy: John falls at the feet of the angel to worship. The angel responds, 'Do not do that! I am a fellow-servant of yours and your brethren who hold to the testimony of Jesus. Worship God! For the testimony of Jesus is the spirit of prophecy.' The angel is doing more here than merely defining the testimony of Jesus. He is pointing to the key theme of all prophecy as well as to Revelation itself: the worship of God. Indeed, the theme of all true prophecy (Old Testament and New Testament) is to distinguish the true God from all other imitators or false claimants.[35] This, then, is the meaning of the testimony of Jesus. It links the contents of Revelation with the prophecy of both the Old Testament prophets and New Testament apostles and, indeed, to the message of Jesus himself: faithfulness to the one true God. Through all circumstances, hardship, persecution, even death, one truth remains, the central core of prophecy, Jesus' message and Revelation itself: worship God, the Alpha and Omega, the first and last, the beginning and end. This is the message of Rev. 1:2, 22:16-20; the reason for John's being on Patmos (1:9); the reason for the martyrdom of the souls under the altar (6:9) and those who had been killed and were reigning with Christ (20:4); the reason why the dragon persecutes the woman's offspring (12:17); and the acknowledgment and worship of the one true God.

[37] Cf. Bauckham, p. 121.

The Holy Spirit

The Holy Spirit is central to the book of Revelation, although he is not described or analyzed directly. The Prologue clearly sets the tone with the Spirit as the origin of the prophecy: 'From him who is, and who was, and who is to come; and from the seven spirits who are before his throne, and from Jesus Christ...' (1:4-5). The Holy Spirit is represented by the symbolism of Zech. 4:2,10, in the number seven, the biblical number of completion. 'The seven spirits of God represent the Holy Spirit in his fullness of life and blessing.'[36] This completeness of the Spirit, along with the other two members of the Trinity, is the source of the Revelation itself. He appears here as an equal component of the Godhead, as equally responsible for what is about to be revealed. This is further suggested by his place in heaven – before the throne of God (see 1:4; 3:1; 4:5; 5:6). In every throne-room scene the Spirit is present, emphasizing the significance of the role of the Spirit in the prophecy; the Spirit is the means by which the message of God is conveyed. Indeed, he is integrally involved in the messages to the individual churches ('the Spirit says to the churches...,' 2:7,11,17,29; 3:13,22), as well as the means of conveying the message to the writer himself ('in the Spirit' weaves together the entire tapestry of visions, 1:10, 4:2, 12:3; 21:10).

Equally significant is the dynamic quality presented by the imagery used to describe the Spirit: 'The seven lamps of fire burning before the throne are the seven spirits of God (4:5); the seven eyes of the Lamb are the seven spirits of God, sent into all the earth' (5:6). Each figure conveys the dynamic quality of the Spirit, his power and warmth (fire), his omniscience (eyes), his active and vital role on the earth ('sent into the earth', 5:6).

---

[38] Beasley-Murray, p. 54. For an extensive discussion of the Spirit in Revelation see R. Waddell, *The Spirit of the Book of Revelation* (Blandford: Deo Publishing, 2006).

Revelation 1:1-8

Commentary

Prologue 1:1–8

The opening verses of the prologue introduce several concepts: the purpose of the book, the method of communication, the source of information, the urgency of the message, and the blessing on the hearers. The author designates his work as the *apokalypsis*. This term, from the verb 'to unveil' or 'to reveal', has come to designate a body of literature written between 250 BCE and 100 CE. Typical characteristics of this literature include symbolism, visions, dreams, and a revelation of heavenly secrets. The message usually requires a divine word of interpretation given by an angel and has to do with future triumph of good over evil.

The book of Revelation fits this general description and therefore should be understood as an 'apocalyptic' book. It is unique, however, in that it is also referred to as 'prophecy' (1:3) and a letter (1:4).

The opening words of v. 1 suggest that the revelation is either *of* Jesus or mediated *by* him. Both options are grammatically possible and could be taken to mean that both are in fact happening: Jesus Christ is the only one worthy to open the scroll (5:5-7), the only one able to 'unveil' or reveal the contents of the prophecy. He is also the central figure as he walks among the churches (1:13) until the time of his reign in the new Heaven (ch. 22). Therefore, while Jesus plays a significant role in communicating the message of Revelation, he is also the key figure in the events which are described.

The source of information is important in both apocalyptic and prophetic literature. In v. 1, God is designated as the originator of the revelation. He then passes it on to Jesus, who sends it by an angel (interpreter) to John who communicates it to his fellow servants (members of the churches).

This chain of communication is common in apocalyptic literature, for God is often portrayed as the source of heavenly secrets. He is the one who has knowledge not even possessed by Jesus (Mk 13:32) and is eager to relate that knowledge to the righteous for encouragement and hope. The message, full of figurative and symbolic terms, requires a guide or interpreter, a role assumed by the angel. This interpreter-angel is seen often in both apocalyptic and prophetic literature.

Thus, the message is 'communicated' to John. This word literally means 'signified' and suggests the concept of figurative or symbolic representation. This should alert the reader to the nature of the book and should lead him/her to expect unusual, symbolic material.

The contents of the revelation have to do with 'the things (events) which must shortly take place'. There are at least three possible ways to interpret this phrase. First, it could mean that the events will take place 'soon', that is, in the author's own time. Second, an alternative translation to 'shortly' would be 'quickly,' meaning that, once begun, the events would take place in rapid succession. Finally, and most likely, the phrase could point to the imminence of the events. The 'soonness' would not be limited to the author's time but would be understood in an eschatological sense of being possible any day.[1]

John is described as the one who 'bore witness to the word of God'. This phrase reflects the language of the fourth Gospel, where 'to bear witness' appears several times and Jesus is repeatedly referred to as the Word (Jn 1:1,14). The word of God also is a common phrase in prophetic literature to denote the way that prophecy was sent (Hos. 1:1; Joel 1:1; Mic. 1:1; Ezek. 1:1-3, etc.). Therefore, the phrase may actually have a double meaning: the author observed the revealing of God's message, which was actually the unveiling of Jesus Christ.

Verse 3 includes the first of seven beatitudes found in Revelation; both the one who reads and those who hear are blessed. This may be a reference to the Jewish liturgical tradition which promised a blessing on those who read a biblical text in the synagogue. The hearers are also blessed if they 'keep the prophetic words'. This is the first reference to the recurring theme of 'keeping' (3:10; 22:7,9). It is particularly significant that this reference to 'those who keep the words of the book of prophecy', is echoed in the final chapter (22:7) where the text reads, 'Blessed is the one who heeds (or *keeps*) the words of the prophecy of this book.' The blessing should invoke an adherence to the message, but the author adds another reason for obedience, 'the time is near'. This shows the author's idea that the time of fulfillment was possible at any time and, therefore, the warnings should be taken seriously by his readers. This concept is further developed in chs. 2 and 3 in the message to the churches.

Verses 4-8 include a salutation and a doxology, concluding with a strong statement from God, the source of the revelation. In v. 4, John

---

[1] Johnson, p. 417, and Mounce, p. 65, support this rendering.

designates himself as the author of the book. Most apocalyptic books are pseudonymous, but tradition strongly supports the apostolic authorship of Revelation. Although he never designates himself as 'apostle' in Revelation, John writes as one who is a known authority in the church whose message will be taken seriously. This fits the traditional view of the disciple John who lived in Ephesus and ministered to the Asian churches. As one of the last living disciples of Jesus, John was a worthy link in the prophetic communication.

The book is addressed as a letter to seven specific churches in Asia Minor. These should be understood to be historical churches in the Roman Empire existing around the end of the first century CE. These particular churches may have been selected by the Lord for several reasons. First, they may represent the church age from John's time to Christ's second coming. Second, they may reflect the church problems found throughout history. Finally and most likely, they were important church centers known to John and since they were located on an important postal route, a message sent to them would spread easily and quickly to other parts of the church. Since John is not identified he must have been well known as an authority whose prophetic message would be read and obeyed by these churches.

In v. 4 there is a typical Christian greeting of grace and peace. This wish of spiritual well-being is known in Paul's epistles and so was no doubt common in the early church. The source of grace and peace is threefold: God, the seven Spirits, and Jesus. The reference to peace particularly recalls the emphasis on peace in the Gospel of John (see especially 14:27 and 16:33, where Jesus promises his disciples that he will give them *his* peace).

God is described as eternal, which is significant, for it implies his knowledge and control over prior and future history. The seven spirits may imply the multifaceted dimension of the Holy Spirit, as discussed below, or they may merely be some of the creatures of the throne room. In any case they are significant enough to be included with God and Jesus as the message is revealed.

The phrase 'seven spirits' deserves special mention. It appears here, as well as in three other places in the book: in the message to the church at Sardis (3:1) and in the throne-room visions in chs. 4 and 5. In both of these throne-room scenes, the spirits are before God's throne, and are identified as the seven lamps of fire (4:5) and as the seven eyes of God sent into the earth (5:6). This imagery clearly reflects Zech. 4:2b, 10b, which John shapes to convey his own message. The equation of the divine Spirit with fire and eyes probably emphasizes the Holy Spirit's power and warmth (fire) as well as his vitality and omniscience (eyes). The sevenfold character of the Spirit may imply the multifaceted dimension of the Holy Spirit, particularly the spirit of prophecy, as well as the Spirit's completeness and perfection. In sum, the 'seven spirits' most likely illustrate the fullness of life found in the Holy Spirit.

Throughout the New Testament Jesus is given many titles. The ones designated in 1:5 are significant for his relationship to the readers and to the message of the book. First, Jesus is described as the 'faithful witness'. The Greek word for witness (μάρτυς) comes into the English language as martyr. Although today the word is associated with one who dies, the emphasis of the word in the time of Revelation was on 'witness', one who testifies to or verifies something, possibly resulting in death (see Blount, *Witness*, pp. 47-49). So this reference would remind the readers that Jesus himself suffered and died while remaining faithful and steadfast to the testimony of God. Therefore, to the churches who are suffering persecution he stands as an example of perseverance and courage.

The second title of Jesus is 'firstborn of the dead'. This again would remind readers that although Jesus suffered death, he also was the first example of the power of the resurrection. This title, even more than the others, sets Christ in the context of kingship.[2] Being the firstborn was the criteria of kingship. Here, Jesus appears as not only the rightful heir to the throne (as the firstborn), he is also 'ruler of the kings of the earth'. Both of these titles are found in the messianic psalm, Ps. 89:27. After experiencing martyrdom and resurrection Jesus finally gains ultimate triumph over all the others. The authority offered inappropriately by Satan to Jesus at the temptation (Mt. 4:8-9) is now rightfully achieved: Jesus is supreme ruler over all the kings of the world.

In vv. 5 and 6 Jesus is given glory and dominion because of his work for humanity: he 'loves us', he 'released us from our sin', and he made us to be a 'kingdom, priests to his God and Father'. This suggests a progression of Jesus' saving work: his love for humanity, his sacrificial death, which has rendered us holy enough to be considered priests before God. This final aspect fulfills the promise found in the Old Testament (Exod. 19:5-6; Isa. 61:6), and because of Jesus' work for humanity he is given praise for ever and ever (see also Rev. 5:9,10).

The author interprets these two Old Testament promises of a kingdom and the priesthood (Exod. 19:5-6; Isa. 61:6) for his readers: corporately they are a kingdom (with Christ as their ruler, Rev. 1-5), and individually they are priests (with individual access to God because of Christ's sacrificial death). The immediately following doxology (v. 6b) appropriately responds to this idea of the exalted Christ: 'glory' connotes the praise and honor due him as king and 'dominion' refers to his

---

[2] R. Hollis Gause, *Revelation* (Cleveland, TN: Pathway, 1983), p. 32.

power and might as ruler of the kings of the earth. This is, then, a strong statement about Christ as king as well as an admonition that he should be appropriately responded to as such.

John then describes the future event of Christ's coming to earth in power and might, which will be seen by all (Rev. 1:7). The promise is a combination of the messianic references of Dan. 7:13 and Zech. 12:10 and it refers to the event later described in Rev. 22:7,12,20. The mourning referred to in 1:7 is probably not the mourning of repentance as found in Zech. 12:10–12 but rather the sorrow resulting from judgment and destruction.

Verse 7 may conclude the description of Christ begun in v. 5, which describes his work of salvation (faithful witness, firstborn of the dead, releasing from sin), the results of that work (he made us to be 'a kingdom of priests') and his final vindication, triumph and rulership (he is ruler of the kings of the earth). Verse 7 describes the manner in which Christ will take his position of power. It is a cosmic, supernatural event rather than a war (cf. 22:7,12,20). Yet, Christ will come to earth and even those who were hostile to him (those who had pierced him) will respond.

The manner of Christ's coming is described as 'with the clouds' rather than 'on' or 'in' the clouds. This is similar to Dan. 7:13, where the Son of Man also comes 'with the clouds'. In Old Testament literature the cloud suggests divine presence (Exod. 13:21; 16:10; 1 Kgs 8:10; cf. Mt. 17:5; Acts 1:9), so Christ is seen as coming surrounded by clouds and, therefore, affirmed by God. (This might also recall the Transfiguration experience of Matthew 17.) Unlike other references to the 'cloud' where God himself is not seen, the coming of Christ will be visible to all, even those hostile to him, and the response is one of mourning rather than joy. Matthew 24:30 refers to this eschatological coming as a 'sign'. Perhaps the reader is to understand that his coming visibly with great power will signify the time of judgment and therefore is cause for sorrow. Note that 'the people of the earth will mourn over him'. Although the word φυλαί literally means 'tribes' and is usually used in reference to Israel, here (1:7) John uses the term to refer to all people (cf. also 5:9; 7:9; 11:9; 13:7; 14:6). Verse 7 should bring hope to John's readers, for though they may be facing persecution and hardship, they can also look forward to Christ's powerful coming as God's ultimate triumph. Christ will be vindicated in the eyes of all people.

The section 1:4-8 concludes with a statement from God himself, who defines his own character in terms of five strong titles: 'I am' may recall the title God used for himself in the Old Testament (Exod. 3:14); 'Alpha and Omega', as the first and last letters of the Greek alphabet, symbolize his completeness – he is over everything; 'Lord God' suggests his rulership; 'who is and who was and who is to come' points out his everlastingness in the sense of time; 'Almighty' suggests 'the one who has his hand on everything'. These titles declare God's character, his power, omniscience and control. It is this God who is the source of the information given to John. Because of such a source the message must be taken seriously and obeyed.

Reflection and Response (Part 1)

Reflection
In this section the theme of God's almightiness seems deserving of reflection and meditation. As self-disclosed to John, the Almighty alone is the source of life and all that exists. He is the Everlasting One, the Ruler, who has his hand on all things in time and eternity. History from beginning to end is under his complete authority, power and control.

With this in mind, in what way does this text, and in particular this theme, converge upon our present situation in the Church? What is the perception of today's church concerning the God they serve? Is he the Almighty in our midst? Are the pastors, programs, budgets and projections of our congregations conceived from and submitted to His authority, power and control, or have we succumbed to the forces of lesser gods? How concerned is the modern church with the Almighty's Lordship and what criteria could be used to evaluate that concern? Do you have any close personal friends that have traded His Lordship for worldly leadership in hot pursuit of money, prestige, vice or power? What would you say to them in light of this portion of scripture?

Our reflection upon this text would be incomplete if it were to end here, but it is essential to our walk with God to allow the scriptures to search our own hearts as well as others'. On a more personal level then, let us probe further with some additional questions. Am I submitted to the I Am? Are the actions, decisions and plans of my life conceived from and subject to his authority and control? In what way does my life demonstrate and reflect this? How would I respond if the Almighty asked me to part with something dear to my heart and replace it with a matter that I perceive as inconvenient, unfair or distasteful?

Response
As these questions were being considered, perhaps there were some issues earmarked by the Holy Spirit that call for a response. You may like to consider the following steps.

1. Invest some time working back through the preceding questions, coming to your answers prayerfully and meditatively. It would be good if you could record your responses on paper, perhaps in a personal journal.
2. Confess any disobedience, resentment or complacency that you may have discovered during this process first to the Lord, and second to a trusted brother or sister so they can keep you in prayer.
3. Make things right. Reconciliation with God's Lordship requires submission and therefore change. Though this will not be easy, it is the surest way to determine the measure of our commitment to him.
4. Keep things right. Cultivate a tender and responsive heart to the Lord. Although this is the goal of daily devotional time with God this might be reinforced through added participation in personal and corporate activities, such as once or twice a week for the next five weeks.
5. Memorize a portion of Scripture that speaks in particular to the importance of yielding to and walking in obedience to Christ's Lordship of our lives.
6. Fast and pray, seeking God's confirmation, direction and input concerning the major areas and issues of your life.
7. Join a congregational or interdenominational prayer group for corporate prayer. Allowing the body of Christ to join your intercession on these matters of Lordship can deepen and solidify them in ways that nothing else can.

Revelation 1:9-3:22

The Commission: 1:9-20

This section begins with another identification of the author, John. He is commissioned to write to specific churches and actually sees an awesome vision of the exalted Christ. The designation of himself as 'brother' suggests a close peer relationship to his readers rather than one of authority. 'Brother' was a term commonly used in the early church for believers and it reflects a close bond of fellowship and sharing.

John also describes himself as a participant in tribulation, the kingdom, and perseverance (v. 9). 'Tribulation' refers to trials and suffering. Eusebius relates that John was banished to Patmos by Domitian in 95 CE and released about eighteen months later by Nerva (Eusebius, *Chronicle*, cited by Aune, lix). This was no doubt due to his preaching of Christ and his Kingdom, which would have been seen as a political threat to Rome. Alone and in prison on the island, John identified with other Christians who were suffering and dying for Jesus' sake (2:10-13).

John says he was a fellow-partaker in the kingdom. This could be a reference to v. 6, where believers are said to be a 'kingdom'. John felt that he was participating with the church at the present time in the rule and reign of Christ. The kingdom concept here may also suggest an eschatological future hope.[1]

Finally, John shares in his readers' perseverance. To be faithful and steadfast in spite of persecution is an important theme in the book of Revelation (chs. 2 and 3). By using this term, John identifies himself with Jesus as a faithful witness (1:5) and uses himself as an example for his suffering congregations.

John states his location as Patmos, a small, rocky volcanic island off the coast of Asia Minor in the Aegean Sea. Tacitus (*Annals* III 68; IV 30; XV 71) describes the use of the island for political prisoners and, as

---

[1] Mounce, p. 75.

mentioned earlier, Eusebius records that John was banished there by Domitian in 95 CE. He was not there in order to preach the Word of God, but because his preaching was seen as a political threat to Roman authority. The Word of God and the testimony of Jesus seem to refer to the content of his preaching, as in Rev. 1:2 John considered himself a 'witness' to the 'Word of God and the testimony of Jesus'. This may also recall Jn 1:1-34, where Jesus is described as the Word of God revealed to the world. His coming was 'witnessed' (attested to) by John the Baptist (1:7,8,15,19,32,34). 'Testimony' (1:9) suggests giving of evidence or proof of a fact. In v. 9 it may refer to John's preaching (testimony) of the Lordship of Jesus, which was most likely the political affront to the Roman empire. These may also recall Jn 15:20-27, where Jesus tells his disciples to expect persecution 'for my name's sake' (Jn 15:21) and to bear witness 'because you have been with me from the beginning' (15:27). John was indeed suffering because of the Word of God and his witness of Jesus.

The first occurrence of the phrase 'I was in the Spirit' occurs in v. 10. This probably means John was in a spirit of worship and prayer. It may also allude to a prophetic spiritual trance inspired by the spirit of prophecy. Such a spiritual state was experienced by Ezekiel (Ezek. 3:12,14; 37:1), Peter at Joppa (Acts 10:10; 11:1-5) and Paul at Jerusalem (Acts 22:17). Paul also describes a person in the Corinthian church who had a spiritual experience in which he was caught up to the third heaven (2 Cor. 12:2-4) but was not permitted to speak of his visions. In this prophetic state in Revelation, John was commissioned to write (Rev. 1:10,11). He also hears the Spirit speak to the churches (chs. 2; 3) and later is taken up to heaven (4:2). John records that this experience took place on the Lord's Day, which most commentators take to mean Sunday, a day designated for worship of the Lord by the late first century.[2]

While in the Spirit, John received his commission to write his visions in a book (1:10-11). He describes the voice as like the sound of a trumpet (σάλπιγγος). In Judaism the trumpet was an important instrument. It was usually constructed from a ram's horn, but the horns of the ibex or antelope were also used. The trumpet was used to signal events such as the new moon or Sabbath. It also warned of danger and was used in exorcisms, magical healing, and war (Judg. 7:19–20). This kind of trumpet was never used with other instruments and was not considered to be a musical instrument. Its function was to make a loud noise to attract attention. The trumpet here (v. 10) would have at-

---

[2] Johnson, p. 425.

tracted John's attention and announced the beginning of the apocalyptic message.

The trumpet voice announces the seven churches which are to receive the message. Although there is a specific message for each individual church (chs. 2-3), the churches most likely also stand for churches throughout history. Indeed, the strengths and weaknesses of these seven churches can be found in one way or another within most churches through the ages. In this sense, then, these seven churches symbolize the universal Church from John's day until now. As discussed in the introductory material, the churches in this particular sequence follow the geographical order of the ancient postal route.

Important introductory information is presented in the first nine verses of Revelation: the source of information, line of communication, author, readers, purpose of the book. Then immediately follows a spectacular vision. In this vision John is commissioned to write. He is also given an audio-visual experience of Christ, who commissions him and who is the central figure in the book. John is shown the relationship of the speaker to the readers (Christ walking among the candlesticks), and a picture that shows the character and role Christ is playing in regard to the churches.

As John turns to see the speaker (v. 12), he is impressed with the setting of the vision: seven golden lampstands with a figure walking among them. The scene would not recall the Temple or tabernacle, for the lampstands are not a version of the single candelabrum with seven lamps (cf. Zech. 4) found there. These lampstands seem to be separate portable stands holding individual lamps and as such could be considered individually.

Later, in v. 20, Jesus interprets the lampstands as representative of the seven churches. This is significant, for in the Gospels Jesus describes the disciples as lights: 'You are the light of the world' ... 'nor do men light a lamp, and put it under the peck measure, but on the lampstand' ... 'let your light shine before men' (Mt. 5:14-16). The purpose of the Church is to be a witness to affect the world as a light in the darkness (Jn 1:5,8,9). If the light ceases to shine, the purpose of that church no longer exists (Rev. 2:5).

The figure which John sees walking among the lampstands is described as 'like the Son of Man'. This phrase recalls Dan. 7:13,14, where the Son of Man comes before the Ancient of Days and is given a kingdom and power that will not pass away. John describes Christ by this messianic phrase, yet he goes on to describe his clothes, which appear to be those of a priest. The long garments were worn by all priests, but only the high priest wore a breastplate interwoven with gold (Exod. 28:4; 29:5; 39:30). It is significant that Christ inspects the churches as a high priest rather than a king or warrior. He is an intercessor who is concerned about their spiritual condition.

John continues to describe the speaker in terms of his hair, eyes, feet, and voice. The white hair, while suggesting age, also would be connected with dignity and wisdom (Dan. 7:9; *1 En.* 46:1). His flaming eyes suggest a penetrating gaze before which nothing is hidden. His bronze feet reflect strength and stability, having endured the refining oven.[3] The NAS version follows the most accepted reading: 'His feet were like burnished bronze when it has been caused to glow in a furnace. His voice is powerful, awesome and strong like a mighty waterfall' (Ezek. 43:2; Rev. 14:2; 19:6; see also *4 Ezra* 6:17).

This dignified, powerful figure holds in his right hand seven stars, identified in v. 20 as the angels of the seven churches (2:1). The right hand suggests a place of prominence and, in this case, scrutiny. The stars (angels) may refer to heavenly representatives for each church or may be a figurative representation of the leader of each church. Regardless, the idea is that Christ is considering each church very carefully while holding them in an intimate place of safety and protection (Jn 10:28).

A sharp two-edged sword is seen in Christ's mouth. This is the only warrior aspect of the figure and the position of the weapon is unique. The sword described reflects the large broad one used by the Thracians.[4] It is not wielded by hand but comes from Christ's mouth. This is consistent with Rev. 2:16 and 19:15,21, Lk. 2:35, and Heb. 4:12, where divine judgment is meted out by Christ's word rather than in a warlike fashion. One might also be reminded of Christ's encounter with Satan in the Temptation account, where Christ declares, 'Man shall not live by bread alone, but by every word that proceeds out of the mouth of God' (Mt. 4:4; see also Lk 2:35; Heb. 4:12; *4 Ezra* 13:10).

John concludes his picture of Christ by describing the shining brightness of his face.[5] This recalls the Transfiguration experience where Jesus' face 'shone like the sun' (Mt. 17:2), distinctly showing Christ's deity (Mt. 13:43; 17:2; Rev. 10:1; *1 En.* 1:4). John's reaction to this dramatic vision was to fall at Christ's feet (v. 17). This response may refer to a trance-like or ecstatic state into which the prophet falls while receiving a divine message. The phrase occurs often in apocalyp-

---

[3] The words and phrasing are difficult to translate here.
[4] Johnson, p. 428.
[5] The Greek word occurs three other times in the New Testament and may refer to his entire appearance rather than just his face (Mt. 17:2; cf. Exod. 34:29; Judg. 5:31; Mt. 13:43).

tic literature and seems to be a sort of waking dream-like state.[6] While in the spirit the prophet can remain on earth, receiving visions, or he may be transported to Heaven or other geographical locations. The idea is that the divine revelations are too extreme (either of impending disasters or of wondrous glory) to be absorbed in a conscious state.

Christ responds with assurance and comfort, touching John and telling him, 'Do not be afraid' (Rev. 1:17). This was a familiar gesture used often by Jesus with the disciples during his earthly ministry (e.g. Mt. 14:27; 17:7). Here, however, the reason to abandon fear is partly based on Christ's identification of himself as the First and Last,[7] both sovereign and everlasting. He is also the Living One, having by resurrection overcome death forever. He holds the keys of death and Hades, which denote access and authority. In Jewish literature God is described as holding these keys (Tg. Jer. on Isa. 22:22; *Sanh.* 11.3a), and the fact that Christ holds them here points to the power of his triumph.[8] Thus, John has no reason to fear because Christ overcame death and in fact holds it as a servant (v. 18).

In v. 19 the commission to write is repeated and expanded. Commentators differ on the division of the phrase, 'the things which you have seen, and the things which are, and the things which shall take place after these things'. While there are a variety of proposed interpretations, perhaps the easiest rendering is suggested by Johnson:

> John is told to write down a description of the vision of Christ he has just seen, what it means and what he will see afterward, i.e., not the end-time things, but the things revealed later to him. Whether they are wholly future, wholly present, or both future and present depends on the content of the vision.[9]

This interpretation allows for more flexibility when one analyzes the chronological progression of the rest of the book. In some cases events seem to follow in a chronological sequence. At other times they might occur simultaneously as on two screens. The context helps to determine each case.

In v. 20 Christ himself interprets the 'mystery' of the stars and lampstands. 'Mystery' in the New Testament usually refers to that which

---

[6] Cf. Ezek. 1:28; Dan. 8:17; 10:15; Mt. 17:6; Acts 26:14; *4 Ezra* 10:59; *1 En.* 71:11.

[7] Ἐγω εἰμι is used 24 times in the Gospel of John as well as a few times in the Synoptics.

[8] Tg. Jer. on Isa. 22:22; *Sanh.* 11.3a. Death and Hades are linked throughout Revelation (6:8; 20:13,14). In the LXX the Hebrew term is translated 'sheol' or grave.

[9] Johnson, p. 419. This view is based on the translation of ἅ εἰσιν as 'what they mean' rather than the usual 'what is now'.

was secret but was revealed by an interpreter (Mk 4:10-13; Rev. 1:17-18; 10:7).

The seven stars and seven candlesticks, according to Christ (v. 20), represent the seven churches. This imagery provides a message of encouragement and comfort as the churches face hostility, hardship and persecution. Christ, himself, is among them, walking in the midst of his churches (1:13). The seven stars are the 'angels of the seven churches' (v. 20). Several interpretations of these angels are possible, but the most likely meaning is that the 'angel of the church' is a way of personifying the spirit or character of the church. Support for this interpretation is strengthened by the fact that each message is addressed to separate angels, one for each church. The message, however, is clearly meant for the congregation as a whole rather than for a single person. Hence, it seems best to associate the 'angel' with each church rather than with the pastor or representative person.

The Churches: 2:1–3:22

The book of Revelation is addressed to the seven churches of Asia (1:4,11). These churches may have been chosen by Christ because the cities in which they were located were major commercial centers as well as distribution sites for the postal districts of Western Central Asia Minor. They were situated 30–50 miles apart on a circular route and are addressed by Christ in the geographical sequence in which they occur. Some commentators see additional significance in the order in which Christ speaks to them: that they present a preview of church history, each church reflecting the challenges of a specific historical period. Others maintain that the churches reflect the problems of the church universal. Regardless, these churches existed during John's time and were experiencing the problems of heresy and persecution reflected in Rev. 2; 3.

The messages to the individual churches follow a particular form:

1. The Angel is named.
2. Christ is identified as he appears to that church. In each case a particular aspect of Christ's appearance is taken from the vision in ch. 1 and is significant for that church's situation.
3. The church is commended and/or rebuked.
4. Action to be taken is declared.
5. A reward is promised to the faithful.

In each case the church is admonished by the statement, 'He who has an ear, let him hear what the Spirit says to the churches'. It is interesting to note that 'churches' is plural. This may suggest that the message is relevant to all seven of the churches. It may also be a literary cue to the readers to listen and take heed.

Chapter 2
The Church of Ephesus: 2:1-7

The church of Ephesus is addressed first, possibly because the city was the largest, most important export and trade center for Asia Minor at that time. Not only did it boast a large harbor, it was also the converging point for three overland trade routes. It was situated on the Cayster River and was part of the Kingdom of Pergamum bequeathed to Rome in 133 BCE by Attalus III. By the end of the first century CE, the population of over a quarter million was ethnically diverse, made up of Greeks, Romans and Jews. Ephesus enjoyed self-government, granted by Rome, and was a center for Roman judicial trials. It had a major stadium and a theater which seated approximately 25,000. A beautiful marble colonnaded street connected the harbor to the agora, a large 'mall' with shops for food, clothing and silver objects.

There were temples to the Emperors Augustus, Claudius, and Domitian but the most impressive was to the main goddess of Ephesus, Artemis (Diana). Considered to be one of the Seven Wonders of the World, the temple was 425 x 220 ft, and 60 ft high, four times the size of the Parthenon. It had 127 marble pillars overlaid with gold and jewels and functioned as a bank and asylum. A gymnasium, aqueduct, library (holding 12,000 rolls), and imposing statues combined to make Ephesus a worthy place for the wealthy and influential.

According to Acts, the Christian church at Ephesus was founded by Priscilla and Aquila about 52 CE (Acts 18:18-21). Later Paul stayed there for two or three years encountering philosophies, exorcists, magicians and angry silversmiths who were threatened by Paul's preaching against idol worship (Acts 19; 20). Timothy and Apollos also ministered there (1 Tim. 1:3; Acts 18:24). Tradition says the Apostle John lived and taught there.

Christ is identified in Rev. 2:1 as the One who holds the seven stars and who walks among the lampstands. Since the stars are symbolic of the seven churches, Christ's position in relation to them suggests his role as one who inspects their condition, for commendation as well as for warning. The detail that they are held in God's *right* hand suggests they are in a special place for perfection and control.

For the church at Ephesus the commendation is significant since its activities and faithfulness were maintained in spite of attacks by false teachers. In fact, Christ commends them for their work, patience and testing of evil individuals. Apparently, the church appropriately tested the spirits and accurately discerned evil (2:2). This sort of testing of doctrine by the early church was also encouraged by Paul (1 Thess. 5:21; 1 Cor. 14.29) and John (1 Jn 4:1; Mt. 7:20).

The problem confronting the church seems to stem from an earlier problem involving false teachers – 'evil individuals and those who unjustly call themselves apostles' are probably the same group. Apostles were usually considered to be the twelve disciples, or those who were directly commissioned by Jesus (Gal. 1:1; 1 Cor. 9:1). By the end of the first century the original twelve disciples had died (except John) and teachers rose up in the church to claim special leadership privileges (1 Cor. 15:13-23; 1 Jn; 2 Jn). These self-appointed 'apostles' may have been some sort of self-styled apostles. In any case, these people were not pagans but 'brethren' who denied the Lordship of Jesus, often promoting idolatry and immoral practices. In Acts 20:28-31 Paul warned the people of Ephesus about the emergence of such false teachers. Evidently the church responded effectively because later Ignatius wrote to the same church commending them for refusing to entertain a heresy.[10] Hence, the Ephesians, as Rev. 2:2 also points out, listened to Paul's admonition: they correctly evaluated teachers and were not influenced by heresy. Jesus also points out that the Ephesians had worked hard, endured, and not grown weary (2:2,3). It is interesting that in these two verses the word steadfastness or perseverance (ὑπομονήν) occurs twice, as well as endured (ἐβάστασας) and have not grown weary (κεκοπίακες). The repetition suggests they have held out for a long time and in a commendable fashion.

The need for testing doctrine was evidently widespread in the early church (1 Thess. 5:21; 1 Cor. 14:29; 1 Jn 4:1). Jesus himself gave the disciples a simple, usable criteria: 'You will know them by their fruits' (Mt. 7:20). The *Didache* also includes the test for a true prophet: 'He has (will have) the behavior of the Lord', 11:8 (Hermas, *Mand.* xi.16). Evidently when the Ephesians applied these tests to their teachers, the teachers proved themselves to be deceivers and liars (2:2). Unfortunately, however, this is not enough. The Lord still has something to bring to the attention of the Ephesians: they have lost their first love (2:4).

This problem found by Christ in Ephesus may have actually resulted from the climate of suspicion mentioned above. The Ephesians evidently overreacted and then lapsed into a rigid orthodoxy, an institutionalized 'form' of religion without the warm enthusiasm of their first love in Christ. 'First (πρώτη) love would suggest that they still loved, but with a quality and intensity unlike that of their initial love.'[11]

---

[10] Ignatius, *Letter to the Ephesians* 6,7,9,16.
[11] Johnson, p. 434.

Christ's warning to the church is a sharp command to remember from where they had fallen. They were to reassess their present spiritual condition in light of their first zeal for God. Then they were to repent, which means to change their mind, to reverse their position to the one held before.[12] Finally, they were to do again the deeds they had done at first. This no doubt refers to the original quality rather than quantity or type of deeds since their activities seem to be commended in v. 2. The point is that the church now lacks the warm intensity for Christ that it once exhibited. Disobedience to the warning would bring drastic results: 'Or else I am coming to you, and will remove your lampstand out of its place – unless you repent' (2:5). Good deeds alone do not merit a church's existence. Without the necessary zeal, enthusiasm and warm outreach of love there is no reason for the church's lampstand to continue in its location. This recalls the church's role, as a light, without which it is useless. Although this message seems harsh, there is the sense that God expects them to obey, for a promise for the overcomer follows.

The Lord adds one more commendation before he gives his promise to the overcomers: the Ephesians follow the Lord in hating the deeds of the Nicolaitans (v. 6). This group is also mentioned in the message to Pergamum (2:15) and is probably implied in the letter to Thyatira (2:20-21). Who the Nicolaitans were is difficult to ascertain. The name is made up of two Greek words: to conquer or consume (νίκαν) and people (λαός). Whether this was a name they gave themselves or whether it is a derogatory description given by Christ is not possible to know. It is certain that they were a heretical sect associated with idolatry and immorality.[13] Evidently, the Ephesians rejected their libertine view of behavior and were hence commended by Jesus.

The phrase 'he who has an ear, let him hear what the Spirit says to the churches' introduces the reward to the overcomers. The first part of the sentence occurs often in the Synoptic Gospels and is a call to hear and also understand the message. The 'Spirit' refers to the prophetic function of the Holy Spirit as he mediates the message.

For each church there is a promised reward which refers to some aspect found at the end of the book of Revelation. The reward promised to Ephesus looks ahead to the new earth (Rev. 22:12). It also recalls the Garden of Eden, where eating of the tree of life was forbidden after

---

[12] 'Remember' is a present imperative in contrast to the aorist imperative 'repent'. Mounce suggests this shows a 'continuing attitude over against a decisive break', p. 88.

[13] D.M. Beck, 'Nicolaitans', *IDB* III, p. 548. Eusebius states that the sect lasted only a short time, *Hist. Eccl.* III 29.1. E. Schüssler-Fiorenza points out that they evidently infiltrated itinerant missionaries as well as the prophetic teachers of the early Christian community ('Apocalyptic and Gnosis in the Book of Revelation', *JBL* 92 [1973], p. 570).

the fall. It is interesting to notice that after Adam ate of the tree of knowledge of good and evil in the garden, he was able to discern good and evil (Gen. 3:22). Death was then introduced into the earth. Since eating of the tree of life would have reversed the death sentence causing Adam and Eve to live forever (Gen. 3:22), God put them out of the Garden. Thousands of years later God promises the overcoming church of Ephesus the right to eat of the tree of life, insuring eternal life. This tree is also found in apocalyptic writings as a reward for the righteous (*1 En.* 24:4–25:6; *Test. Levi* 18:11; *4 Ezra* 8:52; *2 En.* 8:3). For example, in *Test. Levi* 18:10-11, God promises to open the gates of paradise so that the saints can eat from the tree of life. The tree is located in the Paradise of God, a Persian term which means park or garden. For the church to eat in that garden suggests an eschatological state of restored fellowship between God and humanity.

The Church of Smyrna: 2:8-11

Known as the 'Ornament of Asia', Smyrna was located 35 miles north of Ephesus. It was the terminus of a major route into the interior, and in New Testament times was second only to Ephesus in exports. Smyrna was founded in 1000 BCE by Aeolean immigrants from Greece. Although it suffered decline during the sixth and fifth centuries BCE it was later refounded on a new site three miles south of the old city and established as a Hellenistic town by Antigonus. Cicero spoke of it as one of the most flourishing towns of Asia. Strabo called it the finest of Ionian cities, probably because it had a good harbor, a famous library, a stadium and large public theater seating 20,000 on the north western slope of Mount Pagos. The state agora had a courtyard 120 x 80 meters with a two-story portico. Known for its paved streets, it even boasted a throughway called the street of gold.

In New Testament times Smyrna held a strong allegiance to Rome and included several temples to the emperors. Coins portray busts of Nero, Titus and Domitian as well as temples to Tiberius and Hadrian. In the city there was a large temple to Zeus and one to the goddess Cybele. The population of 200,000 was made up of Gentiles and Jews. Inscriptions found in the city suggest the presence of a synagogue. The birthplace of Homer, Smyrna was a place of learning especially in the sciences and medicine.

The Christian church at Smyrna was probably founded during Paul's time in Ephesus.[14] Ignatius (early 2nd cent. CE) describes it as well organized with a bishop (Polycarp), deacons and elders.[15] Tradition says

---

[14] Cf. Pionius, *Life of Polycarp*, pp. 1, 2.
[15] Ignatius, *Smyrna*, XII 2.

Polycarp was bishop there and martyred along with others in the stadium because of his belief in Christ as King.[16] In Revelation Christ appears to the church at Smyrna as 'the first and last, who was dead and has come to life' (cf. 1:17; 2:8). First and last may suggest Christ's presence in and control over all history. He was also the conqueror of death, having experienced resurrection.

The church of Smyrna was surrounded by an atmosphere which was antagonistic to Christianity: emperor worship, wealth, and a large Jewish population. Since the Christians did not engage in worship of pagan gods or emperors and since pagan worshipers often were an intrinsic part of financial commerce, economic survival would have been difficult. The Greek word for 'poverty' suggests extreme poverty, so perhaps the church was without even basic necessities. In spite of this, Smyrna was commended for being spiritually rich (2:9). Christians also encountered persecution from the Jews. This may have been because the Jews found it difficult to accept a poor Galilean peasant's claims or because of the success of Christianity in Smyrna. Revelation 2:9 suggests that the blasphemy came from self-professing Jews who are a 'synagogue of Satan' (2:9). Since there is no evidence of a Satanic synagogue this statement probably refers to the motivation of the persecution – Satan. Ethnically the people may have been Jewish, but they carried out the activities of Satan (see Rom. 2:28; Jn 8:31-47). For example, in the burning of Polycarp, Jews were said to have helped to bring wood for the fire.[17]

This rebuke by Jesus can also be interpreted as a comment on the true nature of being Jewish. Paul in Romans 2:28,29 distinguishes between one who is a Jew inwardly, or spiritually, and one who is outwardly Jewish. For Paul, the true Jew is one who is of the spiritual seed of Abraham, rather than the physical (outward) seed. The purpose of the synagogue was a gathering place for the people of God, but the Smyrneans had distorted the purpose of gathering to worship God. Hence, their synagogue had become the gathering place of God's adversary, Satan.[18] The word used here for Satan ($\Sigma\alpha\tau\alpha\nu\tilde{\alpha}$) is a Greek transliteration of the Hebrew and means 'adversary'. The Greek equivalent means 'false accuser' or 'slanderer'. These people were, in fact, carrying out the activities of God's opponent and adversary, Satan.[19]

---

[16] *Martyrdom of Polycarp*, XIII 1; Eusebius, *Hist. Eccl.* IV 15.25.

[17] Charles, I, p. 325, lists other church fathers (Justin, Tertullian, Ignatius, etc.) who refer to Jewish opposition.

[18] Gause, p. 53.

[19] Mounce, p. 93.

The church at Smyrna is not rebuked for any sin. Rather they are encouraged to 'fear not' (2:10; cf. 1:17), when additional suffering (πάσχειν) occurs. The word used for fear (present imperative φοβοῦ with μή) probably means 'stop being afraid' and conveys the idea of an existing environment of fear. Again the church is reminded that the source of persecution is the devil (2:10 can be seen as a reference back to v. 9) rather than human authorities. Also, they are assured that tribulation would last only ten days. This may be a literal ten days, or if taken symbolically, it could refer to a prolonged yet limited time. The type of persecution they could anticipate was prison and, since prison normally preceded execution, they should be prepared in fact to face death, which John states explicitly (Rev. 2:10). To this courageous church, Christ appears as the one who also died but rose again (2:8). Christ (the One who is alive) promises to give the imperishable *Crown of Life* (Jas. 1:12; 1 Pet. 5:4) to those who remain faithful in spite of the adverse social and religious situation, possibly even death. This is not the royal diadem worn by kings, but a garland or wreath (στέφανον – *stephanon*) given to the victor of athletic games (for which Smyrna was famous). Such a garland was also worn by worshipers of the pagan gods in Smyrna. In addition, the overcomer was promised exemption from the second death. The 'second death' was a rabbinic term for the fate of the wicked in the next world.[20] In Revelation it is described as the Lake of Fire (20:14; 21:8), which has no power over the righteous (20:6). The promise is given to him 'who has an ear to hear ...' and is very strongly emphasized by the Greek double negative: 'He who overcomes shall not be hurt ...' Jesus, who has conquered death, and is now alive, makes this promise.

The Church of Pergamum: 2:12-17

Pergamum was described by Pliny as the most distinguished city in Asia.[21] Located fifteen miles inland, sixty-five miles north of Smyrna and two miles north of the Caicus River in Southern Mysia, it was known for its beauty and wealth, and was a center for education and religion. It had several palaces, a large library with over 200,000 volumes (parchment was invented there), and a theater which had a magnificent view of the plain. The main street curved up the Acropolis with shops and homes on each side. The system of water supply and drainage was well engineered, and during Claudius's reign a new pipe for drinking water was installed. There was also a large auditorium and a beautiful marble hall which served as a shrine for departed heroes.

---

[20] *Targum of Jer.* on Deut. 33:6, cited by Mounce, p. 94.
[21] Pliny, *Hist. Nat.*, V, 30.

Seven gymnasiums functioned as civic centers, club houses, schools, places for emperor worship, lectures, and leisure sports.

Pergamum was one of the first Asian cities to welcome Rome and become a center for emperor worship. One of the first Asian temples to Augustus was built there, and choirs performed for his birthday as well as for other festivals.[22] There were also temples to the mystery cult of Demeter and Persephone and to the Egyptian cult of Serapis and Isis.[23] The temple to Serapis is the largest structure still standing (328 ft x 656 ft. Another hall, recently excavated, is believed to be the sanctuary of the cult of Mithra or Attis.[24] A pit holding animal bones supports this theory since sacrifices of a bull was central to these mysteries.[25]

Dominating the city is an altar to the ethnic god Zeus, which is a large colonnaded structure in the shape of a horseshoe (120 ft x 112 ft). The podium of the altar is almost eighteen feet high. At the base is a great frieze showing a battle of the gods and the giants, a striking example of Hellenistic art.[26]

Located southeast of the acropolis was the Asklepion healing center. The main deity was the god Asklepios,[27] who was believed to have healing powers. The cult was introduced into Pergamum about 350 BCE and seems to have reached its peak of popularity around the second century CE. The temple and court covered a large area (361 ft x 426.5 ft) with porches on three sides. In one corner there was a library with lavatories for men and women nearby. The healing center itself was a two-story cylindrical building eighty-seven feet in diameter. There were several sacred pools connected to the center by a long tunnel (262.5 ft) and a spring which provided water and mud for treatments. The tunnel seems to have been used in the ritual religious ceremonies for healing. The center was not only a site for religious worship, but also for medical experiments. It is interesting to note that Pergamum was the birthplace of Galen (129 CE), who became a famous physician to several emperors, including Marcus Aurelius.[28]

---

[22] Yamauchi, p. 42.

[23] Both cults (Demeter & Persephone and Serapis & Isis) emphasized death and rebirth; included initiation rites involving drugs and included immoral and sexual practices as a means of communicating with the gods.

[24] Mithraism was a popular Roman cult in which Mithra, symbolizing good, kills the bull, symbol of evil. Virtues of courage, strength, loyalty were emphasized. Unlike most of the other mystery cults, Mithraism did not include sexual rites.

[25] Yamauchi, pp. 43-45.

[26] Ibid., p. 36.

[27] Asklepios was symbolized by the form of the serpent and even today is the sign representing medicine.

[28] Yamauchi, p. 47.

There is no mention of the church of Pergamum in the New Testament except Revelation 2. It was probably founded by Paul during his stay in Ephesus and, like the other six churches, was experiencing the problems of persecution and heresy. Christ appears with a sharp sword. It is interesting that Pergamum had been granted the authority by Rome to carry out capital punishment which was also symbolized by a sword.[29] Christ's appearance with the sword suggests that he was coming in judgment to divide between good and evil and that he is the One who has the ultimate power over life and death.

Christ first acknowledges that he is aware of the church, its works and environment in Rev. 2:13. The description of Pergamum as the location of Satan's throne may be due either to the actual shape of the city, which was like a throne towering over the plain, or to the presence of mystery cults and emperor worship. Christ found two groups in this church: those who had maintained faith in spite of persecution and those who had followed false teachings. He commends those who had endured, calling Antipas 'his faithful witness', the description used of Christ in Rev. 1:5.[30] Apparently, even the death of some among them did not weaken the faith of certain members of the church. These members 'held fast' to the name of Christ and did not deny his (Christ's) faith. Since this city was a center for emperor worship (there was also a throne-like altar to Zeus overlooking the city from the citadel), public allegiance to Caesar would have been emphasized. This included a ceremony in which each person would declare 'Caesar is Lord'. For Christians, this was impossible; for them, 'Christ is Lord' even unto death. The Christians at Pergamum held fast to the name of Christ and did not deny their faith even in the face of possible death.

The Lord, however, finds 'a few things against you' (v. 14). The wording here indicates that the problem is not widespread in the church. In view of these Christians' strong stand for Christ, this is a problem affecting only a few. It is, however, important and needs to be addressed. The problem involves adherence to heresy, characterized as the 'teachings of Balaam'. Most likely the word 'teaching' (διδαχή) does not refer to a body of doctrine.[31] Rather, the teaching of Balaam more likely involves a view of behavior. It reflects the Old Testament background of Balaam leading Israel astray with participation in pagan meals and immoral relationships (Num. 24; 25; 31:16f.).

---

[29] Johnson, p. 440.

[30] Tradition says that Antipas was roasted to death in a brazen bull during the reign of Domitian (Mounce, p. 97).

[31] διδαχή in the New Testament does often have this passive sense; cf. Mt. 16:12; Jn 7:16,17, etc. (cf. Mounce, 97).

The Nicolaitans seem to be closely associated with the problems of the Balaam group. They evidently were promoting compromise with the world, specifically eating meat sacrificed to idols and practicing fornication (2:14). Since these sins are connected in this verse, one can infer that members of the congregation were participating in the sacrificial meal of the pagan gods, which also included cult prostitution. Christ exposes the heresy by identifying it with Balaam, who deceived the Israelites into idolatry and immorality (Num. 25; 31). He calls the church to repent, for even those who have tolerated the teaching are considered to be guilty. He warns that he will 'come quickly'. This probably suggests his judgment of the church's condition rather than his second coming, for Christ warned that he would fight with the sword. (It is interesting that Balaam was also killed by the sword, Num. 31:8.)

The overcomers are given three promises: hidden manna, a white stone, and a new name. Hidden manna may be a reference to the manna hidden in the Ark (Exod. 16:33-36). When Solomon's Temple was destroyed, Jeremiah is said to have hidden the Ark under Mount Nebo (2 Macc. 2:4-7). It was believed that at the return of the Messiah, it would be brought out and be placed again in the restored Temple (*2 Bar.* 29:8; *Sib.Or.* 7:149). The second promise is a white stone. White stones were used by ancient jurors to signify the innocence of the person on trial. Stones known as 'tessera' were also used as tokens for admission to a banquet, given by emperors to ensure a supply of corn, or awarded to victors of games.[32] Although any of these meanings could be appropriate, it seems that the most meaningful is that by giving a white stone, Christ would be declaring the church members innocent by admitting them to his banquet. The third promise is a new name written on the stone. It is not clear whether the name is of Christ or of the person receiving the stone. In Egyptian culture, the god's name was kept secret and given only to select individuals. This gave a particular status and power to the few who knew it.[33] The combination of these three symbols suggests that the eschatological promise was assured the church at Pergamum: the manna speaks of a messianic restoration; the white stone signifies either innocence and/or a ticket for admission to the Lord's special feast and the new name designates the church as selected and protected by God. These promises are significant in light of the religio-sociological situation of Pergamum: Christ, who discerns and separates good and evil by the sword of his mouth, recognizes those who have not succumbed to the immorality

---

[32] Mounce, p. 100.
[33] *ANET*, p. 12.

so prevalent where 'Satan dwells' (2:13). This church 'held fast to my name' (2:13) even though faced with death, therefore they will escape the 'war' (2:16) and share in the messianic blessing of salvation (manna, a white stone and a new name, 2:16).

As is so often the case in Revelation, the promise of 'coming quickly' (see also 16:15; 22:7,12) should be viewed on two levels. First, if the people of the church do not repent, then the Lord will 'come quickly', undoubtedly in immediate judgment. Second, this is a statement of the recurring theme of Christ's imminent final coming (cf. 1:7; 3:11; 16:15; 22:7,12,20).

The Church of Thyatira: 2:18-28

Located 35 miles inland and southeast of Pergamum, Thyatira was situated on the Lycus River in the northern part of Lydia. It lay in a valley surrounded by gently sloping hills and was founded by Seleucus I as a military outpost to guard one of the approaches to his empire. Most of the current knowledge about the activities of Thyatira is from inscriptions and coins found in excavations of the city. This evidence shows a prominence of trade guilds, unions of clothiers, bakers, tanners, potters, linen-workers, wool merchants, slave traders, coppersmiths, and dyers. When Paul preached at Philippi, a woman, Lydia, from Thyatira, was converted (Acts 16:14,40). She is described as a seller of purple cloth. This may be a reference to the clothing industry and also to the Turkish-red color dye made from the madder root which abounded in Thyatira.[34]

The chief deity was the god Apollo/Trymnaeus. Coins found in Thyatira depict temples built to him as well as to the goddess Athena.[35] There was also a sanctuary located outside the city dedicated to Sybil Sambathe, a prophetess who claimed to utter divine sayings accepted by the people as oracles. There is no other biblical reference to the founding of the church at Thyatira. It may have grown out of the ministry of Paul or Apollos in Asia Minor. Some even suggest it was founded by Lydia.

Christ appears to this church as the Son of God, with blazing eyes and burnished bronze feet. This title, which occurs only here in Revelation, is a summation of the vision of Jesus in ch. 1: Christ stands in contrast to the god Apollo, in the authority and power only attributed to the Son of God. His flaming eyes suggest the ability to perceive and

---

[34] Homer Hailey, *Revelation: An Introduction and Commentary* (Grand Rapids, MI: Baker Book House, 1979), p. 135.
[35] Yamauchi, p. 52.

penetrate evil, discerning between correct teaching and heresy. His burnished feet convey the idea of strength and splendor.[36]

Christ found this church committed in love, faith and ministry to such an extent that there was an increase in works (Rev. 2:19). These virtues appear to be significant throughout Johannine literature, the Gospel, as well as 1, 2 and 3 John. Unlike the church at Ephesus, this church had a relationship with God (love, faith) that had intensified to the extent that ministry in their community had actually multiplied. 'Greater than at first' (v. 19) probably refers to quantity as well as quality. They had also persevered in spite of the pagan hostility. Nevertheless, Christ questions whether or not they can endure to the end in light of the corruption which was taking place within the church itself. The problem was that they tolerated a false teacher. This person is described as a prophetess who is given the metaphorical name Jezebel. From the passage, she seems to be a woman of leadership ability who professed prophetic gifts. Perhaps because of the gifts she was able to influence members of the church to follow her teachings, and like Jezebel in the Old Testament, the wife of Israel's king Ahab, she encouraged immorality and idolatry (1 Kgs 18:4,19; 2 Kgs 9:22).[37]

The prophetess of Thyatira probably taught compromise with the local guilds and maintained that church members could participate in the pagan practices associated with them. These practices would have included worship of the ethnic gods (which involved prostitution) as well as eating meat sacrificed to idols. Some scholars suggest that Jezebel may refer to Lydia who, being a connected business woman, would see the advantage of compromise. There is, however, no evidence for this. Others suggest she may be the prophetess Sibyl Sambathe, the fortune teller. It is unlikely, however, that such syncretism could have affected the Christian church by this time, and it seems from the context that the prophetess was within the church community, for she is given the opportunity to repent (Rev. 2:21).

The problem for the church was twofold: some had been led astray to follow her teachings, and, perhaps even more damaging, the church had failed to rebuke or expose her sin. Apparently, God had given ample time for repentance but she refused (v. 21). Therefore judgment was necessary. Since the church had tolerated her sin they must also repent or share her judgment. The reference in v. 23 to 'her children' most likely refers to her followers rather than to her physical off-

---

[36] The rare word translated 'burnished bronze' (Rev. 2:18) may be a reference to the special alloy used by local metal workers (Yamauchi, p. 53).

[37] The gift of prophecy was highly respected in the early church and women often filled this role (1 Cor. 12:28; Eph. 4:11; Acts 21:9), Johnson, p. 444.

spring.[38] The statement is constructed so as to convey severe intensity: 'I will kill her offspring with death' (v. 23), a Hebrew idiom possibly denoting pestilence.[39]

Judgment upon Jezebel is drastic: she will be cast ('hurled') on a bed of suffering. This is probably a prediction of physical illness rather than a funeral bed or couch used for feasting at the guild banquets. Disease as punishment for sin was a known and accepted idea in the early church (1 Cor. 11:27-29).[40] The adultery of which she and her followers are accused may be a reference to spiritual unfaithfulness to God rather than a literal physical state. Regardless, her followers are promised exposure of sin and repayment according to their deeds (Rev. 2:23). Christ describes himself as he who searches hearts and minds, which suggests that his judgment is based on the knowledge of a person's inner condition as well as their outward deeds. Such a discernment exposes the deception of false teachers who would appear holy, even exercising spiritual gifts.

Christ's warning extends to the entire church in spite of the fact that they did not follow Jezebel into learning the 'deep secrets' of Satan (v. 24). By this phrase Christ may be identifying the source of the deceptive teachings or the text may refer to a form of Christian gnosticism which held that liberty to sin actually proved one's righteousness. According to Johnson:

> By experiencing the depths of paganism (the deep things of Satan), one would better be equipped to serve Christ or be an example of freedom to his brothers (cf. 1 Cor. 8:9-11).[41]

Regardless, there are no other charges to the rest of the church except that they hold on to what they possess (Rev. 2:25). This probably refers to the basic salvation, love and faith acknowledged by Christ earlier (2:19). The words 'hold on' suggest an active adherence to the teaching they already know and a resistance to prevalent alternative teachings (see earlier reference to their strong holding to the name of Christ, vv. 12-17). Their perseverance should continue until Christ's return (v. 25). This could be a reference to his appearance to aid or judge the church or to his second coming.

---

[38] Isbon T. Beckwith, *The Apocalypse of John with a Critical and Exegetical Commentary* (New York: Macmillan, 1919), p. 467.

[39] Johnson, p. 445.

[40] The point is that Jezebel no longer had opportunity for repentance, but her followers are given a warning to repent of her deeds lest they also suffer her fate (vv. 22, 23). Cf. Mounce, p. 104.

[41] Johnson, p. 445.

The overcomer who endures to the end will share in Christ's rule. The phrase used here, ἄχρι τέλους, is stronger than the one used by Paul in 1 Cor. 1:8 and 2 Cor. 1:13, and means 'even unto the end'.[42] This interpretation suggests that doing God's will must be continued to the eschatological end of time. At that point, the church will be granted the reward of sharing in Christ's authority and rule over the nations (Rev. 2:26). The 'rule of iron' is probably a reference to the earthly millennial kingdom as expressed in Pss. 2; 110:5-6; Isa. 11:14; Rev. 12:5; 19:15. There is an interesting combination of words here, for 'rule' literally means 'to shepherd'. Yet v. 27 suggests power and the crushing of resistance. This is probably a reference to the shepherd's club, which was often capped with iron and used to ward off animal attacks.[43] The believer can look forward to sharing in a future rule in which Christ, the true leader, nurtures the flock yet wards off evil. This is possible because Christ's authority has been given by God the Father (2:27).

The promise of the morning star is a further reward (v. 28). There are many suggestions as to how this metaphor should be interpreted: it could refer to Christ himself (Rev. 22:16), the immortality of the righteous (Dan. 12:3), the dawn of eternal life, the planet Venus, or the Holy Spirit.[44] There is not sufficient evidence to support any of these suggestions; hence one must be content to see the promise as an eschatological blessing to the overcomers. It is unlikely that there is a connection between this title and the 'stars' held in Christ's right hand since they have already been interpreted as representative of the angels of the seven churches (1:20).

Chapter 3
The Church at Sardis: 3:1-6

Sardis was located fifty miles east of Ephesus on the spur of Mount Timolus, overlooking the fertile plain of Hermus. The acropolis rose 1,500 feet above the lower valley, creating an inaccessible and natural fortress. The lower city developed to the north and west of the acropolis and, like many Roman cities, had a theater and a stadium. An impressive temple to Artemis measuring 160 ft x 300 ft[45] equaled the famous temple in Ephesus for splendor and size, but it was never completed. Another impressive feature was a cemetery 'of a thousand hills',

---

[42] Hailey, p. 141.
[43] Mounce, p. 106.
[44] Cf. Mounce, p. 107, for further discussion of these views.
[45] Yamauchi, pp. 49, 66.

so called because hundreds of burial mounds were visible on the skyline.

The patron deity of the city was the Greek goddess Artemis or Cybele. She was believed to possess the power of restoring the dead to life. Other deities honored by altars were Zeus and Aphrodite. Sardis was also supportive of the Roman emperors, for 21 inscriptions of Emperor Augustus have been found there. Sardis was repaid for this solicitude toward the emperors. When in 17 CE an earthquake leveled twelve important Asian cities, Tiberias chose to rebuild this city.[46]

Sardis was a city of wealth and fame, retaining this prosperity through the second century CE. Its political brilliance, however, lay in the past.[47] It was a city of peace – not from battle but from lethargy. Although it was a natural fortress and virtually impregnable, it was captured twice through negligence. One example will illustrate this. When Cyprus attacked Sardis, one of the Persian soldiers observed a Sardian descend the southern winding path to retrieve a fallen helmet. He followed the Sardian back up to the summit and the Persians captured the city.

There is no biblical record of the founding of the church at Sardis. To this church Christ is identified as the one who holds the seven spirits and the seven stars. The seven spirits represent the Holy Spirit, who plays an important role in discernment and prophecy. This is significant, for Sardis is in a lethargic spiritual condition, and perhaps this shows Christ's extreme concern. He holds the seven stars (the churches), again an allusion to the focus on this church's condition. It is interesting that Christ also appeared to Ephesus as the one with the seven stars. Such a description points to Christ's protection and close scrutiny of the church since it is held in his hand.

A sharp warning comes to this church without a previous commendation. The problems parallel the history and character of the city: both have reputations of being alive, but are experiencing incomplete works. Politically as well as spiritually, members did not remain watchful during times of crisis. The rebuke by the Lord that 'you have a name that you are alive, but you are dead' probably refers to their reputation of failure due to negligence. Although the city (as also the church) looked strong, it was, in fact, open to defeat because of lethargy and neglect. Apparently, this did not apply to each individual in the entire church (vv. 4,5), but the majority must have been involved in spiritual compromise for this state to have come about (vv. 1,2).

---

[46] Cf. Yamauchi, p. 67, for more details about the devastation.

[47] Gold and silver coins were struck there and the art of dyeing wool was discovered there (Mounce, p. 109).

Apparently this church had been involved in significant ministry, for it was known by the general church (vv. 1,2) and had an ongoing reputation. One of the problems, however, was that the church did not complete what it had begun. Here incompleteness probably refers to quality rather than quantity, for the deeds described as love, faithfulness, keeping Christ's words and not denying his name are usually considered to convey acceptability.[48]

The message implies that this church was suffering neither heresy nor physical persecution. Rather it had come to terms with the pagan environment, becoming lethargic and 'soiled' (v. 4). In Judaism, as well as in ethnic religions, soiled clothes disqualified the worshiper and dishonored the god. So also for the church, such an appearance was unacceptable to Christ.

The church is commanded to 'wake up', to 'remember' (present imperative meaning 'keep remembering') what they had previously received (a perfect tense indicates that indeed they had received the message previously) and to strengthen what remained. This suggests that the church had become ritualistic with a lack of missionary zeal so as to represent no threat to the pagan environment. They are commanded to remember and reinstate the apostolic doctrine and standards. Failure to respond would result in Christ's coming unexpectedly – like a thief. This no doubt refers to his coming in judgment to discipline their spiritual condition rather than his second coming, which will occur regardless of the church's actions. There is also the urgent sense that if they do not repent as soon as possible, the Lord will most likely come 'as a thief' (quickly and unexpectedly). Very likely they would be unaware of his arrival. The command to be watchful and alert recalls Jesus' words of Mt. 24:42, where the faithful, wise servant is described as the one who is found working when the master returns (see also Mt. 25:13).

The church is commanded to build on the few who have remained faithful and unsoiled (see also Jas. 1:27; Jude 23). They are promised fellowship with Christ and white clothing, which is symbolic of their justified, pure state (Isa. 1:18; Dan. 12:10). White clothing is indicative of righteousness, and throughout Revelation various groups are identified as holy by their white clothing (cf. Rev. 6:11; 7:9,13,14; 19:7,8). The church at Sardis is promised that those who overcome will be clothed in white (considered holy). Perhaps this has an eschatological future meaning, looking ahead to Christ's coming kingdom in Rev. 19:14, where the armies of saints wear white. Furthermore, the over-

---

[48] Johnson, p. 449.

comers are assured mention in the Book of Life and acknowledgment before the Father (3:5).

In ancient cities the names of citizens were recorded in a book and at death their names were erased or marked out (cf. Exod. 32:32-33; Ps. 69:28; Isa. 4:3). Here (Rev. 3:5) the overcomer is promised that his name will never be taken out and, in fact, will be 'confessed' (a strong word used in courtrooms) before God.[49] Having one's name in the book suggests belonging to the Kingdom of God (Dan. 12:1; Lk. 10:20; Phil. 4:3; Heb. 12:23) and thereby possessing eternal life. Christ promises that even in death there will be no separation. The Book of Life is referred to again in Rev. 20:12-15. At the white throne judgment of God the books are opened and checked in a scene which resembles a courtroom, where evidence is produced to determine a fair judgment. The few 'unsoiled' ones in Sardis are promised that they will not be erased from the Book and will be presented by Jesus to the Father. They are 'worthy' to receive these messianic blessings because they have been faithful, even as Jesus was considered 'worthy' to take the Book because he was faithful (Rev. 5:9,10). It seems that these few faithful ones will receive their promise regardless of the response of the rest of the church.

The Church at Philadelphia: 3:7-13

The city of Philadelphia was located at the eastern end of a broad valley, on the southern side of the river Cogamis, tributary of Hermus. Since it was at the juncture of trade routes leading to Mysia, Lydia and Phrygia, it achieved the title 'Gateway to the East'. The volcanic plain to the north was fertile for growing grapes, resulting in an economy based on agriculture and industries of textile and leather.[50]

Philadelphia was established by the Pergamenian king Attalus II (159–138 BCE) for the purpose of disseminating Greco-Asiatic culture and language. It was one of the twelve cities devastated by the earthquake of 17 CE. After it recovered it temporarily took the name of Neocaesarea. Later, under Vespasian (69-79 CE), it was called Flavia. Later still, on account of its many temples and festivals it was called 'little Athens'. Although emperor worship was practiced there, the worship of Dionysius was the chief pagan cult.

The speaker to this church is described by three messianic identifications: holy, true, and holding the key of David (v. 7). 'Holy One' is a familiar title for God (Isa. 40:25; Heb. 3:3; Mk 1:24) but here it is joined with 'True One' and most likely designates Christ. 'True' sug-

---

[49] *Ibid.*
[50] Mounce, pp. 114-15; cf. also Johnson, p. 451.

gests genuine and may be in opposition to Jews who say that Christ is a false messiah.[51] The fact that Christ holds the Key of David probably denotes his authority and access. Together with the messianic title David, Christ in this passage appears to have control over the royal household with authority to include or exclude persons from the New Jerusalem. This powerful figure with its background in Isa. 22:15-25 may appear to bring encouragement to the Christian Jews who were experiencing excommunication from the synagogues. Christ appears with divine authority to open or shut, not only the doors of the synagogues, but all doors, particularly the one to the eternal kingdom.

Nothing is known of the exact origin of the Christian church at Philadelphia, although Eusebius (100–160 CE) describes it as prospering under the ministry of the prophetess Ammia.[52] It receives no rebuke but is commended for its faithfulness in spite of 'little power'. This may be a description of the number of members or the economic and social status of the church in comparison to other wealthy groups in Philadelphia. In spite of this hindrance, the church remained faithful and did not deny the Lord. The two aorist verbs used here suggest a particular period of trial in the past. The church was commended by Christ based on his knowledge of their situation: 'I know your deeds' (Rev. 3:8). Deeds, as in the other churches, had to do with service to the community and missionary activity as evidence of the church's condition (Rev. 2:2,13,19; 3:1,2,8,15). The concept that actions (deeds) are proof of the inner spiritual condition is also seen in 1 John (e.g. 3:18: 'Little children, let us not love with word or with tongue, but in deed and truth'; see also 3:12). Although Philadelphia's deeds are not specifically enumerated, their faithfulness is recognized 'for keeping Christ's Word' and not denying his name in spite of 'little power'.

To this 'weak' church the promise is given of an open door (Rev. 3:7,8). Most commentators see this as parallel to the city, which was the 'Gateway to the East'. As such, it represents an open door for missionary opportunity. Paul also uses 'door' in this manner (1 Cor. 16:9; 2 Cor. 2:12; Col. 4:3). While this may be the case, the door may also have an eschatological meaning that Christ has opened a door to the eternal kingdom for church members in contrast to the door of the synagogue in Philadelphia that was closed to them.[53] Presented here is a beautiful contrast between Christ with his open door and the excom-

---

[51] Mounce, p. 116: The word ἀληθινός (true) is used 22 times in the Gospel of John, although it is rarely applied to Jesus (Jn 7:18; cf. Mk 12:14//Mt. 22:16). In Rev. 19:11, it is the name of the rider on the white horse.

[52] Eusebius, *Hist. Eccl.* V 17.2.

[53] Mounce, p. 116, supports this view.

munication, closed door, of the synagogue. Christ appears as greater than external earthly circumstances – people might close physical doors, but Christ holds the keys to the eternal kingdom.

The reference to the Synagogue of Satan (Rev. 3:9) further supports the idea that the church was experiencing persecution by the Jewish community, which refused to acknowledge Jesus as Messiah. There is no reason to think this is an allusion to Satan worship. Rather, as Jewish worshipers opposed Christianity, they are considered to be supporters of Satan's cause and attackers of God. Many early churches were planted in synagogues only to have members excommunicated when Jesus was rejected as the promised Messiah. Such a situation seems to have occurred in Philadelphia, but Christ appears to the Philadelphians with the authority of the Davidic Messiah. He affirms his authority to open and close doors (3:7) and is in fact opening a door for this church which cannot be closed by any other. Christ assures the Christians that their opponents will eventually have to acknowledge Christ's presence in the church (v. 9). The interpretation of this verse is awkward, with at least two possible solutions. First, the falling down could refer to the conversion of Jews to Christianity. A preferred rendering, however, is that the Jews would be forced to recognize that the church is of God, who loves them.

Furthermore, to the small church of Philadelphia Christ promises deliverance from the hour of trial (v. 10). There are two issues of concern in this passage: the identification of the hour of trial and the sense of being kept from the trial. First, the hour of trial must refer to more than the general distress of the Philadelphian church, for it will affect the whole earth (v. 10) As such, the hour is generally taken to refer to the time of tribulation and testing preceding the establishment of the eternal kingdom (Dan. 12:1,2; Mk 13:19; 2 Thess. 2:1-12).[54] With this interpretation, the promise would refer to the Church Universal – the Church would in some way be delivered from the extreme distress of the Tribulation. The question then follows, in what sense are believers delivered? Does the promise suggest deliverance from the period of trial or safekeeping through it? The Greek phrase is inconclusive and has the sense of 'exempt from'. One can either be 'exempt from' the worldwide distress of famines, earthquakes, wars, floods, etc. by the rapture[55] or by a miraculous method of protection.[56] While neither

---

[54] Ladd, p. 62, Mounce, p. 119, John F. Walvoord, *The Revelation of Jesus Christ: A Commentary* (Chicago, IL: Moody Press, 1966), pp. 86-87.

[55] Walvoord, p. 87.

[56] Johnson, p. 459 (this position is also held by Mounce, pp. 119-20, and Ladd, *Commentary on Revelation of John* [Grand Rapids, MI: Eerdmans, 1957], p. 62).

proposal suggests a definitive means of exemption, it can be encouraging that in a very real sense the believer is promised divine protection. There is a wonderful play on the word 'keep' here: the Lord says that because they have kept 'the word of My Perseverance' he will also *keep* them from the hour of trial (v. 10). Finally, he admonishes them to 'hold fast' (keep) what they have so no one can take their crown (v. 11).

Christ says, 'I am coming quickly' (3:11), a comforting promise of vindication and deliverance rather than a threat of judgment, as in the case of Ephesus, Pergamum and Sardis. Nevertheless, he stresses the necessity for the church to 'hold fast to what you have, in order that no one take your crown' (v. 11). 'Crown' probably refers to the laurel wreath presented to the victor at festivals and athletic games for which Philadelphia was known.

It was necessary for athletes to endure to the end of a race in order to be awarded the victor's crown. Thus, in the same way, Christ admonishes the church that it cannot grow complacent or over confident in itself. Rather, it must continue vigorously to seek to attain the goal lest another win. The idea that someone could take 'your crown' can be understood in the sense that 'evil powers could lead the believer away from the gospel of eternal life'.[57] It seems in the context of a race, however, that if the Philadelphia church lost heart because of the persecution and their small size, they would not complete the task given them (finish the race) and therefore forfeit the reward. The crown would be taken by another. Regardless, the point is clear, that although no one can shut the door of opportunity, lack of endurance to the end can cost a person the winners' crown.

The overcomer is promised stability and permanence in God's Kingdom (vv. 11,12). This would have been particularly significant since Philadelphia had a history of earthquakes.[58] Also, in Greek cultures a person could be honored for faithful civic work by the erection of a special pillar inscribed with his name. Christ pronounced such an honor to the overcomers at Philadelphia: believers would be made into a pillar in God's Temple. On it would be written God's name, the city's name and Christ's new name (v. 12). This promise would have been encouraging to the Philadelphian church, for their apparent weakness (little power) would have been made into strength (supporting pillars). In addition, the pillars would be in the Temple of God

---

[57] Robert W. Wall, *Revelation* (NIBC; Peabody, MA: Hendrickson, 1991), p. 85.

[58] Pliny refers to the quake of 17 CE which leveled twelve cities. It was particularly hard on Philadelphia which felt tremors long after. (See Pliny, *Hist. Nat.*, II 86-200; Tacitus, *Annals*, II 47; Strabo, 12.8.18.)

forever, and engraved with the names of God, the New Jerusalem, and Christ. This implies that a permanent place would be given to the overcomers in the eschatological Messianic Kingdom of God, clearly identified and protected.

The Church of Laodicea: 3:14-22

Situated in the fertile valley south of the Lycus River, Laodicea was located ten miles west of Colossae and six miles south of Hieropolis. It was called 'Laodicea' and 'Lycum' to distinguish it from the eight other cities which were called Laodicea. The city was established by Antiochus II between 261 and 253 BCE and named after Laodicea, his wife or sister.[59]

Laodicea was quite prosperous, becoming a banking center and having a court which hosted such outstanding lawyers as Cicero to hear cases.[60] It was also affected by the earthquake of 17 CE and was aided by Tiberias. By 60 CE however, it was wealthy enough to provide its own restoration after another quake. The Flavians were especially partial to Laodicea, and Laodicea responded by dedicating public buildings to them, e.g. a stadium was dedicated to Vespasian and a gymnasium to Hadrian and his wife. A large Greek theatre was also dedicated to Aelius Caesar and then to Hadrian.[61] Evidently, stadiums and games were important to the Laodiceans and as early as 50 BCE gladiatorial games were held there (Cicero, *Ad Atticum* 5.15). Musical contests were also held in Laodicea.[62]

Laodicea honored many gods and goddesses, among them Dionysius, Helios, Nemesis, Hoder, Serapis, Mithras, Hera, Athena, Tyche, the Syrian Aphrodite, and the founder of the city of Laodicea. Isis was one of the more important goddesses since there was a colossal statue of her found in the excavation of the site of an elaborate nymphaeum, or fountain house, built around the third century CE.[63] Particular reverence was also paid to Apollo (god of prophecy) and Asklepios (god of healing). A famous medical school related to Asklepios was situated about a dozen miles northwest of Laodicea along with the temple of Men Karou. One of the specialties of the medical school was the dispensing of collyrium, used as an eye salve and cosmetic.[64]

---

[59] Yamauchi, p. 137.
[60] Cf. Yamauchi, p. 137, and R.K. Sherk, *Roman Documents from the Greek East*, LII (Baltimore: Johns Hopkins University Press, 1969), pp. 272-76.
[61] Yamauchi, pp. 140-43.
[62] Cf. Yamauchi, p. 145.
[63] *Ibid.*, pp. 141-43.
[64] Cf. Yamauchi, p. 145; Ramsay, *The Letters to the Seven Churches*, pp. 316-17.

Since there were no springs in Laodicea, the Laodiceans used aqueducts to bring water from hot springs in other areas. By the time the water reached Laodicea it was no longer hot, but tepid. To make matters worse, it would have built up calcareous deposits from the hot springs so that it would taste particularly terrible. In addition, cold, clear water was brought through the aqueducts from Colossae. Unfortunately, by the time the water arrived at Laodicea, it was also lukewarm. Like the water at Laodicea, the church was neither hot nor cold, but lukewarm. As Blaiklock puts it, 'The sickly mixture (of soda-laden water), neither refreshingly cold, nor beneficently hot, and burdened with alien content, disgusts.'[65]

Christ appears to the Laodicean church as 'the Amen, the faithful and true witness and the beginning of the creation of God' (Rev. 3:14). These are three important, related titles that present the speaker in a position of great authority. The title 'Amen' probably reflects Isa. 65:16, where it is used as a title for God. This is particularly significant christologically, 'since it attributes to Christ a title associated only with God'.[66] The word 'amen' literally means 'yes' and is often used to validate something, such as an oath or blessing (Isa. 65:16). In this passage 'amen' is amplified by the following title, the 'faithful and true witness' (μάρτυς is also used in Rev. 1:5). It is not entirely clear whether this refers to Jesus' earthly death or to the Christ of Revelation, who guarantees the truth of the message given to John. The second option is better supported by the context since μάρτυς is used of Jesus in 1:5 as a name for the messianic white horse rider of Rev. 19:11, and as the exalted Christ who testifies in Rev. 22:20.[67] Thus, Christ appears to an unfaithful and deceived church as one who is completely trustworthy and true.

The third title, 'the beginning of the creation of God', may reflect Col. 1:15,18, where Paul describes Christ in a similar manner. The two churches may have been closely associated since the cities of Laodicea and Colossae were located a short distance apart in the Lycus valley. Laodicea is mentioned four times in Colossians (2:1, 4:13,15,16). Some scholars hold that the author of Revelation may have known the Colossian epistle.[68]

---

[65] E.M. Blaiklock, *The Cities of the New Testament* (London: Pickering & Inglis, 1965), p. 125.

[66] Aune, *Revelation 1-5*, p. 255.

[67] See Aune, pp. 37, 55.

[68] Mounce, pp. 124-25; Johnson, p. 457; and Charles, pp. 94-95, support this. See also an extended discussion in Aune, p. 249. This connection with Col. 1:15,18 suggests that the Greek word used here (ἀρχή) should be translated 'origin', 'source', or 'beginning' (Mounce; Aune, p. 255), rather than 'ruler' (Johnson).

The emphasis on the *temporal* priority of Christ to all creation is found frequently in early Christian literature and was perhaps the product of the identification of Christ with the wisdom of God. According to John 1:2-3, 'He was in the beginning (ἐν ἀρχῇ) with God; all things were made through him'.[69]

Therefore, Christ speaks to the church of Laodicea as the trustworthy, truthful One, the source of creation. As such, the authenticity of his message is guaranteed.

Unlike most of the previous churches, Laodicea received no commendation. Rather, the church is rebuked for being 'neither hot nor cold' (Rev. 3:15,16). As previously mentioned, this problem is commonly explained by the geographical situation of Laodicea, whose water supply came either from the hot springs of Hierapolis or the cold mountain water of Colossae. By the time the water reached Laodicea via aqueducts, it was tepid, distasteful and useless. For the church, the temperature of Laodicea's spiritual condition was not necessarily in question, but the problem of its effectiveness was. The church was neither useful in providing spiritual refreshment (cold water) nor effective for spiritual healing (hot pools). Christ found this unacceptable. 'I will spit you out of my mouth' reveals an intense rejection by Christ, for the word 'spit' literally means 'vomit'. Thus, Laodicea's indifference made the Lord 'sick'; his rejection was from his deep inner being. It suggests an intense emotional reaction rather than a formal judgment of their deeds, and is in sharp contrast to the church's apathetic indifference.

Furthermore, Christ rebuked the Laodiceans for their self-sufficiency, complacency and lack of spiritual self-discernment (Rev. 3:17). With smug satisfaction the city boasted of financial wealth, an expansive textile industry and a popular eye salve. Church members may have considered their affluence to be a sign of God's blessing (see also Hos. 12:9, Zech. 11:5, *1 En.* 97:8,9). Christ, however, graphically describes their spiritual condition in terms of poverty, destitution and misery. 'Wretched' is a term used to describe life when all of one's physical possessions have been destroyed or plundered by war.[70] The description is linked with poverty, blindness, and nakedness, terms usually associated with the very poor and sick. The connecting of these adjectives by the repeated conjunction 'and' heightens the intensity of their condition.

A major part of the problem was the Laodiceans' lack of awareness of their spiritual condition; they felt no need to ask the Lord for any-

---

[69] Aune, p. 256; see also LXX Prov. 8:22.
[70] Johnson, p. 458.

thing. One can see a possible parallel with Jesus' parable of the rich man who stored up his wealth in barns. In his boastfulness he failed to realize that material wealth would not sustain him after death (Lk. 12:15-24). God instructs the church to buy from him three items for true wealth (Rev. 3:18): gold refined by fire, white garments, and eye salve. All three items reflect Laodicea's natural possessions, but the recommended source of purchase emphasizes the needed spiritual dimension of their wealth. The church considered themselves in need of nothing and yet, in Christ's evaluation, they required basic necessities of spiritual clothing and healing. The gold suggested by God was that which had been refined by fire. Part of the process of refining gold was to put it into a very hot furnace, so when the melting took place, imperfections were separated out. In 1 Pet. 1:7, this idea, used as a metaphor for Christians who are suffering, suggests that persecution, though difficult, tests and purifies. God advises that the testing of persecution would result in their spiritual wealth (1 Pet. 1:7-9 says that the 'proof of your faith ... even though tested by fire, may be found to result in praise and glory and honor at the revelation of Jesus Christ ...') The church should also buy white garments from God. The color white symbolizes righteousness throughout Revelation and in this passage. The clothing should cover their nakedness and shame. It is striking that the church does not even realize they need clothes, an even worse situation than that of Sardis, which had 'soiled' garments. In the Old Testament, nakedness was a sign of judgment, humiliation and shame, while receiving fine garments was an honor (1 Sam. 18:1-4; Ezek. 16:37-39; Gen. 41:42; Esth. 6:6-11).

Furthermore, spiritual blindness seems to have been the cause of the church's problem in that they did not discern their condition. God advises eye salve purchased from him which would heal their blindness. Although they sell eye salve to help physical eye problems, the Laodiceans, themselves, needed God's eye salve to heal their spiritual blindness. The resulting sight would make repentance possible, for change cannot occur unless the problem is recognized.

Therefore, Christ appears to the Laodiceans as the One who speaks truth and exposes unrighteousness. He advises the Laodiceans to change their perspective of what is valuable, useful and effective, which may lead to persecution but will result in holiness and spiritual insight.

There is some debate as to whether Rev. 3:19-22 should be regarded as the conclusion to the Laodicean message or if it should be taken as a final exhortation to all of the churches. Most scholars consider that these verses complete the pattern evident in the seven letters and are therefore necessary to conclude the letter to the Laodiceans.

As such, v. 19 seems to be a concluding statement to Laodicea, strengthening the motive for the rebuke – it is love that results in discipline. Discipline as a means of training and testing for approval appears elsewhere in the Scriptures.[71] Nevertheless, the message is clearly declared: 'Be zealous, therefore, and repent' (3:19). 'Repent' is an aorist imperative, which demands a decisive act, while 'be zealous' is present imperative and suggests a continuing practice. Thus, God requires an immediate action of repentance with a continued change in their lifestyle and ministry. Christ 'spits out' those he does not love, but he rebukes and reproves those he does. With this assurance, Christ urges them to repent.

Verses 20-22 probably conclude the entire section of the messages to each church. With such a conclusion, the message itself should be understood to be intended for all churches as well as for the universal church through the ages. The imagery of v. 20 is often seen in a context of evangelization: Christ knocks at the heart's door, waiting to bring salvation. In this context, however, the individual in the house more likely represents the church which has excluded Christ from fellowship. Repentance is possible, for Christ is at the door knocking for entrance. Fellowship requires a response from the person within, so the intimate relationship suggested by sharing a meal would be strong motivation for a positive action. In the oriental culture sharing food indicates a strong bond of affection.

Some interpret v. 20 in terms of the eschatological return of Christ, for sharing a meal is seen as a positive reward in the Messianic Kingdom (*1 En.* 62:14; Lk. 22:30; Rev. 19:9). The phrase 'if anyone hears my voice' may recall the often repeated phrase in the Gospels, 'he who has an ear, let him hear', a variation of which is spoken to the churches (Rev. 2:7,11,17,29; 3:6,13,22). It urges attentiveness and an immediate response to the commands in Rev. 3:18.

The promise to the overcomers is the right to sit with Christ on his throne (v. 21). This recalls the promise given to Jesus' disciples (Mt. 19:28) and suggests a position of honor and authority in the eschatological kingdom for those who endure.[72]

Verse 22, which concludes the Laodicean letter with the familiar admonition to hear, may also be taken as a summary warning to all churches.

---

[71] Prov. 3:11-12; Ps. 94:10-12; Job 5:17; 1 Cor. 11:32; Heb. 12:5-6.

[72] Paul N. Benware, *Understanding End Times Prophecy on the Davidic Covenant* (Chicago, IL: Moody Press, 1995), pp. 136-44, makes a distinction between God's throne in heaven where Jesus sits at God's right hand and Christ's throne on earth in the Messianic Kingdom which disciples will share.

Reflection and Response (Part 2)

Reflection

One of the most significant aspects of this section involves the relation of Christ to his Church. This is reflected in the messages to the seven churches. In each case, Christ conveys his intimate knowledge of what the church is doing. As the One who holds the churches in his hand, he commends their faithfulness, good deeds, and perseverance, and comforts those being persecuted (especially Smyrna and Pergamum). He also constructively rebukes those who are losing their fervor (Ephesus, Laodicea, and Thyatira). To each of them, he stresses the rewards which await those who overcome the trials and tribulations they are confronting. He warns others to repent and stand firm in the face of the pressures of the surrounding pagan environment.

The reader of Revelation is immediately struck by the familiar issues which resonate between these ancient churches and the churches of today. It is beneficial to hear Christ speaking through these messages. In this light, let us consider the following questions. If Christ visited our modern churches, would he commend our faithfulness and perseverance in the face of pressure from the worldly environment? To what extent would he find perseverance in persecution? Would he find us being persecuted at all or would he find elements of compromise, unfaithfulness and apathy? If there is compromise, unfaithfulness and apathy, how extensive is this problem? What signs are evident which lead you to this identification? In view of this, what opportunities are available for the Spirit to convict his Church and to call them to repentance? Are there some churches which would be commended of the Lord? In what ways do they differ from the churches which are being unfaithful? What community actions might be offered in order to alert the unfaithful churches to appropriate action?

Sometimes it is easier to identify compromise or apathy in the church at large rather than in our own lives. Hence, it is important to raise several additional questions on a more personal level. Am I involved in any situations in which I feel pressured to conform with the ungodly environment in which I live? To what extent am I being influenced by teachers or leaders in the church who are very persuasive, but whose lives include behaviors which are designated by this text as ungodly? What signs indicate this to me? What behaviors of mine would enable Christ to commend me for faithfulness and perseverance, or would he rebuke me for compromise, ungodly behavior, or apathy? How often do I reflect on my life in terms of behavior which mirrors the Lordship of God? In what ways do I take the Holy Spirit's conviction seriously when he indicates areas that need improvement? If my life does not seem to reflect any of these negative issues, what kind of witness does my life suggest? In what way does it clearly suggest the Lordship of God?

To what extent do I take the issue of faithfulness to God seriously, or is my attitude characterized by apathy and indifference?

Response
As we reflect on these questions, it may be helpful to consider the following steps as a response to the guidance of the Holy Spirit.

1. Spend some quality time prayerfully considering the above questions, perhaps with a trusted brother or sister.
2. Identify areas which need particular attention and confess before God those items which are displeasing to him. It may be helpful to make a list of these areas.
3. Join a prayer group in which you can commit to a plan of action in order to strengthen and energize your spiritual life.
4. Join a weekly Bible study on passages which would strengthen your weak areas.
5. Reflect periodically on your progress with a trusted friend who can encourage and motivate you to continue toward your goal.
6. Participate in some form of corporate worship as it enhances and strengthens one's spiritual life.

Revelation 4:1-5:14

Chapter 4

The Throne-Room: 4:1-11

Chapters 2 and 3, in summary, record the letters to the seven churches of Asia, an intense, urgent call to remain faithful in the face of physical persecution and heresy. These letters are now followed by a dramatic, vivid scene shift to where the seer, John, is invited to ascend from earth to heaven. Since the words 'after this' (μετὰ ταῦτα) occur here and again in 7:1, one can assume that chs. 4–6 form a single textual unit. Revelation 4:1-2a may, in fact, function as an introduction to both the seal narrative and the entire central section of Revelation (4:2–22:9).

The placement of the throne-room vision in the literary structure of Revelation is important, for it shows the readers the source of the visions which follow – they are not mere imaginings of a human being, but originate from the majestic throne of God in heaven. Throne-room visions are typical in prophetic and apocalyptic literature,[1] and in Revelation they serve to show the persecuted church that a powerful God is in control of history. Chapter 4 sets the scene for the action of the Lamb in ch. 5 and the opening of the seals in ch. 6: the destiny of the world, both righteous and wicked, is determined and orchestrated from the very throne of God.

John is invited to heaven (the term 'heaven' [οὐρανός] occurs in the singular throughout Revelation except in 12:12) where John sees a door standing open. The passive perfect participle translated 'opened' (ἠνεῳγμένη, 4:1), suggests it had been opened and left open for John's arrival.[2] The imagery of the open door recurs throughout Revelation

---

[1] *Test. Levi* 3:4-9; *Ladder of Jacob* 2:7-22; *1 En.* 45; 55; 62:3-5; 1 Kgs 22:19; Amos 3:7.

[2] Aune, p. 280. Most scholars agree that this does not necessarily reflect the rapture of the Church (Mounce, Johnson, Aune and Walvoord).

(see particularly Jesus knocking at the door, 3:20) and the open Temple (11:19; 15:8). This particular scene is significant since the door provides access to God's throne-room itself.

A connection between this vision and the vision of Christ in ch. 1 is made by John's allusion to the same voice (like a trumpet) which he had first heard speaking (Rev. 1:10; 4:1). The promise is made, 'I will show you what must take place after this' (4:1). Christ had commanded John to write of 'the things which shall come to pass hereafter'. Now he will show him those things.[3]

This appears to imply that the following events in Revelation are to be fulfilled in the future, that is, at a time later than the writing of Revelation, and after the time of the seven historic churches.[4] The time described in Rev. 4:2 then would refer to a time which is yet future, a time in which God will ultimately triumph over evil.

Verse 2 describes John's state as 'in the spirit'. This phrase (ἐν πνεύματι) occurs four times in the book of Revelation (1:10, 4:2, 17:3, 21:10) and probably suggests more than the presence of the Spirit of God; John is experiencing a visionary trance, which is an out of body spiritual state also found in apocalyptic literature.

The first thing John sees is the throne itself and he is aware of someone sitting on it (4:2).[5] He describes the picture in terms of brilliance rather than by particular body features, as found in ch. 1. The vision may recall Ezek. 1:26-28, where colors are associated with God's throne[6] and 'portray in symbolic form the majesty of God, resplendent and clothed in unapproachable light'.[7]

The colors themselves are interesting: jasper was an ancient stone, a translucent rock crystal, perhaps like a diamond; sardius was a blood red stone named after the city Sardis. The rainbow is like an emerald that was either green or a colorless crystal which would refract a prism of colors. These stones are mentioned by Plato as precious (*Phaed.* 110e); they were used by the king of Tyre (Ezek. 1:26; 28:13), and were included on the Jewish high priest's breastplate (Exod. 28:17). Combined, they must have presented an astounding profusion of brilliant, sparkling, shimmering colors.

John continues to describe the throne-room in terms of a series of concentric circles of worshipers: the 24 elders (Rev. 4:4), the four living creatures (v. 6) and the angelic host (5:11; see also *1 En.* 71:6-8; *3*

---

[3] Mounce, p. 133.
[4] Johnson, p. 461.
[5] Aune says this is a circumlocution for the name of God, p. 284.
[6] See also Ps. 104:2; 1 Tim. 6:16; 4Q405 20-22 I 10-11.
[7] Mounce, p. 134.

En. 33:1–34:2). Included in the scene are seven fiery lamps (Rev. 4:5) and a sea of glass (v. 6).

The 24 elders are difficult to identify. Some options include that they are taken from the astronomical tradition of Babylon, the Judaic levitical system of 24 courses of Aaronic priests (1 Chron. 24:5) or the church universal, which combines the twelve patriarchs and the twelve apostles. The most plausible interpretation seems to be that they are a special angelic order which surrounds the throne, serving God as the heavenly counterpart to the 24 priestly orders in the Judaic system (1 Chron. 24:4; 25:9-31).[8] As such, they join the other throne-room beings, participating in worship and adoration of God. Their designation as 'elders', a title often used in biblical times for leaders of tribes, cities, and later the Church, suggests a position of authority.

The author of Hebrews describes the tabernacle that Moses made in the wilderness as 'a copy and shadow of the heavenly things ... for "See", he says, "that you make all things according to the pattern which was shown you on the mountain"' (Heb. 8:5). He also writes of the 'true tabernacle' in which Jesus serves as high priest (Heb. 8:1,2). Later, in Heb. 9:23,24, he speaks of the 'copies of the things in the heavens' and states that 'Christ did not enter a holy place made with hands, a mere copy of the true one, but into heaven itself, now to appear in the presence of God for us ...' Therefore, if the tabernacle in the wilderness with its furniture and 24 priesthood system was a 'copy' of the one in heaven, it follows that the 24 elders most likely would be the 'original' heavenly order of worship, upon which the earthly 'copy' was based. Since in a broad sense, the earthly priesthood existed to bring about acceptable worship of God, it would follow that the heavenly order exists to promote worship in the throne-room.

One of the strongest supports for this interpretation is the description of the elders' praise before God (5:9-10) where they refer to those who were 'purchased by his blood' and are thereby made to be a 'kingdom and priests'. Apparently, the elders set themselves apart from the redeemed.[9] Later, in Rev. 20:4, the 24 elders appear to be functioning sacerdotally as well as administratively in the reign of Christ. In addition, when they first appear before God's throne (4:4-5), they are accompanied by thunders, lightnings and other dynamic sounds, symbolizing God's presence, awesome power and majesty. God's presence is often accompanied by such signs in the Old Testament. For exam-

---

[8] Mounce (p. 135), Beasley-Murray (p. 115), and Johnson (p. 462) also support this concept.

[9] Cf. Mounce, pp. 135-36; see Gause, p. 90, for a discussion of the view that they do represent the redeemed.

ple, the dynamic forces of nature declare God's arrival in Ps. 77:18: 'The sound of thy thunder was in the whirlwind, the lightnings lit up the world'. In Ps. 18:12-16, hailstones, lightning, thunder and fire indicate God's presence. Most importantly, these dynamic natural activities heralded God's theophany on Mount Sinai (Exod. 19:16). The throne-room scene sets the 24 elders within this Old Testament context by describing the accompanying light and sound displays.

John usually describes the clothing of the people in his visions. In this case the elders wear white robes, which suggest their purity and social dignity. In Judaism white suggested joy, purity and social dignity, while dark, which suggested inferiority, was worn by women and lower class men. Jesus himself is associated with white in Rev. 1:14; 19:11. White was also worn by priests. The Jewish tradition that angels wore white is reflected in the New Testament.[10] In the Roman culture wreaths and white garments were worn for praying, sacrificing and marching in religious processions. The elders' golden crowns (Rev. 4:4) recall the wreaths worn for athletic victory or in religious processions, rather than the 'diadems' of royalty. Thus, the elders' manner of dress signifies their position of dignity and worthiness. This heightens the drama: the elders relinquish their crowns, delegating their authority in honor to God (vv. 10-11).

Also around the throne are four creatures (see Isa. 6:2-3; Ezek. 1:5-25; 10:1-22). Although their exact location in relation to the throne is unclear, their function is definitely to lead the worship of God, for Rev. 4:9 says whenever they give honor, the others follow (v. 10).

The four creatures are described in terms of four categories of earthly creatures: a lion, a calf, the face of a human, and a flying eagle. These may reflect the creatures of Ezek. 1:5-10. In Revelation the forms of the creatures are mentioned, except for man, whereas in Ezekiel each of the four creatures have four faces: 'of the lion, ox, man and bird'. There is some manuscript evidence (P 1 2059s pm sy^h TR) that the word translated 'face of a man' is actually the construction that would indicate the entire form of a human rather than only the human face. The evidence is not conclusive, but does support the interpretation that these creatures are related in some way to those in Ezekiel. For whatever reason, Ezekiel was impressed by the four faces of each creature whereas John was impressed by the four forms. John's vision of six wings follows Isaiah's description of the seraphs (Isa. 6:1-2). The wings possibly symbolize swiftness to carry out the will of God. Certainly the wings recall Old Testament passages such as 'He (God) came swiftly upon the wings of the wind' (Ps. 18:10), and Ezekiel 10, which

---

[10] Cf. Mk 16:5; Mt. 28:3; Jn 20:12; Acts 1:10; see also 2 Macc. 11:8, *Test. Levi* 8:2.

shows God's chariot-throne being carried by cherubim, who 'lifted up their wings to mount up from the earth' (Ezek. 10:16).

There are many suggestions for the symbolic interpretation of the four creatures: they could represent the categories of living things in creation, the four Gospels, the character of God or, most likely, another angelic order of beings in heaven. It is also possible that they symbolize, as Swete suggests, 'whatever is noblest, strongest, wisest in animate Nature'.[11] They are covered with eyes (the actual description is 'eyes round about and within'), which probably means that the eyes covered them totally, even the underside of the wings. This may suggest that they have some guardian function, and it no doubt points to their knowledge and watchfulness. Their wings may also suggest a messenger role. These creatures appear throughout Revelation and engage in worship with the elders (Rev. 5:6, 8-14; 6:1; 7:11; 14:3; 15:7; 19:4).

From the throne come thunders and lightnings (4:5). The present indicative verb 'come' suggests the continuous nature of the heavenly phenomena. The sounds recall the Sinai theophany and further point to the powerful character of God. In fact, cosmic manifestations such as earthquakes, thunder, lightning, and fire, etc. should be seen as direct manifestations of who God is. It is noteworthy that there are four references to these cosmic manifestations all in relation to God's presence, usually in judgment: thunders, lightnings and sounds proceed from God's throne (4:5); they follow the opening of the seventh seal and accompany the pouring out of the golden censor containing the prayers of the saints (8:3-5); they introduce the seven trumpets (8:6) and the seven vials (11:19) and finally, they accompany the outpouring of the seventh and final vial which destroys Babylon (16:17-19). The judgments should be understood as emanating directly from God himself and as reflecting his very presence. There is little wonder that the wicked respond in terror (16:20-21).

Along with his worthiness because of his work in creation, God is also given glory for the establishment of his reign (4:10; 11:15; 12:10; 19:1-7). In each scene, the praises for God's reign intensify until his reign is actually established in the Holy City (chs. 21; 22). The praises of hallelujahs (19:1-7) introduce the marriage supper of the Lamb. The glory of the reign is finally described: in the reign of God, the consequences or reward for 'giving God glory' is that the presence of God himself will be at the very center of existence so there is no need for natural light and limitations of human existence cease to exist (7:15-17;

---

[11] Henry B. Swete, *The Apocalypse of St. John* (Grand Rapids, MI: Eerdmans, 1906, 1951), p. 71.

21:3-4; 22:1-5). The consequences for not worshiping God are also clear, as noted earlier: the Lake of Fire (20:14). Whereas the ultimate existence of the righteous will be characterized by light, the glory of God himself, the final end of the wicked will also be characterized by the presence of God – but in terms of judgment by fire (20:15).

Before the throne, perhaps directly in front of it, are seven lamps. It is possible to translate this phrase as 'blazing torches'.[12] These may represent the seven-branched menorah (the easiest interpretation) or they may be another angelic order based on the Jewish idea that angels are made of fire.[13] In apocalyptic literature, there are also references to beings around the throne who are made of wind and fire (*2 Bar.* 21:6; *4 Ezra* 8:21-22). John himself interprets the lamps as the seven spirits of God (Rev. 4:5), referred to earlier in 1:4. Probably the spirits represent 'the activity of the risen Christ through the Holy Spirit in and to the seven churches'.[14] The imagery certainly echoes Zech. 4:1-14, where the prophet describes his vision of seven bowls of oil taken from two olive trees. The seven spirits are mentioned four times in Revelation (1:4; 3:1; 4:5; 5:6). Each time they are closely associated with the victory of the Lamb by means of divine power.[15] In short, the role of the Spirit is the key component in Revelation – the prophecy itself is communicated by the Spirit, and God's ultimate victory will be brought about by the power of the Holy Spirit (see our remarks on pp. 21f. above). In any case, the spirits are always distinct from the saints and are directly associated with God and his throne as the means by which he carries out his plans.

Also in front of the throne is a sea, like glass. This may reflect Ezekiel's vision of an 'expanse, sparkling like ice', Ezek. 1:22. (Other references to a heavenly ocean occur in Pss. 29:10; 104:3; 148:4; *Test. Levi* 2:7; *2 En.* 3:3.) The sea seems to reflect the attitude of God, for here it appears quiet and clear while in Rev. 15:2, it is filled with fire, reflecting the wrath and judgments of God taking place on earth. The 'sea' in this passage seems to be different from the one in Rev. 13:1, for the beast arising out of the 'sea' is not described as near the throne, probably not even in heaven (the sign described in ch. 12, however, is said to appear in heaven). Furthermore, in the new heaven and new earth there is no sea (21:1), not because it is evil, but because it represents separation of God and humanity.[16] In the throne-room scene of ch. 4, the sea appears

---

[12] Aune, p. 295.
[13] Mounce, p. 136.
[14] Johnson, p. 420.
[15] See Bauckham, pp. 109-15, for a fairly extensive discussion of the seven spirits.
[16] Wall (p. 94) suggests evil is located in the sea and as such it represents the old order, which has been replaced by the new order.

clear, reflecting the perfect worship of the angelic beings and providing a separation between God and the earth. Perhaps it is into this sea that all sins are cast, to be remembered no more (Mic. 7:19). It is then possible for humanity to approach the holy throne of God.

Chapter 4 includes the first of the hymn sections in Revelation.[17] Verse 8 says of the four creatures: 'Day and night they never stop saying "Holy, holy, holy, Lord God Almighty, who was, and is, and is to come."' Ceaseless praise is also found in apocalyptic descriptions of heaven.[18] The concept that angels participate in heavenly praise is common in Jewish apocalyptic literature.[19] The hymns are important to the literary structure of Revelation, tending to function like the chorus in a Greek play, as a comment on the events that are occurring. In chs. 4 and 5 the first hymn is addressed to God, the second to the Lamb and the third to both. The size of the choirs also expands.

The first hymn is short and may reflect Isa. 6:3 and Exod. 3:14. It is sung by the four creatures to God for his greatness. The repeated phrase 'Holy, holy, holy' is significant.

Johnson explains:

> In Hebrew, the double repetition of a word adds emphasis while the rare threefold repetition designates the superlative and calls attention to the infinite holiness of God.[20]

The creatures also praise God for his everlastingness, 'who was and is and is to come' (Rev. 4:8). This description echoes Rev. 1:4, which introduces the sender of the message – God himself. As mentioned earlier, it is interesting to note the relation of these living creatures to the seraphs of Isaiah 6 and the living beings of Ezekiel 1. In all three accounts the creatures are directly connected to God's throne: in Rev. 4:6, they are 'in the center and around the throne'; in Isa. 6:1-2, they are above the Lord, who is sitting on his throne; in Ezek. 1:4-26, God's throne is in the expanse above their heads. In all three accounts they are multi-winged (six wings in Rev. and Isa.; four in Ezek). One of the most striking aspects of the creatures in all three accounts is their dynamic and vital character, shown by their many eyes (in Rev. 4:6,8, 'full of eyes around and within'); by their motion in Ezek. 1:14,16, (they run to and fro like lightning bolts and are involved with the motion of the wheels); and by their relation to the burning coals in Isa. 6:6. The many wings also add to this dynamic imagery. Their function

---

[17] See Aune, pp. 314-17, for an excursus on hymns in Revelation, with bibliography.
[18] *1 En.* 39:11-14; *2 En.* 21:1-2; *Test. Levi* 3:8.
[19] See *2 En.* 18:8-9; 19:3-6; 42:3-4; *3 En.* 24-40.
[20] Johnson, p. 463.

is intrinsically linked to worship of God himself (see also Rev. 5:8-14; 7:11; 15:7-8; 19:4). They worship ceaselessly day and night (Rev. 4:8). The words of their worship are very similar in Revelation 4 and Isaiah 6: 'Holy, holy, holy is the Lord God Almighty' (4:8), 'the Lord of Hosts' (Isa. 6:3), 'who was, and is, and is to come' (4:8), 'the whole earth is filled with his glory' (Isa. 6:3). In Ezekiel, the living beings are pictured slightly differently, particularly because of their relation to the actions of the Spirit in the wheel (Ezek. 1:20-21).

The second hymn is sung by the 24 elders in response to the first hymn (4:8) and is also addressed to God, this time for his worthiness and his work in creation (4:11). 'Worthy' (ἄξιος) means what is fitting or proper and is appropriate because of the work that God performed in creation. The term, rarely found outside Revelation is used in 5:9,12 of the Lamb, based on his death. God is given the titles 'our Lord and God', which attribute to him complete sovereignty.[21]

Worship is given to God also because by his will all things were created (4:11). This is a difficult phrase to translate but it has the sense that all things existed first in God's will and then were created in material form.[22]

As constant praise is offered to God by the living creatures (v. 9), the 24 elders fall down and give their crowns to God (v. 10). 'To fall down' in prostration was an act performed before rulers or emperors and implies worship as well as submission. The act of giving up their crowns suggests that the elders gave to God the authority and honor which they themselves had earned. They attribute 'worthiness' to him (v. 11), for God alone is worthy of such praise. Also, God is proclaimed 'Lord and God', a title adopted by Domitian for himself.[23] It implies complete rulership. It is interesting to note that the elders proclaim '*our* Lord and *our* God', suggesting that they recognize God as their own master. The awesome majesty and power of God does not deprive each individual of intimate access to God, however. A personal relationship is also available to everyone. Worship is the only way the creature can give anything to God. Even then, the worshiper does not bestow anything on God. Rather, 'the praise of his name ascribes to

---

[21] Some see it as an application of titles given to the Roman emperors. See Aune, pp. 109-11, for an extended discussion.

[22] Mounce, p. 140. Aune, p. 314, discusses this hymn in light of early Christian and Jewish liturgy and concludes: 'In spite of some traditional elements that certainly had a place in Jewish as well as Christian liturgy, the throne-room liturgy appears to be a Johannine creation based on his knowledge of Roman imperial court ceremonial, as well as aspects of Jewish and Christian liturgical traditions.'

[23] Suetonus, *Dominicana*, 13.

him the glory, honor and praise that are his from eternity to eternity'.[24] The reason for this acclaim is God's work in creation (as mentioned above). He alone is worthy to receive glory, honor and power (v. 11).

The vision of ch. 4 reflects the vision of ch. 1 and repeats the description which God gave himself in Rev. 1:8: 'Lord God, who was and who is and who is to come, the Almighty'. In ch. 4, God is recognized in this way by the angelic creatures and proclaimed in this way as the ultimate Lord (4:8-11). This is important, since the church was faced with emperor worship and needed to be reminded that God is in fact recognized as all-powerful by heavenly beings as well as creation. He is worthy of this acclaim because of his timelessness and work in creation, two attributes which even Roman emperors could not claim. Such a God was in control of the world's history and therefore would ultimately triumph over all evil which might be challenging the church. Also, since he existed in the past, present, and will exist in the future, his message concerning things to come should be received, believed and obeyed.

The dramatic vision of God's throne-room sets the stage for ch. 5 and the following seal narrative. Mounce says:

> Since the vision moves on naturally to the breaking of the seals and ultimately to the unveiling of the close of history, it is best to understand it as referring essentially to a time yet future. While God is eternally adored in heaven, the book of Revelation reveals those specific events with which history is brought to a close.[25]

Chapter 5

The Scroll: 5:1-4

As John observes the throne-room worship scene, he notices more detail in the figure sitting on the throne. Whereas before he had described mostly brilliance (ch. 4), he now notices a scroll held in God's right hand (5:1). The word for scroll (βιβλίον) is sometimes translated 'book'. This translation is also favored by some since it is literally 'on' the hand. The description of the document fits a scroll, however, for it is written 'on the inside and on the back' (ὄπισθεν). Such a scroll is known as an 'opistograph', usually made of parchment or papyrus. Although normally written only on one side, a scroll could have writing on both sides to complete a text or for economic reasons. It could also have been a doubly written legal document, or text written twice,

---

[24] Gause, p. 93.
[25] Mounce, p. 132.

once on the inside and once on the back. The most convincing idea, however, is that the scroll was modeled after Ezekiel's scroll (Ezek. 2:9,10) which was also held in a divine hand and written on the front and back. This indicates that the entire writing area of the scroll was used up and implies completion.

The scroll was sealed by seven seals. A seal was a blob of wax, often impressed with a ring, to protect its contents.[26] Official private documents were sealed in order to keep the contents secret until the appropriate person was present to break the seals. In some cases, certain documents were sealed by seven witnesses. The number seven for John's sealed scroll, however, probably suggests divine completion, as used in other contexts in Revelation, rather than seven different witnesses. The seven seals may also suggest the level of secrecy of the document. This fits with a common prophetic/apocalyptic theme that God's message of future divine retribution is kept secret until the appropriate time and even then is revealed only to the righteous or wise.[27] The scroll could be read only after all of the seals were broken. This further supports the possibility that the document was in the form of a scroll, since if it were a book the seals could have been opened one at a time and the contents read.

A major issue of this passage has to do with the contents of the scroll. There are many options. First, it could be the Book of Life containing the names of the saints. This is unlikely, however, since when the seals are broken, much is revealed that has to do with woes and judgments. Other options include the views that the scroll contains the record of the sins of humankind, for which the Lamb has made atonement, or that it is Scripture, the Old Testament or the Torah. Again, the details in Rev. 5:6-20, which follow the opening of the seals, suggest something more inclusive. Finally, and most convincing, the scroll held by God could be a 'Book of Destiny' containing the final outcome of God's redemptive plan, the judgment of evil, the final exaltation and reign of Christ; it is the consummation of history – of the righteous and wicked as well as the final Messianic Kingdom of God.[28] Ezekiel's scroll is a similar type of scroll with lamentations and woes (Ezek. 2:10). Other passages reflect the day ordained for the righteous (Ps. 139:16; cf. *1 En.* 81:1-2; 47:3; 106:19; 107:1).

---

[26] Gottfried Fitzer, 'σφραγίς, σφραγίζω, κατασφραγίζω', *TDNT* VII (1964-1976), pp. 939-53.
[27] See Dan. 8:26; Isa. 29:11; *1 En.* 89:71; Ezek. 2:9-10; Jer. 36:2.
[28] Aune, pp. 344-45, Mounce, p. 142, and Beasley-Murray, p. 120, follow this option.

In this particular location in the structure of Revelation (ch. 5), the scroll may function as a literary device to introduce the subsequent events. It also focuses the reader on the Lamb and his unique role in opening the seals and thereby inaugurating the eschatological events.

John sees God holding the book in his right hand ready for action. Then a strong (powerful in authority) angel proclaims the necessity for someone to open the seals and to reveal the contents of the book. The picture is striking because even an authoritative angel cannot perform the task. An extensive search is apparently carried out, for no one in heaven, earth, or under the earth is found to be worthy (5:3).[29] 'Worthiness' has to do with qualification rather than ability and fits the metaphor of the scroll, for only the designated person could open such a sealed document. Thus, John spotlights Christ's uniqueness by using the heavenly council motif, where the call goes out 'Who is worthy...?' (cf. Isa. 6:8; 1 Kgs 22:20), then someone is produced and commissioned.

Revelation 5:4 describes John's reaction to the scene prior to the Lamb's arrival: he weeps heavily. The 'weeping prophet' motif is found often in prophetic/apocalyptic literature and most likely suggests more than his own disappointment. Rather, it may dramatize the importance of the event; John would be aware that the failure to open the book would postpone God's actions in bringing about Messianic fulfillment.[30]

Nevertheless, John is not left to mourn. One of the elders introduces Jesus (Rev. 5:5) as 'the Lion from the tribe of Judah, the Root of David'. A divine interpreter appears often in apocalyptic literature, but the typical dialogue with the seer does not take place here. The lion figure, as well as its relationship to David, suggests the warrior King-Messiah, the one who answers prophetic expectations of first century Judaism.[31] The reason Jesus is worthy, as described by the elder, is that he 'overcame', again a conquering messiah concept (Rev. 5:5). In dramatic contrast, John looks for a lion and sees a lamb appearing in the midst of the throne. This scene appears as incredibly dramatic; the imagery itself is profound – a lion is announced; the reader along with the seer expects a lion but sees a lamb. In addition, the lamb has been sacrificed. Instead of the victorious conqueror, symbolized by the king of the beasts, a lamb emerges, a lamb that has been 'slaughtered'.[32] The imagery merges the two concepts further by the vocabulary used: the

---

[29] For the concept of these cosmic levels see Phil. 2:10; Ignatius, *Trallians* 9:1.
[30] Cf. Aune, p. 346; Mounce, p. 144.
[31] Cf. *4 Ezra* 11:36-58 where the lion was used to designate the conquering Messiah.
[32] See Blount, Witness, ch. 3 for a discussion of the imagery. Cf. also Skaggs and Doyle, "Three Critical Questions".

Lamb has 'prevailed' or overcome so as to open the book (v. 5). The word prevailed conveys the idea of overcoming through conquest, particularly by royal military power.[33] The dynamic paradox of this image is powerful: as the conquering warrior, he has attained his position, but the means of doing this is by being the sacrificial lamb. Victory has been achieved through death. The exact location of Jesus in relation to the throne is unclear, but it seems most likely to be in front of the throne, in the midst of the worshipers.

The word used for lamb (ἀρνίον), means a young sheep. This lamb title for Christ occurs 28 times throughout the remainder of the book of Revelation and is the most frequent title used for Jesus. Here it is joined to the adjectival participle 'slaughtered' and suggests that the lamb has actually been slain.[34] The sacrificial lamb metaphor (also in Rev. 5:12, 13:8) would recall the Passover festival of Judaism (Isa. 53:7). Thus, the conquering Davidic Messiah imagery is joined with the suffering servant idea of Isa. 42–53. The lamb is also a dominant theme in the four Gospels, particularly in the Gospel of John.

This passage can perhaps be considered as one of the most profound in the entire Apocalypse, since these verses 'relate Jewish messianic hopes to the distinctively Christian good news of the advent of the Messiah in the person of Jesus of Nazareth'.[35] Both titles are rooted in Old Testament Jewish messianism: the Lion of the Tribe of Judah reflects Gen. 49:9-10, where Jacob in his final blessing on his twelve sons calls Judah 'a lion's whelp' and promises him an everlasting scepter 'until Shiloh come'.[36] The second title, the Root of David, echoes Isa. 11:1-10: 'there shall come forth a shoot out of the stock of Jesse ... who will judge in righteousness and peace'. This strong messianic idea is directly linked to the Lamb who was slain. The Lamb is described as having seven horns and seven eyes. The 'horned' idea may reflect apocalyptic literature (*1 En.* 90:9; *Test. Jos.* 19:6,8; *1 En.* 90:37) and might suggest amazing physical power, while the many eyes would imply knowledge and insight (cf. Jer. 48:25; Ps. 18:1-3; Dan. 7:20,22; *1 En.* 90:35). The number seven, as mentioned earlier, may be an eschatological number used by John to imply completeness.

The Lamb is 'standing' before the throne, in sharp contrast to all the others who are seated. This may highlight the commissioning of Jesus by the heavenly council, as it suggests he is prepared to carry out what

---

[33] Gause, p. 96.
[34] Aune, p. 353.
[35] R.H. Preston and A.T. Hanson, *The Revelation of St. John the Divine*, Torch Bible Commentaries (London: SCM Press, 1962), p. 75.
[36] Cf. also *Test. Judah* 24:5 and *4 Ezra* 12:31 for a similar idea of the lion as Messiah.

is required. This should not be taken as a coronation event for Christ, or as occurring immediately upon his death at Calvary. Rather, here Christ is found 'worthy' to open the book and to introduce the future end-time events because of his death, which has already happened.

As John watches, Jesus, the slain Lamb, takes the book out of God's hand. The word for 'take' may be translated 'seize' and implies taking with authority. Immediately the scene erupts with singing and worship (Rev. 5:8-14) of the Lamb. This time the creatures as well as the 24 elders fall down in worship (5:8b-14). The worship centers around the worthiness of the Lamb to take the book and break the seals. He is worthy because he redeemed people by his sacrificial death and made them to be a 'kingdom and priests to God' (vv. 9-10). This, indeed, is the content of the 'new song' sung by the four creatures and 24 elders who begin the worship (v. 8). Each of them is holding a harp (or lyre, κιθάραν) and a golden bowl of incense. The harp is mentioned two additional times in Revelation (14:2 and 15:2) and only one other place in the New Testament (1 Cor. 14:7).

In both of the other occurrences in Revelation (14:2 and 15:2) the harps are played by the heavenly singers in the context of the worship of God. In the Old Testament and early Jewish literature there is a close relation between the harp and praise.[37] The 24 elders are also holding golden bowls of incense which, according to John, contain the 'prayers of the saints' (v. 8). The term 'holy ones', or saints, most likely should be translated 'God's people', since the point here is their relationship to God rather than their sanctity.[38]

The song of the four living creatures and the 24 elders is 'new', probably because it is not the usual song of praise to God for creation. This category of song ('new') is mentioned seven times in the Old Testament (Pss. 33:3; 40:3; 96:1; 98:1; 144:9; 149:1; Isa. 42:10). The phrase refers to a new composition introduced for a special celebration or to replace traditionally used songs.[39]

As mentioned earlier, the content of the song focuses on redemption and echoes the Passover (Exod. 19:5,6). Whereas the sacrificial animal's blood redeemed the Israelites (cf. Num. 3:13), Christ has redeemed

---

[37] Cf. Pss. 33:2-3; 43:4; 57:7-9; 71:22; 81:1-3; 92:1-3; 98:4-6; 108:1-3; 147:7; 150:3-5; 1 Macc. 4:54; Test. Job 14:1-3.

[38] Cf. J.P. Louw and E.A. Nida, eds., *Greek-English Lexicon of the New Testament Based on Semantic Domains*, I (New York: United Bible Societies, 1988), 11:27. The term ἁγίων occurs 12 times elsewhere in Revelation (8:3,4; 11:18; 13:7,10; 14:12; 16:6; 17:6; 18:20,24; 19:8; 20:9). Cf. Aune, p. 359, for a discussion of the use of the term in OT and early Jewish literature.

[39] Robert C. Cully, *Oral Formulaic Language on the Biblical Psalms*, IV (Toronto: University of Toronto Press, 1967), p. 58.

people to God with his sacrificial death on the Cross. There are people 'out of every tribe, and tongue, and people, and nation' (Rev. 5:9; 7:9; 11:9; 13:7; 14:6). Four ethnic units are specified here, and most certainly the emphasis is on the universality of the redemption by Christ. He has effectively broken down the division between Jew and Gentile (Rom. 1:14-17) and humankind generally (Eph. 2:13-17; Acts 1:8; 13:47), efficiently destroying divisions as prophesied by the ancient prophets (cf. Isa. 42:6; 49:6). By Christ's redemption, people have been transformed into a 'kingdom and priests' (cf. Lk. 22:28-30; Mt. 8:11). Again, divisions have been resolved into unity in the one reign of God. In the Old Testament only a privileged few had access to God for worship and service.[40] It is interesting to note, however, that apparently, although divisions are resolved, diversity still exists. The song lists 'tribes, tongues, nations, and people' (v. 9). Perhaps this indicates that individual differences will still exist; although, most likely, negative connotations about aspects like race or even size would most certainly not be present.

'Myriads and myriads' of angels join the heavenly beings in worship (vv. 11-12); see similar passages in Dan. 7:10; 1 En. 14:22; 40:1; 60:1; 71:8-9). The song of the angels is similar to the preceding one of the creatures and elders, although the concept of 'worthiness' is somewhat different. Angels are not redeemed, but evidently they still worship Christ as Redeemer.[41] It is interesting that Christ's worthiness as praised by the angels includes a list of qualities such as are ascribed to kings and benefactors.[42] Further, these qualities are applied to God and are occasionally bestowed on a king by God.[43] Power (δύναμις) and might (ἰσχύν) are synonymous for strength, and when paired emphasize this quality.[44] Wealth (πλοῦτον) is often associated with kingship (Rev. 18:17), but is never ascribed to God as King in the Old Testament and only occurs here in Revelation in relation to Christ. Wisdom (σοφία) is also used in the hymn in 7:12 and is also considered a quality bestowed on a king by God.[45] Honor (τιμή) is applied twice to God in Revelation (4:11, 7:12) and once to both God and the Lamb (5:13)

---

[40] Gause, p. 99.
[41] Ibid., p. 100.
[42] Cf. Josephus, *War* VII 71: 'power, wealth, wisdom, might, honor, glory and praise' (Rev. 5:12).
[43] Aune, p. 365.
[44] Marc Z. Brettler, *God is King: Understanding an Israelite Metaphor*, JSOTS 76 (Sheffield: Sheffield Academic Press, 1989), pp. 57-68. In other places in Revelation these terms are applied to God, but not to Christ (Rev. 4:11; 7:12; 11:17; 19:1). See also 1 Sam. 2:10 and Ps. 28:8, where this quality is bestowed on a king by God.
[45] Brettler, pp. 55-56.

and 'denotes the honor, respect and status that a person enjoys when his position, wealth and office are appropriately recognized in the community to which he belongs'.[46] Glory (δόξα) is attributed to God alone (4:11; 7:12; 19:1) and once to God and the Lamb (5:13). The meaning of this term sheds light on the nature of worship, and hence on the entire message of Revelation. The oldest and most concrete meaning of δόξα is 'light' or 'radiance'. Although this is found only occasionally in the Greek of the LXX, in the New Testament the word is used in a unique sense which is not found in secular Greek at all except for one reference in Philo. It denotes 'divine and heavenly radiance' and refers to the 'loftiness and majesty of God' and even the 'being of God' or his very essence or presence. In order to understand this unique sense, one must consider the Old Testament word *kabod*. This Hebrew word means 'honor' and refers to the quality which gives importance or impressiveness to someone – something 'weighty', which gives someone importance. In relation to God, it refers to 'that which makes God impressive to man, the force of his self-manifestation'.[47] So, when worshipers 'give glory to God', they are actively acknowledging who God is, the quality of his presence, and are extolling his magnificence. In 4:8,11, the heavenly beings extol God because of his work in creation; they glorify Christ (5:13), for his redemptive work. Praise (εὐλογία) is only applied to God in Rev. 4:11 and 7:12. The angels and creatures have thus ascribed in praise to the Lamb the qualities of power, riches, wisdom, strength, honor, glory and praise (5:12). As Gause comments,

> He is the inheritor of all power in heaven and earth (Mt. 28:18). His wealth is the riches of his grace (Eph. 1:7). In him are hidden all the treasures of wisdom and knowledge (Col. 2:3). His strength lies in His triumph over all principalities and powers; He ascends to the right hand of the Father (Eph. 1:19-20, 6:10). Honor, glory and praise are the vocabulary of worship ... the worshiping creatures cannot bestow them upon Christ, but by the act of praise, they ascribe to him what is his as a divine person.[48]

The third group joins the heavenly creatures and angels, 'every creature which is in heaven and upon the earth and under the earth and in the sea and all things in them' (v. 13). Curiously, this is almost an exact repetition of 5:3, where no one in heaven or creation is able to open the book. The point is clear that all creation joins the heavenly beings

---

[46] J. Schneider, 'τιμή', *TDNT* VIII (1972), pp. 169-80.
[47] G. von Rad, *Old Testament Theology*, II (Evanston, IL: Harper & Row, 1962-65), p. 238.
[48] Gause, p. 100.

in praise of the worthiness of the Lamb: 'blessing, honor, glory and dominion forever and ever' (v. 13). The praise is to both God and the Lamb (cf. Phil. 2:9-11). These four attributes (blessing, honor, glory and dominion) correspond to other doxologies in Revelation (1:5-6; 4:9,11; 5:12-13; 7:12; 19:1). The first doxology (1:6) includes only two terms, 'glory and honor'. There are three terms in 4:9-11; four in 5:13 and seven in 5:12 and 7:12. Since all of these terms are similar in meaning to one another, the progressive addition of terms should be interpreted as the progression of intensity. This progressive intensity is found in the other cycles as well (e.g. the judgments become more severe, etc.). The main point here appears to be the universality of praise in both heaven and on earth and the eternality of worship – for ever and ever (v. 13).

The four living creatures close the worship with 'Amen', after which the 24 elders fall down in worship. It appears that the four living creatures function almost like worship leaders, beginning and ending the worship as well as responding to the various hymns with 'Amen', 'Amen'. These actions strongly affirm what has preceded. The imperfect tense 'they kept saying "Amen"' would indicate a repetitive response. In fact, owing to the tense of the verb 'said' (iterative imperfect), it is possible that their 'Amen' is said after each attribute.[49] In any case, the picture is of continuous praise including songs and prostrations. The final response is the worship of the 24 elders, who fall down (v. 14). This scene is pivotal in Revelation. Whether or not it is an enthronement scene,[50] it is certainly the scene in which the ultimate triumph of Jesus is pictured: 'all power is given unto me in heaven and in earth' (Mt. 28:18).

Reflection and Response (Part 3)

Reflection
The primary theme in this section is worship. Indeed, the entire text of Revelation is set within the context of worship: worship of God as Lord, worship of Christ as sacrificial Lamb. Infinite numbers of heavenly beings prostrate themselves before the Throne, praising God for his work in Creation, praising Christ for his sacrificial death, and crying, 'Holy, Holy, Holy, Lord God Almighty!' The main theme of their worship is that God reigns, he is holy and almighty, and is altogether worthy of eternal praise.

---

[49] Verse 12; cf. Mounce, p. 150.
[50] Gause, p. 102.

In light of this, in what way does this text inform our worship today? What role does worship play in our services? What is the central focus of our worship? Indeed, does our worship revolve around the fact that God is in control of our lives? Or has it become a sort of 'role' part of the service, merely a 'warm-up' or prelude to the sermon? Is the music itself more central than the message? In other words, does the medium detract from the message? What opportunities are available for the musicians and worship leaders to reflect on the meaning of worship and how best to enhance the worship experience?

The text has meaning not only for the church as a whole, but also for each of us individually. It is beneficial to reflect on some additional questions. How do I approach the worship part of the service? Is worship the means by which I come into his presence, acknowledging his Lordship, his holiness, his worthiness, his power to transform my life? Or have I become so familiar with the songs that my mind wanders and I merely say the words without meaning them? What role does the music itself play in my worship: am I so focused on the medium that I lose the message itself? How can I participate in worship so that I maintain the praise of God as the central focus of my worship?

Response
The following are suggestions for response.

1. Examine the ministry of worship in your church. If you are not a member of the worship team, suggest such a review to the music leaders so that they might agree with you in prayerful assessment of the ministry. The use of scriptural passages about the nature and purpose of worship would help to facilitate this process.
2. Prayerfully identify ways in which worship is a meaningful aspect of the service and ways which would enhance its meaning to the church community.
3. Form a prayer group of worship among the musicians themselves. The more you unite as a prayerfully reflective group, the more possible it will be to convey this same sense to the entire church community.
4. Commit as a group to such a periodic review so that the focus on the intention of worship will be on-going.

Revelation 6:1-9:21

Chapter 6

Chapter 6 continues the vision begun in ch. 4: the Lamb who has taken the scroll from God's hand amid wondrous worship (ch. 5) now begins to open the seals. It appears that the actual contents of the scroll are not revealed until all seals are broken (ch. 8). There are many suggestions as to the relationship of the seals to the judgments found in the scroll, mostly having to do with the question of whether the events of the seal are preparatory to the final judgment, or if they are actually part of it. Certainly there is a time sequence to the seals and therefore 'the seals represent events preparatory to the final consummation'.[1] In fact, each opened seal introduces the reader to 'a sense of preliminary judgments representing forces operative throughout history ...'[2] Apparently the seals introduce the characters and characteristic forces which lead to and then play important roles in the final pouring out of judgments described in succeeding chapters. For example, as the four horses are introduced no specific events are described; rather, John is shown a dynamic warrior-leader (6:2) and the characteristics of his rule: warfare (6:3,4), famine (6:5,6), death and hades (6:7,8). When the fifth seal is opened the martyrs under the altar in heaven are told to wait (6:11). The sixth seal reveals judgments which are imminent (6:12-17).

The first six seals seem to parallel Jesus' Mount Olivet discourse (Mt. 24): False christs will come (24:5); there will be wars, famines and earthquakes (vv. 6-8). Persecution is also predicted (v. 9) and, like the souls under the altar of Rev. 6:11, the disciples are told that the (eschatological) end is not yet, and that only the one who endures to the end will be saved (Mt. 24:12,13). The sign of the Son of Man's coming is described in terms of earthly cosmic, cataclysmic events (vv. 29-31), which are said to occur 'after the distress of those days' (vv. 24-29). At

---

[1] Johnson, p. 472.
[2] Mounce, p. 151.

that time, the Son of Man appears with great power and the nations of the earth mourn (v. 30). John sees a great earthquake, the sun blackened, and the stars falling (Rev. 6:12-14). He also sees terror and confusion as the wicked attempt to escape the wrath of the Lamb (6:15-17). In the Olivet discourse Jesus does not reveal the judgments of the wicked to the disciples, for his address seems to be in answer to their questions: 'What will be the sign of your coming and of the end of the age?' (Mt. 24:3) and has to do primarily with the church.

Therefore, the seals of Revelation should be understood as introducing the specific characters which lead into the final judgments. Like all of the visions in the book of Revelation, John is shown events in heaven and on earth which often occur simultaneously, much like a multilevel screen: as he sees the progression of war, famine, and death on earth, he also sees the righteous in heaven wearing white robes, and praising God and the Lamb.

As the Lamb opens the first seal, one of the four living creatures calls out with a loud voice, 'Come!' (Rev. 6:1). The call should be understood as addressing the horsemen rather than John or the Lamb, for it is the horsemen who respond. Perhaps the idea presented here is that only after being commissioned by God can the Lamb initiate the events (by opening the seal). Even then, the riders must be called out by those close to the throne – one of the four living creatures. The call 'come' functions in a similar fashion as in first-century circuses, where charioteers were summoned by such a call.[3]

The first four seals introduce four apocalyptic horses. They are described by colors and their riders perform certain tasks in the earth. The imagery of the horses may reflect Zech. 1:8-17 and 6:1-8, but the meaning of John's figure is quite distinct. In Zechariah the colors have no significance; the horses are sent out by God to patrol the earth, but the riders are not described. In contrast, the colors of the horses in John's vision actually give an insight into the character of the riders. Although these horses apparently originate from God, they are *destructive* and are symbolic of God's *judgment* rather than his grace. The imagery of horses suggests powerful, swift messengers which can cover ground quickly. Also, horses were used by people of wealth and authority, often in war. As such, they are appropriate to usher in the eschatological events.

The first horse introduced is white. It is interesting that John does not see his entrance; rather, the horse seems to appear on the scene suddenly. The rider is described as holding a bow (note: arrows are not included). He is given a crown (perhaps as John watches) and he rides

---

[3] Johnson, p. 472.

out in conquest (6:2). Though the identity of this rider is a critical issue, it is interesting that he is not more closely identified, since the descriptions of the next horses leave little to question. One option is that the white horse rider is Christ, who brings the triumphant spread of the gospel. The strongest argument for this view has to do with the white horse, for Christ is seen later on a white horse (Rev. 19:11), and in Revelation white is usually an indication of righteousness.

At this point the similarities cease, and significant differences are evident. While the rider of Revelation 6 has no name, Christ is called Faithful and True, the Word of God, King of Kings, Lord of Lords, and a name which he alone knows. The first rider (6:2) carries a bow, a rather unsubstantial weapon (especially without arrows; and it is usually associated with God's enemies, e.g. in Ezek. 39:3), when contrasted with the sharp sword proceeding out of Christ's mouth (Rev. 19:15). The first rider is 'given a victor's wreath' (στέφανος) while Christ has many diadems (διαδήματα πολλά), symbolic of royal authority.

The first rider goes out like a conqueror out to conquer. There is no word of his success. Christ is described as judging and making war (19:11), his robe is stained with blood (perhaps of his enemies, cf. Isa. 63:1,3), which suggests military victory; and he goes out with an iron scepter, implying his rule after conquest. The white horse rider of Revelation 19 presents a striking picture of a successful warrior returning with his untouched armies in glorious victory, prepared to establish rule over all nations, while the rider of Revelation 6 is granted authority and goes out as one who is seeking to conquer. Perhaps the 'final and fatal objection' to the identification of this rider as Christ is the phrase 'there was given', used throughout Revelation to refer to 'the divine permission granted to evil powers to carry out their nefarious work (e.g. the denizens of the abyss [Rev. 9:1,3,5], the monster [13:5,7], and the false prophet [13:14.15]).[4] In addition to these differences, the events which follow the emergence of the rider of Revelation 6 are war, famine and death, which do not seem to imply a revival of the gospel. In contrast, the rider of Revelation 19 confronts the beast and destroys him and his followers (19:19-21). The marked contrast between the rider of ch. 6 and the one in ch. 19 can be summed up: the rider of ch. 6 'receives the victor's crown', not the crown of royal rule (ch. 19). It is a symbol of conquest and not a symbol of rulership. The rider is not primarily a king; he is a conqueror. The crown

---

[4] G.B. Caird, *A Commentary on the Revelation of St. John the Divine*, Harper's New Testament Commentaries, 17 (New York: Harper & Row, 1966), p. 81.

was given to the rider. It is not his by right, but is bestowed on him by someone else.⁵

A more likely identity of the white horse rider of Revelation 6 is the world leader, Antichrist, although the term does not occur in Revelation. He is symbolized in various forms, as in Rev. 11:7 and 13:17.⁶ He types Christ but has relatively little power, and even that is granted temporarily by God. He reflects the messianic deception of Mt. 24:24, which characterizes the period of the end time (cf. also Dan. 7:23-27, 8:23-25). In contrast to Christ, who is faithful and true, judging justly (Rev. 19:11), this rider brings war, bloodshed, famine and death (6:3-8). Perhaps his description reflects the beast of Rev. 13:7, who is given power to make war.

When the second seal is broken a red horse is called out by the second living creature. One cannot tell whether the seals are stacked one upon the other or if they are lined up along the edge of the scroll. Regardless, only one at a time can be broken, which suggests some sort of progression. The color of the horse is red (πυρρός) like fire and its rider is granted power to take peace from the earth by turning people against each other (Rev. 6:4). The Greek word used here (σφάξουσιν) means to kill or murder and suggests the violence and savagery of civil rebellion rather than war.⁷ This may recall Zech. 14:13, which describes a day when people will kill each other after a panic from the Lord falls on them.⁸ It may also parallel Paul's prediction that the last days will be a time of lawlessness (2 Thess. 2:6). The rider is given a 'large sword' (μάχαιρα μεγάλη), which further illuminates the picture of the internal strife and violence that will follow the conquest of the first rider.⁹

The opening of the third seal introduces a black horse whose rider holds measuring scales in his hands. He is told by a voice from among the four living creatures to ration the wheat and barley but not to touch the oil and wine (Rev. 6:5,6). Black usually symbolizes mourning, sorrow, and despair (cf. Isa. 50:3; Jer. 4:28) while the horseman represents famine, with its resulting poverty and hardship. In antiquity, black usually had strong negative connotations because of its association with darkness. Hence, it was often used to symbolize death and

---

⁵ Gause, p. 104.
⁶ Cf. M. Rissi, 'The Rider on the White Horse: A Study of Revelation 6:1-8', *IJBT* 18 (1964), pp. 405-18.
⁷ Cf. Louw-Nida, §20.72.
⁸ Cf. Isa. 19:2; *1 En.* 10:12; *4 Ezra* 5:9; 6:24; *2 Bar.* 48:37; 70:2-8.
⁹ Aune, *Revelation 6-16* (52b), p. 396, interprets the sword in terms of authority and power over people's lives. Governing authorities often carried daggers or swords as symbols of the power of their offices.

the underworld.[10] In this passage, the black horse clearly represents famine, for the cost of a measure of wheat or barley, basic food commodities, was a denarius, which was equivalent to a day's wage. It suggests a time of scarcity when food costs ten to twelve times the usual amount (cf. Cicero, *Verr.* III 81). Famine is probably due to invasion and/or drought. The warning to leave the oil and wine untouched can be interpreted several ways, the most likely being that God limits the effect of the destruction. Thus, only the weaker crops would be affected, while the deeper roots of olive trees and grape vines would not be destroyed. This idea of limited judgment fits well with the phases of destruction seen in Revelation: a fourth of the earth is affected (6:8), then a third (8:7-12), then there is complete destruction (16:17).

When the fourth seal is broken the fourth living creature calls out the final horse and rider, a pale horse bearing Death. Hades follows closely behind. This is perhaps the ghastliest image, for the color (χλωρός) is a pale, sickly greenish color typical of a corpse or a person in terror. This is significant since Death is his rider. Death and Hades (the grave) are usually linked together (1:18,20; 20:14) although it is not clear if Hades is on foot or riding the same or another horse. Power was given the rider to kill by sword, famine, plague or wild animals (cf. Ezek. 14:21). This seems to be an intensification of the first three seals, with its grim picture of bloodshed, famine, and death. Plagues and wild beasts are often a result of the carnage of both famine and war. Nevertheless, God again limits the destruction to a fourth of the earth. This is probably not a reference to a geographical area but to the proportion of humanity affected.

With the opening of the fifth seal (6:9), the scene shifts to a group of righteous martyrs in heaven. They are under the altar and are crying for God to vindicate them by judging evil on the earth. They are given white robes and told to wait until their number is complete. This 'interruption' in the destruction which is occurring on earth may serve several purposes. First, it shows that the righteous are also affected on the earth as the seals are broken. It may also show that the atrocities of the first four seals lead to but do not represent the end time of judgment itself (cf. Mt. 24:14) for they are told to wait. Ultimately, this passage suggests that God is in control of all history and even his judgments will be done according to the correct conditions.

The scene is an altar in heaven. The idea that heaven is God's Temple can be found in Jewish thought[11] and may reflect the altar and burnt offering where animals were sacrificed and their blood poured out at

---

[10] Aune, p. 396.
[11] Hab. 2:20; Ps. 18:6; *Test. Levi* 18:6; cf. Heb. 8:1,2; 9:11,12,23-25.

the base (Lev. 4:7; Exod. 29:12). Blood was sacred in Jewish rituals, for it was thought that the life or spirit was in the blood (Lev. 17:11). 'That the souls of the martyrs were underneath the altar is a way of saying that their untimely deaths on earth are from God's perspective a sacrifice on the altar of heaven.'[12] The word translated 'soul' (ψυχάς) may refer to a disembodied soul or it may also mean a person. If taken as a living person, then John sees those who had been killed on earth alive in heaven.

These people (with all witnesses to God's prophetic message; see the Introduction) had been slain because of the Word of God and their testimony. The theme of martyrdom is predominant in Revelation. Jesus is called the 'faithful martyr' (1:5); John himself is on Patmos because of 'the Word of God and the testimony of Jesus' (1:9); the churches are commended for enduring persecution even when some of their congregation are killed (e.g. 2:10,13); Jesus is worthy to open the seals because of his death (5:9). Thus, John's readers would be encouraged to see that there is a special place for the persecuted and that their concern over God's delay of vindication was heard. The cry of the souls under the altar seems inconsistent with Jesus' and Stephen's forgiveness of their persecutors. Rather, their plea for vengeance seems more in keeping with Jewish thought (Pss. 79:10; 94:3; Hab. 1:2). It also can be found in apocalyptic writings that the prophets complain over the injustice that the wicked prosper while the righteous suffer. God tells them to be patient; vindication will come in time. It seems that the cry of John's martyrs is for God ultimately to triumph and to obliterate the evil which has opposed his people for all time, rather than a prayer for personal revenge (cf. Rom. 12:19).

The souls address God as 'Sovereign Lord, holy and true' (Rev. 6:10). The word 'despot' is used in a slave/master relationship and suggests ownership;[13] 'holy and true' suggests that God is above sin and is fair, just and righteous. Therefore, he is able to distinguish between right and wrong and is implored as their master to avenge their wrongful deaths. The souls, however, are given white robes and told to wait. Sometimes these white robes are interpreted as glorified bodies (see 1 En. 62:16; 2 En. 22:8; Ps. 104:2). It seems more consistent within the book of Revelation, however, to understand them as actual white robes given to reward the righteous for their endurance. For example, the few righteous in Sardis are promised to 'walk with me, dressed in white, for they are worthy' (3:4). Overcomers at Sardis are promised to be clothed in white (3:5); the Laodiceans are counseled to buy white

---

[12] Mounce, p. 157.
[13] K.H. Rengstorf, 'δεσποτής', *TDNT* II (1964), pp. 44-49.

clothes from Christ (3:18) and righteous groups in heaven wear white robes (e.g. 7:9, 19:14). Thus, the martyred ones in heaven are rewarded and comforted by white robes and told to wait until their number is complete.

The concept of predetermination is found often in apocalyptic thought (e.g. *2 Bar.* 23:4,5; *4 Ezra* 4:35-37) as is the notion that the end will not come until there are particular numbers of righteous (*1 En.* 47:4, *4 Ezra* 2:41). It is not clear whether these are martyrs of all times or if they reflect only the church age or the end time period. Neither is it stated whether these are Christians, Jews, or both. It is certainly clear that they are righteous saints, since their fellow servants and brethren who will yet be killed are referred to in v. 11. Nevertheless, they have endured persecution even to death and are rewarded with white robes and told to rest; their time of struggle is over. Although the time of God's final vindication and triumph over evil is not complete (more seals need to be broken), it is imminent.

The revelation of the sixth seal extends from 6:12 to 7:17. It is heightened by the phrase 'I watched' (6:12), repeated from Rev. 6:1. John once again sees the earth, which itself is responding to the Day of Judgment. Verse 17 may be taken as a key to the section 6:12–7:17, 'For the great day of his wrath has come, and *who can stand?*' The cosmic events of 6:12–7:17 do not seem to be the actual judgments which are poured out later during the trumpets and the bowls; rather, they may be preparatory and the reactions may reflect the inadequacy of even the creation to stand in the face of the Lamb's wrath, which is to come.

Earthquakes typically characterize divine visitation, as when God descended on Mount Sinai (Exod. 19:18). Cosmic phenomena were also described by the prophets as preceding the Day of the Lord.[14] Jesus himself described the darkened sun and the falling stars (Mt. 24:29). John describes the scene in vivid detail: the sun turns black like sackcloth, the moon turns blood red (6:12). Sackcloth, a rough cloth made of black goat's hair, was worn during times of mourning. Jewish prophets wore such cloth as a sign of Israel's repentance (Isa. 20:2) and the people of Assyria wore it as a drastic measure to invoke God's mercy. The dark appearance of the sun may be due to an eclipse or the presence of a pervasive substance in the atmosphere. The moon's color is probably a reflection of the sun's darkened state. Volcanic eruptions have been known to resemble earthquakes, with the ash darkening the sun and affecting the color of the moon. Stars falling were often

---

[14] Isa. 2:10-21; 13:10; 34:4; Jer. 4:28; Ezek. 32:7-8; Joel 2:31; 3:15; Zeph. 1:14-18.

viewed by the ancients as omens needing interpretation[15] or a sign of impending judgment.[16] Stars as part of cosmic disturbance are common in apocalyptic literature.[17] Hence, falling stars as indications of the end of the world are appropriate in this context. The stars falling in conjunction with other heavenly events occur elsewhere in Revelation (cf. 8:10; 9:1; 12:4) and in the Synoptic Gospels (cf. Mk 13:25; Mt. 24:29; Lk. 21:26). The sky itself is also affected, rolling up like a scroll and the earth (mountains and islands) are moved about. This suggests the extent of cosmic disturbance. Whether or not this passage is to be taken literally, it follows that as all creation worshiped God and the Lamb (chs. 4; 5), it now is in a state of terror and mourning before their wrath.

Revelation 6:15-17 describes the reaction of the people who are usually in control on earth: kings, princes, generals, the rich and the mighty. They, like the slaves, are reduced to terror and to taking refuge among the mountains. Their calling for the rocks to fall on them seems drastic: it suggests that the fear is not just due to cosmic disturbances, but to the divine presence (6:16). They declare, 'The great day of his wrath has come, and who can stand?' John's description may reflect Isa. 2:10,19,21 and Hos. 10:8, which speak of a time when God will reduce to terror the mighty and powerful on earth who have not recognized his sovereignty. John's picture presents a seeming paradox, for he refers to the 'wrath of the Lamb'. Since lambs are rarely, if ever, violent, the figure appears incongruent, but the joining of the Lamb with 'him who sits on the throne' (Rev. 6:16) shows the unity of the Godhead. God's mercy for humankind, exhibited by the giving of his own Son as the sacrificial lamb, has now reached an end, and retribution is justifiably enforced upon those who have been confident in their own positions of authority. The question 'Who is able to stand?' is no doubt taken from Nahum 1:6: 'Who can stand before his indignation? Who can endure the heat of his anger?' (See also Mal. 3:2; Isa. 13:7,8.) In this passage, Christ is no longer seen as the slain Lamb examining and warning his church (chs. 2; 3). Rather, the Lamb joins God in wrath and divine retribution in response to wickedness. In the face of such wrath the question is posed, 'Who can stand?' The earth cannot (6:12,13); the heavens cannot (6:14); the powerful, wealthy and slaves cannot (6:15,16).

In contrast, the two groups described in Revelation 7 can endure the perilous times: those sealed (protected) by God (7:1-4) and those who have washed their robes in the blood of the Lamb (7:14).

---

[15] Cf. *4 Ezra* 5:5; Josephus, *War* VI 289; Marcus Manilius *Astronomica* I.814-875.
[16] Ezek. 32:7; Joel 2:10, 3:15; Mk 13:25; Mt. 24:29.
[17] Cf. A.D. Nock and A.J. Festugiere, *Corp. Herm.* 2:381 n218.

Chapter 7

The 144,000 and the Great Multitude

The breaking of the sixth seal opens the curtain on a multi-screen presentation of vivid contrasts: earth and heaven, the wicked and the righteous, the terrified and the rejoicing. Rev. 6:14 says, 'The heavens departed as a scroll', giving John a glimpse of both heaven and earth entering the time of God's wrath.

On one 'screen' kings, great men, slaves and freemen are crying out in great terror to be hidden from God's wrath (6:15-17). 'After this' (7:1-8) John's gaze shifts to another 'screen' on which he sees a select group, the 144,000, being prepared to endure the time of destruction (they are sealed for protection). Finally, 'after this' (7:9) John lifts his eyes to yet another 'screen', one showing the most glorious and captivating scenes of the entire revelation: an innumerable crowd representing all ethnic groups, tongues and nations. These have joined the angels, elders and heavenly creatures in God's throne-room. They are clothed with purity and righteousness (white robes), celebrating victory (waving palms) and praising God ceaselessly. The words 'after this' may serve to separate each 'screen' rather than to denote a chronological sequence of time.

The description of these three groups is striking as portrayed on the 'screens'. The first group is described in terms of their social positions and represents those usually in control, as well. Their social distinctions are reduced to equality as they run for cover from God and the Lamb. It is interesting that while they recognize God, their relationship to him is one of terror as they seek escape from his impending wrath. They cry out to the *earth* for protection rather than to God for mercy, once again showing their trust in material (earthly) things rather than God.

John does not see the second group until later (Rev. 14), although he sees the angel descend with the seal (7:2) and he *hears* the number of those to be sealed, 144,000, from a select group: 12,000 from each tribe of Israel. The sealed ones are called 'the servants of God' (7:3), which implies that they enjoy a close relationship with God. (The Lamb is not mentioned here, but appears in 14:1,4.) The response of the group is not recorded by John, probably because he does not see them. The implication is that this group is protected in some supernatural way in order for them to endure the time of wrath on earth. Although the exact role of the group is not described at this time, they seem to represent the righteous remnant spared as an answer to the promises in Jewish prophecy that God would honor his covenant with Israel as he establishes the eschatological Messianic Kingdom.[18]

The third and final group is described in the most detail and stands in contrast to the two preceding groups. They have 'come out of the tribulation' and have washed their robes in the blood of the Lamb (7:14). They seem to be the group anticipated in Rev. 5:9, for they represent 'every tribe and tongue and nation and people'. In this passage the multitude praise God and the Lamb for their salvation (7:10).

Chapter 7 includes several important interpretive challenges. As the chapter begins, one anticipates an impending disaster: four angels stand at the four corners of the earth holding back the four winds (7:1). Winds are often used as metaphorical agents of God, usually for destructive purposes (1 En. 76, 34:3; Dan. 7:2; Jer. 49:36). That their function is destructive is suggested by the later command to wait to 'hurt the earth', etc. until the group is sealed (Rev. 7:3). In apocalyptic literature nature is often under angelic control. The phrase 'four corners of the earth' was an ancient expression much like the 'four points of the compass', showing the comprehensive nature of the phenomena.

The idea that the agents of destruction are in place and detained only by certain divine preparations seems to heighten the tension of God's timing/control and emphasizes that everything must go according to plan. At this point, the major preparatory event is the sealing of a select group.

The seal (Rev. 7:2) is most likely a signet ring used by officials to authenticate and protect private documents. It also implies ownership and divine approval. In this case, the seal appears to be the name of the Lamb and the Father (14:1). A similar passage in Ezekiel 9 describes a man sent by God to mark the foreheads of those who lamented over the corruption of Jerusalem. The mark was the Hebrew letter *tau* made like an X or T. It is interesting that this mark was also used by early Christians to identify themselves with Jesus' cross (see 2 Tim. 2:19). The seal of Rev. 7:2 gave protection from God's wrath in a similar manner to the blood on the doorpost during the Exodus. Furthermore, the seal in Rev. 7:2 is of the 'living God,' which implies an actively involved deity in contrast to the pagan gods of the Greco-Roman world. (See also Josh. 3:10; 2 Kgs 19:4,16.)

---

[18] See Benware, pp. 252-53. Some scholars interpret these two groups as actually the same group: John *hears* the number (144,000) and turns and *sees* the more diverse group. However, the many differences in the two groups as well as the identification of the group in ch. 14 as the 144,000 support more strongly that they are indeed two distinct groups (cf. Skaggs and Doyle, "Three Critical Questions").

A major interpretive challenge of ch. 7 has to do with the identity of the 144,000 and the great multitude, as well as their relationship to each other. The following chart shows the striking differences. It should be noted that since the 144,000 also appear later, information from Revelation 14 must also be considered. The great multitude does not appear until much later (Rev. 19) and must be interpreted within the immediate context of Revelation 7.

144,000	**Multitude**
A limited number	Great multitude
Multiples of 12	Innumerable
A homogeneous group	All tribes, nations, peoples, tongues
On earth, Mount Zion (ch. 14)	In heaven before the throne
Clothing is not specified	Wear white robes
	Wave palms
Sing a new song unique to them	Sing to God and the Lamb
Not joined by heavenly creatures	Joined by angels, creatures, elders
Have been purchased out of the earth (ch. 14:3) 'First fruits unto God and the Lamb'	They have come out of the great Tribulation
Not been defiled with women	Have washed their robes in the blood of the Lamb
Blameless, no lie	Follow the Lamb wherever he goes
Therefore they serve God unceasingly	Servants of God
God spreads his tabernacle over them	No more hunger, thirst, sun striking, heat
Lamb stands with them on Mount Zion	Lamb is their shepherd
They follow him	Will guide them unto fountains of Water of Life
	God will wipe away tears
Their names are heard by John (7:4)	These are seen and heard by John in ch. 7.
Seen later in ch. 14	John does not see them again, until ch. 19, so must be interpreted in this context

Given the extent of the differences, one must conclude that these groups are not the same.[19] Considering the description of the 144,000

---

[19] See Aune, pp. 491-95, for an extensive discussion on various positions; see also Skaggs and Doyle, "Three Critical Questions".

from Rev. 7:4-8 and 14:1-5, this group is a homogeneous ethnic group limited to a predetermined number (12,000 per tribe). Since the number twelve suggests completeness, the multiples of twelve (144,000) further emphasize that the group includes the full number of faithful servants of God. The exact order and content of this list are not found anywhere else in the Old Testament, but it should be noted that few lists of the tribes of Israel in the Old Testament are exactly the same by order and content.[20] Judah is listed first, probably because it is the messianic tribe of Jesus; Dan may have been omitted because of his connection with idolatry (Judg. 18:30-31; 1 Kgs 12:25-33); Ephraim–Manasseh (Joseph's sons) have been included in order to bring the number to twelve. John hears the number of those sealed (7:4), which may imply that names are called out.

The description of the sealing of the 144,000 in Revelation 7 locates the group on earth and implies that they are susceptible to the destructive elements. Later, in Revelation 14, they are located on Mount Zion, which may be taken in either a spiritual or literal sense. In any case, they are on a specific mountain, perhaps in Jerusalem. The group's clothing is not described, as is usual with righteous groups in heaven, where white robes are given as rewards. This may also support their location on earth.

The 144,000 are called 'servants of God' (7:3); they are truthful and without blemish (14:5), have not been defiled with women, being celibate (14:4), were purchased from among men out of the earth (14:3,4), and are 'first fruits' unto God and the Lamb (14:4). They alone are able to sing the new song. Thus, this group enjoys a privileged relationship with God and the Lamb – they have a dual name and follow the Lamb.

Scholars debate the identity of this group.[21] Most recent opinion suggests they are a specific group of Christians selected for sealing (ch. 7) but reunited later (ch. 14).[22] It seems better, however, to allow the group to be distinct from the church.[23] Throughout the Old Testament a righteous remnant of Israel is spared so that God's plan can be

---

[20] See Aune, p. 464, for discussion. Bauckham (*Climax*, pp. 217-20) shows that such lists are "always a reckoning of the military strength of a nation", which would suggest the 144,000 are a military group preparing for war.

[21] See Aune, pp. 440-48. Cf. also Skaggs and Doyle, 'Three Critical Questions'.

[22] Cf. e.g. Mounce, p. 267. Aune, p. 445, states: 'The fact that some but not all of the twelve tribes of the sons of Israel were sealed means that the group from which the sealed were selected was obviously not sealed and hence cannot be Christians. To understand "sealing" as baptism these scholars must ignore the basic character of the metaphor that presents the 144,000 as sealed from a presumably larger "unsealed" group.'

[23] See Aune, p. 474.

achieved. Furthermore, a number of Jewish apocalyptic, eschatological references describe a remnant of Israel being protected by God from the woes of the great eschatological battle in order to experience the messianic triumph at the end time.[24] Their survival seems to be linked to their location in the land of Israel and implies the regathering of the twelve tribes.[25] Their being Jewish would account for: (1) the connection with the tribes, (2) their location on Mount Zion, (3) their identity as 'servants of God', and (4) the absence of church-related terminology such as the white robes, having been washed in blood, etc. But they are righteous and have been purchased from the earth. The reference to their celibate nature (probably meaning faithfulness to God rather than physical celibacy) would be consistent with the metaphor of Israel as the faithful wife of God, which is often used in the Old Testament.[26] The idea that a righteous remnant of Israel would be spared in order to enter the Messianic Kingdom suggests that God will honor the Abrahamic and Davidic covenants and fulfill the prophecies, such as *4 Ezra* 13:35,39-40, in which the Messiah is expected to appear on Mount Zion with a great multitude.[27] The group of Revelation 7 is unique from the Old Testament Jews and/or New Testament church, however, for (1) they are considered 'first fruits' to God and the Lamb (14:4); (2) they sing a *new* song which no other could learn (14:3); (3) they have the mark of *both* God and the Lamb (14:1); and (4) they follow the Lamb (14:4). It may be that they do not fit into the particular categories of Jews, Jewish Christians or martyrs, etc. seen in Revelation, for the passage suggests that they alone are a unique group. It seems likely they are not a select group of the larger multitude. To judge by this description, they could be righteous Jews preparing for holy war who accept the Lamb as their leader who will take them into the Messianic Kingdom.

The great multitude is described in more detail, making identification easier. John first notes their vast size 'which no man could number' (7:9). Aeschylus describes the Persian army in such terms[28] and the Church father, Origen, later refers to early Christian converts as innu-

---

[24] See Dan. 12:12; *4 Ezra* 5:41; 6:25; 9:7-8; 12:34; 13:48; *2 Bar.* 29:1-2; 32:1; 40:2; 71:1; Mk 13:13; 1 Thess. 4:15-17.

[25] For discussion of this see W.D. Davies, *The Gospel and the Land* (Berkeley, CA: University of California, 1974), pp. 49-52.

[26] Bauckham (*Climax*, pp. 230-2) argues that celibacy should be considered the requirement for participation in holy war. Most scholars now agree.

[27] See also Mic. 4:6-8; Joel 2:32; Isa. 11:9-12; *2 Bar.* 29:2; 71:1. See Benware, pp. 31-74, for discussion on covenant promises.

[28] See Aune, p. 445.

merable.²⁹ Also, the multitude is diverse, including every nation, tribe, people, and tongue. The breakdown into these specific categories stresses the internationality and the comprehensiveness of the group – no people is omitted.³⁰ This characteristic is in striking contrast to the 144,000 and quite different from the typical apocalyptic literature, which defines a select group that is rewarded as being wise and righteous.

The great multitude are standing before the throne and the Lamb in heaven (7:9), a position usually reserved for angelic beings. They are wearing white robes, waving palms, and singing praises to God for salvation. In Revelation, white robes denote the reward of the righteous (Rev. 3:4,5; 6:11) as well as purity and absence of sin. In Rev. 7:14 we are told that the group have washed their robes in the blood of the Lamb. The idea that blood could make a garment white is taken from Isa. 1:18, which speaks of scarlet sins being made white as snow. The Lamb's death resulted in cleansing atonement and, as such, had purified this multitude.³¹ White robes were also used for festive occasions (Eccl. 9:8).

The multitude hold palms, a symbol of victory in Judaism as well as in the Greco-Roman world. The Jewish Feast of Tabernacles included a procession in which palms were carried into the Temple in celebration. These were actually a bundle of palm, myrtle and willow branches tied together (Lev. 23:40; Neh. 8:15; Jos. *Ant*. III 245). When the Maccabees captured the Temple Mount the people carried palms (1 Macc. 13:51; 2 Macc. 14:4), and Jesus' triumphal entry into Jerusalem was characterized by a palm-waving crowd (Jn 12:13). Palm fronds were given to Olympic winners at athletic games in the Greco-Roman world.³² After 293 BCE, Roman generals celebrated military victories by waving palms (Livy X 7.9), and there are coins and drawings depicting gods or goddesses in triumphal processions holding palms. In very early times in Egypt the palm was a symbol of life after death and length of life.

Thus, John saw an incredible picture of the throne room of God crowded with diverse people, as far as the eye could see, wearing white robes and waving palms, celebrating the victory of salvation. The term used here for salvation (σωτηρία) is generally linked with eschatological victory in Revelation and possibly refers to deliverance or victory over

---

[29] *Contra Celsum* 1.27. See also Justin Martyr, *Apology* 15.7; Tacitus, *Annals* XV 44; Livy, II 39.9, IV 33.2, V 7.2; *1 Clem.* 6:1.
[30] See also Rev. 5:9; 10:11; 11:9; 13:7; 14:6; 17:15.
[31] See 1 Cor. 10:16; Eph. 1:7; 2:13; 1 Pet. 1:19; Heb. 9:14; 10:19; 1 Jn 1:7; Lev. 17:11; 14:52.
[32] Pausanias 8.48.1-2; Hermas, 2nd cent. *Sim.* 8.2; Livy X 47.3; Virgil, *Aeneid* VI 111.

persecution.[33] It may echo the hosanna of Ps. 118:25, a phrase often used at the Feast of Tabernacles.[34] It certainly has a strong association with praise for deliverance from trials and temptations. Probably the trials referred to are more than their recent persecution.[35] The deliverance may refer to the broader perspective of the trials of human existence enumerated in vv. 15-17. A particularly vibrant translation reads: 'To our God ... and to the Lamb we owe our salvation' (Weymouth translation).

The triumphant song of the multitude is joined by the angels, elders and the four living creatures (Rev. 7:11-12). It is a seven-fold doxology of praise heightened by the definite article before each attribute: '*the* blessing, *the* glory, *the* wisdom', etc. This doxology consists of several interesting components. First, it begins and ends with 'Amen' (v. 12). The first amen may actually be a response to the praise of the great multitude (v. 10). Second, it serves to heighten the dynamism of the praises – they were apparently continual, overlapping one another. The doxology itself includes seven attributes, all of which occur elsewhere in Revelation (see 4:9, also 5:12; the attribute of wisdom occurs elsewhere in the New Testament, Lk. 11:49; 1 Cor. 1:24; 2:7). The attributes are highly descriptive: 'blessing' can be defined as 'that spontaneous act of thanks which men utter when they realize more vividly than ever before their happiness';[36] 'glory' probably has reference to the radiance and/or essence of God himself. (See our discussion of δόξα above.) 'Wisdom' refers to the divine knowledge disclosed in his redemptive plan (cf. Eph. 3:10); 'thanksgiving' is appropriate praise for salvation; 'honor' is public acknowledgement of the final two attributes; 'power' and 'might' are both essential components of God's presence in human existence. The final phrase 'to our God' again puts the praise in the context of personal relationship – God is not an abstract principle but a personal, interactive God, to be praised. All heaven rejoices over the salvation made possible by the Lamb.

In the midst of the praising, one of the elders speaks to John (v. 13). It is interesting that the text says the elder 'answered' and yet one does not hear the question. The implication is that the elder was aware of the question in John's mind. The question/answer form is often used in prophetic and apocalyptic literature to introduce the meaning of a

---

[33] Cf. Werner Foerster, 'σώζω, σωτηρία,' *TDNT* VII (1971), pp. 998-600; W. Bauer and B. Aland, *The Text of the New Testament*, trans. E.F. Rhodes (Leiden: Brill; Grand Rapids, MI: Eerdmans, 1987), p. 1598.

[34] Cf. R.J. McKelvey, *The New Temple: The Church in the New Testament* (London: Oxford University Press, 1969), p. 163.

[35] Cf. Caird, p. 100.

[36] Preston and Hanson, p. 47.

vision.[37] John's response 'You know' reflects the usual apocalyptic/prophetic position that mere mortals cannot know and understand the mysteries of God (Rev. 7:14).

The elder's explanation of the group raises yet another interpretive point of concern: 'These are they that come out of the great Tribulation' (Rev. 7:14). The use of the definite article implies that the Tribulation refers to the final series of trials that precede the end, as expected in both Jewish and Christian tradition.[38] Daniel 12:1 describes a time of trouble worse than any known before, when God will deliver his people. John's readers would understand that while only a select number (144,000) would be divinely protected to go through this period, all others would 'come out of it'. There are a variety of explanations for this phrase. Some scholars see those coming (οἱ ἐρχόμενοι) as martyrs who are being killed and arriving on the scene as John watches.[39] Others interpret these as having 'escaped' the Tribulation, perhaps by the Rapture. Aune shows that the verb of those coming (οἱ ἐρχόμενοι), though in the present tense, represents action which is occurring at the same time as washed (ἔπλυναν) and made white (ἐλεύκαναν). Since both these main verbs are in the past tense (the aorist tense indicates once-for-all actions which took place in the past), they influence the understanding of those coming (ἐρχόμενοι). The construction suggests that the group is complete, having died, having been martyred or raptured.[40] They are not 'coming out' as John watches.

The great multitude (7:9-15) is before the throne praising God ceaselessly ('day and night' suggests 'without stopping for rest'). Their service seems to be in terms of worship rather than ritual like that performed by levitical priests (see also 22:3-5). In return the group is sheltered and protected by God and is no longer susceptible to the hardships of daily life: 'The one who is seated on the throne will shelter [tabernacle over] them' (Rev. 7:15). This would recall the tabernacle in the wilderness (Lev. 26), God's guiding presence in the pillar of cloud and fire (Exod. 13:21-22), and perhaps be the fulfillment of Isa. 4:5-6: 'It will serve as a pavilion, a shade by day from the heat, and a refuge ...' (see also Ezek. 37:27-28; Zech. 2:10). One is reminded of John 1:14 at this point: 'And the Word became flesh and lived among

---

[37] See, for example, Zech. 4:5; Ezek. 37:3; Jer. 1:11,13, 24:3; Amos 7:8, 8:2; cf. *1 En.* 18:14,15; 21:6,10; 22:3,7,9; 23:4; 25:3; *4 Ezra* 10:44-48.
[38] *Test. Moses* 8:1; *Jub.* 23:11-21; *4 Ezra* 13:16-19; *2 Bar.* 27:1-15; Mk 13:7-13; 1 Cor. 15:24-25; Rev. 3:21.
[39] E.g. Charles, I, p. 213. See Skaggs and Doyle for discussion of this phrase.
[40] Aune (52b), p. 473.

us, and we have seen his glory, the glory as of a father's only son, full of grace and truth.'

It is interesting that God promises protection from daily elements, such as hunger, thirst, and sadness rather than persecution or martyrdom. The terminology may be taken from Isa. 49:10, where God promises relief from hunger, thirst, heat, and sun. The promise reflects physical needs, and there may also be the hope of spiritual satisfaction as well (see Mt. 5:6; Jn 6:35). It is noteworthy that the opposite will happen to the inhabitants of the earth when the bowls are poured out (Rev. 16).

This section concludes with the assurance that the Lamb will be 'their Shepherd'; he will guide them to fountains of living water, and wipe away tears (Rev. 7:17). Shepherd imagery is often used of Jesus, particularly in the Johannine literature (e.g. Jn 10:1-30; 21:15-17). The metaphor builds on Ps. 23:1, 'The Lord is my Shepherd, I shall not want', and Isa. 40:11, 'He will feed his flock like a shepherd'. It may at first seem strange that the Lamb will also shepherd the flock, but the concept is no doubt a development on the Davidic Messiah figure (cf. *Ps. Sol.* 17:40), recalling prophecies such as Ezek. 34:23, where the expected Messiah is connected with David.[41] Like a good shepherd, the Lamb guides his flock to running water (a river or spring), which is preferable to the cistern or well water typically available to shepherds in ancient times (see also Jn 4:14; 7:38; *1 En.* 48:1; Rev. 21:6). The image of living water certainly recalls John 4, where Jesus explains that he has water which will eternally quench the Samaritan woman's thirst. Here in Rev. 7:17 the promise in the Gospel is about to be fulfilled for the group before the throne.

Finally, the Lamb will wipe away all tears (Rev. 7:17). This phrase suggests parental loving and concern and provides a very personal promise to John's readers (see Isa. 25:8; Jer. 31:16; Rev. 21:4). This dramatic scene of God seated on his throne with the Lamb nearby, surrounded by worshiping angelic creatures and an innumerable crowd of white-robed, palm-waving people, becomes even more striking, for God himself wipes away their tears. These are probably not tears shed on the scene, but a lingering reminder of the pain and sadness endured on earth. It is worth noting that God's protective and comforting presence and the reward enjoyed by the multitude in Rev. 7:15-17 are promises described in the new heaven and new earth (Rev. 21:3-4), which are granted immediately to the multitude. Furthermore, the multitude is not described again in Revelation until the new heaven and earth, which implies that the church will 'escape' the worst of the

---

[41] Cf. Aune, pp. 477-78, for background on shepherd imagery.

Tribulation (chs. 8–19) and immediately enjoy rest in the Messianic Kingdom in heaven. It is possible that this group is already in the final eternal state of the righteous (cf. the parallel description in 21:3-4); however, the fact that they serve in the Temple (not found in the future state according to 21:22) speaks against this.

In summary, with the opening of the sixth seal, John is shown a multi-screen view of the end time: many will be facing God's wrath in fear and terror; a few will be sealed so as to endure the destruction (144,000), while the privileged multitude in white robes who have been faithful to God will have entered into eternal blessedness in heaven.

Chapter 8

Following the scenes of ch. 7, which describe the 144,000 and the Great Multitude, the narrative of the seals is taken up once again: the seventh seal is opened and a great silence occurs in heaven for about half an hour. The abrupt quietness is in shocking contrast to the joyful shouts of the Great Multitude and the worshiping praises of the throne room creatures. Commentators differ as to the purpose of the silence. It may be that God can hear the prayers of the saints which follow (Rev. 8:3-5), or it may be an eschatological return to the primal silence which preceded creation (cf. *4 Ezra* 6:39; 7:30; *2 Bar.* 3:7-8). In the Old Testament, silence is seen as a prelude to divine manifestation (cf. e.g. Job 4:16; Zeph. 1:7; Zech. 2:13) and necessary to be maintained in God's presence (Ps. 62:1; Hab. 2:20; *4 Ezra* 7:30), especially during the incense offering in Jerusalem Temple practice.[42]

The silence creates a dramatic pause, marking the eschatological beginning of the revelation of the contents of the book itself. As Zeph. 1:7 says, 'Be silent before the sovereign Lord, for the Day of the Lord is near.'[43] During the pause the angels prepare to announce God's wrath upon the earth. It seems that the silence in this context serves to heighten the tension in anticipation of what is to come: the seals have been broken; now the reader must prepare for the contents of the book. In essence, the seals (chs. 6-7) have introduced the characteristics and main players of the end-time drama: the world leader (the white horse rider of 6:1-2 and the beast of ch. 13) play a dominant role with bloodshed, famine and death characteristic of his rule (6:1-8). Meanwhile, the martyrs in heaven cry for vengeance (6:9-10), the 144,000

---

[42] Cf. *m. Talmid* 5:1-6, *Test. Adam* 1.12.

[43] Cf. *4 Ezra* 7:29-31, which describes a seven-day period of silence between this age and the age to come.

are selected for protection to endure the wrath of God (7:1-8) and the Great Multitude (the church) praise God for salvation, enjoying the Messianic reward and escaping the horrors which will fall on the earth.

The opening of the seventh and final seal introduces the trumpet plagues. Rev. 8:1–9:21 appears to be a textual unit, for it begins with the introductory scene in heaven: the angels prepare to blow the trumpets and an incense offering is made before the throne. Then an angel casts the incense with the saints' prayers and fire to earth. The first four trumpet plagues which follow have a partial effect on the earth, while the final three trumpets are combined with 'woes'. These 'woes' serve to indicate intensification of the plagues which now affect humankind (ch. 9). The section ends with a comment that humankind does not repent (9:21), a tragic, yet recurring response to God's activity.

The use of trumpets at this point in Revelation is in order, for trumpets were used in ancient times to announce events (Num. 10:5-6,10; 29:1), to herald royal entries such as coronations (1 Kgs 1:34,39; 2 Kgs 9:13), and to call troops to battle (Num. 10:9).[44] In the Revelation context, the trumpets herald God's wrath.[45]

The seven angels appointed to blow the trumpets appear to be a specific group, as the definite article is included (*the* seven angels, 8:2).[46] The role of the angels is to 'stand before God' (v. 2), which means that they attend or serve him. It is these angels that God chose to announce the opening of the book, unleashing the eschatological end-time events. The trumpets announce God's attack on the earth and his ultimate victory leading to the Messianic Kingdom. It does not appear that the trumpet players are a recapitulation of the seven seals, but an announcement that the activity leading to the end has begun. Trumpet imagery is used in other early Christian apocalypses in this way (Mt. 24:31; 1 Thess. 4:16; 1 Cor. 15:52; *Did.* 16.6). References to a series of trumpet blasts before divine judgment can be found in the Old Testament and other Jewish literature (see Josh. 6, the destruction of Jericho, and 1QM 7:14).[47] Quite early, the trumpet imagery was adopted into Jewish apocalyptic literature and, while it was used to announce

---

[44] Zeph. 1:9-12 is an apocalyptic text which makes use of the trumpet as a structural device, but the trumpet's contents are quite different from Rev. 8,9.

[45] See also Zeph. 1:14-16; *4 Ezra* 6:23; *Apoc. Abr.* 31.

[46] *1 En.* 20:2-8 names them: Uriel, Raphael, Raquel, Michael, Saraquel, Gabriel and Remiel. They are also called archangels (*1 En.* 81:5; 90:21-22; *Test. Levi* 3:5), and angels of the presence (Isa. 63:9; *Jub.* 1:27,29; 2:1-2,18, 15:27, 31:14; see also Lk. 1:19).

[47] Cf. Aune, p. 510, on the use of trumpets in early Judaism; G. Friedrich, 'σαλπίζω, σαλπιστής', *TDNT* VII (1971), pp. 71-88, provides extensive information on the trumpet in ancient times.

eschatological salvation (Isa. 27:13; Zeph. 1:14-16), it more often introduced eschatological judgment.[48]

Before the angels actually sound their trumpets, another unidentified angel stands before the altar and performs the priestly function of offering incense (see Exod. 30:1-10; 1 Chron. 28:18; Heb. 9:4; Lk. 1:9). Exodus 30 describes the altar in the wilderness tabernacle as made of acacia wood overlaid with gold, square in shape with 'horns' on top. The incense was a fragrant blend of spices such as gum resin, onycha, galleanum and frankincense, and was burned twice a day – in the morning and evening. The altar stood before the Ark of the Covenant separated by a curtain (Num. 16:40). The bowl that held the incense (the censer) in the tabernacle was made of brass (Exod. 27:3) while in Solomon's Temple it was made of gold (1 Kgs 7:50).

Many ancient censers were ladles shaped like a hand holding a shallow bowl. Incense was used in several Jewish Temple rituals, where it was burned with the grain offering (Lev. 2:1,15; 6:8,14-15). There was also a separate incense offering where the incense was offered in a long-handled censer. Fire from live coals on the brazen altar was prepared for this and then incense was added (Ezek. 8:10-11; Lev. 10:1-3; Num. 16:6,17; Lev. 16:12). Incense was also offered on the golden incense altar twice a day in coordination with the lamb offering. Coals from the great altar were spread out on the altar and incense added on top. Special incense offerings were made on the Day of Atonement (Lev. 16:11-14).

The altar of incense is mentioned four times in Revelation (8:3 [x2], 5; 9:13). It is not mentioned in other Jewish apocalyptic literature, although there are references to incense.[49]

In Rev. 8:3-5 an angel performs the priestly role of bringing the censer filled with incense to the altar. It seems that the incense was not offered on behalf of the prayers, but rather that the prayers were added to the incense as a means of ascending before God (see Ps. 141:2). The prayers may have been for divine vengeance on evil and, as such, were actually the prayers prayed by the souls under the altar (Rev. 6:9-10), for they appear to play a role in the judgments which follow. The angel adds fire to the incense/prayer combination, then hurls the contents of the censer to earth. The resulting explosion includes peals of thunder, flashes of lightning and an earthquake (8:5). These reactions, which recall the theophany of Mount Sinai, suggest God's own presence in the activity and anticipate the actual judgments which follow the trumpet blasts. They also echo 4:5, where lightning and thunder

---

[48] Isa. 58:1; Joel 2:1-3; Zeph. 1:14-16; *4 Ezra* 6:23; *Sib.Or.* 4.74-75.
[49] *Apoc. Paul* 44; *Test. Levi* 3:5-6.

accompany God's presence on his throne. There may be a parallel to Ezek. 10:2-3, which states that God sent his messenger to throw burning coals on Jerusalem after he had punished those who had been unfaithful to him (Ezek. 9). In the Ezekiel passage the coals appear to purify the disobedient people of God after his punishment of them (see also Isa. 6:6). In the Revelation passage, however, the action precedes the judgments which are poured out on the pagan world. At various places in Scripture, fire that falls to earth symbolizes divine judgment,[50] and earthquakes have significance often suggesting theophanies (Exod. 19:18; Ps. 68:8; Isa. 64:3). They also symbolize God's presence (Judg. 5:4; Pss. 68:8; 114:6-7; 1 Kgs 19:11; Mt. 28:2); anticipate divine judgment (2 Sam. 22:8; Isa. 24:18-20; Hag. 2:6-7,21; Heb. 12:26); and even accompany Christ's resurrection (Mt. 27:51).

The seven angels sound their trumpets one at a time without an obvious cue from the throne or a divine agent. The first four trumpets, which take place quickly, affect one third of the earth and recall the Egyptian plagues. The final three coincide with the three 'woes', have more detail and affect more of humankind. The section concludes by reporting that in spite of the horrors experienced by the plagues, people do not repent (9:20), a similar motif to Exod. 7:14.

In the Greco-Roman world, the sounding of trumpets symbolized warning of divine anger,[51] heralded a new age[52] and was thought to be a sign of divine activity.[53] In the Old Testament, trumpets signaled the Day of the Lord.[54] In Christian literature trumpets will announce the return of Christ (e.g. 1 Thess. 4:16; Mt. 24:31; 1 Cor. 15:52; *Did.* 16:6). Furthermore, it is a common expectation in apocalyptic literature that cosmic catastrophes will accompany the Day of Judgment:[55] *2 Bar.* 27:1-13 says that history will be divided into twelve periods (see also *4 Ezra* 14:11-12; *Apoc. Abr.* 29:2); tribulation will affect humankind before the Messiah comes (*2 Bar.* 27–30:1; cf. *1 En.* 80:2-8; *4 Ezra* 5:4-13). The idea that eschatological plagues will precede the end of the world is also found in Jewish apocalyptic literature (*1 En.* 91:7-9; *3 Bar.* 16:3).

The first trumpet announces a storm of hail, fire and blood (Rev. 8:7). It begins in heaven and is cast to earth. Ancient literature describes the sixth heaven as a storehouse of hail and storm maintained

---

[50] Gen. 19:24; 2 Kgs 1:10, 12, 14; Job 1:16; Ps. 11:6; 2 Thess. 1:8.
[51] Caesar, *Civ.* 3.105; *Lucan* 1.578; *Cassius Dio* 47.40.2.
[52] Plutarch, *Sulla* 7.3-4.
[53] *Did.* 16:6; *Sib.Or.* 4.124.
[54] Zech. 9:14; Zeph. 1:14,16; *4 Ezra* 6:23; *Apoc. Abr.* 31:1.
[55] Joel 2:30-31; Isa. 13:9-10, 34:4; Ezek. 32:7-8. See also *Sib. Or.* 2.196-213; 3.81-92, 669-701; 4.171-78; 7.118-29; 8.225-43, 336-58.

within the gates of fire.[56] The phenomenon of blood raining from the sky also appears in Roman literature.[57] The imagery may echo the seventh Egyptian plague (Exod. 9:13-35) or may reflect Joel's prophecy of the last days (Joel 2:31; Acts 2:19). In the context, the fire most likely refers to lightning. The blood may reflect the color of the storm like the blood-red rain containing fine red sand from the Sahara Desert, which occasionally falls in southern Europe. Finally, especially when taken together with Rev. 8:8, the catastrophe could be a volcanic eruption, throwing stones and fire into the air, some of which burns the grass while other parts fall into the sea. Pliny records an eye witness account of Vesuvius' eruption on August 24, 79 CE.[58] He reports extensive land destruction as well as the effect of the volcanic eruption on the sea and sea animals. Whether John sees a volcanic eruption or another cosmic phenomenon, the context suggests divine activity and control: the storm of Rev. 8:7 is announced and begins in heaven. It affects one-third of the trees and green grass. The fraction may suggest that the first plague is a warning, God's extension of mercy. Although one-third destruction appears to be drastic, that devastation will be thought to be relatively minor when compared with the total destruction of Revelation 16.

The second trumpet sounds and a fiery mountain is thrown into the sea, turning one-third of it to blood. As mentioned before, this may describe volcanic activity as well as reflect Jewish apocalyptic imagery: *1 Enoch* describes seven stars like great burning mountains (*1 En.* 21:3; 108:3-6). This recalls the first Egyptian plague, in which the water of Egypt was turned to blood (Exod. 7:20-21). It affects the sea, the sea creatures and ships. Again, the destruction affects one-third of the sea and its life. The purpose appears to be to warn of the coming judgment.

The third trumpet also announces a fiery phenomenon: a blazing star, like a torch, falls, affecting one-third of the springs and rivers (8:10-11). The star, named Wormwood, poisons the waters, resulting in death. Wormwood is a plant belonging to the daisy family, native to various parts of the world, including central and southern Europe and North Africa. It was known in the ancient world as a plant which could cause intoxication, hallucinations, convulsions and damage to the nervous system. Though bitter, it was not usually lethal. Wormwood is mentioned in the Bible and is associated with sorrow (Prov. 5:3-4;

---

[56] *M. hagigah* 12b; *Sib. Or.* 5:377; Mounce, pp. 184-85.

[57] E.g. Cicero, *De div.* V 1.43.98, 2.27.58; Pliny, *Hist. Nat.* II 57.147; *Sib.Or.* 5.77-80, quoted in Aune, p. 519.

[58] Pliny the Younger, *Epistulae* VI 16.20; cf. Tacitus, *Annals* IV 67; Josephus, *Ant.* XX 144; Suetonius, 'Titus', *The Twelve Caesars* 8.3-40.

Lam. 3:19). Because Israel had forsaken God he gave them wormwood (Jer. 9:15). Wormwood itself is not poisonous, but its very bitterness can be lethal. As before, a part of humanity was affected, suggesting the warning aspect of the judgment. This is the first of the trumpets to directly affect human life.

The fourth angel's trumpet blast was directed at the sun, moon, and stars (Rev. 8:12). The light intensity was affected (the luminosity of a third of these turned dark) as well as the length of daylight (a third of the day and night was without light). The text says that the sun was 'struck' (πλήσσω), a word used only here in the New Testament and in the Septuagint version of Exod. 9:31-32, to describe the devastating effects of hail on crops.[59] If the first four trumpets reflect volcanic activity, it follows that the ash could cause darkness for several days.[60] Again, one is reminded of the Egyptian plague, which covered the land with darkness for three days. It is interesting to note that on the fourth day of creation, God created the sun, moon and stars (Gen. 1:14-19). Here, with the blast of the fourth trumpet, God reverses that creation with a drastic cosmic destruction – the sun is blackened, the moon turns red and stars fall.

The first four trumpets may have been warnings to repent. Recalling the Egyptian plagues, they would bring to mind that God will punish those hostile to him and his people. Darkness is a symbol of judgment in the Old Testament (Amos 5:18; Joel 2:2; Isa. 13:10) and is associated with demons in the New Testament (Mt. 8:12; 2 Cor. 6:14-15; Col. 1:13). Most drastic is the sudden darkness at the death of Jesus (e.g. Mk 15:33). It is no surprise that the plague of darkness provides a transition from the divine warnings to the demonic woes.[61] God's anger and judgment are definitely evident as the four trumpet plagues relate the fire imagery to the fire taken from the altar in heaven. The first four plagues are controlled, however, affecting one-third of the earth. Thus, some have suggested that God's mercy is extended yet a while longer, giving an opportunity for humanity to repent.

Like the seal narratives, the trumpet narratives are divided into a 4+3 pattern. The final three trumpets are introduced by a bird flying in midheaven – the location of the sun, moon and planets. The bird speaks, announcing an intensification of the plagues; the call is not a call for repentance. The bird may be a vulture (Hab. 1:8), although most commentators think of it as an eagle. In apocalyptic literature

---

[59] Mounce, p. 188.
[60] Cf. Vesuvius described in Pliny, *Ep.* VI 16.7; VI 20.15.
[61] Mounce, p. 188.

birds speak for God[62] and sometimes are associated with angels (*3 En.* 2:1; 24:11; 26:3; 44:5). The eagle was also a messenger for Zeus in the Greco-Roman world.[63] Whether the bird is a vulture or an eagle, the symbolism is clear: it has a predatory nature and is a messenger for God to announce that the final three plagues will be worse than before.

Possibly the trumpet plagues are an 'eschatological application' of the ten plagues inflicted on Egypt (Exod. 7–12). Although the plagues are a recurring theme in early Jewish literature, they are in a primitive form in this passage and do not lead to the possibility of repentance.[64]

Revelation 8:13 marks the transition from the four trumpet plagues, which have affected nature, to the final three trumpet plagues announced as three woes. These final three are carried out by demonic forces from the abyss, and hence are appropriately announced by a bird of prey. At the conclusion of trumpets 5, 6, 7, the author states 'the first woe is past, behold the second (or third) woe is coming' (9:12; 11:14). Hence, it is fairly clear that the three woes are actually the final three trumpets. It is interesting to note that these first three plagues affect particularly the pagan and wicked world (see 9:4,20 which indicate that the sealed righteous are not affected).

Chapter 9

Chapter 9 describes the last three trumpets, which also correspond to the first two woes mentioned in Rev. 8:13. The third woe may refer to the seventh trumpet, which is not blown until ch. 15, the judgment of Babylon. Thus, the trumpet blasts (like the other series of sevens, i.e. seals and bowls) begin with a short sequence of four (8:1-13). Then as they combine with the woes, the fifth and sixth trumpet plagues intensify. There is a pause after the sixth blast, preceding the final trumpet, the most disastrous of them all (ch. 15). It is noteworthy that the first four plagues affect nature and originate from above the earth, whereas the fifth and sixth afflict people and come from the 'abyss' (9:1).

As John's vision progresses, he is shown a star which has fallen from the sky to earth. Commentators suggest that John did not actually witness the fall, for fallen (πεπτωκότα) is a perfect active participle modifying 'star', suggesting John saw it after it had fallen.[65]

Stars have a variety of connotations in biblical and apocalyptic literature. Isaiah 14:12 describes the king of Babylon as a star fallen from heaven; in

---

[62] Cf. *4 Ezra* 11:7-8, *2 Bar.* 77:19:26.
[63] Sophocles, *Elec.* 149; *Anth.Graec.* 9.223.1-2, quoted in Aune, p. 523.
[64] Aune, p. 499; cf. Aune, pp. 502-506, for extensive discussion on the plague traditions.
[65] *Ibid.*, p. 525.

1 En. 21:6, fallen angels are stars of heaven who sinned against God; Jesus describes Satan's fall as like lightning from heaven (Lk. 10:18). Judges 5:20, Job 38:7, and Dan. 8:10 refer to stars as angelic beings having personalities, while *1 En.* 86:3; 88:1; 90:21-24; *Test. Sol.* 20.14.17 and Jude 13 refer to them as *evil* beings. *Sib. Or.* 5.155-61 describes a star as a messenger of God sent to earth.

In Rev. 9:1, the star functions as a messenger sent to carry out God's will. The idea of 'fallen' does not have a negative connotation, but takes on the simple meaning of 'descent'.[66] His role is to open the abyss and release the plagues. Possibly the star is responsible for/or representative of the social, political, economic and religious institutions which promote evil.[67]

That the star (or the person it symbolizes) is given the key suggests that God controls the opening of the abyss and limits access to it. The use of the definite article for both *the* key and *the* abyss, suggests that the concept was known to John's readers. The Greek word ἀβύσσου means 'without depth, fathomless, boundless'. In the LXX it is used for the Hebrew word for 'sea', the deep primeval ocean below the earth. Thus, it is consistent with the three-level concept of heaven, earth and abyss found throughout Revelation. In apocalyptic literature it is the final prison of fallen angels, the place of fire (*1 En.* 21:7; 18:11). In biblical references it refers to the depths of the earth (e.g. Ps. 71:20), the underworld abode of the dead,[68] and the place where demons are imprisoned (Lk. 8:31; cf. *1 En.* 18:12). The 'shaft' of the abyss occurs only in Rev. 9:1, and suggests a locked passageway, preventing access to the main underworld. The abyss of Revelation is the origin of the demonic forces (9:11); the beast emerges from it (11:7; 17:8); and Satan is later imprisoned there (20:1-3). When the abyss is opened smoke pours out (9:2), darkening the sky and the sun. This phenomenon could resemble the smoke which arises from an active fiery volcano, or it could describe the cloud of the locusts, which resembles smoke as they pour out of the shaft (Philo *Moses.* 1.123 describes such a locust scene).

When the star unlocks the abyss a swarm of locusts pours out. The locust is a grasshopper-type insect. They travel in a column up to 100 feet deep and four miles long. Stripping the vegetation to the ground, they cover crops in waves. Joel describes their effect in stages, for the first wave eats the top of the vegetation, the next wave attacks the

---

[66] See Charles, I, pp. 238-39; Mounce, p. 192.
[67] Wall, p. 128.
[68] Ps. 71:20; Rom. 10:7; see also *1 En.* 17:7,8; *Joseph and Aseneth* 15.12.

stalks, continuing until the land is bare.[69] In the Old Testament the locust is a symbol of destruction (Deut. 28:42; 1 Kgs 8:37; Ps. 78:46), is the eighth plague sent by God on Egypt (Exod. 10:1-20), and is used to describe the Day of the Lord (Joel 1:2–2:11; cf. *3 Bar.* 16:1-3).

In Revelation 9, the locusts are given specific commands and authority to carry out their mission (9:3-5). Although the source of the instruction is not specifically described, one can assume they are acting under God's direction, for the three passive verbs ('was given', v. 3, 'were instructed', v. 4, and 'was given', v. 5) are used elsewhere to denote divine activity, avoiding the mention of God's name.[70] It is noteworthy that the locusts are not allowed to perform their usual function, that is to devastate grass, plants or trees. Rather they are to attack people. Even this activity is limited, however, for they are restricted to tormenting their victims and cannot kill them (see Job 2:6 for God's limits). The mission of the locusts appears to be to inflict pain and suffering on the wicked. Whether the intention is to bring about repentance is not entirely clear. In any case, nothing indicates that people repent after any of the woes. In fact, vv. 20-21 state explicitly that the people who were not killed did not repent.

The locust plague is limited to five months (Rev. 9:5-10). This could refer to the locusts' actual life cycle, which is five months – spring to late summer, or it may emphasize that their time was limited, since in New Testament writings the number five often is a way of describing 'a few'.[71]

The locust's torment is likened to the sting of a scorpion. A scorpion is a 4 to 5"-long lobster-like creature which belongs to the arachnida class (spiders, ticks, mites). It has a claw on the end of its tail which secretes a poison not usually fatal to humans, though very painful. It is most active at night and is common in the southern parts of the Mediterranean world. In the Old Testament the scorpion is used by God as a metaphor for punishment of the wicked (e.g. 1 Kgs 12:11,14).

God directs the plague of locusts in Revelation 9 by giving them authority (ability) to terrorize humanity (see also 2 Chron. 7:13). The pain inflicted by their sting is so great that people seek death because of fear and suffering. The locusts are led by the 'angel of the abyss' whose name is Abaddon (Hebrew) and Apollyon (Greek). The name means 'destruction'. This description makes it clear that the plague is evil,

---

[69] See Joel 1:4 and W. Wright, *The Chronicle of Psalms – Joshua the Stylite* (Cambridge: Cambridge University Press, 1982), ch. 38, which gives an eyewitness account of the locust-caused famine of 499-500 CE, quoted by Aune, p. 529.

[70] See Aune, pp. 527-28.

[71] Cf. Mt. 17:17-19; Lk. 12:6,52; Acts 20:6; 24:1; 1 Cor. 14:19, etc.

although commissioned by God. Also, this messenger should not be confused with Satan (also called the Devil and the Dragon in Revelation) or the 'star' who opens the shaft, for 'destruction' comes from the evil realm, the abyss (Rev. 9:11).

The description of the locusts in Revelation 9 implies their power, strength and cruelty: they appear like horses prepared for battle, with gold crowns, human faces, women's hair, lions' teeth and iron breastplates. They make a thunderous noise. An Arabian proverb describes locusts as like a horse, with a lion's breast, a camel's feet, a serpent's body, and antennae like a girl's hair. This description could account for the German word for locust *Heupferd* (hay-horse) and the Italian *cavalletta* (little horse).[72]

The evil origin of this locust plague is obvious, but scholars debate the extent to which it should be interpreted literally or symbolically in this context. A real locust plague as in the Egypt/Exodus tradition may be in view, or this may be a graphic description of the supernatural demonic powers released to torment humanity at the end time. Either way, with this plague God uses evil forces to achieve his purpose in the earth (see also Rev. 17:17 where God controls the plans of the wicked).

In Rev. 9:12 the reader is reminded of the earlier 'woe' announcement: 'the first woe is past; two woes are yet to come'. This structuring device moves the reader ahead to anticipate the next trumpet woes.

With the sounding of the sixth trumpet John hears a voice coming from the altar addressing the sixth angel trumpeter (9:12). The voice may be that of the angel priest mentioned in Rev. 8:3-5 or it may be that the altar itself speaks. In any case, it is not God's voice, since it originates from the altar which is 'before God' (9:13). This is the only time one of the trumpet angels is told to perform an action, and though the action of the angel is not described, one can assume the releasing of the bound angels was carried out by him.

The four bound angels (9:14) are being held by the River Euphrates. That they are bound suggests that they are evil (see Rev. 20:2; Tob. 3:17), although some scholars equate them with the angels of Rev. 7:1 who hold back the winds.[73] Their role is different, however, and the only similarity is their number. The River Euphrates, 1,700 miles long, is the longest river in Western Asia. It figures prominently in the Old Testament, marking the boundaries between Israel and its enemies. It also formed the eastern boundary of the Roman Empire in the first century CE.

---

[72] Mounce, p. 196.
[73] Aune suggests *Apoc. Zeph.* 4.1-4 gives a similar description of 'ugly' angels, p. 496.

The four angels have been kept for the purpose of carrying out this particular judgment at this 'very hour and day and month and year' (Rev. 9:15). John's specification of hour, day, month and year serves to emphasize the exactness of God's predetermined plan.

The angels' role is to kill one-third of humankind. John describes their attack against 'earth dwellers', a designation usually reserved for people who are hostile to God. Their purpose is punishment, a divine judgment on the wicked.[74] The angels' destruction seems to be carried out by cavalry.[75] It appears that the angels release the ground troops who number in the millions (Rev. 9:16). The interpretive problem here is whether these troops should be understood as demonic forces or as human cavalry. The detail that John *heard* the number suggests the reality of the huge army – it was not a mere visual impression. John describes the horses and riders as dressed for battle, wearing 'fiery' colors, red, dark blue and yellow. Their breastplates are the color of fire, of hyacinth (a brilliant blue), of brimstone (like sulfur, a dull yellow). Their heads are like *lions'* heads, breathing fire, smoke and sulfur. Thus, not only are they a terrifying visual phenomenon, they also emit an awesome smell. It is interesting to note that fire and brimstone are associated with God's destruction of Sodom and Gomorrah,[76] in early Judaism and early Christianity as well as in the Old Testament (Gen. 19:24).[77] It is noteworthy that the riders do not play an active role in the assault. Rather, the plague comes from the horses' mouths and tails (Rev. 9:17:19). This description has led some to see a parallel with modern tanks and cannons.[78] Others point out parallels with the ancient creature Chimaera described in Greek and Roman mythology. The Chimaera had the head of a lion, tail of a dragon, and body of a goat. It belched fire.[79] John's vision is unique, in that he describes a plague reserved by God for the end time; the image appears to be more than merely a composite of imagery found in sacred and secular sources.[80]

Revelation 9 concludes with the impact of the plagues on humankind: those who were not killed did *not* repent of their immorality and idolatry (9:10-21). Possibly, the fraction (one-third) of humankind

---

[74] See *1 En.* 53:3; 56:1; 62:11; 66:1; *3 En.* 31:2; 32:1; 33:1 for angels of punishment. Cf. Ladd, p. 135; Mounce, p. 201.

[75] Aune, pp. 538-39, suggests there is no connection between the four angels and the demonic cavalry of vv. 16-19.

[76] Cf. Philo's highly stylized account in *Moses* 2.55-58.

[77] Cf. also Deut. 29:23; Ps. 11:6; Ezek. 38:22; Isa. 30:33; 34:9; Luke 17:29; *1 Clem.* 11:1.

[78] William Hendricksen, *More Than Conquerors* (Grand Rapids, MI: Baker Book House, 1944), p. 148; Walvoord, p. 167.

[79] Homer, *Iliad.* VI 181-82, Euripides, *Ion* 203-204 (see further Aune, pp. 539-40).

[80] See Mounce, p. 201.

represents time left for lost humanity to repent. It was not merely torture or judgment.[81] Also, it is made clear why God chose to 'seal' or protect some, for God always protects his people from his own judgments, as in the Egyptian plague traditions. On the other hand, the purpose of the trumpet plagues could be punishment. The reference to the lack of repentance shows the extent of humankind's commitment to evil.[82]

Humankind's sin is described as idolatry, magic-related worship, murders and immorality (vv. 20-21). These activities were prevalent in the Judaeo-Greco-Roman environment of the first century and were often problematic for Judaism and Christianity.[83] The phrase 'the works of their hands' is a Semitic phrase that is often used to indicate the lifeless, impotent, manufactured nature of idols.[84] This meaning is especially clear in Ps. 115:4, 'Their idols are silver and gold, the work of human hands'. There is a result clause in v. 20. They did not repent, and so did not cease worshiping demons. This construction probably implies that 'demons' here are 'idols of gold and silver...' (v. 20). There is also a common concept in the Old Testament (Deut. 32:17; Ps. 105:37) that worship of pagan gods was actually demonic worship.[85]

Idolatry was denounced by both Judaism and Christianity (1 Macc. 2:23-28; 1 Cor. 10:14; Rev. 22:15). Paul describes the origin of paganism, with its idolatry and immorality, as a result of a refusal to worship and thank the true God (Rom. 1:18-32). Thus, rebellion against God leads to deception and distortion of the truth: humanity worships the creature rather than the Creator (Rom. 1:21-25). Immorality follows, since human depravity occurs when God abandons those who do not honor him (Rom. 1:28). It is interesting to note that this list of vices, murders, sorceries, immorality, and thefts (Rev. 9:20), is echoed closely in the list of those destined for the Lake of Fire (21:8) and those outside of the heavenly city (22:15).

This moral situation can be found in the world described by John: as in the case of the Egyptian plagues, punishment does not bring about repentance, but produces a pronounced continuation of commitment to evil practices.

---

[81] Wall, p. 129; cf. 1 Pet. 3:9.
[82] See Aune, p. 541.
[83] Cf. Deut. 31:29; 1 Kgs 16:7; Acts 7:41; Rom. 13:9; Mk 7:21-22.
[84] Cf. Deut. 31:29; 1 Kgs 16:7; 2 Kgs 22:17; 2 Chron. 34:25; Isa. 2:8, 17:8; Jer. 1:16; 25:6-7; 32:30; Mic. 5:13; Acts 7:41; Justin Martyr, *1 Apol.* 20.5; *Dial.* 35.6.
[85] Cf. *1 En.* 19:1; 99:7; cf. Plutarch, *De def. Orac.* 421 C-E, in Aune, p. 542.

Reflection and Response (Part 4)

Reflection

A major issue for Revelation, as well as for all New Testament and most apocalyptic writing, is the tension between the emphases on eschatological imminence and eschatological delay. In Revelation, God's Kingdom must quickly come to eradicate rampant evil and to vindicate the suffering of the faithful righteous. Certainly, God's justice will triumph. Conversely, God is gracious and patient, allowing more time for more people to repent (see also 2 Peter).

The delay is clearly evident in Revelation. The martyrs under the altar are told to wait a while longer (6:10-11); the pauses or interludes between the sixth and seventh seals and the sixth and seventh trumpets both symbolize and attempt to explain the delay. The angel with the small scroll (10:3-6) finally states that there will be no more delay and that the final judgments of God are at hand, but then in 11:3 there appears to be another delay.

Since the text of Revelation is so expansive, the author of Revelation is able to use this tension to make a particularly significant point about God's final purpose in history. Indeed, it is at the point where the tension between eschatological imminence and eschatological delay is strongest, that the value and meaning of history is clearest. The significant point is that this present life must be lived in light of both eschatological imminence and eschatological delay. In fact, every moment of present life must be lived in relation to the imminent coming of God's Kingdom.[86]

In light of this perspective of the present and future, it is extremely important to reflect upon our lives, both in community and as individuals. How does the belief in the imminence of God's Kingdom impact the lives of the believing community? To what extent does your church emphasize the seriousness of the possibility that Christ could come at any moment? What differences can you discern between the churches that emphasize the imminent coming and those that focus more on this present life? Do you know people who reflect these different perspectives? What behaviors cause you to make this assessment? Without emphasizing either aspect over the other, what would a church look like which taught that the present life should be lived from the perspective of the imminent Coming? What tangible changes might emerge from this perspective?

On a more personal level, consider these issues. From what perspective am I living? In what ways would this viewpoint affect my dealings

---

[86] Bauckham, p. 159.

with others? In what ways would/should my priorities shift so that my time and energy is taken up more by things that pertain to the furtherance of God's Kingdom rather than by natural things and/or temporary pleasures? On the other hand, the Lord said to 'occupy' till he comes. Scripture also leads us to take care of our home, our children. What could I do so that my life reflects a better balance between the fact that Christ could come at any moment and the reality that he may delay a while longer?

Response
The following are suggestions for responding to these questions:

1. Prayerfully assess your life, identifying your focus and perspective.
2. Relate the words of Revelation to your life, particularly the passages that describe the lifestyle that is pleasing to God in contrast to that which is not.
3. With a trusted friend or prayer group, seek God's guidance about what and how your life might change to reflect better in this present time the urgency of his coming.
4. With the support of your prayer group or friend, allow God to change your attitude gradually so that it would more clearly reflect God's plan for the future.

Revelation 10:1-11:19

Chapter 10

The Little Scroll

After the sixth trumpet and before the sounding of the seventh there is an interlude of two events (chs. 10 and 11). The first describes a mighty angel who descends from heaven with a small scroll. With one foot on earth and one on the sea, the angel declares that there shall no longer be a delay (10:6). John is told to eat the little scroll and to prophesy concerning many people, nations, tongues and kings (10:11). The second episode is also directed by the angel: John is told to measure the Temple (11:1) and that God intends to empower two witnesses who will preach and perform miracles (11:2-6), only to be killed by the beast (11:7). After three days they rise from the dead to the astonishment of the world (11:11). John records that this signals the end of the second woe (11:14). The seventh trumpet woe comes quickly, announcing the coming kingdom of Christ (11:15-19).

The trumpets and woes continue to serve as literary devices to keep the reader aware of the progress of the plagues. It is interesting to note that there is also an interlude between the sixth and seventh seals during which the four angels who are holding the winds back (7:1) are told *not* to let the destructive winds blow. Next, John hears the sealing of the 144,000. Following the sealing, John sees the multitude celebrating in heaven (vv. 9-17). A pause follows the opening of the final seal and then the trumpet plagues begin.

In the interlude of chs. 10 and 11 one mighty angel descends and initiates action. There is a shift in the narrative viewpoint here (10:1) for John is no longer in heaven (he was 'called up', 4:1). Also, there is another scroll (10:2) and another commissioning of John (10:11).

The strong angel with the great voice (ch. 10) is different from the trumpet angels. While it is possible to think he may be the same strong angel of 5:2, who was looking for someone to open the scroll of destiny, the reference to his strength and the scene having to do with scrolls are the only similarities. It is more likely that he may be identified with the angel who plays a role in the communication of the vision (1:1; 22:16).[1] He is definitely not Christ, for Christ is always identified by name and never appears as an angel.[2]

This strong angel appears to reflect Dan. 12:5-7, where a figure described as a man in linen stands on the river. His physical description is different from the strong angel's, however, and he does not have a scroll. Daniel's angel raises both hands and swears by God concerning the time of the end: 'It shall be for a time, times, and an half; and when he shall have accomplished to scatter the power of the holy people, all these things shall be finished' (Dan. 12:7). These prophetic words were to be sealed up until the end (Dan. 12:9). Daniel states that there will be 1,290 days from the end of the daily sacrifice until the abomination (Dan. 12:11).

In John's vision the angel is described in a much more glorious state: clothed with a cloud, a rainbow upon his head, a face like the sun and legs like pillars of fire (Rev. 10:1). These are details often found in theophanies where clouds function as a means of transport.[3] The rainbow may be the result of the bright light from the angel's face refracted by the clouds. His legs may recall the pillar of fire which gave the Hebrews protection in the wilderness (Exod. 14:19,24; 13:21-22; cf. Wis. 18:3; Sib.Or. 3.50). The description of the angel fits his message: 'the affirming of God's fidelity to his covenants' (Rev. 10:7); the rainbow recalls the Noachic covenant of Genesis: the clouds, God's wilderness presence, and the scroll, the Mosaic Covenant.[4]

The great angel's stance, with one foot on land and one on the sea, may symbolize his authority over the earth and/or the universality of his message. It may also correspond to his oath, in which he appeals to God, creator of heaven, earth and sea. He holds a small scroll which is open. The description is in contrast to the large scroll of Revelation 5, which is securely sealed with seven seals. Since it is 'open' it is ready to be read. The book originates in heaven, but its message is intended to be communicated to people. It is not exactly clear how this small scroll relates to the scroll of destiny (ch. 5). Perhaps, if the larger scroll contains the destiny of the world, the small one contains a fragment of that purpose.[5] It may reflect Ezek. 2:9-10, which describes a scroll containing lamentations and woes. As such, it would refer only to the later period of the Tribulation times, a mere fragment of the larger scroll

---

[1] Aune, p. 557, cites Bauckham, 'Conversion', pp. 254-55.
[2] Mounce, p. 207.
[3] Aune, p. 657.
[4] Mounce, p. 208.
[5] Ladd, p. 142.

which contains information on the entire end-time events for both wicked and righteous.

The angel's great voice is likened to a lion's roar. Divine beings are often described as speaking loudly, perhaps to emphasize the importance and authority of the speaker (cf. Hos. 11:10; Joel 3:16; Amos 1:2; 3:8; Jer. 25:30). The seven thunders respond to the angel's cry (Rev. 10:3). In Revelation, thunder is often associated with divine retribution (8:5; 11:19; 16:18) and here it anticipates that retribution. The number seven corresponds to the other series of sevens found throughout Revelation (seals, trumpets, bowls), but here it seems that the thunders themselves actually talk (10:3,4). This is the only passage in Revelation where a speech is mentioned but not produced. The message of the thunders must have been understandable because John was prepared to write it down (10:4). As he is about to record the utterances, however, a voice from heaven forbids him, commanding him to seal up the message and to refrain from writing. This double command seems strange, since if John had not written the words down, he would be unable to seal them up. The command probably emphasizes that the thunder's message is not to be written, spoken or in any way passed on. This follows the apocalyptic motif of secrecy (*Test. Sol.* 6.6; *Apoc. Zeph.* 5.6; 2 Cor. 12:4), but differs in that the material is usually to be revealed only to the wise.[6] The message was probably another series of plagues. Commentators suggest several reasons for the forbidden disclosure: (a) people's lack of repentance, seen in 9:20,21, would make another series of plagues futile; (b) as Paul suggests in 2 Cor. 12:4, some heavenly things are not to be communicated; perhaps (as in apocalyptic motifs) they would be incomprehensible or unaccepted by mere mortals, and (c) it may be that the additional plagues would cause a delay in God's plan (see 10:6).

The voice that forbids the thunder's disclosure comes from heaven and, though the speaker is not identified, it can be assumed it is either God or Christ speaking.[7]

Revelation 10:5-7 continues the narrative interrupted by the thunders: the angel raises his hand to heaven and swears by God, who created heaven, earth and the sea, as well as the things in each sphere, that 'there should be time no longer'. It is interesting that many oaths use heaven or earth as witnesses because they are perceived as stable. In this case, however, the only stable reality is God, for heaven and earth will

---

[6] Cf. *4 Ezra* 14:5b-6; 14:37-48; Dan. 12:4, 8:26; Josephus, *Ant.* III 90.

[7] See Old Testament parallels: Num. 7:89, Ezek. 1:28, Dan. 4:31-32, 8:16. For references in early Judaism, cf. *4 Ezra* 6:3; 7:11-13; *2 Bar.* 13:1-2; 22:1.

pass away (21:1).[8] The angel raises his hand to heaven, perhaps in an appeal to God himself to witness the oath. This seems appropriate also, for since God created the heaven, earth, and sea, he alone could witness its end.

The shocking announcement is that there will be no further delay – time is at an end (10:6,7). John is told that with the sounding of the seventh trumpet, as he begins to sound, the 'mystery of God' will be finished. Probably 'delay' (χρόνος) should not be understood in the sense of postponement, for God controls time and eschatological events happen according to his plan. Rather, Rev. 10:6,7 reflects Dan. 12:7, where the disclosure of events is to be sealed until the end. John is told that the end has now come (cf. 2 Thess. 2:3; Dan. 12:1; Mt. 13:19). The reader should connect this passage also to Rev. 6:11, in which the souls under the altar are told to wait for God's vengeance on evil. With the sounding of the seventh trumpet the common apocalyptic question of 'How long?' is answered.[9]

A major interpretive challenge in this passage is the understanding of 'mystery' (10:7). Literally the word means 'secret'. In apocalyptic literature the concept is commonly understood that there are secrets treasured in heaven and revealed only to a select few, the wise and righteous.[10] The idea is that God communicates to prophets heavenly mysteries that will only be understood when properly communicated and interpreted. The word for 'preached' (εὐηγγέλισεν, v. 7b) is the word for 'preaching the gospel'. This would appear to indicate that the 'mystery' referred to here has to do with the good news of the gospel message. God revealed it to his prophets both in the Old Testament and the New Testament (cf. Rom. 1:1,2; Gal. 3:8). It is possible that this message also includes the coming of God as judge and savior.[11] This is the usage of early Palestinian Jewish Christianity.[12] The angelic voice appears to underscore the fact that God's judgment is not coming unannounced. Rather, God has revealed his plan to his prophets in ancient times, although full understanding will not be possible until the events actually take place.

Following the mighty angel's announcement, John is told to take the little book from the angel (10:8). It is unlikely that John would

---

[8] Aune, p. 565.
[9] Wall, p. 138.
[10] *1 En.* 40:2; 71:3; Tob. 12:7,11; Wis. 2:22.
[11] Cf. Peter Stuhlmacher, *Evangelium – Schriftauslegung – Kirche* (Göttingen: Vandenhoeck & Ruprecht, 1997), pp. 210-18; Joachim Jeremias, *Jesu Verheissung für die Völker* (2nd ed.; Stuttgart, 1956); ET: *Jesus' Promise to the Nations*, SBT 24 (rev. ed.; London: SCM, 1967), pp. 19-20, 59.
[12] See Rev. 10:7; 14:6; also Mt. 11:2-6; Lk. 18:23; 14:16-30; Mk 1:14-15.

have approached the angel if he had not been commanded to do so. John obeys and is given further instructions by the large angel to eat the book. He is warned that it would taste like honey but result in a bitter stomach (10:10). The figure is based on Ezek. 2:8–3:6, where the prophet is also told to eat a scroll and that it would taste like honey. The sweet taste is often associated with God's Word in the Old Testament (Pss. 19:10; 119:100-103). Eating the scroll suggests that the prophet must ingest and assimilate the message before he can adequately communicate it. Like Ezekiel's scroll, the immediate result is a sweet taste, but for John the final ingesting results in bitterness (a sour stomach).

The scroll episode represents a reaffirmation and renewal of John's prophetic ministry. The actual content of the scroll is debated, particularly whether it contains any or all of the end of ch. 10 and ch. 11.[13] Although we cannot know for certain, Rev. 11:1-13 seems the likely content, for the scroll must contain negative words of judgment to affect John with bitterness. Also, Rev. 11:14 provides a break – the end of the second woe and beginning of the final trumpet/woes. Thus, the scroll may contain a message of impending judgment, yet a final appeal for repentance (the preaching of the two witnesses). There is no positive response to the preaching, and though there seems to be a forced recognition of God (as in the Exodus tradition) it is no doubt ineffective in the long term. Hence the prophet's initial reaction is of sweetness turning to bitterness.

One critical interpretive element is how the word translated 'about' (ἔπι) is used in Rev. 10:11. Is John commissioned to prophecy 'about', 'before', or 'against' many peoples, nations, tongues and kings? 'About' and 'before' suggest a more neutral prophetic attitude but 'against' may be more consistent with the apocalyptist's attitude toward ungodly nations. This last option also seems to be supported by Ezek. 2:9-10, Mt. 10:18, and Mk 13:9.[14] The reference to 'peoples, nations, tongues and kings' suggests the universality of the message (see 10:9). It may be that John's message is to denounce wickedness as he turns to prophesy against a society hostile to God.[15]

---

[13] Options include (1) Rev. 10-11, G. Bornkamm, 'Die Komposition der apokalyptischen Visionen in der Offenbarung Johannis', *ZNW* 36 (1937), pp. 132-49; (2) Rev. 11:1-13; Charles, I, pp. 260-69; Gottlob Schrenk, 'βιβλίον', *TDNT* I (1964), p. 618; Ernst Lohmeyer, *Die Offenbarung des Johannes*, 3rd ed., Handbuch zum Neuen Testament 16 (Tübingen: Mohr-Siebeck, 1970), pp. 87-89; Mounce, pp. 213f.; (3) Rev. 11:1–15:4; Schüssler Fiorenza and Beasley-Murray (cited in Aune, pp. 571-72).

[14] See Aune, p. 573, for further discussion.

[15] Ladd, p. 216.

Chapter 11

Measuring the Temple

Chapter 11, which continues the interlude begun in ch. 10, contains a coherent literary unit in two parts: vv. 1-2, the measuring of the Temple and vv. 3-13, the activity of the two witnesses. Verses 15-19 report the seventh trumpet and lead into the next section. Revelation 11:1-13 is presented like a narrative prophecy rather than a vision which John saw and wrote down.[16]

A major problem with this section is whether the passage should be taken literally or allegorically. On the one hand, *if taken literally* the temple will be rebuilt during the Tribulation. The altar, worshipers and holy city have something to do with the Jews and God's plan for Israel. The two witnesses are two people who will return to prophesy in the eschatological end time tradition. On the other hand, *if taken allegorically* the Temple could represent the Christian church, and the witnesses could symbolize their prophetic preaching during the end time period. In recent scholarship there is a trend to interpret this passage symbolically to represent the Christian church.[17] There does not seem to be any basis for this in the text, however, which would require only an allegorical interpretation of these verses.[18]

John himself is drawn into the activity and told to measure the temple. The actual performance of the task is not described but it should be assumed by the reader that John carried out the command. The measuring activity should be understood in a spiritual sense, and one can assume that John is on earth, since no location change is mentioned after 10:1.

John is given a reed like a rod. Reeds grew abundantly in the Jordan Valley and were like bamboo, long and stiff (cf. Ezek. 40:5). With this rod John is told to measure the Temple. Although the speaker is not identified it most likely is the angel of ch. 10. The action parallels the symbolic prophetic action found often in the Old Testament.[19] In this passage, measuring suggests preservation and divine protection, much like the sealing of the 144,000 (7:1-8). Scholars differ as to the extent of protection; God could protect against spiritual danger and defilement, ensuring entrance into the Messianic Kingdom.[20] Or, as Aune

---

[16] Aune, p. 585.
[17] Martin Kiddle, *The Revelation of Saint John*, The Moffatt New Testament Commentary (London: Hodder & Stoughton, 1940), pp. 174-88; Mounce, p. 218; Aune, p. 499.
[18] Aune says the temple here is certainly the one in Jerusalem, p. 605.
[19] 1 Kgs 22:11; Isa. 8:1-4; 20:1-6; Jer. 13:3-11; 27:1–28:16; Ezek. 24:3; Acts 1:11.
[20] Mounce, p. 219.

points out, the protection could be from physical death and persecution, which seems to be more consistent with the meaning of the text, for the witnesses are protected physically until God lifts that protection when their testimony is complete.[21] Also, the areas not measured are overrun, trampled, which suggests physical damage (cf. Ezek. 40:3–48:35).

John is told to measure the Temple of God, the altar and the worshipers within (11:1). Two Greek words are used in the New Testament for temple: one, ἱερόν, refers to the structure, including the three courts, colonnades and outer courts (Mt. 4:5; Jn 2:14) and the other, ναός, refers only to the sanctuary or inner house (Mt. 23:35; 27:51). The latter term is used in Rev. 11:1 and probably refers to the sanctuary and three courts which were separated from the outer court by a low stone barrier enclosed in the area known as the rampart. Warnings were posted forbidding Gentiles to pass through on pain of death.[22]

The altar referred to is the stone altar of sacrifice in the court of the priests. The worshipers included would be those in the three courts: the court of priests, the court of Israel, and the court of women. Since they are included in the measuring, the worshipers represent the righteous who recognize and accept God. It is interesting to note that they are counted.

John is told to exclude the outer court. Frequented by a mixed group of Gentiles and unbelievers it was not protected in any sense. In fact, it is 'given' to the Gentiles (Rev. 11:2). This suggests God permitted it to be overrun by Gentiles, which term may be taken in the general sense of the 'nations' (Mt. 24:9,14; Lk. 24:47) or in a specific sense of Gentiles in contrast to Jews (Mt. 4:15; 10:5; Lk. 2:32), or as people in rebellion against God.

Regardless, 'given to the Gentiles' suggests that God permits defiling persons to overrun the outer court, while the inner court and those who are within are preserved and protected. This recalls Old Testament stories of God's protection, such as the sparing of all who were in the Ark, all who were in Rahab's house, and Israelites in Egypt who had the Passover blood on the doorposts of their houses.

Finally, the holy city is to be trampled underfoot for 42 months. The 'holy city' refers to Jerusalem. Three reasons may be offered in support of a literal interpretation of the city: (1) the Old Testament use of 'holy city' for Jerusalem;[23] (2) the proximity of the term to the temple reference (11:1); and (3) the mention of the 'great city where our

---

[21] Aune, p. 604.
[22] See Josephus, *Ant.* XV 410-17.
[23] Cf. Neh. 11:1; Isa. 48:2, 52:1; Dan. 9:24; Mt. 4:5; 27:53.

Lord was crucified' (11:8).[24] 'Trampling', therefore, means destruction or defilement. The idea is that God will permit the outer court and the city itself to be persecuted and overrun by the ungodly people of the beast. The time period (42 months) is also consistent with the reign of the beast.[25] Daniel is the basis for this time period known as the Tribulation, for Dan. 9:27 tells of a week of sevens, each of which seems to represent seven years. The seven years of the end time are divided into two sets of three and one-half years, during which the world leader (symbolized by the beast) reigns. This time frame is also seen in the length of the witnesses' testimony (11:3f.) and the time the woman is protected from the dragon (12:6).

If understood literally, then, in the Tribulation period the Temple in Jerusalem will be rebuilt and its sacrificial system revived. The worshipers will be recognized by God as holy and protected from the beast's persecution. This could be another reference to the 144,000 sealed (protected).[26] Other recent scholars, however, have adopted a more symbolic interpretation of this passage. The holy city will be a symbolic designation for the church, which will be persecuted for 42 months by the beast, but will be spiritually protected from defilement.[27] In this view, it is not quite clear why God would protect some Christians (the measured Temple) and permit others to be overrun (the holy city). It seems more likely that God protects a remnant of Jews who are faithful to him (the 144,000 and the worshipers in the Temple who are also counted) in order for them to survive the reign of the beast. It is not clear exactly how they are protected, but the symbolic imagery of sealing (ch. 7) and measuring (11:1) makes them untouchable by the beast for 42 months. It seems that the Jewish imagery of the Temple, the altar, courts and Jerusalem should be taken as references to God's plan for Israel during the Tribulation. Also, protection of a remnant while the rest are allowed to perish is an Old Testament concept found in God's dealings with Israel. In the New Testament the church is tested as a whole and never separated into a spared remnant.

It is not entirely clear how this protection of certain Jews relates to the problem in the church of Philadelphia (3:9), 'those who claim to be Jews, but are not'. Most likely, this church problem has to do with the spiritual issue of what constitutes true Jewish identity. Paul clarifies that 'it is those who are of faith that are sons of Abraham' (Gal. 3:7),

---

[24] Johnson, p. 502.
[25] Dan. 8:10; Rev. 11:2; cf. *Pss. Sol.* 17.24-25,42-47, which says Jerusalem will be trampled by pagans until restored by the Messiah.
[26] See Johnson, p. 502.
[27] Mounce, p. 221; Johnson, p. 502.

rather than those who are outwardly Jewish. The problem of the church of Philadelphia would represent the problem in churches throughout history: that there is a distinction between those whose faith is genuine and those whose faith is not.

The Two Witnesses

The second section of ch. 11 has to do with the two witnesses. The passage continues as a prophetic narrative, probably told by the angel of ch. 10. The section (vv. 3-10) is dominated by verbs in the future tense which shift to past tense in vv. 11-13. The passage can be outlined in the following manner: (1) mission and authority of the two witnesses (vv. 3-6), (2) killing of the two witnesses (vv. 7-10), (3) victory of the two witnesses and punishment of their enemies (vv. 11-13), and (4) response of the survivors (v. 13).

The introduction of the two witnesses follows the measurement of the Temple sanctuary with its inner courts and the exclusion of the outer courts, which are left to be trampled on (with the 'holy city') for 42 months. Since the narrative follows so closely, it seems that the witnesses will testify during the same time period as the Temple measurement. (The 1,290 days of Daniel [12:11], is another way of counting 42 months.)

Although no specific mention is made of the witnesses' origin, one can assume they were commissioned and sent by God: they are called 'my' witnesses (v. 3) and they stand before the Lord of the earth (v. 4). Prophetic terms and imagery abound in the description of the individuals: they prophesy, they are clothed in sackcloth, they are described by the prophetic images of Zechariah (olive trees and lampstands), and they perform miracles like prophets of old (v. 6). The concept of two prophetic witnesses returning at the end time may originate from early Jewish expectations of two messianic figures based on Aaron and David (Zech. 4:2-3, 11-12).[28] Both Old Testament and New Testament references support the idea that a prophet like Moses would be raised up (Deut. 18:18) and that Elijah would return before the Day of the Lord (Mal. 4:5; cf. Mk 9:11; Mt. 11:14; Jn 6:14; 7:40). Some identify one of the eschatological prophets as Enoch, probably because of his translation to heaven. Moses, Elijah and Enoch are named because of their unusual departures from earth, but Moses and Elijah are more commonly suggested because of the miracles and prophetic references to them (Deut. 18:18; Mal. 4:5).

---

[28] John J. Collins, *Daniel with an Introduction to Apocalyptic Literature*, FOTL 20 (Grand Rapids, MI: Eerdmans, 1984), pp. 71-90.

The witnesses are clothed in sackcloth, a rough cloth made of goat's or camel's hair. This material, used for grain sacks, was also worn by prophets or others to show mourning and national distress (Gen. 37:34; 2 Sam. 3:31; Isa. 15:3; 22:10), submission to God (Jer. 4:8; Dan. 9:3), repentance (Neh. 9:1; Isa. 20.2; Jonah 3:5-8; Mt. 11:21), and prophetic mourning in anticipation of God's coming judgment (Isa. 50:3; cf. 1 Clem. 8.3). In Revelation 11, the wearing of sackcloth gives an impression of the witnesses' role and message – one of mourning, lamentations and impending divine judgment.

The witnesses are identified as the two olive trees and lampstands that stand before the Lord (Rev. 11:4). The imagery is based on Zech. 4:1-14, and describes Zerubbabel, claimant to the Davidic throne and a Joshua-like priest who was to restore Judah. Although modified, the images as used by John would reflect the eschatological expectations of prophetic figures who would return at the end time once again to preach repentance and warn of God's judgment on wickedness.

The witnesses have power to do miracles: breathe fire from their mouths, cause drought, turn water to blood and bring about plagues on the earth. These types of miracles recall Elijah, who called fire down on the king's emissaries (2 Kgs 1:10f.) and who caused drought during Ahab's reign (1 Kgs 17:1). The plagues, especially the turning of water into blood, would recall Moses and the Exodus tradition (Exod. 7–8). These were done in response to the people's desire to harm the witnesses. The phrase 'if anyone tries to harm them' is a first class conditional sentence that emphasizes the reality of the situation. The miracles can be taken literally (real fire was called down) or the fire from their mouths could be a symbolic way of describing the burning Word of God which would be spoken as rebuke and condemnation (cf. Jer. 14:10; 4 Ezra 13:10, 37-38; Ps. 18:13). Regardless, the witnesses tormented the earth by their miracles, plagues and punishments. It is not clear how these plagues are related to the earlier trumpet plagues. Since the two witnesses seem to be part of the sixth trumpet (and second woe) these may be generally considered as part of God's acts of judgment on the world.

At the time designated by God – when their testimony is complete (v. 7), the beast attacks and kills the witnesses. This is the first reference to the beast in Revelation. He is described as coming from the abyss, suggesting his origin as demonic. The reference anticipates Revelation 13, where the beast is described in more detail. God allows the witnesses to be killed. Revelation 11:7 says the beast 'attacks and overpowers them'. Apparently the power that protects the two witnesses (their power to smite earth with plagues and fire, 11:6), will be limited so that 'when they have finished their testimony' (v. 7), the beast will be allowed to kill them. The word used for completed or finished, τελέσωσιν, has more than a temporal sense of completion; it also conveys the notion of accomplishment of a goal.[29] Apparently the plagues and fire which were used to fight off the attackers for three and one-half years were no longer available.

The response to the witnesses' death is great joy and celebration. People even give gifts to one another, a custom usually reserved for major celebrations. That their bodies are left unburied in the street is the height of indignity, a demonstration of the hostile feelings of the people for these witnesses. They are said to lie in the streets of the 'great city, figuratively called Sodom and Egypt, where also our Lord was crucified' (Rev. 11:8). The city is most likely Jerusalem, especially since that is where Jesus was crucified, and there is no scene shift from Rev. 11:1-2.[30] The city is 'figuratively' called Sodom and Egypt. This may point to the spiritual atmosphere of Jerusalem under the beast's influence. Sodom suggests rebellion against God: it was immoral and doomed to divine judgment; Egypt reflects enslavement of God's people and is symbolic of idolatry.

The fact that all nations could see the bodies left in the streets could reflect the cosmopolitan nature of Jerusalem, but there is also the possibility that through modern media techniques this type of monumental activity could be communicated to and followed closely by the entire world. The passage reports that the bodies are left in the streets amid raucous rejoicing for three and one-half days. At that time, God resurrects the witnesses, and in the sight of all they are called up to heaven. The resurrection language reflects Ezekiel 37, where life again comes into the dry bones. It is an indication that God has power over life and death. Following the ascension (11:13), a great earthquake levels a portion of the city, killing 7,000 people (cf. Ezek. 38:19-20; Zech. 14:1-5). The earthquake may recall the Sinai tradition of God's presence as well as the earthquake on the day of Jesus' death (Mt. 27.52ff.).

It is interesting to note the response of those who watched these events: there was joy after the witnesses' death (Rev. 11:10),[31] but there was terror after the resurrection. The word for terror (φόβος) can indicate a collective response of awe or a reaction to supernatural powers.[32] Two events immediately follow the resurrection: (1) a heavenly voice summons the witnesses and they ascend to heaven in the sight of their 'enemies' (v. 12), and (2) a great earthquake immediately follows 'in

---

[29] Mounce, p. 225 n. 23.
[30] Aune, p. 620.
[31] Swete describes their delight as 'at once fiendish and childish', p. 138.
[32] Cf. Exod. 15:16; 1 Macc. 3:25; 2 Macc. 3:24; Lk. 1:12; Acts 19:17.

that hour' (v. 13). The quake results in major damage – a tenth of the city is destroyed and 7,000 people are killed (v. 13). Following the ascension and earthquake, the survivors were even more terrified and 'gave glory to the God of heaven' (v. 13). This is an unusual response from the hostile world, and it can have two meanings: (a) praise and honor to God as in acknowledgement of his power, or (b) a verbal indication of conversion, but this would be the only instance in Revelation of people turning to God because of miracles.[33] It seems more likely that the people's response was to recognize God as all powerful because of their terror. As the Egyptian pharaoh was forced to acknowledge Moses' God because of the plagues, and the same way that acknowledgement was short lived, so the response to God's judgments on the people of the Tribulation was not a response of true repentance (being sorry for their sin and willing to turn from their commitment to evil); it appears this response will also be temporary. The title 'God of heaven' is a title used by non-Jews, and therefore could suggest that the response was from all people and nations and not necessarily from Israel.[34] In any case, although the wicked give 'glory to the God of heaven' (v. 13), there is no response from God. This perhaps suggests the position that this is merely an acknowledgment of God's power, or it is 'too little, too late' because God does not respond and the author notes that the 'second woe is past and the third woe is quickly coming' (v. 14).

A major question in this passage has to do with the interpretation and identity of the witnesses. Options include the following:

a. They are Moses and Elijah (or Enoch) as expected in early Jewish tradition.
b. They are two prophetic individuals raised up by God, empowered in the spirit of Moses and Elijah.
c. They are symbols of the witnessing church before the end of the age. As such they are not limited to two individuals, but reflect the prophetic ministry of the church, which could perform miracles in the prophetic tradition.[35]

It seems probable that the witnesses are eschatological prophetic individuals. In other times of God's judgment He sent individuals to preach repentance and warn of impending judgment, such as Noah, Lot, and Jonah. The performance of miracles would be consistent with

---

[33] Aune, p. 628; Bauckham, p. 6; cf. Ladd, 'Why Not Prophetic-Apocalyptic?', *JBL* 76 (1957), pp. 192-200.
[34] Aune, p. 629.
[35] See Johnson, p. 504; Aune, p. 612.

the actions of individuals. The two witnesses being killed, resurrected, and then called to heaven seems more plausible than for the whole church to be resurrected. Finally, the Jewish and early Christian tradition expected one or two eschatological prophet figures to appear before the Day of the Lord (see especially the tradition developing from Deut. 18:15 and Mal. 4:5-6). There are no known prophetic references to a righteous body of believers appearing at the end time. Finally, the terminology of the chapter does not seem to reflect the church. There is a focus on the Temple, the altar, and the worshipers therein (11:1,2). Jerusalem seems to be the location and the witnesses are consistent with Jewish eschatological prophetic expectations. There is no mention of Jesus, the Cross or the church.

Revelation 11:14 concludes the interlude with a reminder that the second woe is past and the readers should expect the third soon.[36]

Then the seventh angel sounds his trumpet (11:15), but instead of the expected 'woe', John hears an announcement by 'loud voices' that the rule of the world now belongs to God and Christ (v. 15). The 24 elders again lead worship as in chs. 4, 5 and 7. This group, which last appeared in 7:11 kneeling before God's throne, have fallen on their faces before God, worshiping (11:16). The voices are singing a hymn of victory that the rule of the world has been transferred to God 'and his Christ, who shall reign for ever and ever' (v. 15). The extensive use of these particular tenses indicates the absolute certainty of the events to come ('You have taken [εἴληφας, perfect tense] your great power and begun to reign' [ἐβασίλευσας, aorist tense], v. 17). These praises actually serve to introduce the major themes of the remainder of Revelation found in the eschatological events which will usher in and establish forevermore the universal reign of God.[37] The actual kingdom is not taken over by Christ until his return in Revelation 19, but this section anticipates the millennial kingdom, judgment of the wicked, rewarding of the righteous and the reality of God's presence.

The group that is worshiping in Rev. 11:15-19 is an angelic host, not the glorified church, for they proclaim 'the kingdom of the world has become the Kingdom of our Lord and *of His Christ!*' (11:15). This hymn uses names belonging to covenant language, especially Old Testament terminology, 'Lord, God, the Almighty' (v. 17; 4:8).[38] The name 'the Almighty' asserts God as sovereign ruler. 'The One who is, and the One who was' recalls 1:8, an articulation of God's eternality, his infinite power and existence. In fact, the perfect tense (εἴληφας)

---

[36] For source criticism of this, see Aune, pp. 588-603.
[37] Mounce, p. 230.
[38] Beasley-Murray, p. 189; Gause, p. 157.

indicates that something which occurred in the past is continuing into the present: God has taken his great power and is now continuing to exercise it. Even when it appeared that Satan or human rebellion was in control, in reality God had never lost control. He always has been and eternally is ruler of humanity.[39]

The angelic host announces the great eschatological events prophesied in Old Testament scriptures, such as Dan. 2:31-45,49, where the Kingdom of God would replace all others (cf. Zech. 14:9). One is reminded of the temptation of Jesus, that he was offered all the kingdoms of the world by Satan, and rebuked him (Mt. 4:8-9). God's final reign will be established by the judgment and annihilation of wickedness. It is only then that God's rule can be supreme in the earth.

So, the reign of God is established by the judging of the wicked (cf. 16:9-11,21). Human rebellion, with its anger against God (see Rom. 3:9-18), has been judged throughout history. God has allowed time for repentance. Now the time has come when the possibility for repentance is past. It is appropriate that God is now meeting wickedness with extreme wrath.[40]

The final reign of God is preceded by one last attack by 'the nations' (11:18). This final violent assault upon God's authority is a common theme in apocalypticism,[41] and certainly reflects Ps. 98:1, 'The Lord has begun to reign and the people are enraged'.[42] The theme is a recurring one in Revelation (16:14; 17:14; 19:19; 20:9). Apparently the mention of the judgment of the dead is an anticipation of the judgment of the wicked dead described in 20:11-15.[43] The rewards of the righteous, also mentioned in 11:18, are carried out in the vision of the New Jerusalem (21:9–22:5). Although all righteous receive the reward of grace (Rev. 1:4-5; 14:4), each person is also rewarded for his/her deeds (1 Cor. 3:8). There appear to be categories of the righteous here in 11:18 (prophets, saints, 'those who fear thy name'). In 19:5, the groups appear to be consolidated into 'you who fear, the small and great' (see also Ps. 115:13).

---

[39] See Gause, p. 157.

[40] Cf. Hanns Lilje, *The Last Book of the Bible*, trans. Olive Wyon (Philadelphia: Muhlenberg Press, 1957), p. 167, who calls the holy wrath of God a 'majestic antithesis'.

[41] Mounce, p. 231.

[42] See also Exod. 15:14. The two motifs are also connected in other eschatological scenarios: Pss. 2:1-2; 46:6; 65:7; *1 En.* 99:4; *4 Ezra* 13:30-31; *Jub.* 23:23; *Sib.Or.* 3.660-68; Lars Hartman, *Prophecy Interpreted*, CBNT, 1 (Lund: CWK Gleerup, 1966), pp. 77-101; Aune, p.644.

[43] Cf. Gerhard Delling, 'καιρός', *TDNT* III (1965), for significant points about 'the time' (ὁ καιρός), pp. 460-62.

Revelation 11:19 concludes the prophetic summary by describing the opening of God's temple in heaven. Within the temple is the Ark of His Covenant. The Ark was the special chest that God instructed Moses to make for the tabernacle in the wilderness. It was placed in the holiest room, guarded by two cherubim and separated from the public by a heavy curtain. In the Ark were placed the stone tablets bearing the Ten Commandments and other sacred articles. The original Ark was lost in the Babylonian Captivity (586 BCE). A legend is recorded in 2 Macc. 2:7 that the Ark will be hidden until the time for God to gather his people for the expected messianic eschatological event.

It is highly significant that the doors of the Temple of God open (17:19). Even in the secular world, temple doors that opened by themselves were considered a marvel.[44] Obviously, this is a moment of awesome significance: the temple doors open in response to the hymn of praise (vv. 17,18) and the Ark of the Covenant itself is revealed (v. 19). Such an event would appear 'to represent the fulfillment of the covenant of redemption claimed in the services of the temple'.[45]

In the Old Testament as well as Revelation, the Temple is the location where the glory of God is revealed; where sin is judged and atoned for; where God is worshiped. In the Old Testament, people were allowed to approach the Ark only by God's permission (cf. Exod. 30:10; Heb. 9:7). The Ark itself symbolized the abiding presence of God, his faithfulness to bring about his covenant promises.[46] The revelation of the Ark in heaven (v. 19) is an explicit statement that God is faithfully bringing about these promises – the rewards for the righteous and the judgment of the wicked (v. 18). This heavenly Ark appears as the true Ark, the archetype for the construction of the Ark housed in the earthly tabernacle and temple.[47] As usual, cosmic disturbances follow the revelation of the Ark, symbolizing the presence of God.[48]

---

[44] Xenophon, *Hellenica* VI 4.7; Tacitus, *Hist.* V 13; *Dio Cassius* LXVI 8.2; see also a parallel to 11:19 in Vergil, *Aeneid*, III 90-95.

[45] Gause, p. 158.

[46] Mounce, p. 233.

[47] Cf. Exod. 25:9,40; 26:30; 27:8; 1 Chron. 28:19; Wis. 9:8; Acts 7:44; Heb. 8:1-5; 9:24; *b. Hag.* 12b; *Gen. Rab.* 55.7; *Midr. Cant.* 44; *Str.B.* 3.702-704; David Winston, *The Wisdom of Solomon*, Anchor Bible 33 (Garden City, NY: Doubleday, 1979), pp. 203-205.

[48] See lightning and thunder, 8:5; 16:18; earthquakes, 6:12; 8:5; 11:13; 16:18; hail, 8:7; 16:21.

Reflection and Response (Part 5)

Reflection

One of the major themes of Revelation is 'witness'. Indeed, it is the first title given to Jesus (1:5; 3:14). Although today the Greek word (μάρτυς) has the connotation of one who suffers and dies for a cause (consider the English translation, martyr), in the time of Revelation, it had the meaning of one who bears evidence for a cause. This is affirmed by the close association in Revelation between witness and the 'Word of the Lord' (1:2,9; 6:9; 20:4; also 12:11). It is also closely linked to keeping the commandments of God (12:17). Certainly, there is a strong implication that this witness will lead to suffering and death (2:13; 11:17; 12:17; 17:6), but the word primarily means the evidence presented for a cause.

Usually, 'witness' in Revelation is linked directly with Jesus himself ('the witness of Jesus'). This most likely refers to the witness given by Jesus, the witness he himself bore to the true God and his righteousness (see John 3:32f.; 18:37) rather than to the witness about Jesus.

The author vividly contrasts the authentic truth of the witness of Jesus and his followers and the falsity and deceit of the beast and his followers. The imagery is of a courtroom drama in which Jesus and his followers present evidence for the truth which exposes and condemns the wicked. In the final phase of the text, the faithful witness (3:14) becomes the faithful judge, 19:11.[49] Jesus' witness condemns evil itself, symbolized by the beast and Satan.

Like Jesus, his followers also bear witness to the true God and will often suffer and die for it (2:13; 11:7; 12:17). Those who are faithful, however, will participate in the millennial kingdom (ch. 20) and in the New Heaven and New Earth (chs. 21-22).

The text of Revelation concludes with the witness of Jesus himself to the words of the prophecy (22:16-20). Because of the faithfulness and truth of Jesus' witness so far, the reader is expected to rely on his faithfulness in the future cataclysmic events.

When reflecting on this theme, it might be beneficial to challenge oneself with questions like these. What sort of witness is the church of today bearing? In what ways does it expose the falsity and deception of the world around it? Does it challenge its own members to live lives reflecting the holiness of God? Has the church become so comfortable with and in its surroundings that it no longer seeks to challenge its environment like Jesus did? What characteristics of the church would

---

[49] See Bauckham, pp. 72-73.

support your answer? What actions could be taken to call for a return of the church to this aspect of its mission?

On a more individual level, I might ask myself the following: What is my own witness for God? When was the last time I challenged those around me to live more authentically in relation to God? In what ways do I tend to blur the distinction between myself as God's witness and the world around? Is there any noticeable difference between myself and the surrounding world? What actions or behaviors could be strengthened so that I would have a stronger witness for God?

Response
Consider these suggestions for response:

1. Perhaps with a trusted friend, evaluate and acknowledge the condition of your witness.
2. Develop a scriptural understanding of 'witness' by examining the use of this word in the Bible.
3. Earnestly seek God's guidance in developing an action plan for strengthening your witness.
4. With your friend, and perhaps others in your spiritual community, commit to this plan of action, to live more visibly as a witness to God.

Revelation 12:1-19:21

Chapter 12

The Sun-Clothed Woman

Chapters 12-14 form a break in the series of sevens. This section follows the blowing of the seventh trumpet (Rev. 11:15) and precedes that of the seven last plagues (Rev. 15). It includes vivid symbolic material as John sees a radiant woman, a dragon and a variety of beasts. The section may be introduced by 11:19 where God's Temple in heaven is opened and the Ark of the Covenant is revealed to him. The signs in the heavens are a result of this revelation.[1]

Chapter 12 shows John's readers a metaphorical representation of the spiritual warfare occurring behind events on earth. God and Satan struggle for dominance, and as the symbolic figures portray, this conflict influences events on earth. As Ladd describes it, the vision 'completely transcends the usual categories of time and space' and represents 'the struggle in the spiritual world which lies behind history'.[2]

Current scholars describe the genre of ch. 12 in terms of the 'combat myth' which was common in the Greco-Roman world. These myths depict cosmic struggles between divine beings, in which one usually represented order and fertility, while the other represented chaos and sterility. In Jewish tradition eschatological combat myths developed out of protological combat myths, such as Dan. 7, where the four beasts represent empires. These beasts are conquered by divine intervention (v. 12) and an everlasting kingdom is then introduced (vv. 13,14).[3] In this Jewish tradition, God is expected to overcome current historical enemies just as he did the mythological opponents. Apocalyptists (e.g. Isa. 27:1) added a futuristic element by maintaining that

---

[1] Aune, pp. 663-64.
[2] George E. Ladd, *A Commentary on the Revelation of John* (Grand Rapids, MI: Eerdmans, 1972), p. 166.
[3] Aune, p. 668.

God will do in the future what he did in the past (depicted mythologically). A major function of the combat myth was to explain the current situation of suffering and evil in terms of a cosmic adversary, Satan.[4]

Chapter 12 focuses on two main characters: a pregnant woman and a dragon (Rev. 12:1-4a). The drama unfolds in terms of three scenes of conflict:

a. The birth and escape of the woman's child and the woman's subsequent flight (12:4b-6).
b. The defeat and expulsion of the dragon (12:7-12).
c. The dragon's pursuit of the woman and her offspring (12:13-17).

The woman clearly represents the righteous element. In spite of the evil dragon's efforts to destroy her and her children, God preserves her and the dragon (evil) is overthrown.

The passage begins when God's Temple is opened in heaven (11:19) and a 'sign' appears (12:1),[5] a portent, or significant spectacle, in the stars, perhaps a constellation. John calls it a 'sign', which would indicate to his readers that the material which follows should be taken symbolically as having deeper meaning. John is no doubt on earth when he sees this spectacle: he has not changed his location since ch. 11, where he measured the Temple in Jerusalem. From that vantage point, he sees the woman's child caught up to heaven (12:5) and the dragon cast down to earth, where the dragon pursues the woman (12:13).

As John watches he sees a woman clothed with the sun, with her feet upon the moon. She is crowned with twelve stars. Such a picture portrays the woman as righteous, glowing with divine light and in an authoritative role. The stars on her crown (royal diadem) may represent the twelve signs of the zodiac. Such a portrayal would not be unique in Jewish tradition, for several Jewish synagogues of late antiq-

---

[4] Scholars have found parallels to ch. 12 in Greek, Egyptian and Babylonian mythology. One issue of discussion revolves around the extent to which John made use of the imagery from these sources. Robert H. Charles, *A Critical and Exegetical Commentary on the Revelation of St. John*, I, pp. 291-314, finds two major sources: 12:7-10,12, an original product of Judaism (even though some of its subject matter may go back to the Zen religion), and 12:1-5,13-17, a primitive international myth applied messianically by a Pharisaic Jew about 67-69 CE and then borrowed and transformed by the seer to give spiritual insight into the underlying cause of the final persecution of the Church. See Aune, pp. 670-79, and Mounce, p. 235, for discussion. (It seems that John may have used some imagery common to his thought world in order to communicate his visions to his readers, but it seems unlikely that he would have used pagan tradition consciously when he was so averse to the influence of paganism on the churches, see Rev. 2; 3).

[5] ὤφθη, 'appeared', is an aorist passive verb which occurs only in this context, 11:19, 12:1,3, and further supports the connection of 11:19 with 12:1,3 (Aune, p. 679).

uity have been found with mosaic floors depicting the zodiac signs.⁶ They may also represent the twelve Jewish tribes (cf. Gen. 37:9).

The impressive picture of the 'queen of the cosmos' shifts radically, for the woman is pregnant and in labor pains. Israel in distress is frequently compared to a woman in birth pains.⁷ Also, there is a messianic text (Isa. 66:7) with a metaphor of Israel bearing a male child to indicate the period of salvation (cf. 1QH 3:7-12). From this perspective it can be said that the woman is in 'pre-messianic agony of expectation'.⁸

A major interpretive issue of Revelation 12 is the identity of the Sun-Clothed Woman. Options include: (1) Mary, the mother of Jesus, (2) the Church, (3) Faithful Israel, (4) the Bride, the heavenly Jerusalem of Rev. 19:7-8, (5) an astrological constellation, (6) Isis, the Egyptian queen of heaven, and (7) Ideal Zion, mother of both Messiah and the Church. There are strengths and weaknesses with each option, and a particular challenge is to harmonize the woman giving birth to the son (v. 5) with the woman and her offspring pursued by the dragon (vv. 13-17). It is unlikely that the woman represents Jesus' historical mother, for vv. 13-17, which reveal pursuit by the dragon, would in that case be difficult to explain. It is also difficult to see the woman in v. 5 as the Church, for the Church did not give birth to the Messiah. As mentioned above, it is unlikely that John would use pagan mythology such as Isis in his portrayal of the righteous character. One view maintains that the woman in v. 5 is Faithful Israel and that she later, in vv. 13-17, represents the Church. This is not a problem because they are all people of God, the ideal Israel.⁹ Another view holds that since the woman is the mother of both Messiah and the Church the woman must be the Ideal Zion (Isa. 54:1; 66:7-9).¹⁰ Finally some acknowledge the Jewishness of the messianic texts and the eschatological trials preceding the end, but point out that only one Old Testament passage personifies Israel as a mother giving birth to a child messiah.¹¹

It seems that the woman most likely represents faithful Israel for the following reasons:

1. Ancient cities and peoples were often identified as women.¹²
2. Israel is sometimes depicted as a woman in birth pains (e.g. Isa. 66:7).
3. Isa. 66:7 depicts the birth of a male son in the time of salvation.

---

[6] See Aune, p. 681, for names and examples.
[7] Isa. 21:3; 26:17-18; 37:3; Jer. 4:31; 6:24; 13:21; 22:23; 30:6; Mic. 4:9; 1QH 3:8-9.
[8] Kiddle, p. 220, quoted by Mounce.
[9] Mounce, p. 167.
[10] Ladd, *A Commentary on the Revelation of John*, p. 167.
[11] Aune, p. 688.
[12] Cf. Bauckham, p. 126.

4. The symbols of stars, moon and sun, although used in pagan astrology and mythology, were also used to represent the Twelve Tribes of Israel (e.g. Gen. 37:9).
5. Both Jewish and Christian tradition maintain that Jesus the Messiah came through the nation of Israel (12:5).
6. The woman, protected in the wilderness, could represent the 144,000, the righteous remnant of Israel preserved to endure the Tribulation. (The woman is hidden for a time, times and half a time [v. 14], a reference to Dan. 9:27, which is consistent with the time of Tribulation.)

As John continues to watch the sky, another spectacle, or 'sign', appears (v. 3), a large red dragon with seven heads, ten horns and crowns on his heads (v. 3). Dragons often figure in mythology representing evil. This is the case in the Old Testament (cf. Pss. 74:14; 89:10; Isa. 17:1; 51:9; Job 40:15), where there are also references to sea monsters (Job 7:12; Ezek. 32:3) and serpents (Amos 9:3; Isa. 27:1).

A dragon, called Draco, with a long coiling tail, was a constellation known in the Hellenistic period. The red color of John's dragon may not be significant, although red in Revelation seems to have a negative connotation; for example, the red horse (6:4) and the scarlet beast (17:3). Red may also relate to the character of the dragon as in murder or blood.

The dragon has seven crowned heads and ten horns. This is an unusual description, but may serve to connect him with the beast imagery in Revelation 13. The crown (diadem) is one worn by a king or priest. It usually had gold strips embossed with various designs and decorated with pendants. Such crowns were not worn in Jewish courts until the Hellenistic period.[13] Coins have been found showing such a crown on Herod the Great. The dragon hurls one third of the stars to earth, which may reflect Dan. 8:10, where the small horn grows powerful until he even casts the stars to earth. It may also allude to the story of the watchers, in which the stars represent the fallen angels who follow Satan (*1 En.* 6:1-11; 18:14; 21:3-6; 86:1-3; 88:3; cf. Isa. 24:21-22). The picture is of a powerful beast lashing his tail, confronting a vulnerable, pregnant woman.

The dragon stands expectantly, intending to devour the woman's child (Rev. 12:4). This may correspond to the violence with which the Messiah was met when Herod the Great (Mt. 2) sought to kill the baby Jesus, as well as his later temptations and final crucifixion. In spite of the dragon, the woman gives birth to a male child who is identified as

---

[13] See Josephus, *Ant.* XX 241.

the One to rule all nations with a rod of iron (v. 5). This may reflect Ps. 2:9, in which the judicial authority of the Messiah is described.[14]

The life and ministry of the child is not recorded; rather John mentions that he was 'caught up to God and to his Throne' (12:5). Most scholars agree that this describes the ascension and enthronement of Christ.[15]

The woman flees to the wilderness, where she is sheltered for 1,260 days (12:6). The wilderness was important in Jewish tradition, usually representing a place of refuge and nourishment (cf. e.g. Hos. 2:14; 1 Kgs 17:2-3; 19:3-4). The Qumran community considered the desert a retreat in which to await the eschatological battle (1QS 1:1-3). Some suggest the woman's flight may reflect the escape of the Palestinian church to Pella in 66 CE, recorded by Eusebius.[16] Be that as it may, the focus of the passage is the woman's protection rather than her flight. Since the same woman is said earlier (v. 6) to be nourished for 1,260 days, these two time phases must be equivalent. By this calculation, a 'time' equals one year. A similar locution is used in Dan. 9:25-27; 'sevens' are used to indicate a period of seven years. In fact, Daniel 9 can shed light on Revelation 12, since both passages discuss aspects of the same time period.

Daniel, prophesying to a Jewish audience, relates the future of the Jews in terms of 'weeks of sevens'. He states that an official proclamation to rebuild Jerusalem will be decreed and 69 'weeks' later, i.e. 493 years, the Anointed One will come and be cut off. Many scholars see in this statement a prophecy of the crucifixion of Christ, the Anointed One, who was 'cut off'.[17] What is of concern here, however, is Daniel's vision of the 70th week.

The 70th week of Daniel's prophecy, which clearly concerns the Jews, continues with matters of sanctuary and sacrificial cult. Daniel is apparently not given any information regarding the Church Age. He skips from the events of the first century CE, to a discussion of the 'end' (Dan. 9:26). This 'end' will include war and desolation. Most significantly, a ruler will arise during this eschatological seven-year period who will confirm a covenant with the people for one seven-year period. In the middle of this period, 'he will put an end to sacrifice and

---

[14] Aune, says, 'The gloss is intended to identify the male child as the Messiah of Jewish eschatological expectation and to place that rule in the future', Aune, p. 688. (A. Yarbro Collins, *The Combat Myth in the Book of Revelation* [Missoula, MT: Scholars, 1995], p. 105, shows this description of the Messiah and his role to be Jewish rather than Christian.)

[15] Cf. e.g. Johnson, p. 515; Gause, p. 166; Mounce, pp. 238-39.

[16] Eusebius, *Ecclesiastical History*, III 5; Mk 13:14.

[17] Cf. Gleason L. Archer, Jr., 'Daniel', in *EBC* VII (1985), p. 57.

offering and ... he will set up an abomination that causes desolation' until finally he himself is destroyed' (Dan. 9:27).

Some commentators equate this 'abomination' in the Temple with the statue of Zeus which Antiochus Epiphanes set up in the Temple in the third century BCE. However, this cannot be the entire fulfillment, since Jesus refers to this same event as still to come, in particular, in the end times. In the Olivet Discourse, Jesus warns his disciples: 'So when you see the desolating sacrilege standing in the holy place, as was spoken of by the prophet Daniel (let the reader understand), then those in Judea must flee to the mountains' (Mt. 24:15-16). The passage continues with a description of the trouble coming on the world before the second advent of Christ. This 'abomination' of Daniel to which Jesus referred could be some action taken by the Antichrist which desecrates the Temple and indicates to the Jews that the Antichrist is indeed not the anticipated Messiah. This would necessarily lead to their rejection of him and his mark and, ultimately, to his persecution of them (the dragon persecuting the woman in the desert).

The second scene of conflict in Revelation 12 is between the angel Michael and his angels and the dragon (12:7-12). This section seems to be an intrusive narrative between the sections 12:1-6 and 12:13-17, interrupting the story of the woman and the dragon. As such, it gives a reason for the dragon's continued pursuit of the woman, a sort of glimpse into the spiritual warfare behind events on earth.

There was a concept in Old Testament times and early Judaism that each nation was represented in heaven by an angel who often acted in a guardian role fighting, if necessary, against evil (cf. Isa. 37:36; Dan. 10:20). Michael is the archangel mentioned in such a role in Dan. 12:1, as the guardian of Israel, and *1 En.* 9.11-14 states that he will be instrumental in the eschatological deliverance. He contended over the body of Moses (Jude 9) and stands against evil (*Test. Dan.* 6:2).[18]

According to Jewish thought, Satan was also an angel but one who sought equality with God (*2 En.* 29.4-5). Some traditions suggest that he flies continuously in the air (cf. Eph. 2:2); Isa. 14:12 refers to his once held position as Son of the Morning, and Mt. 25:41 suggests he has angels under him, which would make him an archangel.

Because of Satan's attempt to elevate his position to be like God, tradition suggests that he was cast out of heaven (Isa. 14:12; *2 En.* 29.4-5), but passages such as Job 1:6-9 and Zech. 3:1-2 imply that he continues to have access to heaven. John alludes to several of his titles: Satan, the Devil, the Serpent and the Dragon (Rev. 12:9). Satan means 'adversary', a term used to describe the paid informer in the Roman

---

[18] For a detailed account of Michael tradition see Aune, pp. 693-94.

courts who made a profession of accusing people before authorities. Some passages suggest that Satan was a member of the heavenly court (cf. 1 Kgs 22:19; Pss. 82:1; 89:5-7; Jer. 23:18-22).[19] By biblical times 'Satan' was a proper name used to describe the Evil One and his role of accusing the saints (Job 1:6-11; Zech. 3:1-10; cf. *1 En.* 40.7). Devil means 'Slanderer', which also characterizes Satan's role of presenting people in a negative light before God. John goes so far as to describe him as the one 'who leads the whole world astray' (Rev. 12:9). This composite description parallels the Gospels and Pauline writings, in which Satan causes Judas to betray Jesus (Jn 13:2), seeks to 'sift' Peter (Lk. 22:31), uses evil devices (2 Cor. 2:11), deceives Eve (2 Cor. 11:3; 1 Tim. 2:14) and accuses Job (1:20). There is evidence that a final celestial battle between God and Satan is expected preceding the end time,[20] and there are references that describe the battle between the Sons of Light and Sons of Darkness, where Michael joins in the fight.[21]

The titles for the Evil One, 'Dragon' and 'Serpent', may reflect mythology, as discussed above, and may also connect with the Genesis story, in which a serpent deceives Eve (Gen. 3:1-19). It is interesting that John records so many names for the evil beast while never naming the pregnant woman at all.

The war in heaven between Michael and Satan as described by John (Rev. 12:7-12) is difficult to fit into a time sequence. It may represent an attempt by Satan to regain his position in the presence of God prior to the end times, or it may describe his original expulsion from heaven. The first option seems most likely in relation to the hymn of Rev. 12:10-12. As such, it would be the cosmic prelude to the end time and would explain Satan's heightened outrage against the saints. As Satan is defeated and loses his access to heaven, he is cast into the earth with his angels (Rev. 12:9). This is the beginning of the end (the Tribulation era). Knowing his time is short (12:12), Satan turns his rage on the *righteous* (God's people).

Supporting the first option, above, is the fact that Jesus saw and rejoiced over his fall (Lk. 10:18). Thus, Satan, who has been accusing the people of God since the beginning of time, has finally lost any means of presenting his accusations to God. Losing this prestigious position, he turns on the saints on earth during the Tribulation. That he recognizes that his time is short (Rev. 12:12) suggests that he knows at least

---

[19] William Barclay, *The Revelation of John*, DSB Series, 2 (2 vols.; Philadelphia, PA: Westminster Press, 1960), p. 102; Mounce, p. 242.

[20] *Sib. Or.* 3.796-909; cf. 2 Macc. 5:14.

[21] *Test. Levi* 3.3; 1QM 15.19; 17.7; cf. *1 En.* 10.11-16; *Test. Judah* 25.3.

some of God's plans for the end time, and probably looks ahead to the final battle, after which he will be cast into the Lake of Fire (20:10).

An outburst of praise follows Satan's expulsion from heaven. A loud voice announces the impact and significance of the event: 'Now have come the salvation and the power and the Kingdom of our God and the authority of his Christ' (12:10). The voice may be from an angel or one of the elders. The announcement is given that the battle is over. It may be a legal battle (accusing the brothers, 10,11), rather than a military one, and the loser is disbarred.[22] Satan is also conquered by the faithful's word of testimony and the blood of the Lamb (12:11). This provides a striking courtroom scene, for Satan, the adversary who accuses the saints before God, is defeated partly by the powerful words of their testimony. Ultimately, all of evil is defeated by the defense of the powerful Word himself (Rev. 5:1-14).

That the reign of God and Christ has come is a reiteration of Rev. 11:15. Once again, it seems that victory has been achieved and recognized in heaven before it is actually carried out on earth. Revelation 12:10 is the only reference in Revelation to the 'authority' (ἐξουσία) of the Messiah. As the Greek word most commonly used for supreme administrative power it serves to emphasize Christ's rule in the Messianic Kingdom.[23]

The expulsion of Satan is cause for rejoicing in heaven, but a cause for 'woe' to the earth (12:12) because Satan takes out his rage on it. The intensity of his fury also stems from the short time that is left to him (12:12). The term 'woe', which occurs 14 times in Revelation, is also found in the Synoptic Gospels as a prophetic denunciation to suggest impending disasters.

The third scene of conflict resumes the story of the dragon and the woman (Rev. 12:13-17). After being hurled to earth the dragon pursues the woman, but she is given wings of an eagle to escape to a prepared place in the desert for a time, times, and half a time. The story reflects Exodus typology – the pursuit by Pharaoh (Exod. 14:8), God's rescue by eagles' wings (Exod. 19:4) and the rivers of water bringing death (Exod. 1:22). The opening of the earth may recall the episode of Korah's rebellion when the earth devoured those who disobeyed God (Num. 16:31-33). John's readers would, no doubt, connect the woman's deliverance by God's supply of eagles' wings to the past rescue of Israel as on eagles' wings. The imagery suggests the woman herself was given wings, a concept also found in Greek mythology in which people are given wings or are transformed into birds by the gods

---

[22] Caird, p. 155.
[23] Cf. Rev. 12:5 (Aune, p. 700).

to escape death.[24] Rescue by wings is also a general theme in the Old Testament, where God often bears his people up on eagles' wings (cf. Deut. 32:10-11; Exod. 19:4; Isa. 40:31).

As mentioned earlier, in Jewish tradition the desert often represents a refuge, and in this passage it has been prepared to preserve the woman for 42 months – the length of the Tribulation (Rev. 12:14; cf. Dan. 7:26-28). This protection seems to be physical rather than spiritual; in some way God is able to protect these people from the physical harm which the beast seeks to inflict on the righteous during the Tribulation.

Again, it is helpful to consider Daniel 9;[25] the parallels between Revelation 12 and Daniel 9 are too striking to ignore. In both, a wicked ruler rises up against Israel (Dan. 9:27; Rev. 12:13). In both, she is protected for three and a half years (until the 'middle of the seven', Dan. 9:27; '1,260 days', Rev. 12:6; 'time, times and half a time', Rev. 12:14). Daniel perhaps provides the reason for the wicked ruler's attack on Israel, namely, she refuses to follow him when he desecrates the sanctuary (the abomination of desolation, Mt. 24:15). Perhaps the wicked ruler sets himself up as God, even as Antiochus Epiphanes ('god manifest') demanded the worship of the Jews in Hellenistic times.

One of the ways the dragon seeks to destroy the woman is by a flood, but the earth swallows the water. This should probably be taken symbolically. Although the dragon pursues the woman (note: she must be on earth to be threatened by the flood), she is supernaturally protected.

The dragon, in fury, then turns on the 'rest' of the woman's offspring. This is interesting for there has been no previous reference to her children besides the male child. The identity of the woman's offspring, probably the most difficult interpretive issue of this section, causes some scholars to shift the woman's identity from earlier in the chapter. As mentioned before, the woman in v. 5 is no doubt Israel, for it is through that nation that the Messiah came. But many commentators argue that she represents the Church,[26] probably because of the description that her offspring 'hold to the commandments of God and the testimony of Jesus' (12:17). It seems, however, that the woman in 12:13-17 is the same as in 12:5 for she is identified in the same way

---

[24] Aune, p. 705.

[25] Although John (Revelation) attributes the pursuit of the woman to the dragon and Daniel associates this persecution with the world leader, it must be noted that for John, the dragon empowers the beast who actually carries out his command.

[26] See Mounce, p. 247; Gause, pp. 167-68; and Aune, pp. 708-709, who hold to this shift.

as giving birth to the male child and fleeing to the desert (12:13-14). Furthermore, Isa. 66:7-10 speaks of Zion being in labor and bearing a son (66:7), then giving birth to 'children' (66:8). Thus her offspring could also be Jewish. Perhaps, the woman protected could represent faithful Israel, the 144,000 who are supernaturally preserved, hidden by God to endure the Tribulation. Since the beast cannot attack God himself, he turns on the rest of Israel, those who hold to the moral code of the Mosaic Law and to the testimony of Jesus (12:17). These would be the rest of Israel (not the 144,000) who reject the beast as Messiah after the desecration of the Temple. These will most likely be martyred because they will not accept the mark of the beast.

The Testimony of Jesus
I do not believe a shift in the meaning of the symbol of the woman is necessary. The woman could represent righteous Israel throughout the passage. Nevertheless, there is an interpretive problem: the 'offspring' are described as 'keeping the commandments of God and the testimony of Jesus' (12:17). The question is: what is the testimony of Jesus, and what light does it shed on the identity of the woman's offspring (v. 17)? These issues are addressed in the Introduction. The point here is that the testimony "of Jesus" is not necessarily "about Jesus" but more likely his message, including the sovereignty of God as proclaimed by the prophets, the apostles, and the righteous through the ages.

This understanding of the 'testimony of Jesus' sheds considerable light on 12:17. The offspring of the woman are those who acknowledge God and are faithful to him in spite of the pursuit of the dragon. They also obey the commandments of God, most likely the Ten Commandments. This context does not designate these people as the Church. The main thing is that they are righteous – they acknowledge the one true God. There is no need to shift the meaning of the symbol of the woman to include the Church. She remains representative of Israel (see the earlier discussion of Daniel 9, and Daniel's 70th week). The Messiah came through Israel, and the same way God protected Israel when she fled from Egypt into the wilderness, he will again protect her from the reign of the beast.

Several additional aspects that support this interpretation should be noted. (1) The woman is protected in the wilderness (12:14). The only group in Revelation that is designated as protected by God is the 144,000 who were 'sealed' (Rev. 7:4-8; 14:1-5; 15:1-4). Probably, then, the woman symbolizes this group. (2) The rest of Israel reject the beast as Messiah because he has desecrated the Temple (Dan. 9:27). This rejection would most certainly include the refusal to take the mark of the beast. (3) The Church has most likely already been raptured.[27] It is not mentioned in Revelation (except for the great multitude in Rev. 7:9-17).[28]

The woman's offspring (Rev. 12:17), then, is most likely symbolic of Israel, excluding the 144,000: they have rejected the beast and his rule and are thus persecuted and probably martyred by him for refusing to take his mark. As such, the faithful 'rest of Israel's offspring' could be those Jews who keep the Commandments and hold to the prophetic hope of a Messianic Kingdom to come. This interpretation of the woman and her offspring (12:13-17) allows for a consistent view of the woman's identity and avoids an awkward shift at the end of this section.

In summary, Revelation 12 seems to be a metaphorical representation of the spiritual warfare leading up to and during the Tribulation times. The Messiah's birth and ascension are recorded, but any detail of his ministry or of the Church age is omitted. Rather, the reader is taken from the Messiah's ascension (12:5b) to the Tribulation (1,260 days, 12:6), a time, times and half a time (12:14). The reader is not told how long the war in heaven lasts between Michael and Satan but his expulsion from heaven appears to precipitate the Tribulation period and his intensified persecution of God's people. Satan's demotion is cause for celebration in heaven, for Christ is now in authority (12:10). The accuser of the brothers has been overcome by the faithful's word of testimony (12:11). This victory over Satan occurs *before* his final furious attack on the righteous (12:12), which results in part from his short time left on earth during the Tribulation.

Thus, this chapter could reflect Israel's role in relation to the Messiah's birth, and the spiritual warfare behind Israel's persecution during the Tribulation times. In addition, it could represent the metaphorical warfare between good and evil behind and before history. As such, it stands at the very heart or core of the text of Revelation.

Chapter 13

The Two Beasts

Revelation 13 is a highly symbolic chapter describing the activity of two beasts. It is linked with ch. 12 by the dragon motif as well as by the theme of persecution of the saints. Chapter 12, a metaphorical depiction of the warfare between God and Satan, concludes with the dragon's (Satan's) pursuit of the woman's offspring (righteous people). Then, 12:17 leads into the arrival of the beasts (ch. 13) with a picture

---

[27] Gause, p. 173.
[28] The formidable debate about the time of the rapture will not be addressed here.

of the dragon standing on the seashore.[29] Thus, 12:17–13:18 forms a coherent unit loosely linked together by the dragon imagery.

There are two sections in ch. 13: one of the beast from the sea (12:17–13:10) and another of the beast from the land (13:11-18). If 12:17 introduces this section, then the dragon standing on the shore can be seen as initiating the arrival of the beast from the sea. The sea may represent many peoples, nations and languages (see Rev. 17:15), another description of the abyss (17:18), or the social and political condition out of which tyrannies arise. In ancient literature the sea is usually associated with evil or chaos.

In Jewish literature the dragon (δράκων) is also a symbol of chaos[30] and is a term for Satan.[31] The extensive beast imagery of Revelation 13 may be inspired by Genesis 1:21, which records God's creation of the great creatures of the sea. There is also the Jewish myth of Leviathan, the female monster from the sea, and Behemoth, the male from the desert.[32] The myth records that God appointed each beast to inhabit its specific environment.[33] Then at the end time the evil Leviathan and Behemoth will serve as food for the righteous.[34] Although these references place the monsters in the last days, their activity is quite different from that of John's account, for the beasts of Revelation are ultimately thrown into the Lake of Fire (19:20).

Many scholars hold the theory that John may have shaped the character of the beast after the Roman emperors – maybe Nero or Domitian. One view suggests that the beast coming out of the sea might, in fact, be a type of the Roman governor who arrived in Asia Minor by sea.[35]

The beast is a curious combination of animals. He has ten horns and seven heads, probably based on Daniel's fourth beast which has ten horns interpreted as ten kings (Dan. 7:7,24). The seven heads could connect the beast with the seven-headed dragon of Revelation 12. Revelation 17:3 also describes a beast with ten horns and seven heads and interprets the horns as kings (v. 12), while the heads are both seven hills and seven kings (vv. 8, 9). Thus, the beast is related to other kings, most likely uniting them under his power. The beast of Revelation 13

---

[29] In some MS traditions 'he stood' is changed to 'I stood' (13:1). Most textual scholars support the third-person singular reading which implies that the dragon is in some way summoning the beast from the sea who is empowered by the dragon (v. 2).

[30] *Sib. Or.* 8.85.

[31] *Apoc. Abr.* 23.7.

[32] *1 En.* 60:7-11,24; *4 Ezra* 6:49-52; *2 Bar.* 29:4.

[33] Job 41:1-34; Ps. 104:25-26; *4 Ezra* 6:51-52; Job 40:15-24.

[34] *1 En.* 60.7-11,24; *4 Ezra* 6:52; *2 Bar.* 29:4-5.

[35] Aune, p. 733.

has ten crowns (diadems) on his ten horns, again supporting his relationship to kings. On each head is a blasphemous name (v. 1). These names could be related to the titles used by the Roman emperors, 'divus' (deified), 'savior' or 'dominus' (Lord). Most of the emperors accepted worship as a sign of political allegiance, e.g. Augustus and Tiberius, while others, e.g. Caligula and Domitian, demanded it.[36] Thus, the beast presents a picture of royal power and authority as well as divine stature.

John's beast looks like a leopard (13:2) but has a bear's feet and a lion's mouth. This combination of Daniel's beasts (Dan. 7) depicts the character of a great, terrifying monster. Zechariah 11:16-17 describes a 'worthless shepherd' who will not only deceive people, but will intentionally harm and even destroy them.[37] The text of Zechariah (11:16b) clearly describes this: 'he will devour the flesh of the fat ones, tearing off even their hooves'. One version translates this last phrase as 'throw away their broken bones'. Certainly, this is a world leader who cares nothing for his people's welfare. John tells his readers that the dragon empowers the beast (Rev. 13:2). This is consistent with Paul's description of the lawless one who is an agent of Satan (2 Thess. 2:9) and recalls Lk. 4:1-13, where Satan offers his power even to Jesus.

Apparently the beast suffers a serious (fatal) wound which heals. Zechariah 11:17 describes the 'worthless shepherd' who will come at the end time and will be wounded in the arm and the eye. Perhaps the references to these particular body parts suggest that these are special areas of competence for this leader.[38] Revelation 13:3 says that one of the heads was injured, and the next verse implies that it was the beast itself who was wounded and healed. This is only a problem when one attempts to identify each horn with a particular emperor or king. In any event, the ability of the beast to recover from such a wound astonishes the whole world (13:3) and causes people to worship the dragon (v. 4). One can see parallels with the temptation of Jesus. Satan's suggestion that Jesus jump off the Temple pinnacle would have brought astonishment and worship by the people. Satan also tempts Jesus to worship him, promising authority over the nations. Jesus rejects each option and defeats Satan (Mt. 4:4-10).

In Revelation 13, after the healing of the beast's fatal wound, there is an intensity of worship – not only of the beast, but of his source of

---

[36] Cf. Suetonius, *The Twelve Caesars*, pp. 164, 309.

[37] Hannah Harrington, 'Zechariah', *The Book of the Twelve* (Blandford: Deo Publishing, forthcoming).

[38] Cf. Harrington (forthcoming); E. Cashdon, 'Zechariah' in *The Twelve Prophets*, ed. A. Cohen (1994), p. 328

power – the dragon (v. 4). The words of praise, 'Who is like the beast? Who can make war against him?' are similar to Exod. 15:11, where God is praised: 'Who in the skies can compare...?' Both are praised for their awesome power, but only God is praised for his moral greatness.

Worship in the Roman world included prayer to the emperor and sacrifice on his behalf. It is interesting that the beast uses religious worship to fulfill his political agenda. The combination, well known in Egypt as well as in the Roman imperial cult, gave the ruler an amazing power over the people.

Revelation 13:5 suggests that God permits the beast to operate in his arrogant, blasphemous manner for 42 months – the length of the Great Tribulation (see Dan. 7:8,20,25; 11:36; Ezek. 28:2 for pride and blasphemy). Such pride and blasphemy is described in Dan. 8:10-12, where the little horn speaks against God. It is also characteristic of Lucifer, who challenges God.[39] The time of the beast coincides with the preaching of the two witnesses (11:12-13), the trampling of the holy city (11:2) and the protection of the woman (12:6; cf. also Dan. 9:27). Apparently John wants his readers to understand that these events occur simultaneously. The fact that God controls the activity of the beast is obvious from the phrase 'was given' (13:5; cf. also 17:17-18).

The beast 'opened his mouth to blaspheme God' (13:6). The phrase 'opened his mouth' suggests that he speaks for an extended time (cf. Mt. 5:2; Acts 8:35) in an official, formal manner (cf. Job 33:1-2; Ezek. 3:17; Dan. 10:16). The blasphemous character of the beast recalls Dan. 7:25; 11:36; 8:9-14, and fits with the lawless one predicted by Paul in 2 Thess. 2:4.

Three objects of the beast's blasphemy are the name of God, the tabernacle, and those who dwell in heaven (13:6). The first and second imply that the beast speaks against God's character, his reputation, and his dwelling place. The third object, which is a bit unclear, could refer to angelic beings as well as righteous people in heaven (cf. Eph. 2:6; Col. 3:1). Thus, the beast speaks at length against God himself, against where he lives and his people.

God permits the beast to attack the righteous, to conquer them (13:7) and to have authority over 'every tribe, people, language and nation'.

Furthermore, *all* people will worship the beast – 'all whose names are not in the Book of Life' (13:8). This passage builds on Dan. 7:21, where the saints are overcome and the arrogant king is allowed by God to have power for a time. But, ultimately, the saints will be victorious,

---

[39] Isa. 14:13-14; *2 Bar.* 67:7; *4 Ezra* 11:43; *Apoc. Elijah* 4.8-12.

for they keep the faith even to death (cf. Rev. 15:2). The reference to 'all the inhabitants' is the only time John alludes to *all* people; therefore it may point to a future time rather than past or present.[40] The Book of Life refers to a kind of heavenly register where the names of the righteous are recorded, much as in a book which lists the citizens of a town (cf. Rev. 3:5; 13:8; 17:8; 20:12,15; 21:27). In this case John wants his readers to be aware that all the inhabitants of the earth who worship the beast are not included in the Lamb's Book of Life, for to worship Satan's agent is to be alienated from God and to be excluded from his book (see Rev. 21:27). An issue of interpretation is whether the *names* were written in the Lamb's book ('before the foundation of the world', 13:8, which would imply predestination), or if the *death of Christ* was preordained before eternity. Although both options can be argued, it seems that the second alternative is more consistent with Revelation, for names can be blotted out of the book (3:5). Also, it would fit with the apocalyptic notion of predeterminism: that God planned Jesus' atoning death before the world's existence.

Revelation 13:9 recalls a phrase that occurs frequently in the Gospels: 'He who has an ear, let him hear'. This designates the importance of the words that follow and demands the attention of the reader. It is also a recurring phrase to the seven churches (Rev. 2:7,11,17,29; 3:6,13,22), omitting reference to the Holy Spirit. In Revelation 13:9,10 the phrase introduces a sort of proverb based on Jer. 15:2 (LXX). John omits the reference to pestilence and famine. In Jeremiah's time death was due to sins of the people, whereas in Revelation death is the punishment by the beast of people keeping the faith. At first, this passage seems to have little relationship to the broader narrative of the book, and this difficulty has resulted in a number of textual variants. It may, however, simply suggest that captivity and death will happen, and that the righteous response to persecution should be endurance and faithfulness. John's admonition, therefore, both to his readers in his present situation of persecution and to saints in the future is to endure and be faithful.

The major question at this point is, 'Who is the beast?' Many commentators see parallels with the Roman Empire of John's day and the emperors Nero and/or Domitian as models for the evil, deceiving, persecuting, blasphemous beast.[41] Most scholars, however, also explain that while John's vision may have grown out of his historical situation (90-100 CE) there are strong prophetic implications for the future.

---

[40] Aune, p. 746.
[41] Cf. Johnson, p. 522, for a discussion of the Nero legend.

There are two major interpretive challenges in this issue: (1) Do these figures of the beast represent persons or other entities such as heresies or situations in the Church? (2) Is the rule of the beast future or does it reflect a continuous presence of evil in Church history? Answers to these challenges arise extremely early in Church history, denoting that interpretive problems emerged early. It would exceed the purpose of this commentary to survey the extensive history of this issue, but a summary is helpful.

There is some ambiguity in 1 John as to whether the writer views the Antichrist as an individual (seemingly implied in passages like 2:18), or rather a more general 'spirit' of negation that rejects Christ (see 1 Jn 2:22; 2 Jn 7). The personhood of such a leader is more clearly found in Dan. 8:9-14,23-25; 9:25-27; 2 Thess. 2:3-4,9. Certainly the eschatological beast figure in Revelation reflects the figure in Daniel's visions. Daniel 7:23-28 describes a kingdom that will appear on the earth, different from all other kingdoms. It will devour the earth, trampling and crushing it. One particular king will arise and exalt himself above other rulers, even God himself; he will speak against God and persecute the saints, who will be handed over to him for a time, times, and half a time. At the appointed time, God will destroy this ruler and set up an everlasting kingdom of righteousness (Rev. 17:8-16). Daniel 8:9-14 further describes a ruler who will interrupt the daily sacrifice and desecrate the sanctuary (see also Dan. 8:23-25; 9:25-27).

Paul describes a 'man of lawlessness' who will arise in the end time. He will exalt himself, set himself up in the Temple, and proclaim his divinity (2 Thess. 2:3,4). He will do miracles and signs by Satan's power, deceiving many (2 Thess. 2:9; cf. Rev. 13:11-15; 17:8-14).

Early interpreters argue that the beast represents a person, a world leader reflective of Daniel's 'little horn' (Dan. 7:24), and the *Epistle of Barnabas* (c. 70-100 CE) warns readers to watch for the imminent appearing of 'the final stumbling block', who is identified with Daniel's 'little horn' (Dan. 7:24).[42] The *Didache* (early 2nd century) describes a 'world deceiver (who) will appear in the guise of God's Son. He will work "signs and wonders" and the earth will fall into his hands; he will commit outrages such as have never occurred before' (*Didache* 16.4). Justin Martyr (d. 165 CE) also anticipated during his own lifetime the appearance of the 'Antichrist', like Daniel's world leader, who would reign for three and one half years (cf. Dan. 7:25).[43] Irenaeus (d. 202 CE) gives probably the most extensive ancient discussion of the 'Antichrist'. He links the beast of Revelation 13 with the unrighteous king

---

[42] *Ep. of Bam.* 4.3-6,9-10; ANF 1.138-39.
[43] Justin Martyr, *Dialogue*, 32; ANF 1.210.

(Daniel's 'little horn', 7:8), who rules over the world for the last half of Daniel's 70th 'week' (Dan. 9:27). Irenaeus also identifies this 'Antichrist' with Paul's 'man of lawlessness', or sin (2 Thess. 2:3-4), who will exalt himself in the restored Temple of Jerusalem.[44] Several Church fathers follow Irenaeus's view: Hippolytus (*Treatise on Christ and Antichrist*, 2.235, ANF 5.204-205); Tertullian, d. 220 CE (*Against Marcion*, 5.16; ANF 3.463-64); and Victorinus, d. 304 CE (*Commentary on the Apocalypse*, 1; ANF 7.356-57).

The alternative view, that the beast is symbolic of something other than a person, is also suggested by early sources. Polycarp (d. 155 CE) suggests that the Antichrist appears in the heresies of his day (Polycarp, *Philo* 7.1; ANF 1.34). A student of the apostle John, Polycarp bases his position more on the concept of the 'spirit of Antichrist' found in 1 Jn 2:18,22; 4:3; 2 Jn 7. Tertullian links the Antichrist with the false prophets of Docetism, and also identifies them as the precursors of the eschatological Antichrist, who will produce 'all kinds of counterfeit miracles, signs and wonders' to deceive those who 'have not believed the truth, but have delighted in wickedness' (2 Thess. 2:9-12; see *Against Marcion* 5.16; ANF 3.463-64). Tertullian's view is particularly attractive since it merges the two positions, recognizing the spirit of the rejection of Christ inherent in all heresies, while still anticipating the eschatological world leader described by Daniel. Indeed, 1 Jn 2:18 seems to suggest that there is 'an Antichrist' while at the same time there will be 'many antichrists': "Little children, it is the last hour and as you heard that *Antichrist* is coming, even now, *many* antichrists have arisen..."

If the descriptions of the beast in Revelation 13 are linked with Dan. 7–9, Zech. 11:16-17, and 2 Thess. 2:3,4, a picture emerges of a world leader (Rev. 13:5-7; 17:11,12; Dan. 7:24-26; 8:23-25; 9:27; 11:36,38,41,45) who is lawless, wicked, arrogant (2 Thess. 2:3-9), deceptive (Dan. 8:23-25), destructive (8:23-25; Zech. 11:16), skilled in intrigue (Dan. 8:23-25), idolatrous (11:36-39), and blasphemous (7:24-26; Rev. 13:5-6). He is empowered by the dragon [Satan] (Rev. 13:2,4; 2 Thess. 2:9; Dan. 8:24), comes from the abyss (Rev. 17:8), has the power to do miracles, signs and wonders (13:3,13) and will ultimately be cast into the Lake of Fire (19:20). The beast, then, is symbolic of a world leader who will arise from among the people of the world. Along with a group of kings, he will reign as a dictator, deceiving many and persecuting the righteous. He will blaspheme God by setting himself up as 'Lord' and 'Savior', and will demand worship of all.

---

[44] Irenaeus, *Adv. haer.* 5.25.1-5; 5.28.2; ANF 1.553, 556-59.

Whether or not John bases his imagery on Jewish mythology (Leviathan and Behemoth), Jewish tradition (Daniel's visions), or on his own historical situation (the emperors), it appears that he is predicting a world ruler who will come in the end times and who will be unlike any before in wickedness, deception and power. He may also be anticipated in evil leaders and heresies throughout history.

The second section of Revelation 13 describes a second beast who arises from the earth, maybe from a cave or fissure. The meaning of the earth (v. 11), which is not clear, may represent people. The beast appears gentle (two horns like a lamb), but he speaks in a powerful manner (like a dragon, 13:11). The dragon imagery may connect this beast with the dragon of 13:1-10 and suggest that this beast is also controlled by Satan (cf. Mt. 7:15, where Jesus warns against false prophets who appear to be sheep, but are wolves).

This beast appears to assist the first beast. Irenaeus calls him the 'armor bearer' of the beast.[45] As such, he promotes the first beast, acts as his representative (Rev. 13:12) and causes people to worship him (vv. 11-15). Later, in Rev. 19:20, he is called the 'false prophet'. He seems to have a religious prophet-like character, for he does miracles and signs, makes the image speak and causes people to worship the beast (cf. Deut. 13:1, which warns against a false prophet who would lead people to worship other gods by signs).

The false prophet's miracles imitate those of Elijah (e.g. calling fire down from heaven, 1 Kgs 18:38; 2 Kgs 1:10). It is interesting that in the contest of Elijah and the prophets of Baal, fire from heaven was the sure sign of the true God. The false prophet of Revelation 13 performs such a miracle and as a result deceives many. It is also interesting that the two witnesses do not call fire from heaven, but fire comes from their mouths to devour their enemies (Rev. 11:5).

Evil eschatological figures are often expected to do signs and wonders in order to deceive people.[46] John uses the word 'sign' (σημεῖον) four times in Revelation (13:13,14; 16:14; 19:20). This is the same term used 13 times in the Gospel of John (e.g. 2:23; 3:2; 4:54; 6:2,14,30; 7:31; 9:16). The term denotes that the 'sign' points to something beyond itself. This sign conveys the sense that the beast has superhuman powers. John says that the false prophet was 'given power' to do these signs (13:14). The idea is that God allows him to demonstrate the wonders for a time, during which he performs these signs on behalf of the beast in order to deceive people into following him. The false prophet also sets up an image to honor the beast and he makes it

---

[45] Irenaeus, *Adv. haer.* 5.28.2.
[46] Cf. Mk 13:21-23; *Did.* 16.4, *Asc. Isa.* 4.10, Greek *Apoc. Ezra* 4.26-27.

speak. Anyone who does not worship the image is killed (13:15). This image is most likely a cult-image, perhaps reflecting the story of Nebuchadnezzar's image (Dan. 3:4-6). In Hellenistic and Roman times statues and portraits were often made for the emperors and set up for worship in temples and shrines. It was commonly thought that gods inhabited their statues (Plutarch, *De Iside et Osiride* 379C-D), and ventriloquism was occasionally practiced by priests to give the appearance of animation. Other special effects were also used by magicians and sorcerers to give the appearance that the statues were alive. Apparently the false prophet will cause the image of the beast to speak, and in this present age of technology this is not difficult to imagine! All who do not worship the beast are killed (cf. *Apoc. Pet.* 2), a detail which again recalls the story of Nebuchadnezzar's image and the three Hebrew children (Dan. 3).

People are also forced to be branded with the beast's mark in order to participate in commercial activity. The list of kinds of people to receive the mark stresses the inclusivity of enforcement: small and great, rich and poor, free and slave – no one is exempt. The branding is an individual's action, whereas the enforced worship is public and as such insures each person's loyalty to the beast. An example of such a branding occurs in the Maccabean times when Ptolemy IV Philopater (221-204 BCE) branded Jews who submitted to registering under his reign with an ivy leaf, the mark of Dionysus (3 Macc. 2:29). Any who did not comply were killed.

It is not clear what the mark is like. Some see in it a similarity to the Jewish phylacteries that devout men wore to remember the Scriptures. Others suggest that the mark may be a sort of tattoo such as was given to slaves, soldiers, and religious devotees, similar to the stamp of the imperial seal. Whatever its form, the mark signifies participation with, and loyalty to, the reign of the beast, in much the same way people used to belong to a guild. In Roman times, belonging to a trade guild was very important for particular careers and often determined whether or not one could carry out the basic economic activities of buying or selling. Such guilds were private organizations that included people from all social levels, but they usually had a cultic character including emperor worship and/or worship of a god or goddess. Worship included cultic prayers, sacrifices and eating meat blessed by the gods.

It is clear that the beast's sealing of followers with a mark is a sign of ownership. It can be contrasted with the sealing of God's servants in Revelation 7. In both cases followers are sealed in order to escape their leader's destructive wrath. Thus, the mark, which symbolizes obedience and allegiance to a particular leader, has a protective power. The mark also identifies the beast's worshipers and allows them to buy or sell. Those who do not take the mark are harassed and ostracised (13:17).

Revelation 13:18 may be an explanatory redactional addition by John to the vision of 13:11-17. 'Here is wisdom' may reflect Dan. 12:10 and may draw the reader's attention to the code-like character of the material that follows. 'If anyone has insight' recalls the apocalyptist's concept that only the wise are capable of understanding heavenly secrets. Then the riddle is proposed: the number of the beast is 666, man's number. People throughout the centuries have attempted to decode this number by a variety of methods. Among the early attempts are those of Irenaeus[47] and Hippolytus,[48] who on the basis of the numerical value of letters deduced the name Nero, Nero Caesar or Domitian and an array of modern dictators. No one solution has proven satisfactory, and the search continues for the riddle's solution. It is clear, however, that 666 represents the name of a person. The Greek term used here (ἀνθρώπου, man, person) can be understood in a generic sense, a number calculable according to human reckoning, or it could refer to a specific person in a non-generic sense. The last option is the most likely.

Chapter 14

Chapter 14:1-5

Chapter 14 presents a vivid contrast to the preceding, terrifying chapter, where people are forced to take the mark of the beast. The 144,000 have the name of the Lamb and his Father written on their foreheads and are singing a song before the Throne. The chapter itself, which consists of four textual units (vv. 1-5, 6-12, 13, and 14-20), begins with one of the writer's favorite phrases, 'Then I saw, and behold', which is repeated in v. 14. Verses 6-20 are structured around the appearance of six angels, each of them being introduced by the phrase 'another angel' (14:6,8,9,15,17,18).[49] It is noteworthy that there are two distinct pictures of Christ in this chapter: he first appears as the Lamb (redeemer, vv. 1-5), and then as the Son of Man (the bringer of judgment, v. 14).[50]

The scene opens with the Lamb 'standing on Mount Zion' in victory with his followers, after having been found worthy to open the seals (ch. 5) and to receive the adoration of the heavenly multitude

---

[47] Irenaeus, *Adv. haer.* 5.30.3.
[48] Hippolytus, *De Ant.* 50.
[49] Aune, p. 794.
[50] Gause, p. 187.

(ch. 7). Again there is a sharp contrast between the Lamb, who stands on a mountain, and the beast, who stands on the shifting sand of the seashore (13:1). It is not clear whether Mount Zion is on earth or in heaven. Both positions can be supported by the text, but in either case Mount Zion is associated with messianic deliverance. Both the Old Testament and apocalyptic literature associate Mount Zion with the return of the Messiah to bring deliverance. For example, Joel 2:32 says, 'And it will come about that whoever calls on the name of the Lord will be delivered; for on Mount Zion and in Jerusalem there will be those who escape, as the Lord has said'.[51] The older Jewish portion of *4 Ezra* (chs. 3-4) locates Mount Zion on earth (see especially 13:3-36), but the heavenly site also has some equally valid support: (1) The rest of the scene is obviously in heaven.[52] References to the heavenly beings (24 elders, four living creatures) indicate this (v. 3; see also chs. 4; 5; 7:11; 11:16; 15:7). (2) 2 Esdr. 2:42-47 has a similar vision of Mount Zion with a crowd singing hymns of praise *in heaven*. (3) The remainder of the scene is clearly in heaven rather than on earth since the singers of v. 3 are around the Throne and recall the throne-room scenes in chs. 4 and 5. Probably, this scene is partly in heaven (the singers around the Throne) and partly on earth (the Lamb surrounded by the 144,000 on Mount Zion). As in other places in Revelation, John sees action that is taking place in heaven while at the same time, events are unfolding on earth.

The figure of the Lamb 'standing', rather than sitting, on Mount Zion is noteworthy, for it may represent the Davidic 'Warrior Messiah' prepared to fight in battle (cf. Ps. 2:6). The figure of Christ as the Lamb is also significant since this is one of the more explicit occurrences of this name for Christ. Other references to the Lamb (e.g. 5:6; 6:1) imply by the context that the Lamb is Christ, but do not state this as clearly.

Numbers in Revelation appear to be significant. Since seven connotes completeness and four reflects the world with its four corners (7:1; 20:8) and four divisions (5:13; 14:7, etc.), the fact that the 'Lamb' occurs 28 (7x4) times in Revelation could suggest the 'worldwide scope of his complete victory'.[53] In any case, it is notable that the first four judgments of each plague series affect the world (6:1-8; 8:7-12; 16:2-9). It is also significant that the title for Jesus as the fulfillment of Jewish messianic hope (Messiah, Christ) also occurs seven times, em-

---

[51] Isa. 24:23; 31:4; Mic. 4:7; Zech. 14:4-5; Job 1:28; *4 Ezra* 13:29-50; *2 Bar.* 41:1-4.

[52] See especially vv. 2-3. See, however, George E. Ladd, *A Commentary on the Revelation of John*, pp. 189-90, for the opposing view.

[53] Cf. Bauckham, pp. 66-67.

phasizing the prominence of this theme of victory. The main point of this passage, whether its setting is earth or heaven, is that Christ appears as the Lamb, the fulfillment of Jewish Messianic hope.

One of the challenging issues in this passage has to do with the identification of the 144,000 (v. 1). Are they the same group mentioned in ch. 7, a chosen group of Jews? Do they represent an elite group of Christians? Or, do they represent a redeemed group of Israel, the people of God?[54] A consideration of their description may help towards an answer.

The 144,000 are mentioned only three times in Revelation – once in ch. 7, twice in ch. 14. Some of the material in 14:1-5 clearly parallels ch. 7. The author apparently intends to connect the identification of the group in ch. 7 with that in ch. 14: (1) the number 144,000 (John hears the number of each tribe in ch. 7 while in ch. 14 he sees them on Mt. Zion with the Lamb); (2) their probable location on earth (ch. 7 mentions the winds); (3) although the word 'seal' is not used in ch. 14 it is evident that the inscription on their foreheads clarifies the information in ch. 7 (in ch. 14 it is the names of the Father and the Lamb, suggesting protection and membership in a group ready for holy war); (4) the military census in ch. 7 is complemented in ch. 14 by the group on Mt. Zion with the Lamb, a strongly Messianic, militaristic scene.

This vision of the 144,000 with the Lamb is accompanied by a loud voice that recalls Old Testament imagery. 'Like the roar of many waters' and 'like the sound of thunder' reminds the reader of Ezek. 1:24: 'Like the sound of abundant waters...like the voice of the Almighty, a sound of tumult like the sound of an army camp...' (cf. also Rev. 1:15; 6:1; 19:6). To enhance his description of the voice, the author adds a third simile to the first two (waters and thunder), literally, 'like the sound of harpists harping on their harps' (v. 2). The emphatic repetition of a word, which is characteristic of Hebrew usage, enhances the imagery. He also hears singing, but at first does not understand the words of the song. The song is a 'new song' sung before the Throne, the four creatures and the 24 elders (v. 3). In the Old Testament a 'new song' is associated with joyful worship and praise (cf. Pss. 33:3; 40:3; 96:1; 144:9; 149:1; Isa. 42:10). It is not exactly clear who is actually singing – obviously the four creatures and the elders are not the singers since the song is being sung before them. The third person plural pronoun that begins v. 3 ('They sang') appears to identify the 144,000 as the singers. John's attention is drawn from the scene on Mt.

---

[54] See Aune, p. 804, for an explanation of each of these positions. Most scholars support the identification of this group (ch. 14) with the group identified as the 144,000 in ch. 7. See particularly Massyngberde Ford, p. 245 and Boismard, p. 168.

Zion (on earth) to the singers (in heaven). John hears the thunderous roar of the voices (v. 2) and then begins to identify more specifically the singers as those making the sounds (v. 3). Evidently he hears the song being sung, but does not hear or understand the words. The explanation is given that only the 144,000 can comprehend the words, implying that the 144,000 are not the singers; they are apparently learning the song themselves. The word 'learn' (μαθεῖν) also has the connotation of 'understanding'. John hears the words but is not able to 'understand' or comprehend them because that is possible only for the 144,000. Perhaps this lack of understanding is due to the nature of the song itself: it is appropriately sung and understood only before the Throne of God.[55] A similar idea is found in 2 Cor. 12:4, where Paul is caught up to the third heaven but is not permitted to tell about his experiences. Later (Rev. 15:3-4), John does seem to be able to understand the words of the song and identifies them as the 'Song of Moses and the Lamb' (15:3).

There follows a noteworthy description of the 144,000 as 'celibates' (παρθένοι). Evidently these are males since they have not defiled themselves with women (μετὰ γυναικῶν). This Greek term that means 'to soil, make dirty, stain' (ἐμολύνθησαν) refers to ceremonial impurity. Scholars have offered a variety of interpretations for this celibacy. Caird[56] and others suggest that this is the ritual purity required of soldiers in a military setting (cf. Deut. 20; 23:9-10; 1 Sam. 21:5; 2 Sam. 11:11). This would strongly suggest that the 144,000 are soldiers surrounding the warrior figure of the Lamb. In contrast, Carrington[57] interprets these celibates as those who have not polluted themselves with the sexual rites practiced in the pagan temples such as at Ephesus.[58] The character and purpose of celibacy can take various forms:

1. Total abstinence from sexual activity, something which Judaism and the Essenes (in particular), as well as some of the philosophical sects, like the Stoics, saw as necessary to achieve the pure state needed to commune with God;[59]
2. Faithfulness within marriage, or being married only once, again striving toward purity before God;
3. Faithfulness to God;

---

[55] See also J. Massyngberde Ford, Anchor Bible, pp. 233-34, for the suggestion that the song may be a mystical song only comprehensible to those advanced in prayer.
[56] Caird, pp. 178-81. Bauckham (*Climax*, pp. 229-342) provides convincing evidence.
[57] Carrington, pp. 337-40.
[58] For other possibilities see J. Massyngberde Ford, pp. 234-35.
[59] For this minority view, see Kiddle, p. 268, and Glasson, p. 85.

4. A requirement for participation in holy war. Most scholars now agree with Bauckham (*War Scroll*, pp. 29, 217) that this is the purpose in the present context.

The group is further described as 'following the Lamb' (v. 4), which links them with the group in v. 1 standing with the Lamb on Mount Zion. The nature of this relationship is not fully described but the word ('following') itself connotes discipleship of some sort. The Lamb's role as shepherd is suggested: this group have put their trust in the Lamb and have followed him to Mount Zion. They are further said to be 'purchased from among men as first fruits to God and to the Lamb' (v. 4). The term for 'purchased' can also be translated 'redeemed'. The word is ordinarily used to describe a purchase, as in the market place. The point is that the item purchased then belongs to the buyer. These people have been purchased and now belong to the Lamb. Paul often uses it to describe the state of believers, who have been bought with a price and now belong to Christ and God (see 1 Cor. 6:20; 7:23). Revelation 5:9 states that the price of the purchase was Christ's blood.[60]

'First fruits' is derived from the context of Old Testament offerings and sacrifices. Three kinds of sacrifices were considered acceptable – food, objects, and animals. The 'first fruits' were the most basic and could comprise the first-born of animals and humans as well as cereal and fruit crops. In Old Testament tradition it was considered that the first and best belonged to God.[61] The Greek term used (ἀπαρχή) refers to first fruits of the harvest (e.g. barley, wheat, grapes). They could not be eaten by the offerer but were set apart as holy for the priests. The particular phrase used in Rev. 14:4 (ἀνθρώπων ἀπαρχή) – literally, first fruits of people – is used in various kinds of Greek literature to refer to people given as offerings to gods. These people then became temple servants.[62] In Jeremiah 2:3, Israel is described as the first fruit of God's harvest.

Finally, it is said of the group, 'No lie is found in their mouth; they are blameless' (v. 5). Probably 'no lie' indicates that they did not compromise with the beast. To be 'blameless' literally means to have no blemish, to be uncompromised ethically and sacrificially acceptable.[63] As first fruits these people are holy.

---

[60] Gause, p. 190.

[61] See Gen. 4:1-15; Exod. 13:2-16; Lev. 27:26-27; Num. 3:44-51; 18:13-17; Deut. 14:22-26; Neh. 10:35; Josephus, *Ant.* IV 70; Ezek. 20:25-27.

[62] P. Stengel, 'ἀπάρχαι', *Pauly-Wissowa* 1.26,27; Franz Bomer, *Untersuchungen über die Religion der Sklaven in Griechenland und Rom*, Forschungen zur antiken Sklaverei 14 (1981-1990), 3.10-24; see also Plutarch, *Theseus* 16.2; *Quest Grace* 298f.; *De Pyth, Oraac.* 401a; Diodorus Siculus, 4.66.

[63] Cf. 1 Pet. 1:19; Heb. 9:14; Mounce, p. 271.

This description tells the reader several things about the 144,000: they are pure and faithful to God; they have not compromised with the beast or the pagan environment. As blameless 'first fruits', they are indeed representative of Israel (see also ch. 7). They have in some way acknowledged Christ (the Lamb) as Messiah. They are with the Lamb on Mount Zion (the Messianic site) and are sealed (protected) with the name of the Lamb and his Father (v. 1).

Chapter 14:6-12
The second unit of ch. 14 (vv. 6-12) consists of three angels proclaiming eschatological messages. The first angel proclaims the need for repentance before God's judgment at the end of the world. The second angel heralds the fall of Babylon (probably Rome), which is described in detail in ch. 18. The third angel announces the nature of God's wrath upon those who worship the beast and take his mark. The section concludes with an admonition to persevere to the end.

The angels are introduced by the term 'another angel,' which occurs six times in Revelation 14. There is no immediately preceding mention of an angel, so this usage is curious. Probably the phrase indicates that the first angel is the first of a series of angels. The next one is called 'another angel, a second one' (v. 8), etc. It is possible that John is attempting to relate them to the angel of 8:13, since most of the angels of Revelation do not have wings or fly, except for the cherubim and seraphim. *1 Enoch* 61:1 also mentions angels who acquire wings and fly.[64] The point is that these messengers are flying in 'mid-heaven', an area in which they can be seen and heard by everyone on earth. Probably this assumes the cosmological notion that the world is flat and circular,[65] the prevalent idea of the universe at that time, but this is not significant.

The first angel of ch. 14 proclaims an eternal message (εὐαγγέλιον αἰώνιον) to those on earth. The interpretive question is whether or not this is the 'good news' of the gospel, which is salvation. In Roman times, a messenger from the battlefield would relay the good news of victory to the emperor.[66] The use of the noun εὐαγγέλιον ('message')

---

[64] Cf. J. Weiss, *Die Offenbarung des Johannes: Ein Beitrag zur Literatur- und Religionsgeschichte* (Göttingen: Vandenhoeck & Ruprecht, 1904), p. 96.

[65] Herodotus, 5.49.

[66] See Aune, pp. 825-27, for a detailed discussion of the grammar, background and use of this term in Hellenistic and Christian literature. J. Massyngberde Ford, p. 247, explains that in secular Greek the word was a technical word for the 'news of victory', especially in relation to the imperial or emperor cult. In this context, the author of Revelation would be making a statement markedly contrasting the claims of victory by the emperor with the *eternal* victory by a sovereign God.

rather than the verb ('preach' or 'proclaim the good news') occurs only here in Revelation. The definite article is not used, which suggests it should be understood in the sense of a 'message' rather than as the specific proclamation of the Gospel. In the Synoptic Gospels the term is clearly used to refer to Jesus' preaching the kingdom of God (e.g. Mk 1:14-15, 'Jesus came into Galilee preaching the gospel [εὐαγγέλιον] of God and saying, the time is fulfilled and the kingdom of God is at hand. Repent and believe in the gospel.'). The Gospels never refer to the message as an *'eternal* message', which suggests that indeed this message (Rev. 14:6) has a different content. Verse 7 supports this by describing the message itself in an eschatological context ('saying with a loud voice, "Fear God, and give glory to him; for the hour of his judgment is come: and worship him that made heaven, and earth, and the sea, and the fountains of water."').

Four key words are significant: fear, glory, judgment, worship. In the Old Testament 'fear God' means to regard him with 'awe' and 'respect', which results in obedience. For example, Ps. 111:10, 'The *fear* of the Lord is the beginning of wisdom' (see similar references in Gen. 22:12; Jer. 32:40; Prov. 8:13, etc.). The second phrase 'give him *glory'* further defines the appropriate attitude toward God. One should worship the true God because he created the heavens and the earth and because 'the hour of his *judgment* has come'. The grammatical construction of this phrase lends a sense of urgency, a call to repent, while shedding light on the content of the message of the first angel. The 'eternal message' is not an announcement of the coming of God's *salvation;* rather, it is a proclamation of the necessity to *repent* before God's judgment at the end of the world. Similar passages can be found in Isa. 40:9-10 and 51:7-9. This much is clear: the angel is announcing the urgent need to repent before the judgment of God. The readers are admonished to worship God as Creator.

The next question is whether this call to repentance is 'real', that is, is repentance actually possible or is it already too late since God has already arrived in judgment? There are various responses to this issue, but several aspects are fairly clear and important: (1) The grammatical construction used in this context indicates that eschatological judgment has already arrived. (2) The message does not appear to be one of salvation; it is a call to worship God as Creator. (3) It is universal ('to those who live on earth, every nation, tribe, tongue, and people', v. 6). (4) This inclusivity contrasts sharply with the exclusivity in Jewish apocalyptic.[67] It is not clear from the text whether repentance is possible. The fact is, however, that the text states with clarity that people do

---

[67] *Pss. Sol.* 17-18; *2 Bar.* 53-57; *4 Ezra* 10-13; *Apoc. Abr.* 21-32.

not repent, but respond by blaspheming God (16:9,11). This message of repentance is probably addressed to the readers – they should acknowledge God before the final judgment comes, when it will be too late for repentance.

The second angel heralds the fall of Babylon. The aorist form of the repeated verb ('fallen, fallen', v. 8) indicates the certainty of the fall. In fact, this can be called a 'prophetic perfect', where a future event is described by using a past tense as if the event has already occurred.[68]

The historical city of Babylon was often used symbolically to refer to Rome because both cities were religious and political capitals known for their prosperity and moral corruption. Moreover, the early Church often made this connection.[69] Most likely the readers of Revelation would have done the same. As a symbol for Rome, 'Babylon' recalls Dan. 4:30, where Babylon represents the spirit of godlessness and humanism.[70]

The reason for Babylon's fall is that she has seduced all nations to 'drink of the wine of the passion of her immorality' (Rev. 14.8). The fall itself is described in some detail in ch. 18. Two symbols are joined in this one image. Babylon is shown as a seductive harlot (elaborated on in ch. 17), and God is pictured as pouring his wine as wrath on her to destroy her (14:8-10). Babylon's seductive powers thus merge with God's wrath. Both figures echo the passage in LXX Jer. 28:7 – (MT 51:7): 'Babylon was a golden cup in the hand of the Lord making all the earth intoxicated. The nations drank from her wine; because of this they staggered. Suddenly Babylon fell and was crushed.' The word for 'passion' (θυμοῦ, Rev. 14:8) can also be translated 'wrath'. It suggests an intensity of passion. The word also links the figure with God's wrath discussed in v. 10. Evidently, the passion of Babylon's desire to sin will merge with God's wrath at the end time to bring about the severity of eschatological judgment.

The third angel follows, announcing God's wrath upon the followers of the beast. Verses 9-11 form a counter-proclamation to the imagery of ch. 13 – the beast will kill anyone who refuses to take his mark. However, the third angel announces a worse fate for those who do take the mark, that is, they will drink God's wrath and endure eternal torment by fire. The word 'worship' is in the present tense, probably indicating that the warning is for those who continue to worship

---

[68] Cf. G. Mussies, *The Morphology of Koine Greek, as Used in the Apocalypse of St. John*, GKC (Leiden: Brill, 1971), p. 338; Justin Martyr, *1 Apol.* 26.1.

[69] See, for example, 1 Pet. 5:13, where the author sends a greeting probably from Rome: 'She who is in Babylon ... sends you greetings.' See also *2 Bar.* 11:1; 67:7; *Sib. Or.* 5:143, 159, 434.

[70] Mounce, p. 274.

the beast without heeding the message. In any case, God's wrath is described in vivid terms; wrath (θύμος) means passionate and vehement anger.[71] Wine as a metaphor for wrath is often found in the Old Testament (e.g. Job 21:20; Ps. 75:8; Isa. 51:17; Jer. 25:15-38). The wine is described as 'mixed in full strength' which refers to the undiluted strength of God's anger. Usually, the Greeks mixed water with wine.[72] The emphasis in this passage is on the strength of God's undiluted wrath and the severity of his judgment untempered by his mercy and grace (see the pouring out of the seven bowls, chs. 16-18).

The torment itself consists of 'fire and brimstone' (v. 10). The imagery, which recalls Sodom and Gomorrah (cf. Gen. 19:28), perhaps was intended to startle the readers into realizing the consequences of worshiping the beast: not only will the torment be severe, it will also be forever (cf. Rev. 20:10).

In view of this certain judgment, the seer exhorts his readers 'to keep the commandments of God and their faith in Jesus' (14:12). This comment may refer to those who are being killed for not taking the mark (ch. 13) or it could be a message to John's first readers, the members of the seven churches. In either case, it refers to the commitment of the righteous in terms of their obedience to divine revelation (they keep the commandments) and their constant reliance on God (the faith of Jesus). 'The commandments' undoubtedly refers to the Torah. The second part of the phrase may be the faith *in* Jesus, referring to Christian belief or, the faith *of* Jesus, i.e. the faith that Jesus *had* (*like* Jesus). Either option is grammatically possible, but the second ('*of* Jesus') fits better with the context because it would mean that they believe in God as preached by Jesus (see comments on the testimony of Jesus as the spirit of prophecy, 19:10).

Chapter 14:13-20
A small break occurs after v. 12. Verse 13 links this section (vv. 6-12) with the final section (vv. 14-20). The beatitude ('blessed...') is announced by a voice from heaven. This is the second of seven beatitudes in Revelation (1:3; 14:13; 16:15; 19:9; 20:6; 22:7,14). A heavenly voice commands John to 'write', which emphasizes the importance of the message: 'Blessed are the dead who die in the Lord.' This suggests that they are blessed or fortunate from the moment of their death. A further confirmatory comment elaborates: 'Truly, says the Spirit, that they might rest from their labors'. The emphatic (truly)

---

[71] *Ibid.*, p. 275.
[72] H. Blumner, *The Home Life of the Ancient Greeks*, trans. Alice Zimmern (New York: Cooper Square, 1966), pp. 209-10.

underscores the affirmation of the blessing. These 'labors' are probably not ordinary toil or work, but most likely work relating to the faith of the righteous. 'Rest' is often used in apocalyptic and wisdom literature to describe the state after death.[73] In Revelation 6:11, the martyrs are commanded to rest for a while (see also *4 Ezra* 7:88-99). The righteous dead are blessed because 'their works follow after them'. These 'works' are probably those done in resistance to the beast, not only spiritual attitudes or inward character traits.[74] 'Works' of the righteous are mentioned several other times in Revelation (see 2:2,19; 3:2,15) as well as in apocalyptic literature (e.g. *4 Ezra* 7:35,77; 8:33). The Lord acknowledges good works or deeds in the messages to the churches: 'I know your *deeds*...' They are associated with 'toil and perseverance' (2:2, the church at Ephesus); 'love, faith and service' (2:19, the church of Thyatira); 'your deeds are not completed' (3:2, the church at Sardis); 'you are neither hot nor cold' (3:15, the church at Laodicea). In each case, the deeds seem to be actions taken as a result of commitment to God (Ephesus and Thyatira) or, in their absence, in apathy and indifference (Sardis or Laodicea). The deeds are evidence of the churches' commitment to God and will 'follow those who die in the Lord for their faith'.

The series of angels continues, preceded by a figure like a son of man (v. 14) heralding the eschatological harvest (vv. 15-20). Two images are used to describe the judgment: the grain harvest (vv. 14-16) and the winepress (vv. 17-20). There are two interpretive challenges here: (1) who is the figure in v. 14; and (2) what does the harvest represent? The image of a son of man (literally a human being) in the clouds is most certainly a reflection of Dan. 7:13, where the Son of Man comes on the clouds. One is also reminded of Ps. 110:1 and Mk 14:62, which describe a similar figure. There are small differences such as whether the figure is seated or standing and whether 'cloud' is singular or plural, but generally the echo of these passages is fairly certain. Probably the reader is also meant to recall the vision of Christ as 'Son of Man' in the first vision in Rev. 1:13. The golden wreath on his head represents his status and authority.[75] Golden crowns are also worn by others in Revelation: by the 24 elders (4:4,10), by the rider on the white horse (6:2), and by the demonic locust cavalry (9:7). Probably the crown emphasizes the figure's divine mission. The 'sickle', de-

---

[73] E.g. Wis. 4:7; *Joseph and Aseneth*, 8:11; 15:7; 22:13; *1 En.* 39:4-9; *Test. Isaac* 2:13,15; *Test. Dan.* 5:12.
[74] Mounce, p. 278.
[75] See Aune, p. 172: 'Excursus 2C: Ancient Crown & Wreath Imagery' in *Revelation, 1-5* for more detail.

scribed as a sharp instrument, is a tool used for grape harvesting. It suggests that judgment is about to take place.

Nothing in this description necessitates the identification of the son of man figure as Jesus or an angel; though either is possible. However, since the title is different from that of the other angels and suggests reliance on Dan. 7:13 (cloud imagery), it seems probable that indeed this is the exalted Jesus. The problem remains that the following angels appear to command 'the figure on the cloud' to reap, which could point to this figure being some kind of angel. In any case, the figure's action is to harvest the earth. Both the grain harvest (vv. 14-16) and the grape harvest (vv. 17-20) reflect Joel 3:13 as metaphors for the eschatological judgment of the earth. The first two angels of the series in Revelation emerge from 'the Temple', showing that they have divine authorization. They cry to the figure to begin the harvest. Why one angel should command another to harvest is curious, but it is even stranger for an angel to command Christ. Probably the 'commands' should rather be considered as pleas for help. The parallel passage in traditional Jewish exegesis of Joel 3:13 has God commanding angels to harvest (Midr. Ps. 8.1.73). That the angels are agents of God for eschatological judgment is certain. There are also numerous parallels in Jewish apocalyptic where angels are agents of God for this purpose.[76] When the figure is seen as representative of Christ, the point is fairly clear: he is being urged by the angels to begin the harvest. Again, the imagery suggests that Christ the Savior has become Christ the Judge.

The 'sickle' is a curved knife used to cut grain or grapes.[77] In the Old Testament, 'harvest' was a term to indicate divine judgment.[78] In Matthew 3:11-12, the threshing floor is used as a metaphor to describe the separation of the righteous and the wicked. Although the grain harvest of Rev. 14:14-17 can be interpreted as God's gathering of the elect, the traditional use of the harvest imagery suggests that it is a general picture of the coming judgment, a harvesting of the whole earth, both wicked and righteous. Nothing is said about what happens to the grain in this first harvest (vv. 14-16). The second harvest (vv. 17-20) follows immediately.[79]

---

[76] *1 En.* 53:3-5; 56:1; 62:11; 63:1; *3 En.* 31:2; 32:1; 33:1; *b.Sabb.* 55a; 88a; cf. P.S. Alexander, '3 (Hebrew Apocalypse of) Enoch, (Fifth-Sixth Century AD)', in Charlesworth, *OTP* I (1963), 285ff., on chs. 31-32; Karl-Erich Grozinger, 'Engel III', *TRE* IX (1982), p. 591; Johann Michl, 'Engel II', *RAC* V (1962), pp. 75-76.

[77] Josephus, *War*, III 95, 225; Kurt Galling, *Biblisches Reallexikon*, HAT, I (Tübingen: J.C.B. Mohr [Paul Siebeck], 1977), pp. 475-76.

[78] See Joel 3:12-13; Zech. 14:2-4; *4 Ezra* 13:33-35; cf. Rev. 19:17-21; 20:7-9.

[79] See Aune, pp. 800-803, for an extensive discussion on the alternatives for this. He concludes strongly that the grain harvest here is a metaphor for eschatological judgments.

The third angel emerges from the 'altar', which could refer either to the altar of incense (8:3 [2x], 5; 9:13) or the altar of burnt offerings (6:9; 9:13; 14:18; 16:7). The term can also mean the 'sanctuary' where the altar is located. The altar is not only the place of atonement for sins, but is the source of judgment. Here Christ as judge emerges: he is not only the redeeming Lamb, the fulfillment of messianic hopes (vv. 1-5), but he is also the Judge (vv. 14-20). All of the possibilities suggest that the origin is God himself. This angel is identified as the 'one who has power over fire'. In Jewish and apocalyptic tradition, angels were associated with various spheres, including: thunder, sea, hail, snow, rain (see *1 En.* 60:11-21; the four winds (Rev. 7:1); the abyss (9:11); and the waters (16:5). The Testament of Abraham [Rec. A] 12:14 identifies the angel in charge of fire or the fiery angel as Purouel. His emergence from the altar again indicates the divine authorization of his mission. The crushing of the grapes that follows is an image often used in Jewish tradition for divine wrath upon God's enemies (e.g. Isa. 63:3; Lam. 1:15; Joel 3:13; Rev. 19:15).

The city outside of which this crushing of the winepress takes place is not named but is probably Jerusalem.[80] The treading of the grapes may be a metaphorical reference to an eschatological battle near Jerusalem.[81] It is not clear in this passage who exactly is doing the treading or crushing, but in Rev. 19:15 (which appears to be an elaboration of this crushing) it is the rider on the white horse, the exalted Christ with his heavenly armies.[82]

The link between blood and crushed grapes is widespread in ancient literature.[83] The hyperbole of slaughter can also be found in ancient literature.[84] The explicit mention of horses' *bridles* serves as a particular allusion to a victorious eschatological, heavenly army.[85] The judgment of nations in Joel 3:12-14 takes place in the Valley of Jehoshaphat, which tradition links with the Kidron Valley lying between Jerusalem

---

On p. 799, Aune includes a chart which shows the parallel structure of vv. 17-20 with vv. 14-16, again suggesting strongly that indeed *both* of these harvests are metaphors for eschatological judgment.

[80] E. Lohmeyer, *Theologische Realencyklopädie*, III (NY; Berlin: de Gruyter, 1978), p. 129.

[81] See Joel 3:2-17; Zech. 14:2-4; *4 Ezra* 13:33-35; cf. Rev. 19:17-21, 20:7-9.

[82] Aune, p. 847.

[83] Cf. e.g. Gen. 49:11; Deut. 32:14; Sir. 39:26, 50:15; 1 Macc. 6:34; Achilles Tatius, 2.2.5; Clement of Alexandria, *Paed.*, 2.19.3, 2.29.1; *Strom.* 5.8; 48.8.

[84] Cf. Richard J. Bauckham and Benjamin Drewery, eds., *Scripture, Tradition, and Reason. Essays in Honour of Richard P.C. Hanson* (Edinburgh: T & T Clark, 1988), pp. 40-48; *1 En.* 100:3; *4 Ezra* 15:35b-36.

[85] See Rev. 19:14; Charles, II, p. 26; Yarbro Collins, p. 37; Gunther Bornkamm, 'ληνός, ὑπολήνιον', *TDNT* IV (1977), p. 256.

and the Mount of Olives.[86] Hence, it is fairly certain that the battle is expected to be near Jerusalem.

The specification of 1600 furlongs (approx. 200 miles) can be interpreted in various ways: (a) literally, it could be the length of Palestine or, (b) symbolically, it squares the number four (four winds, four corners of the earth) and multiplies it by the square of ten (number of completeness [see 5:11; 20:6]). In either interpretation it represents and highlights the extensiveness of God's judgment: beginning outside of Jerusalem it will include all people everywhere.[87]

In summary, this section begins with the Lamb standing with his saints on Mount Zion, in sharp contrast to the group who identifies with the beast by taking his mark (ch. 13). The figure of Christ is the fulfillment of messianic hopes. John quickly becomes aware of a loud voice like thunder, a roar like many waters or of many harpists playing. He realizes that this sound is actually the sound of a choir singing a new song understood only by the sealed 144,000 before the Throne. These are identified as persons who are faithful and blameless before God, the representatives or first fruits of Israel.

A series of angels follows, each with an important message from God to the earth. The first calls for repentance and worship of God as Creator; the second announces the fall of Babylon, and the third warns of God's wrath to come on the ones who take the mark of the beast. The latter are subject to the judgment of God with fire and brimstone forever. In contrast, the saints will persevere in obedience to the Torah and in faithfulness to God, and are blessed even if they are killed by the beast.

Another series of three angels brings God's message: the first announces the coming of God's harvest (judgment) and cries for the reaping to begin; two more angels follow, the first proclaiming the grain harvest, the second heralding the grape harvest.

God's judgment of all the earth will be extensive and victorious. Christ, the Redeeming Savior and Messianic Deliverer, will have become the Bringer of God's Wrath and Judgment.

Chapters 15 and 16

With Revelation 15 a new literary unit begins which sets the scene for the outpouring of the seven vials or bowls, the completion of God's wrath (chs. 17-19). The phrase 'Then I saw' again introduces a new

---

[86] Zech. 14:4 also puts the final war on the outskirts of Jerusalem. *1 En.* 53:1 identifies it as the deep valley near Hinnon (Mounce, p. 283).

[87] Cf. Mounce, p. 283.

unit (see 6:1; 8:2; 10:1; 13:1; 14:1; 15:1; 19:11; 20:1; 21:1). For the third time the phrase 'another sign' is used to connect the new section to the previous narrative. The first occurrence has reference to the sun-clothed woman (12:1); the second introduces the great dragon (12:13).

The word used here for sign, σημεῖον, again indicates an awesome event or miracle which serves as a symbol to convey a deeper meaning. John also uses it in his Gospel to refer to the seven major 'signs' around which his Gospel is composed. For example, in Jn 2:11: 'This beginning of his signs Jesus did in Cana of Galilee...' This comment follows the miracle of Jesus turning water into wine. This word for sign can be understood in contrast to δύναμις, which can also be translated as 'miracle' (as in the Synoptics). 'Miracle' denotes the dynamic effect of a miracle whereas *semeion* carries the sense of symbol – the miraculous or awesome event that points to something beyond itself. This suggests that these three sections in Revelation – the sun-clothed woman (ch. 12), the beast (ch. 13), and now the bowls or vials (ch. 15) – should be viewed as symbols that convey a deeper message to the readers of Revelation. The message, which emerges in the action of the angels (chs. 15 and 16) is specifically articulated in 15:1: 'Seven angels had seven plagues, which are the last because in them *the wrath of God is finished*.' Chapter 15 introduces the seven angels who pour out the seven bowls containing God's wrath. The bowls are the unfolding of the seventh trumpet in the same way as the seven trumpets emerge from the seventh seal. It is important to realize that this literary sequence is not chronological. Sometimes events take place simultaneously and/or on various levels: the main focus for the readers is eschatological, not necessarily chronological. In any case, this small introduction actually is an overview, or summary, of what is to follow: the outpouring of each angel is explained in more detail in ch. 16. The key point of ch. 15 is that the action of the angels with the bowls originates in heaven at the very throne of God himself.

The first scene of the chapter is the throne-room of God. It recalls a similar scene in ch. 5, which introduces the seven seals. The scene is the same in ch. 8, which introduces the seven trumpets. The judgments announced by the seven angels (ch. 15) are described as the 'last plagues' because they complete the outpouring of God's wrath (v. 1). There is an interesting relation to the plagues of Exodus.

The scene opens with a group standing on a sea of glass (15:2). The sea of glass is also part of the throne-room scene in ch. 4, where the sea is described as 'like crystal', clear and untroubled. In this scene (ch. 15), it is described as 'mixed with fire', most likely symbolizing the impending judgment, the *final* wrath of God originating from God's throne.[88] Evidently, the sea itself has a special relation to God, appearing to mirror what he is about to do. In ch. 4 it is clear and untroubled, while in ch. 15 it is mixed with fire, symbolizing God's wrath and judgment. The group standing on the sea of glass are directly associated with God since they are standing on the sea in his presence. These are not the object of God's wrath. Indeed, they are described in terms indicating that they have overcome the enemies of God. The aspects of their victory are enumerated: they are victorious over (1) the beast, (2) his image, and (3) the number of his name. The nature of their conquest is not entirely clear. They could be conquerors through martyrdom,[89] but usually the martyrs in Revelation are directly designated as such (e.g. the souls under the altar, ch. 6). Most likely they are simply conquerors because they did not succumb to the power of the beast. They are called 'those who had come off victorious' over the beast, etc. It is significant that the three (the beast, the image and the number) are personified almost as if they are three separate enemies of God.[90] Probably they are distinguished in order to heighten the imagery of enmity against God and to point to the structure of the opposition. The 'beast' in ch. 13 appears to represent the political, economic and religious forces aligned in opposition to God. Chapter 13 associates the beast with the dragon (Satan), 12:9; indeed, the beast is the dragon's representative to carry out Satan's mission against God (13:2). The 'image' (the second enemy) appears to function in a sort of public relations capacity: it is given life and is caused to speak. Miracles and wonders are performed in its presence. In fact, worship is associated with it and is performed in its presence (13:11-18). Anyone who refuses to participate is killed (13:15). Finally, the 'number of the name' of the beast functions as the means by which one demonstrates allegiance to the beast – without it no one can buy or sell (13:16-18).

The group on the sea of glass (15:2) is further described in imagery reflective of Exodus – they are singing a song of Moses and of the Lamb. The interpretive question is how this song actually relates to Moses and the Lamb. There are three songs sung by Moses in Exodus: (1) in Exod. 15:1-18, Moses sings after the deliverance from the Egyptians at the Red Sea; (2) he sings in Deut. 31:30–32:43, at the end of his life. He details the trials of Israel in the wilderness and praises God for his faithfulness and righteousness; and (3) he prays the prayer of

---

[88] Cf. Lohmeyer, p. 130.
[89] Cf. Bauckham, *The Theology of the Book of Revelation*, pp. 98-102, for this view.
[90] Gause, p. 202, calls them the representation of 'spiritual focus' in the attack against the kingdom of God.

Psalm 90, the only psalm called a prayer by Moses.[91] The song in Rev. 15:3-4 most closely resembles Exod. 15:1-19, since both are songs of victory, deliverance and praise to God for his righteous acts.[92] Possibly the song in Revelation 15 is actually an interpretation of the song in Exodus 15, an application of the original Exodus imagery to the eschatological context in Revelation 15. Certainly, the themes are remarkably similar: (1) praise of God for his wondrous acts of deliverance and judgment on the wicked (Exod. 15:1-10,12; Rev. 15:3); (2) the superiority of God over his enemies and their pagan gods (Exod. 15:11-13,17; Rev. 15:4); and (3) the response of the nations in fear, acknowledgment of God and, finally, worship of God (Exod. 15:14-16; Rev. 15:4).

The interpretation of Revelation 15 in light of Exodus 15 sheds some light on the nature of this group. Like the children of Israel in Exodus, they are praising God for delivering them from their enemies (Israel from Egypt; this group from the power of the beast). By their deliverance, God is also bringing judgment upon his enemies (the Egyptians were drowned in the Red Sea; God's final judgments are about to be poured out on the beast and his kingdom in Revelation). By these righteous acts, God has shown his superiority over the pagan gods in Egypt as well as the kingdom of the beast. Finally, these righteous acts have resulted in two responses: (a) God's people worship him; they were brought into his Temple (Exod. 15:13), and there (in Rev. 15:1-4), they are standing before the very presence of God; (b) the second possible response, not addressed until later, is a refusal to acknowledge God. In fact, people blaspheme (16:11,21).

Although the song concludes with the anticipation of universal worship (15:4), the nations do not worship God with repentance. Perhaps this can be best understood by a consideration of what it means to 'fear God' (v. 4: 'who will not *fear* God and glorify his name?'). The word 'fear' has the connotation of respect, but also of dread in God's presence because of judgment. Indeed, to glorify his name is to acknowledge his nature and deeds as just and righteous,[93] to have an attitude of awe and respect. In fact, the final stages of the song indicate the reason for their praise of God (v. 4), 'because you alone are holy; because all the nations shall come and worship before you; because your righteous works have been manifested'.[94] The second response in this scene is that

---

[91] Cf. Peter C. Craigie, *Psalms 1-50* (Waco, TX: Word Books, 1983), pp. 33-35.

[92] For an extensive analysis and comparison of the two songs, see Beckwith, pp. 676-78; Ford, p. 247; cf. also Gause, pp. 202-206; Bauckham, pp. 98-102.

[93] Gause, pp. 204-205.

[94] Translation from Gause, p. 204; see also the second song of Moses in Deut. 32:4.

the whole world does not worship God, they blaspheme him (16:11,21). Although the final judgments do not bring repentance, they do force 'all nations' to acknowledge that the judgments are from God. Like Pharaoh in Egypt, although he refused to worship God, he was still forced by the plagues at least to affirm the power of God. These judgments are elaborated in Revelation 16–19. Finally, the concluding words of the Exodus song ('the Lord shall reign forever and ever', Exod. 15:18) directly relate to the major theme of Revelation, namely the establishment of God's eschatological kingdom.[95]

This description sheds some light on the identification of this group: (1) They have victoriously come through the reign of the beast, probably not by means of martyrdom; (2) the Exodus imagery and language of their song suggest their relation to Israel rather than to a generic group of Christians. In their song there is no mention of salvation as in Rev. 7:9-10. Neither is there any reference to their being 'washed in the blood' as is the case with the group in 7:14. The only reference to the Lamb is that their song is 'of Moses and of the Lamb' (15:3), but taken within the context of Exodus, this could be reflective of the deliverance of Israel from Egypt by means of the blood of the passover lamb. In Revelation, the group are singing about their deliverance by God, the Eternal Lamb;[96] (3) they are described as singing, which connects them with the group in 14:1-5, the 144,000 standing with the Lamb on Mount Zion singing a new song (14:3). Hence, most likely they are the same group, the 144,000, the remnant of Israel sealed by God (see 7:1-4-8).[97]

This interpretation would show a progression of John's view of this group: in 7:4-8, he hears the number of the ones who were sealed: 144,000 – 12,000 from each tribe of Israel. Then in 14:1-5, he sees them standing on Mount Zion with the Lamb, singing. He does not understand the song at this point (14:3). Finally, in 15:2-4, the author *sees* them and *hears* their song of Moses and the Lamb – a song of victory and deliverance which echoes Moses' song of deliverance from Egypt (Exodus 15). The song integrates the deliverance experience from Egypt with the present rescue from the beast. This underscores the Jewish nature of this group and links them with the 144,000 in 14:1: the song connects their past heritage with their present salvation from the beast. Like Moses' song, the song in Revelation emphasizes God's redemptive acts as well as his judgment.

---

[95] See Rev. 11:15; cf. Bauckham, p. 99.
[96] See Gause, pp. 202-203.
[97] Mounce, p. 288 n. 9, explains the manuscript evidence. J. Massyngberde Ford, p. 257, with other scholars, identifies this group as the 144,000 in 14:1-5.

The second scene unfolds with the opening of the Temple of the tabernacle of testimony (15:5). As in ch. 14, the emergence of the angels from the Temple emphasizes the origin and authority of their message. Old Testament imagery continues: the tabernacle of testimony is directly reflective of the Old Testament tabernacle in the wilderness, which was called the 'tent of testimony' because of the presence of the two tablets of testimony from Mount Sinai (Exod. 32:15; Deut. 10:5). The earthly Holy of Holies, which housed the tablets in the Ark of the Covenant, was the special abiding place of the presence of God among Israel. In fact, God promised to speak to his people from between the two cherubim of the Ark (see Exod. 25:22). The Old Testament tabernacle in the wilderness was also called the 'tabernacle of witness' (Exod. 38:21; 40:34) because the Ark of the Covenant (housed within) symbolized the witness of the covenant between God and his people Israel. The earthly witness was the Law engraved on the stone tablets in the tabernacle;[98] the heavenly witness is God himself. The primary significance of John's description in this passage (Rev. 15:5) is to emphasize that the origin of these angels with the bowls of wrath is the very presence of God. The opening of the doors unassisted is significant, for it symbolizes power and authority: the doors that led to the porch or vestibule from the sanctuary in the Temple at Jerusalem were so heavy that several men were needed to open them.[99] The doors opening by themselves would indicate the divine origin of the event and the emergence of divine blessing and/or judgment.[100]

The seven angels are dressed like Jewish priests in linen with golden girdles (v. 6), denoting the sacred nature of their mission (cf. Ezek. 9:2; Dan. 10:5). One of the four creatures from before the throne gives the bowls to the angels to disperse. This action constitutes the commissioning of their mission as in the case of the seven seals (6:6-14) and the seven trumpets (8:2). The 'bowl' mentioned here is the term used to refer to utensils used in sacred offerings.[101] These libation bowls are referred to twelve times in Revelation (5:8; 15:7; 16:1,2,3,4,8,10, 12,17; 17:1; 21:9). In Revelation 5:8, the bowls contain incense representing the prayers of the saints.[102] Here (15:7) they are filled with the wrath of God.

---

[98] *Ibid.*, pp. 206-207.

[99] See Josephus, *Against Apion* II 119, and the *War* V 202; VI 293, for two accounts of how many men were needed to open the doors because of their size.

[100] Josephus, *War*, VI 293-96.

[101] W. Bauer, W.F Arndt, F.W. Gingrich, and F.W. Danker, *A Greek-English Lexicon of the New Testament*, 2nd ed. (*BAGD*), p. 858.

[102] Cf. Josephus, *Ant.* III 143.

As the angels receive their golden bowls filled with God's wrath, the Temple is filled with smoke 'from the glory of God and from his power' (v. 8), so that no one is able to enter the Temple until the plagues, the seven bowls of God's wrath, are finished. In the Old Testament, there is a strong connection between smoke and the glory of Yahweh. Isaiah was overcome by a vision of the Lord and his angels in the Temple. As the angels praised God's holiness and glory, the Temple foundations shook and the house was filled with smoke (Isa. 6:1-4). Similarly, the revelation of God at Mount Sinai was accompanied by thunder, lightening, and a heavy cloud (Exod. 19:16). Occasionally, smoke functions as a metaphor for the presence of Satan.[103] This verse (Rev. 15:8), however, clearly links the smoke with the glory and power of God. The reader is reminded of the shekinah which filled the tabernacle in the wilderness (Exod. 13:21; 40:34). The glory of God is, likewise, pictured here in terms of holiness and power: God himself is prepared to carry out his final judgments before which no one is able to stand.

The scene of the heavenly throne-room concludes with the comment, 'No one was able to enter the Temple until the seven plagues were complete.' This construction recalls similar throne-room scenes in Rev. 4:1–5:14; 8:2-5. It also echoes 1 Kgs 8:10-11 and 2 Chron. 5:13-14, where after the dedication of Solomon's Temple the cloud of God filled the Temple to such an extent that no one could enter. Several interpretations of the Revelation passages are possible: (1) God has become unapproachable because his presence is now one of wrath and judgment; (2) God is unapproachable because of his majesty and power; or (3) now that the final judgment has arrived, no angelic mediator is available (as in 2:8 and 8:3). In any case, the final outpouring of God's wrath now follows.

In summary, 15:1-8 provides an introduction to the commissioning of and pouring out of the bowls of wrath by the seven angels. The 144,000, who are sealed by God, are seen singing the victory song of Moses and the Lamb in God's presence. They have been delivered from the beast and are now praising God for his wondrous acts. The commissioning of the last seven plagues follows.

Several noticeable parallels are found between the above series of judgments and the judgments announced by the seven trumpets (chs. 8-11). The first four plagues of each involve the earth, sea, waters, and heavenly bodies; the fifth includes darkness and pain (cf. 16:10; 9:2,5-6); and the sixth includes threatening enemies from the area of the

---

[103] Cf. Rev. 9:2: 'smoke rises from the abyss'; *Apoc. Sedr.* 5:4-5; J.H. Charlesworth, ed., *OTP* 1:6-10

Euphrates (cf. 16:12; 9:14). Both sets of plagues (the bowls and the trumpets) have recognizable similarities to the plagues of Egypt: the first ones affect nature, progressing to the ones which injure humans (e.g. water turning to blood, Exod. 7:20; the boils, cf. Exod. 9:9; darkness is included in both, cf. Exod. 10:22). It is necessary, however, to notice the differences. First, whereas the effect of the trumpets is partial destruction (one-third of the earth and sea, 8:7-12), the destruction from the bowls is universal ('every living soul died', 16:3-20). Second, whereas the trumpets to a certain extent warn of impending judgment and call for repentance, the bowls pour out divine wrath in an undiluted state. Third, although humankind is not directly affected by the first four trumpet plagues, the judgments of the bowls impact humans immediately and directly. Finally, whereas there is an 'interlude' between the sixth and seventh of the first two series (of the seals and the trumpets), there is no break between the pouring out of the bowls: one immediately follows the other.[104]

A voice from the Temple commands the angels to begin the pouring (16:1). This must be the voice of God, mentioned again in v. 17, since no one else could enter the Temple till the plagues were complete (15:8; cf. Isa. 66:6). The term ἐκχέετε, 'pour out' is often used for the pouring out of libations.[105] The Old Testament prophets also speak of God's wrath being poured out on the wicked (LXX Jer. 7:20: 'Behold, my wrath and anger will be poured out upon this place').[106]

The first angel pours out his bowl specifically onto those who have taken the mark of the beast. It can be said that those who had the beast's 'mark' now receive the 'marks' of God.[107] These marks, described as 'loathsome and malignant sores' (16:2), are most likely ulcerous sores reminiscent of the Egyptian plague of boils (Exod. 9:9-11) and the boils of Job (Job 2:7-8,13).

The second angel pours his bowl into the sea and it becomes blood, killing all the creatures in the sea. The ancients considered blood to be a source of pollution as well as a means of purification.[108] This plague certainly recalls the Egyptian plague of the Nile River turned to blood (Exod. 7:14-25) and it parallels the second trumpet plague of the burn-

---

[104] Mounce, p. 292.
[105] E.g. Phil. 2:17; 2 Tim. 4:6; Josephus, *Ant.* III 234; Isa. 57:6.
[106] Cf. also similar passages in Jer. 10:25; Ezek. 7:8; 9:8, 14:19; 20:8,13,21; 21:31 (Mt. 21:31); 22:22; 30:15; 39:29.
[107] Hanns Lilje, *The Last Book of the Bible*, trans. Olive Wyon (Philadelphia: Muhlenberg, 1957), p. 214.
[108] Robert Parker, *Miasma: Pollution and Purification in Early Greek Religion* (Oxford: Clarendon Press, 1983), pp. 370-74.

ing mountain which falls into the sea, turning it to blood (Rev. 8:8-9). Here water, something necessary for life, is rendered useless.

The third pouring is into the rivers and springs, also turning water into blood. The parallel trumpet-plague turns the rivers and fountains bitter by a great burning star falling from heaven (8:10-11). This also recalls the first Egyptian plague, which turned all the rivers, canals, ponds and pools of water into blood (Exod. 7:14-19; cf. Pss. 78:44; 105:29). Several apocalyptic texts also predict water turning into blood.[109] As mentioned above, although parallels exist between the various series of plagues, the differences are also significant. Most notably, these final plagues are more intense in terms of devastation; for example, the trumpet plagues affect *part* of the water, this plague affects *all* of it.

The 'angel of the waters' responds by affirming the righteousness and justice of God's action (16:5): 'You are just, O Holy One, for you have judged these things; because they shed the blood of saints and prophets you have given them blood to drink. It is what they deserve' (16:5,6). In apocalyptic literature, angels are thought to be in charge of various elements, including water; for example, *1 En.* 60:12-22 refers to angels or spirits of the sea, hoarfrost, hail, snow, mist, dew and rain;[110] and in Rev. 7:1 an angel of water is mentioned and 14:18 speaks of the angel of fire. It is interesting to note that the comment by this angel (16:5,6) is very reminiscent of the Song of Moses and the Lamb of 15:2-4: both praise God for his righteousness, holiness and just judgment of the wicked. There are many parallels to this 'song' (16:5,6) in Jewish and apocalyptic literature that extol the righteousness and justice of God for judging sin.[111] The angel's comment adds the special note that it is especially just that the wicked drink blood, since they 'poured out the blood of saints and prophets' (v. 6). The point is that there is heavenly acclamation to the justice and righteousness of God's judgment on the wicked.

The altar also testifies that God's judgment is just (16:7). Perhaps the voice of the altar represents the souls of the martyrs (6:9) and the prayers of the saints (8:3-5). Both are closely associated with the altar. Throughout Revelation the altar is connected with judgment (6:9; 8:3-5; 9:13; 14:18; 16:7). This comment underscores the heavenly affirmation of God's just judgment.

---

[109] *Apoc. Elijah* 5-7.
[110] Cf. other apocalyptic references to angels of the water in *1 En.* 69:22; *2 En.* 4:6, 19:1-4; *Jub.* 2:2; 1QH 1:8-13; Str-B III 818-20; *1 En.* 61:10.
[111] Mounce, p. 886.

The fourth angel pours out his bowl upon the sun. The intensity of the heat is expressed in the construction translated as 'scorched by the fierce heat' (v. 9). It is noteworthy that the sun 'is given' (ἐδόθη) the power to burn people with fire. Fire is characteristic of divine judgment. This particular plague carries the punishment out with severe intensity. It is interesting to contrast those in that state to those in heaven, who are promised to be kept from severe heat (cf. 7:16). Again, the reader is reminded of the Egyptian plagues; the sun was affected by the ninth plague (Exod. 10:21-29). Although the plagues themselves differ (one Egyptian plague is darkness; here the sun scorches), both affect the sun. The point is clear – the sun itself is subject to God.

Again people do not respond with repentance or acknowledgment of God. This negative response is distinctive in Revelation, occurring twice in this chapter (vv. 11, 21). It is significant to note that the wrongful use of the name of God in blasphemy involves the breaking of the third commandment (Exod. 20:7; Deut. 5:11), which is punishable by death in the Old Testament (Lev. 24:16). The phrases 'to blaspheme the name of God' and 'to give glory to God', which are antithetical, appear together at other times in Jewish literature (see e.g. Test. Job 16.4). The failure to repent recalls the Exodus plagues, which resulted in the hardening of Pharaoh's heart rather than repentance.[112] The point is that in spite of such dynamic appearances of God's power, the people do not repent, but rather blaspheme.

The fifth angel's bowl is poured upon the throne of the beast (16:10) and his kingdom becomes dark. Whether or not the throne represents a city such as Rome, it is certain that the throne refers in some sense to the center of the authority and power of the beast. It is not clear in what way the kingdom becomes dark; possibly this is actual darkness (cf. Joel 2:31, where the sun becomes dark before the great day of the Lord; and note the ninth Egyptian plague, where the darkness is 'felt'). Whatever the nature of the darkness, it causes people to 'gnaw their tongues in pain' (Rev. 16:10). The response to this plague is also negative – the people 'blasphemed the God of heaven because of their suffering and their sores' (v. 11). The exact relation of the darkness to the sores and/or pain is not clear, but the plague again produces blasphemy rather than repentance.

The sixth angel's bowl is poured out upon the Euphrates River, which entirely dries up although it is the largest river in southwest Asia. Because of the dried-up river, an enormous army led by eastern kings is allowed to advance for the purpose of war (vv. 13-14). The

---

[112] Cf. Exod. 7:13,22; 8:15,19,32; 9:7,12,34-35; 10:1,20; 11:9-10; 14:4.

kings of the East (v. 12) can be interpreted in numerous ways.[113] However one interprets them, they appear to be related in some way to the kings of the world (v. 14). Probably, they are the kings which join and support the rule of the beast (17:10-14). The point is that the judgment of God is being acknowledged by the whole world although they are responding negatively by gathering to confront God in battle (the battle and final destruction are detailed in chs. 18-19).

It is possible that v. 13 begins a new section distinct from the sixth bowl of v. 12 because of the phrase 'I saw...' This interpretation, however, would not take into account the seer's usual style. Usually the sixth of each series is more elaborately described, for example, the sixth seal (6:12–7:17) and the sixth trumpet (9:13–11:13). In any case, from the mouth of the dragon, the beast and the false prophet emerge 'three unclean spirits like frogs' (16:13). The dragon is most likely that of 12:9 and 13:4 (Satan, 12:9); the beast is probably the beast out of the sea in 13:1-10, and the false prophet is quite certainly the beast of vv. 11-17. The implication is that these represent the kingdom of the beast, which gathers together to confront God (cf. 17:10-14; 19:19). The emergence of the frogs (considered unclean animals) from their mouths probably indicates persuasive, deceptive propaganda spoken to lead people to commit evil deeds against God.[114]

Most likely the 'kings of the whole world' (16:14) should be identified with the ten kings of 17:12-14 and 16-17. It seems unlikely that two different sets of kings would be involved. They symbolize the extent of involvement of the war with God at the end time: the whole world responds to his outpouring of destruction and display of power and prepares to confront him. The great battle of God against the nations hostile to him is frequently mentioned within the Old Testament and apocalyptic literature.[115] Certainly this battle (16:14ff.) should and must be seen against this backdrop. The Qumran sect, too, envisioned an eschatological battle of all nations, in which the righteous conquer the coalition of the wicked in the war of the 'Sons of Light' against the 'Sons of Darkness'.[116]

The warning in v. 15 is interjected into the account of the great battle. It does not directly connect to the preceding or succeeding passages, and yet it is quite an appropriate and relevant aside to the readers: 'Behold, I am coming like a thief.' This comment obviously

[113] Cf. Walvoord, p. 236.
[114] Mounce, pp. 299–300.
[115] Cf. e.g. Ezek. 38–39; Joel 3:2; Zech. 12:3; 14:2; Ps. 2:1-2; *4 Ezra* 13:34-35; *1 En.* 56:5-8; 90:12-19; *2 Bar.* 70:7-10; *Sib. Or.* 3.663-68; *Test. Joseph* 19; LXX Esth. 11:5-6; 1QM 1.10-11; 15.2-3, etc.
[116] Cf. Aune, p. 896.

echoes Jesus' words in Mt. 24:42-44 and Paul's statement in 1 Thess. 5:2. The word 'blessed' (μακάριος), which is the word used in the Gospels for the beatitudes, conveys the idea of the bestowal of grace. It is associated with staying awake and alert (ὁ γρηγορῶν), while watching for the coming of Christ. This particular kind of watching is not an idle apathy, but is a watchfulness characterized by alertness and vigilance.[117] The message is clear – God's people must be on the alert for his coming. The second part of the verse underscores this: 'lest he walk about naked and men see his shame'. The Mishnah provides an interesting historical context for this.[118] The captain of the Temple in Jerusalem would make his rounds of the precinct every night. If he found a guard asleep, that guard's clothes would be taken and burned and he would be sent home naked. In vivid imagery, the readers are urged to be alert and ready for the Lord's return.

One of the more challenging texts in Revelation is found in 16:14-16, relating to the location of the great battle. Verse 16 locates it in Armageddon. This is a translation of the Hebrew Har-Megiddo, a well-known site on the north side of the Carmel ridge. It has been the scene of numerous battles throughout history. Among many such battles is that of Thutmose III against the Canaanite kings in 1468 BCE, the battle of Deborah and Barak against a Canaanite coalition in Judg. 4:6-16, 5:19, the victory of Gideon over the Midianites (Judg. 7), and the defeat of Saul by the Philistines (1 Sam. 29:1; 31:1-7). At other times, the site was used as a Roman camp and a junction on the trade route from Syria to Egypt. Zechariah 12:9-11 refers to it as the place where the hostile enemies of God will challenge him and ultimately mourn because they failed to recognize the Messiah.[119] The literary problem has to do with the name. If it is seen as Har-Magedon (Mount of Megiddo) then the problem is that no one mountain in the region has this name. It can be translated in other ways, e.g. city of..., or as an adjective modifying Magedon, or Megiddo, but none of these solutions seem to answer all of the issues satisfactorily. The most satisfactory solution is that Megiddo refers to a particular pass in the Carmel ridge which leads into the large valley of Esdraelon. Probably this reference to Armageddon, the site of the final battle, simply refers to this area. Obviously, armies could not fight in the pass, but control of the pass would be essential in order to win. The ancient battles mentioned

---

[117] Gause, p. 215.
[118] Quoted by F.F. Bruce, 'The Revelation to John', in G.C.D. Howley, ed., *New Testament Commentary* (1969), p. 657.
[119] Cf. Mounce, pp. 301-303, and Aune, pp. 898-99, for a discussion of these as well as various other theories.

above were fought in the Valley of Esdraelon. This is also probably a reference to this general area. As is the case with the number of the beast (666) a solution will continue to be sought that will finally reveal the mystery, but for now, the important thing is that there is obviously a great battle at the end time for which all the kings of the world will gather to confront God himself. Wherever it occurs, 'Armageddon' (v. 16) symbolizes the final battle of Christ and the beast, God and Satan, the powers of good and evil.

The final bowl, the seventh, is poured out on the 'air'. This bowl impacts the final of the four elements considered basic to the universe by the early Greek natural philosophers (earth, water, fire, air).[120] A loud voice acclaims that 'it is done' (v. 17). Again, as in v. 1 (reflective of Isa. 66:6), the voice is associated directly with God. This time, however, the voice is associated with both the Temple and the throne and is accompanied with a storm. It is a theophany, i.e. God displaying himself by means of nature, also mentioned in other similar scenes in Revelation (see 4:5; 8:5; 11:19). The statement 'it is finished' points clearly to the final end of the series of God's judgments. The spectacular destruction by nature (v. 18) alludes to Dan. 12:1,[121] and is unique in the world in that it is described as 'such as there had not been since man came to be upon the earth' (v. 18). Several of the seven churches were in areas that regularly experienced earthquakes so the readers of the seven churches would be especially horrified.

Verses 19-21 summarize the final devastating destruction. The 'great city' splits, the 'cities of the nations' fall, Babylon is remembered by God with special wrath (v. 19); every island 'flees away', the mountains 'are not found' (v. 20), huge hailstones (100 pounds) come down 'upon' humans (v. 21).

It is unclear which city should be considered 'the great city' of v. 19. Since Babylon is mentioned directly in the second half of the verse, some scholars suggest that the 'great city' is Jerusalem (cf. 11:8); while Babylon probably refers to Rome. Others have suggested that both references are to the same city, namely Rome; still others have suggested that it symbolizes general civilization. For John, it may have been Rome, since Rome was seen as the center of oppression of the Church at his time. Perhaps for later readers through the ages it stands for whatever city fills this role their day, whenever they are reading Revelation. In this sense, Babylon represents the kingdom and power

---

[120] E.g. 'Empedocles Frags. B96, B98, B107, B115' in Hermann Diels, *Die Fragmente der Vorsokratiker: griechisch und deutsch*, 6th ed., ed. Walther Kranz (Zürich, Hildesheim: Weidmann, 1951).

[121] See also *Sib. Or.* 3.689-92.

of the beast (see discussion of the harlot as the 'great city', 17:18). In any case, the earthquake affects the whole world ('cities of the nations fall', 16:19). Babylon (however interpreted) suffers the worst as the recipient of God's wrathful 'remembrance'.

As often in Revelation, although the fall of Babylon is referred to in 16:19, the details are not described until ch. 18. This can be explained in various ways, but the best explanation seems to be related to the author's literary style. In other places (for example, the pouring out of the seven last bowls in 15:5-8), something is introduced, and later it is described in more detail. In 16:19-21, John anticipates the events that are later described in considerably more detail in 19:11-21: the war of Armageddon, the fall of Babylon (ch. 18), the final destruction by God's wrath.

Again, one can see parallels to earlier sequences of plagues. For example, the sixth seal also includes earthquakes, cosmic disturbances and the moving of mountains and islands (6:12-14). The disappearance of mountains is often connected in the Old Testament with a theophany and/or eschatological judgment (Ps. 97:5; Isa. 40:4; 42:15; 45:2; 54:10; Ezek. 38:20).

Verse 21 completes this introductory summary of the destruction by God's wrath. Huge hailstones rain down upon people. Again, the Egyptian plagues parallel this final event with less intensity – the seventh plague brings about thunder, hail and lightning, 'such as had never been in all the land of Egypt since it became a nation'.[122] In Joshua 10:11, hail is used by God to confuse the Amorites.[123] Although hail did occur on occasion in Mediterranean countries,[124] unusually destructive hail was associated with action taken upon humans by the gods.[125] It was reported that 'hail of incredible size' occurred in Rhodes in ancient times, causing houses to collapse and many deaths.[126] One can only imagine the destruction by hailstones of 100 pounds. Whether this should be understood literally or figuratively, the point is clear – utter destruction.

Again, the response to this devastation is blasphemy (v. 21), 'because its plague was extremely severe'. (See the similar response to the fourth plague in v. 9 and the fifth plague in v. 11.) Since even the pagan

---

[122] Exod. 9:24; cf. Ps. 105:32-33; Josephus, *Ant.* II 305.
[123] Cf. Isa. 28:17; Ezek. 38:22; Hag. 2:17; Job 38:22-23; Ps. 78:47; *Sib. Or.* 3.691.
[124] Cf. Ovid, *Metamorphoses* 5.158.
[125] E.S. McCartney, 'Greek and Roman Weatherlore of Hail', in the *Classical World*, 28, cited by Aune, p. 902.
[126] Reported by Diodorus Siculus, 19.45.2; J.J. Wettstein, *Novum Testamentum Graecum*, II, 2 vols. (1752; repr. Graz: Akademische Druck- und Verlagsanstalt, 1962), p. 819.

Greeks would have interpreted the falling of the great hailstones as evidence of the anger of the gods, the negative response of the people is even more remarkable. Whether repentance is possible or not, the text is certainly clear – they did not repent, but blasphemed God.

In summary, the narrative of the seven bowl plagues (15:1–16:21) concludes the series of plagues in Revelation (the seals and the trumpets). Like the narratives of the seven seals (4:1–5:14) and the seven trumpets (8:2-5), the author introduces the seven bowls with a throne-room scene (15:1-4). This setting clearly establishes the source and authority of these eschatological judgments as the very presence of God. Although neither God nor the throne are directly mentioned in ch. 16, the setting of the sea of glass (15:2) and the words of the Song of Moses (15:3,4) identify this source with the previous throne-room scenes.

Following the throne-room introduction, John watches the seven angels emerge from the heavenly sanctuary (15:5-8). They are given bowls filled with the wrath of God, an Old Testament metaphor for divine judgment (cf. Isa. 51:17-23).

The seven bowls are poured out one by one on earth (v. 2), the sea (v. 3), the rivers and springs (v. 4), the sun (v. 8), the throne of the beast (v. 10), the great river Euphrates (v. 12), and finally the air (v. 17). These plagues go beyond the other two series, utterly destroying in various ways the elements toward which they are directed. The sixth angel's bowl prepares the way for an army to invade, and the spirits from the dragon, beast, and false prophet (vv. 13-14) gather the kings of the whole world to confront God in battle (v. 14). The final bowl unleashes the final display of nature (vv. 19-21) bringing about the destruction of many cities, including the great Babylon (v. 19).

This concluding summary of the final devastation (vv. 13-21) serves to introduce the more elaborately described section on the great war and the fall of Babylon (chs. 17–19). Indeed, this is the final climax of the other two series of plagues (the seals and the trumpets). God himself announces the completion of his judgment of wrath: 'It is done!' (16:17).

Chapter 17

Chapter 17 is part of the larger textual unit (17.1-19:10) that describes Babylon and its destruction by God. Chapter 17 describes and interprets the meaning of the harlot (Babylon) and the beast; ch. 18 describes her destruction; 19:1-10 relates the response in heaven to her destruction. This entire unit (chs. 17–19) provides an elaboration of the fall of Babylon referred to in 16:19, when the seventh angel pours out his bowl of God's wrath.

The vision in ch. 17 is unique in Revelation in two notable ways: (1) It is one of three visions that are interpreted by an angel.[127] An interpreter is noted in Rev. 1:1 and 22:6,8-9, but an actual interpretation occurs only here in ch. 17 and in two later passages, 19:9-10 and (if this is the same angel) in 21:9–22:9. In a few passages the interpreter is the exalted Christ (1:9-20, 4:1) or one of the 24 elders (7:13-14). Otherwise, the angel as interpreter occurs only here and in ch. 19 and 21:9. (2) Another unique aspect of this passage is that it is the only vision described in static or tableau form: the characters do not *do* anything, whereas in the other visions, angels ascend or descend, and various characters worship, sing, or say things. This 'static' form is significant from a literary vantage point.[128] Otherwise, this vision functions in the same way as the other visions.

The judgment of the harlot is evidently part of the final wrath of God symbolized by the pouring out of the seven vials or bowls by the seven angels (15:6–16:21). Along with ch. 18 (the description of the fall of Babylon) the description of the harlot in ch. 17 appears to elaborate in symbolic form the nature and character of the 'great city' mentioned in 16:17-21: the seventh bowl or vial is poured out on the great city (16:17-21); the nature of the city and its abominable character is elaborated (ch. 17); finally the utter destruction by God's wrath is detailed (ch. 18) along with the laments over its destruction.

The harlot herself is introduced with the enumeration of three main characteristics: (1) she is sitting on many waters, (2) she has committed many acts of fornication, and (3) she has intoxicated other nations with her immorality. In Old Testament prophetic literature the imagery of the harlot is associated with religious apostasy. Isaiah 1:21 notes that Jerusalem has become a harlot because she has compromised with the gods of other nations. Jeremiah also associates idolatrous Israel with adultery and 'harlotries' (see Jer. 2:20-37; 13:27; Ezek. 16:15ff.; Hos. 2:5). Isaiah calls Tyre a harlot, again referring to religious apostasy (Isa. 23:16-17). Nahum 3:4 accuses Nineveh of seducing other nations to commit idolatry with her harlotries and charms (cf. Rev. 17:4). In each of these cases, false gods and idols were worshiped instead of the God of Israel.

The 'many waters' upon which the woman sits are interpreted by the angel in v. 15 as 'peoples, multitudes, nations, and tongues', undoubtedly denoting the universal extent and power of her (the

---

[127] A common feature in Jewish apocalyptic; e.g. there is a particularly close parallel in 3 *Bar.* 2:5-6, in which Baruch's angelic guide says, 'Come and I will show you greater mysteries.'

[128] See Aune, pp. 915-19.

woman's) influence (cf. Ps. 144:7; Isa. 8:6-7; 17:12-14; 28:17; Jer. 47:2). Since the harlot is later named Babylon (Rev. 17:5) it is interesting to note that Jer. 51:13 describes Babylon as 'dwelling by many waters'. Perhaps one should see a connection between the many canals of Babylon's Euphrates and the worldwide influence symbolized here in Rev. 17:1. In any case, the 'many waters' most likely represent the widespread influence of the city.

The second and third descriptive characteristics are articulated as: (2) 'kings of the earth commit acts of immorality with her' and (3) 'those who dwell on the earth were made drunk with the wine of her immorality'. These two phrases sum up the details which the author will describe in the remainder of the chapter. Both phrases also support the wide influence and seductive power of the harlot. The Hebrew term for fornicate (זנה, *zanah*) is often used in the Old Testament to refer to Israel's faithless behavior toward God.[129] In some instances in the Old Testament, commercial trade in particular is described using the metaphor of prostitution,[130] probably because of the association of religious practices with some economic relationships; for example, in some cases one had to sacrifice to pagan deities in order to belong to a workers' guild or union.[131] The significant point is that this city (harlot) is unfaithful to God and is also influencing others to follow her faithless behavior.

Verse 3 locates the setting and context of the vision 'in the Spirit' and 'in the wilderness'. The phrase 'in the Spirit' (ἐν πνεύματι) occurs four times in Revelation (1:10; 4:2; 17:3; 21:10). This is probably not a new or different state for John; rather it emphasizes the continuing state in which the vision is given.[132] The phrase is often used in apocalyptic literature to refer to visionary experiences.[133] The location 'in the wilderness' is significant. At various times in Israel's history, the wilderness was the setting for visionary and unusual experiences.[134] In this passage (Rev. 17:3), however, the wilderness is not a location of protection and nurture (cf. 12:6,14, where God nurtures the sun-clothed woman in the desert); rather, it is the location of divine judgment.

The seer describes the woman in the elaborate imagery of a prostitute or harlot (as anticipated in v. 2). The figure of the prostitute, or

---

[129] Cf. particularly Hos. 1:2; 2:4; Mt. 4:15, 9:1; Jer. 2:20; 3:2,9,13, 5:7,11; 13:27; Ezek. 6:9; 16:23; 43:7,9. See also Seth Erlandsson, '(זנה) *zanah*; (זנונים) *zᵉnunim*; (זנות) *zᵉnuth*; (תזנות) *taznuth*', *TDOT* IV (1980), pp. 101-104.

[130] Cf. Georg Kuhn, 'βαβυλών', *TDNT* I (1964), pp. 515 n.17.

[131] See Mic. 1:7; Nah. 3:4; 2 Kgs 9:22, etc.; cf. Aune, pp. 930-31.

[132] Cf. Mounce, p. 308.

[133] Cf. e.g. Hermas, *Visions* 1.1.3.

[134] Exod. 3:1; 1 Kgs 19:4; Mt. 4:1-11 (consider also Jesus' temptation in the wilderness).

courtesan, was often used even by ancient secular writers to personify vices.[135] Old Testament and early Jewish writers also used this imagery to illustrate faithless Israel.[136] In ch. 17, the seer describes the woman as wearing purple and scarlet (πορφυροῦν καὶ κόκκινον) and an assortment of jewelry. Purple refers to a spectrum of colors ranging from red to black.[137] Although many Old Testament and other ancient texts associate purple with status and royalty,[138] other writers hold that it denotes carnality.[139] In the context of this passage, both connotations are relevant and appropriate. The city is rich and lavish, but also promotes worship and behavior that is antithetical to God. In particular, ancient Rome tolerated many religions which included prostitution and/or other sexual activities associated with worship (particularly the mystery religions and the occult). In some cases, the traditional worship of the Greek and Roman gods like Zeus and Aphrodite also included prostitution as part of the religious practices. Elaborate jewelry was characteristic of the clothing of prostitutes.[140] The woman is pictured as holding a gold cup 'full of abominations (βδελυγμάτων) and impurities (ἀκάθαρτα) of her immorality' (v. 4). These terms are used in the LXX to describe the moral and ceremonial impurities associated with idolatry.[141] This further substantiates that this woman represents religious apostasy, which is faithlessness to God.

The woman has names written on her forehead. In ancient times, some types of prostitutes were tattooed or branded on the face and/or forehead to indicate their degradation and low status in society.[142] Other types of courtesans (perhaps those who were rich or had rich customers) wore their names on headbands. The names of the woman of Revelation 17 are cited: 'Babylon the Great, Mother of Harlots and of the Abominations of the Earth' (v. 5). Here she is first characterized directly as Babylon. Her other name, 'Mother of Harlots and of the

---

[135] Cf. *The Tabula of Cebes*, ed. John T. Fitzgerald and L. Michael White (Chico: SBL, 1983), 142 n33.

[136] See e.g. '4Q184', in John M. Allegro, ed., *Qumran Cave 4*, DJD 5 (Oxford: Clarendon Press, 1968), pp. 82-85; R.D. Moore, 'Personification of the Seduction of Evil: "The Wiles of the Wicked Woman"', *RestQ* 10 (1979-81), pp. 505-506.

[137] H. Durbeck, *Zur Charakteristik der griechischen Farbenbezeichnungen* (Bonn: Habelt, 1977), pp. 129-39.

[138] See e.g. Judg. 8:26; Esth. 8:15; Lam. 4:5; Dan. 5:7,16,29; 1 Macc. 10:20,62,64; 11:58; 14:43; Mk 15:17; Jn 19:2; *Gos. Pet.* 3.5; see M. Reinhold, *The History of Purple as a Status Symbol in Antiquity* (Brussels: Latomus, 1970), pp. 15-21, 37.

[139] Cf. Porphyry, *De Antro* 14.

[140] Cf. Lucian, *Piscator of Samosata*, 12; *Dial. meretr.* 286, 294; Alciphron, *Ep. Court*, 9.1.

[141] Werner Foerster, 'βδελύσσομαι', *TDNT* I (1964), p. 600.

[142] Cf. C.P. Jones, 'Stigma: Tattooing and Branding in Graeco-Roman Antiquity', *JRS* 77 (1987), p. 151.

Abominations of the Earth', is not surprising, considering the previous imagery, which emphasizes her debauchery.[143] In addition to these names, she has the title 'Mystery' (μυστήριον). It is uncertain whether this should be taken as her actual name or whether her name has a secret meaning. The latter option is more probable: it underscores the mysteriousness of the name, and the angel's promise to interpret the meaning in v. 7. Names are particularly significant in Revelation and should be interpreted as indicative of the character of the bearer. Christ, the triumphant warrior, wears the name King of Kings and Lord of Lords (19:16) as well as Faithful and True (19:11); the followers of the beast wear his mark as symbolic of their identification with the beast (13:16-18) while the 144,000 are identified as belonging to Christ by having his name written on their foreheads (14:1). Similarly, the name identifies this woman's character with her lifestyle of debauchery and rebellion against God: 'Babylon the Great, the Mother of Harlots and of the Abominations of the Earth' (17:5).

In addition to the vivid imagery of the prostitute, this woman is 'drunk with the blood of the saints, with the blood of the witnesses of Jesus' (v. 6). Certainly this connection of blood and wine echoes Isa. 49:26, where Isaiah prophesies that the enemies of Israel will be 'drunk with their own blood as with wine' (see also *1 En.* 62:12 and Isa. 34:5; 51:21 for similar passages). Roman writers also used this metaphor.[144] This description is striking in that it adds the charge of murder to the woman's other sins: not only is she promoting the worship of other gods, but she is also killing God's saints and prophets. The killing of the saints is certainly characteristic of ancient Rome, where especially terrible persecutions were carried out by Nero and Domitian. Although Nero primarily killed Christians in Rome, Domitian's policies were carried out throughout the empire. The interpretive challenge here is whether 'saints and witnesses' represent two groups or one. Literally the text reads, 'and I saw the woman drunk with the blood of the saints and with the blood of the witnesses (μαρτύρων) of Jesus'. Most likely, this is one group, not two. The Greek grammatical structure best suggests that the second phrase amplifies or explains the first: 'drunk with the blood of the saints, that is, those who were killed for their loyalty (witness) to Jesus'.[145] Further, the parallel phrase in 16:6 ('for they poured out the blood of saints and prophets') suggests this interpretation. The common theme of both groups is indicated: both

---

[143] Cf. Gause, pp. 220-21.
[144] Cf. Suetonius, *Tiber*, 59; Pliny, *Hist. Nat.* 14.28; Josephus, *War* V 8.2.
[145] Aune, p. 936; Mounce, p. 310.

comprise those who were killed for their loyalty to God.[146] Certainly witness or martyr (μάρτυς) refers to those who died because of their loyalty. In any case, the seer is filled with great wonder (v. 6) at the sight. The angelic interpreter responds to his wonder (or amazement) with the promise to explain the mysteries (v. 7) of the woman and the beast.

The two figures (the beast and the woman) should be seen as two parts of one mystery since neither can be fully understood without the other. It is noteworthy that the figure the author mentions first (the woman) is actually the last to be explained (v. 18). He begins with a description of the beast. The seer describes the beast as the same beast discussed earlier, in ch. 13: he has seven heads and ten horns (13:1; 17:7). The description 'was, and is not' (17:8) is not included in the previous description (ch. 13) and probably functions here to contrast sharply with the description of Christ and God, 'The Alpha and Omega, the first and the last, the beginning and the end' (1:17; 22:13). This could also refer to the wound of the beast, which appears to be fatal and from which the beast arises or is healed (13:3,12; 17:8).[147] The irony is striking: whereas the beast exists to be destroyed ('was, and is not, and is about to come out of the abyss and go to destruction', 17:8), God 'is, and was and is to come, the Almighty' (1:8; 22:13). Indeed, while the beast's power and authority is limited and temporary, God's power spans creation and the universe and, in fact, even controls the destiny of the beast and his followers (17:17-18).

It is also notable that the beast is described in terms of his origin (the abyss, associated in ch. 20 with Satan) and his destiny (destruction, the Lake of Fire, 19:20).[148] Finally, all those whose names are not in the Book of Life (the unbelievers) will marvel and be amazed at the powers of the beast (13:3; 17:8). Again, this appears to refer to the world's response to the healing of the fatal wound of the beast ('and the whole world was amazed and followed after the beast', 13:3; 17:8).

The interpretation is introduced by the phrase 'here is the mind which has wisdom' (v. 9). This could mean that the reader should proceed with caution since the following text is the clue to the interpretation of the beast. In other words, the meaning will be clear only to those who ponder with care and wisdom. Another option is to translate the verse more freely: 'this requires deep insight'.[149] This seems to

---

[146] Cf. D. Hill, 'Prophecy and Prophets in the Revelation of St. John', *NTS* 18 (1971-72), p. 409.
[147] Cf. Gause, p. 233.
[148] *Ibid.*
[149] See Aune, p. 959.

underline the difficulty of the mystery and to heighten the reader's awareness of what is necessary for comprehension. However one translates the phrase, the difficulty of understanding is clear. Certainly, anyone who has attempted to struggle with the meaning of this passage with its elaborate symbolism will wholeheartedly agree as to its complexity and deep mystery.

The angelic interpretation begins with the beast with seven heads and ten horns (vv. 8-14). Again, the description suggests that this beast is undoubtedly the same beast as in ch. 13. It rises from the sea and has seven heads and ten horns. The angel interprets the seven heads as seven mountains (17:9). Most likely the first-century reader would associate this immediately with Rome, the city built on seven hills. This designation was common among Roman authors.[150] The seven heads are probably also symbolic of political power. In Daniel 7, Daniel receives a similar vision in which the heads represent political power and kingdoms (see also Jer. 51:25). The beast in Daniel 7, however, has ten horns but does not have multiple heads. The numbers here probably function figuratively for considerable influence, rather than as indicating an actual number of rulers. The imagery of the seven-headed beast in Revelation 17 possibly reflects an ancient Israelite tradition in which a seven-headed beast epitomizes evil and will ultimately be destroyed by God (cf. Ps. 74:12-17; Isa. 27:1). The beast in Revelation 17 is also described as covered with blasphemous names (17:3; see 13:1) emphasizing his antipathy toward God.

The imagery of the seven heads becomes more complex in v. 10, where the angelic interpreter associates them with seven kings, five of which 'have fallen, one is, the other has not yet come; and when he comes, he must remain a little while' (v. 10). Some interpreters think that it is fairly clear that these are the rulers of the Roman Empire, and the 'one who is' refers to the emperor at the time of the writing. The 'five kings who have fallen' would refer to those who have already ruled. The term for 'fall' (ἔπεσαν, from πίπτω) has the connotation of something or someone being overthrown or killed violently.[151] This does not help, however, with the identification of a particular Roman emperor, since most of them died violently (also, there are more than five). The problem is even more complicated when one attempts to identify the emperors by counting them. Part of the problem is the

---

[150] Cf. Vergil, *Aeneid*, VI 782; *Martial*, IV 64; Cicero, *Ad Atticum*, VI 5, etc.

[151] Lohmeyer, p. 143; A. Strobel, 'Apokalypse des Johannes', *NTS* 10 (1963-64), p. 439. Jewish and Greek literature also reflects this meaning: Exod. 32:28; 1 Sam. 4:10; 2 Sam. 1:19,25,27; 3:38; 21:22; Job 14:10 (LXX only); 1 Chron. 5:10; 20:8; 1 Macc. 3:24; 4:15,34; 2 Macc. 12:34-5; Jdt. 7:11; *1 En.* 14:6; 1 Cor. 10:18; *Barn.* 12:5; *Iliad* VIII 67; X 200, XI 157,500; Xenophon, *Cyropaedia*, I 4.24; Herodotus, IX 67.

uncertainty with which emperor one should begin counting. Augustus, of course, is a possibility since he founded the Roman Empire. Julius Caesar, however, was actually the first Caesar. Then, a second consideration emerges – how one should consider the three rulers who succeeded Nero (Galba, Otto and Vitelius), each of whose reigns lasted for only a short time.[152] Perhaps the best way to deal with the issue is to interpret the number seven as symbolic of the power of the Roman Empire as an historic whole rather than attempting to relate the seven kings to particular emperors. This is justified by the symbolic nature of numbers in apocalyptic literature. From this perspective, then, the seven heads would disclose the imminent end of the age, the point clearly being that the eschatological end is near ('five have fallen, one is, and one is yet to come).

The beast is further described as the one 'who was and is not' (v. 11). Clearly this is functioning as a parody of the Lamb who is described as having died, come back to life, and is alive forevermore (1:18; 2:8). It also serves as an intentional antithesis to God himself, 'the One who was, and is, and is to come' (1:4,8; 4:8). Again, it is probable that the beast here is the same as the beast from the sea (ch. 13), who receives a fatal wound and revives (13:3,12,14).

The angelic interpreter explains that the beast is one of the seven kings, but is also the eighth and will ultimately 'go to destruction'. Probably what is meant is that this ruler is part of the political structure to which the seven kings belong, but has not come to power yet. As the eighth king, however, he is distinct from the other seven kings.

Obviously, it is necessary to interpret the beast and the seven heads symbolically. The beast is the beast of ch. 13, who is probably not one of the Roman emperors, but belongs to the eschatological struggle between God and Satan (see discussion on ch. 13). The seven heads from this perspective would symbolize the political power from which the beast emerges. Since the beast is the eighth king, the final king in the series of kings, it is possible that he also symbolizes the culmination of the wicked characters of all the preceding kingdoms of history.[153]

The ten horns (v. 12) are ten kings who have not yet received their power. These are probably not the emperors of Rome since according to the text, the horns have not yet received their kingdoms (v. 12). It is difficult to determine what the ten kings represent in terms of actual kings or rulers. Again, it is probably best to interpret them as symbolic

---

[152] See Aune, pp. 945-50, for an extensive discussion of the alternatives and their significances.

[153] Gause, p. 224.

of the general political structure of the world which will agree to collaborate with the beast (17:13-18).

The ten kings receive their power from the beast for 'one hour' (a short time). Verse 13 states that the ten kings support the beast, have 'one purpose', and are in one accord.[154] This idiom, which is derived from the political sphere, refers to the agreement among citizens of a city or state.[155] Their common purpose is explained further in the comment in v. 17: 'God has put it into their hearts' to accomplish three things: (1) to do his (God's) will (v. 17a); (2) to be in one accord (v. 17b); (3) and to surrender their regal power to the beast (v. 17b; cf. Exod. 35:30-35; Ezra 7:27; 1 Esdr. 8:25). The author here puts the entire passage in perspective: 'until the words of God shall be fulfilled' (v. 17). It is noteworthy that for the author of Revelation, even God's enemies are proceeding according to God's purpose and plan. Ultimately, God is in control of evil as well as good.

The ten kings will also be involved in some way in the destruction of the city (17:16-17). It is not entirely clear how these kings relate to the 'kings of the earth', who mourn over the fall of Babylon (18:19). Most likely, the ten horns (kings) are part of the actual structure of the beast's government, since they join their kingdoms with the beast and receive authority from the beast (17:12). These kings commit immorality with the harlot and then mourn her downfall, probably symbolizing the whole world which has become rich from interacting with the beast's political and economic center. Their fortunes are devastated along with the city (18:9-10). The ten horns, then, most likely reflect the political structure of the beast.[156] Like the seven heads (v. 10), these ten kings (ten horns) should be interpreted eschatologically, as symbolic of the political and economic world powers of all nations of the earth (the number ten represents completeness) united in the reign of the beast.

It is especially noteworthy that although the ten kings (the nations of the world) are unified in their support of the beast (v. 13), they apparently are ambivalent about the woman (they will hate the harlot, devastate her, eat her flesh and burn her with fire, v. 16). Perhaps this can be interpreted as the division within the kingdom of the beast: although the kings cooperate for practical purposes to attain wealth and power, they are also quick to turn against one another in viciousness

[154] See Johnson, p. 560, who suggests that the numbers here should be interpreted qualitatively rather than quantitatively so that the seven heads would represent the fullness of evil power residing in the heart.

[155] Cf. Dio Chrysostom, *Orationes* 36.22; 39.8; Isocrates, 4.138; Thucydides, 1.122.2; 6.17.4; Demosthenes, *Orationes* 10.59; cf. also Gause, p. 255.

[156] See a similar imagery in Dan. 7:7-8,20,24; cf. also *Barn.* 4:3-5.

and greed.[157] In this way God uses them to destroy the kingdom of the beast – ironically, the source of their own power and authority (v. 17). In fact, there is a pattern in political history which suggests that 'every revolutionary power contains within itself the seed of self-destruction'.[158]

Verse 14 anticipates the war between Christ and the nations of the earth (19:11-21). Since the war is mentioned here only briefly, the ten kings who are associated with the beast must have a distinct role in the war as well as in the fall of Babylon (17:16 anticipates the destruction detailed in ch. 18). Apparently, the author's style is to summarize the main points of an event or person which will be discussed in more detail later (e.g. 15:6 introduces the bowl-angels who pour out their bowls in detail in ch. 16; 16:19 briefly refers to the fall of Babylon which is detailed in ch. 18).

It is important to consider, first, that in 17:14 the author gives the reason for the Lamb's victory in the great war – 'because he is the Lord of lords and King of kings'. This is the key factor: in contrast to the perceived power of the beast and his supporters, Christ will overcome because he is ultimately Lord and King (cf. Deut. 10:17; Ps. 136:2,3; Dan. 2:47; 2 Macc. 13:4; *1 En.* 9:4).

The second significant point of this war (again to be expanded in ch. 19), is that the faithful are with the Lord. The question is, who are these faithful? In this passage one is not told precisely, except that they are the 'called, chosen, faithful'. The idea that the righteous take part in the destruction of the wicked is a standard apocalyptic theme. For example, Enoch warns the unrighteous that they will be delivered into the hands of the righteous (*1 En.* 98:12), who will show no mercy (cf. also *1 En.* 38:5; 91:12; 96:1). These are definitely the redeemed, those who are characterized by their commitment and loyalty to God. Faithfulness is an important concept in Revelation. Over and over, the message to the churches commends faithfulness to God (to Ephesus, 2:2-3; to Smyrna, 2:9-10; to Pergamum, 2:13; to Thyatira, 2:19; to Philadelphia, 3:10). The faithful will be given rewards such as the crown of life (2:10), the hidden manna and a new name (2:17); they will be kept from the hour of testing (3:10). These faithful probably include those from the churches. Also, the 144,000 are obviously chosen and protected by God (7:4); and the multitude of the redeemed are purchased for God (5:9). All of these could be classified as 'called, chosen, faithful'. The main point is that they are characterized by their loyalty and

---

[157] Gause, pp. 226-27.
[158] Lilje, p. 229.

faithfulness to God.[159] This factor definitely suggests that these are the righteous rather than angelic or heavenly beings, which are always identified as such (e.g. in the worship scenes of chs. 4, 5, 7, and 15).

The angel finally addresses the main challenge of this passage, the woman. She is identified as the 'great city which reigns over the kings of the earth' (v. 18).[160] There is almost unanimous agreement that this 'great city' is not ancient Babylon. Although the ancient city's hanging gardens were at one time one of the seven wonders of the ancient world, at the time of the Roman Empire ancient Babylon did not exist as a functioning city. In the author's time, Babylon was an accepted code name for Rome, although some scholars suggest that Babylon could be Jerusalem. Jerusalem, however, does not fit as many characteristics of the woman as does Rome. Throughout this chapter Babylon is called 'the great city' (18:10,16,18). This description was often used to refer to Rome. Horace called Rome *princeps urbium* the 'greatest of cities'.[161] Other ancient writers also refer to her as 'the great city'.[162]

Several aspects of this vision of the woman strongly point to Rome; they recall the goddess of Rome, Dea Roma. She is depicted on a Roman coin minted in 71 CE under Emperor Vespasian in the Roman province of Asia (where these churches were located). Dea Roma is pictured on the coin as reclining on the seven hills of Rome. The representation of the god of the River Tiber also reclines against the seven hills on the right side of the coin. Particularly significant is that the Smyrneans claimed to be the first to worship Roma.[163]

The name of Roma (goddess of Rome) was kept secret for security purposes, since she was the goddess and protectress of the city. For her enemies to know her name was thought to make Rome vulnerable to attack. Also pictured on the coin were Romulus and Remus (the legendary twin founders of ancient Rome) with the she-wolf who nur-

---

[159] Cf. Gause, p. 226.

[160] Cf. Bauckham, pp. 125-28, who interprets Babylon with its city imagery in marked contrast to the New Jerusalem.

[161] Cf. Horace, *Carmina*, 43.13.

[162] Cf. Aelius Aristides, *Orationes* 26.3; 26.9; Dio Cassius 76.4.4-5; *Pal.Anth.* 9.59; Athenaeus 1.208b; 3.98c; Porphyry, *De abst.* 2.56.9 (ἡ μεγάλη πόλις): Procopius, *Goth.* 3.22; Vergil, *Aeneid* 1.601-6; 7.272-82; *Eclogues* 1.19-25; Livy 1.16.6-7; Ovid *Festi* 5.91-100; *Metam.* 15.439-49; Manilius, *Astron.* 4.686-95, 773-77; Pliny, *Hist.nat.* 3.38; Silius Italicus, *Pun.* 3.505-10, 582-87; Martial, 1.3.1-6; 10.103.7-12; Aeschylus, Ammianus Marc. 14.6.5-6. (For an extensive list of other ancient authors see Wettstein, 2.826, ad Rev. 17:18.)

[163] M. Mellor, ΘΕΑ ΡΩΜΗ: *The Worship of the Goddess Roma in the Greek World* (Göttingen: Vandenhoeck & Ruprecht, 1975), p. 20. In fact, Smyrna was the first city to establish a temple to Roma in 195 BCE.

tured them. It is interesting that the Latin term for female wolf (*lupa*) also has the connotation of prostitute. In this context, the imagery of the great city as a rich, gaudily dressed, and destitute prostitute would be most appropriate and recognizable to first-century readers. The widespread luxury, political power and influence described in ch. 17 are also characteristic of Rome. Not only could she be said to seduce the nations, but also the other nations could be said to be 'intoxicated with her immoralities' (17:1-2). Religious apostasy would be a relevant and appropriate characteristic of Rome, too. Since Rome was tolerant of most religions, a wide variety of worship could be found there: occultism, sorcery and magic, the mysteries with their wild orgies, initiations, and secret rites, as well as the more traditional pagan worship such as that of Zeus and Aphrodite. Rome was also the center of emperor worship itself.

The woman will ultimately meet a horrifying end (v. 16, also ch. 18). The ten kings who have fornicated with her will destroy her. The language of v. 16 recalls the vision of Ezek. 23:25-26, which speaks of the fate of the harlot. In this passage (Rev. 17), however, the author merely mentions what will be addressed in more detail later (ch. 18).

Finally, the woman is sitting on 'many waters'. This is probably a metaphor indicating the power and influence of Rome. Like the River Tiber upon which she is situated, she extends her influence to many people, nations and tongues by being the center of the Empire.

The question remains, What city does the harlot represent in the eschatological time frame? It is critical to realize that for apocalyptists, one thing or event can represent several ideas and can be relevant to several timeframes. Although it is quite clear that the harlot as Babylon symbolized ancient Rome to the first readers, readers of today would not necessarily expect her to represent contemporary Rome, Italy. Ancient Rome, to Revelation's first readers, was the center of the Empire, the heart of luxury and wealth, the center of trade and commerce. Its political and religious policies and practices controlled and influenced the rest of the Empire. Also supportive of this interpretation of 'Babylon' as a world political structure is the consideration of the seven hills or mountains upon which the woman resides (17:9). Although the readers of Revelation most likely would associate the seven mountains with Rome, it should also be noted that mountains are often used allegorically to refer to world powers by the Old Testament prophets (Isa. 2:2; Jer. 51:25; Dan. 2:35; Zech. 4:7). The identification, then, by the seer of the seven mountains with the seven kings would follow (Rev. 17:9-10), and would suggest that Babylon should be interpreted as a political and economic structure (the kings) rather than as one particular geographical location.[164] This concept of a powerful amoral central headquarters must be applied to eschatological time.

The beast clearly represents the leader of a political and economic center who will rule over the world for a short time (see discussion in ch. 13 on Daniel's world leader). The seven heads and ten horns represent his worldwide political structure and influence. The harlot (the city) rides the beast, an indication that she is supported by the beast and his political structure. As mentioned above, she most likely also includes the religious nature of the beast's reign. Hence, eschatologically, it is best not to associate the woman with any one particular geographical city. 'Babylon' is used in Revelation merely because it was the epitome of an evil, powerful city, headquarters of an empire. Today, one might expect a different city. It is logical that the readers would assume that the beast will have some sort of center or headquarters which will function as the center for his political, economic, and religious programs and reign. Wherever that city is, it is symbolized by the harlot supported by the beast. At the same time, she symbolizes the religious and political apostasy which is antithetical to God himself.[165]

In summary, the seer beholds the vision of the woman on the beast wearing the recognizable clothes and jewels of a prostitute. The imagery remarkably recalls the coin depicting the goddess Roma sitting on seven hills with the representation of the god of the River Tiber. She sits on a beast, which echoes the beast of ch. 13, with seven heads and ten horns and blasphemous names. The seven heads represent seven hills (suggestive of Rome, but also indicative of political and economic powers). Babylon, then, suggests political, economic and religious powers. The ten kings (the nations of the world) support the political structure of the beast and suggest worldwide influence. This structure will exist for a short while, but eventually the beast will confront the Lamb himself in the final battle of the end times (see 19:11-21). The outcome of that war is summarized in 17:14-16. The Lamb will overcome the beast (v. 14) and the ten kings will turn on the woman and destroy her. The vision concludes with a typical apocalyptic perspective: God himself is in control, even causing the enemies of the Lamb to attack one another in order to be defeated. All of this is to be considered within the perspective of 'until the words of God shall be fulfilled' (v. 17).

---

[164] Johnson, p. 559.
[165] Cf. Johnson, pp. 448-60.

Chapter 18

Chapter 18 describes the fall of Babylon (Rome) as anticipated in 17:16. The events are not recorded in chronological or even topical order, but are organized in such a way as to heighten the impact on the readers. The chapter is a violent denunciation of Babylon in the form of prophetic taunt songs and speeches (two announcements by angels in vv. 1-3, 21-24, and one proclamation by a heavenly voice in vv. 4-20). The largest section is made up of the taunt songs by three groups: the kings of the earth (vv. 9-10), the merchants (vv. 11-16), and the sea captains and sailors (vv. 17-19). Taunt songs or laments have no fixed form but include derision and joy over past, present and/or future misfortunes and the shortcomings of others.[166] The Old Testament prophets used them to deride their enemies and predict their downfall (cf. Isa. 23-24; 47; Jer. 50-51; Ezek. 26-27). This particular denunciation of Babylon echoes Isa. 21:9, 'fallen, fallen is Babylon the Great!'

This section is introduced with the phrase, 'After this, I saw' (18:1), which is often used to note the beginning of another textual unit (cf. 4:1; 7:1,9; 15:5; 18:1). The phrase also marks this as another vision. The literary device 'another angel' links the coming unit to the previous text, but also differentiates this angel from the preceding one (17:1,3,7,15). This particular angel, notably accompanied by 'glory' (18:1), is the only angel in Revelation to be so designated. Although usually reserved for the presence of God (cf. Rev. 15:8; 21:11,23) 'glory' is sometimes associated with angels in the Old Testament (Ezek. 9:3; 10:4,18,19; Heb. 9:5; see also Sir. 49.8). Evidently, this angel has a particularly special message, and his authority comes directly from God himself. The earth is illumined by the angel's glory (18:1), probably implying the worldwide impact of his message. This could also suggest the worldwide influence and power of Babylon.[167]

The angel proclaims, 'Fallen, fallen is Babylon the Great' (an allusion to Isa. 21:9; see also Jer. 51:8; LXX 28:8). This same proclamation was previously announced by 'another angel' (Rev. 14:8). The aorist tenses used here are most likely prophetic perfects which emphasize the certainty of the fall.[168] Most scholars interpret Babylon as a code name for

---

[166] Aune, p. 976; cf. examples of taunt songs in 1 Sam. 17:43-44; Jer. 22:14-15; Isa. 23:15-16.

[167] Gause, p. 228.

[168] Prophetic perfects are past tenses which denote a certainty so strong that although the event is in the future, it can be spoken of as if it has already taken place. Indeed, from the perspective of the speaker, the fall has already happened (cf. S GKC 106 n.; G. Mussies, p. 338).

Rome (as discussed in our comments on ch. 17).[169] but a few others interpret it as referring to Jerusalem.[170] The details in the chapter, however, seem to support more strongly the position of Rome (e.g. the seven hills, the worldwide influence, the excessive wealth).

The prediction of utter desolation follows (vv. 2,3): the city will become 'a dwelling place of demons and a prison of every unclean spirit, and unclean and hateful bird' (v. 2). There is probably a reflection of Jer. 51:37 (LXX 28:37) here.[171] Desolation is a recurring theme in prophetic denunciations.[172] The metaphor of 'a prison of unclean spirits and hateful birds' is a particularly vivid picture. The term prison (φυλακή) can refer to a watchtower. One is struck by the imagery of desolation: the devastated city is watched over by evil spirits like vultures in a tower.[173]

The reasons for Babylon's fall are stated in 18:3 (see parallel in 17:1-2): (1) She has influenced other nations with her immorality; the kings of the earth have committed immorality with her. (2) The kings and merchants have profited from their economic alliances with her; in fact, they have become so rich that they have become proud and arrogant. Both of these reasons have to do with the immoral influence of this city on the rest of the world – the nations and kings of the earth, the traders. Perhaps Babylon represents wickedness through the ages (cf. Dan. 2, where the image represents kingdoms through the ages).[174] Verse 3 echoes 14:8, 'Fallen, fallen is Babylon the Great, who gave all nations to drink of the wine of her passionate lust' (also see parallels in LXX Jer. 28:7). Here, as in ch. 17, the imagery of a prostitute is used to designate faithlessness to God. Babylon most likely symbolizes the political, social and religious center for the rule of the beast and, therefore, epitomizes faithlessness to God. Also, the policies of this city would influence the rest of the world. The lure of riches from trade would certainly 'seduce' nations, kings of the earth, and traders to compromise on religious/ethical and even legal matters in order to

---

[169] Cf. Wilhelm Bousset, *Die Offenbarung Johannis* (Göttingen: Vandenhoeck & Ruprecht, 1906), p. 384; Charles, II, pp. 62-63; U.B. Muller, *Die Offenbarung des Johannes* (Gütersloh: Mohn, 1984), pp. 267, 288-89.

[170] Ford, pp. 205-86, 296-307; Alan J. Beagley. *The 'Sitz im Leben' of the Apocalypse with particular reference to the Role of the Church's Enemies*. BZNW 50 (New York: W. de Gruyter, 1987), pp. 92-102; Iain Provan, 'Foul Spirits, Fornication and Finance: Revelation 18 from an Old Testament Perspective', *JSNT* 64 (1996), pp. 91-97.

[171] A similar form is used to describe the destruction of Tyre in Isa. 23:1. See also *Gen. Rab.* 65.21.

[172] Cf. Jer. 4:26-27; 9:10-12; 22:5-6; Ezek. 6:14; Hos. 2:3; Joel 3:19; Zeph. 2:13; Mal. 1:2-3.

[173] Cf. Gause, p. 228, who suggests that it is appropriate that the city which hosted the religious powers of the beast has become the habitation of devils.

[174] Gause, p. 229.

benefit financially from the interaction with this wealthy and affluent city. Ancient Rome would be an appropriate representative for the influence of such a powerful political and social structure. The entire world would not hesitate to participate in beneficial and profitable enterprises even if they strained legal and/or ethical principles. (3) The third reason for Babylon's fall is that the merchants (who probably include the sea captains, since the sea was the main means of transportation from east to west) have profited from these alliances with her. Rome's well-known greed for luxury was a topic of denunciation even by secular Latin writers.[175]

The second message of this chapter (vv. 4-5) is given by a heavenly voice (probably God), urging 'my people' to separate themselves from the city so as not to fellowship with her sins and hence share the plagues. This 'summons to flight' is often found in Old Testament prophetic messages, particularly Jer. 51:45 (see also Jer. 50:8; 51:6; Isa. 48:20; 52:11), so it is appropriate for inclusion here. This is an especially challenging section to interpret since it involves several time frames: (1) the time of the seer and the seven churches; (2) the current readers' time; and (3) the eschatological time after the actual event of the fall of Babylon. There is general agreement among interpreters that since Babylon is a code name for Rome, most likely the summons to flee is to the people of the seven churches, to flee the wickedness of the Roman Empire. Since, however, these churches were not in the actual *city* of Rome, but the Roman Empire, and it would not be possible for the people actually to leave the geographical area of the Roman Empire, the summons should probably be interpreted figuratively: God is calling the people to separate from the wickedness and apostasy symbolized in Revelation by the harlot, Babylon/Rome. The city 'Rome' epitomizes the whole Roman Empire.

This interpretation should apply to the current time frame as well; that is, current readers should also separate themselves from the wickedness and apostasy of the time or place in which they live. The eschatological perspective is the most difficult to understand since it does not appear that anyone has a chance to escape Babylon's destruction. Perhaps, then, the summons should best be understood as the pronouncement of doom rather than as a warning to the eschatological dwellers. The eschatological city may or may not be the city of Rome, Italy, but will be the city which is the headquarters of the beast's rule. The city of ancient Rome, then, serves as a symbol of wickedness and apostasy. At the time of the writing of Revelation, if Babylon is under-

---

[175] Cf. Petronius, *Satyricon*, CXIX, pp. 1-36. See Aune, p. 990 for a further discussion of Roman greed and luxury.

stood to symbolize the city of Rome (cf. 17:9,18; 18:10,16,18,21), this would be the seer's admonition to his readers to leave the city with its wickedness and apostasy. The prophetic call, then, would be for the people to separate themselves from the corrupt and seductive influences of pagan society.[176] A similar instance is found in 2 Cor. 6:17, where the readers are exhorted 'to come out from them and be separate', to abstain from the immoral and idolatrous practices of pagan society. The ancient city of Rome symbolizes the wickedness of the coming eschatological rule of the beast.

The heavenly voice denounces the city for the accumulation of her sins. The term 'accumulate' (ἐκολλήθησαν) in this context indicates the piling up of one sin upon another until the heap reaches outrageous proportions, all the way to heaven. This idiom is also found in the Old Testament as well as in apocalyptic and even secular literature.[177] The Old Testament also uses the metaphor 'to the heavens' to emphasize the magnitude of something (see Gen. 11:4; Deut. 1:28; 9:1; 2 Chron. 28:9). Secular literature similarly includes this hyperbole: for example, Homer, *Odyssey* 15.329, says that excessive pride and violence have reached even to the heavens. The seer in Revelation is making the point that although God has been patient, the magnitude of the city's sin has become outrageous and cannot be overlooked.

Revelation 18:5 is the only place in the New Testament where it is said that God 'remembers'. Usually a petitioner is asking God to 'remember' him/her (e.g. Judg. 16:28; 2 Kgs 20:3; Ps. 74:2; Isa. 38:3). In the Old Testament, God 'remembers' his servants (e.g. Gen. 8:1; 19:29; 30:22); he 'remembers' his covenant (CD^a 1:4; 6:2); he 'remembers' the wickedness of the enemies of Israel and brings vengeance on them (Pss. 25:7; 137:7; 1 Macc. 7:38).[178] God is asked to 'remember' in inscriptions on votive offerings.[179] In this passage in Revelation (18:5), God's 'remembering' can be said to be ironic. Instead of *prayers* reaching God for remembrance, Babylon's *sins* have reached heaven and will provoke a response of justifiable vengeance.

The response to the iniquity of Babylon is that she will be recompensed *double* for what she has done. The justice of this double recompense is not addressed or justified. The idea of paying for one's sins is,

---

[176] See P.A. de Souza Nogueira, 'Der Widerstand gegen Rom in der Apokalypse des Johannes. Eine Untersuchung zur Tradition des Falls von Babylon in *Apokalypse* XVIII' (Diss.: Heidelberg, 1991), pp. 208-209.

[177] Cf. Jer. 51:9; Jonah 1:2; e.g. Ezra 9:6 comments that 'the people's iniquities have risen above our heads and our guilt has grown even to the heavens' (cf. 11:43).

[178] See O. Michel, 'μιμνήσκομαι', *TDNT* IV (1967), pp. 675-83.

[179] H.S. Versnel, 'Religious Mentality in Ancient Prayer', in *Faith, Hope and Worship: Aspects of Religious Mentality in the Ancient World* (1981), pp. 59ff.

of course, a common theme in the Old Testament, but the recompense is usually 'an eye for an eye' (Exod. 21:24; see also Lev. 24:19-20; Deut. 19:21, etc.). The concept of double recompense is rare, most pointedly in Jer. 16:18, where God says, 'I will recompense their iniquities *twofold*'. Jeremiah (50:29b) asks God to 'Requite to her according to her deeds', but this is not necessarily double recompense. Isaiah (40:2) also notes that Israel has paid double for her sins. It is noteworthy that in both cases (Jer. 16:18 and Isa. 40:2) the situation had to do with God's response to Israel's idolatry. Greek literature occasionally includes the idea of paying back double for evil.[180]

The question is, To whom is the voice speaking when it calls for such vengeance? It could be to Christians or Jews ('my people'), but either is unlikely since the concept of double vengeance is not usual (see above). Most likely, the voice, probably of God, is announcing divine retribution to be brought upon Babylon because of her idolatry and religious apostasy. As noted in v. 3, she not only committed these sins against God, she also has influenced the whole world to sin with her. There are several options as to who was expected to bring about the judgment. Chapter 16 describes the plagues and judgments of God's wrath as the result of the pouring out of the bowls by the angels. It is not clear how this is going to occur. Angels as messengers of divine judgment are familiar within Jewish apocalyptic literature.[181] Certainly, God could bring about the judgment mentioned in ch. 16 through nature. Or some of the destruction could possibly result from human war. In any case, it is certain that, however it happens in the end time Babylon will pay double for her sins against God by being utterly destroyed.

Verses 7-8 reiterate that as 'Babylon's' deeds have been, so will her judgment be. She has been arrogant in her sin; literally, 'she has glorified herself' (v. 7). Hence, she will be utterly devastated with the fire of divine judgment because 'the Lord God who judges her is strong' (v. 8). The emphasis here is on the might of God. The statement serves both as a conclusion to the prophecy of vv. 4-8 and as an introduction to the following section about the actual destruction. Indeed, it is God's actual power that will bring about the destruction of Babylon's perceived power, for although Babylon/Rome appears to be powerful,

---

[180] See e.g., Hesiod, *Works*, pp. 709-11; Homer, *Iliad*, 13.445-47; *Theognis*, 1189-90; Sophocles, *Oedipus Rex* 1320; Aeschylus, *Agamemnon*, 537; Plato, *Laws*, 642e; Xenophon, *Anabasis*; 1.9.11; *Memorabilia*, 2.6.35; cf. Aune, p. 993, for extensive discussion of this concept.

[181] See *1 En.* 53:3; 56:1; 62:11; 63:1; 66:1; *3 En.* 31:2; 32:1; 33:1; *b.Sabb.* 55a, 88a; cf. Alexander in Charlesworth, *OTP* I, p. 285 nn. 31f.; Grozinger, p. 591; Michl, 'Engel II', *RAC* V, pp. 75-76.

God's actual power is greater. Judgment by fire is particularly characteristic of God's divine judgment (for example, Sodom and Gomorrah were destroyed by fire, Gen. 19).

Verses 9-19 consist of three laments, or 'hymns of defeat'.[182] The first is by the kings of the earth who have committed acts of immorality with Babylon (vv. 9-10). These are probably the ten kings of ch. 17 who join with the beast against Christ. Most likely they represent the economic and political structure of the nations of the world who have made alliances with the commercial center of the world (Rome) in order to become rich. Likewise, the merchants of the earth (vv. 11,17) have become rich by establishing commercial links with this center. Verses 12-14 list a catalog of imports, of mostly luxury items, which would have been familiar to those involved in Roman commerce. They fall into several primary categories: (1) precious metals and stones; (2) expensive fabric; (3) ornamental pieces; (4) expensive spices, probably for perfumes and incense; (5) foodstuffs; and (6) animals and humans. The list undoubtedly impresses the reader as to the extravagance and fortunes involved in this commercial center. It also indicates the extent of the destruction: not only are luxury items involved, but also more necessary, ordinary items.[183] The extent and nature of this trade with Rome can perhaps be inferred from the writings of ancient authors such as Pliny and Aristides.[184] Ancient Roman life was extravagant and lavish; for example, the Egyptian roses at one of Nero's banquets cost the equivalent of almost $100,000. Vitellius spent $20,000,000 in one year for food, including delicacies such as peacocks' brains and nightingales' tongues.[185] If this kind of extravagance of ancient Rome is symbolic of the outrageous wealth of the eschatological center of commerce, it is no wonder that the merchants mourned the loss of the source of their financial fortunes. The main point is that the lament of these groups is not for the loss of a great city, but rather for the loss of their own source of fortune. The language of v. 14 'and they shall not be found any longer' in Greek is a triple negative. This construction is not found in English, but in Greek it is used to emphasize something intensely negative. In this case the desolation is absolute.[186]

---

[182] Gause, p. 232.
[183] See Mounce, pp. 329-30, and Aune, pp. 998-1002, for further information.
[184] Pliny, *Hist. Nat.* VI 26; Aristides, *In Rom.*, 200.
[185] Mounce, 329.
[186] Gause, p. 234.

The third group to lament is the sea captains and sailors. This group has posed a major problem for translators.[187] However the individual terms are translated, it appears that all the people whose livelihood is derived from the sea are indicated: pilots, seafaring men, sailors, everyone that works the sea. These men also lament the loss and comment on the swiftness of the destruction. All three of the groups (kings, merchants, and sea traders) survey the destruction 'from a distance' (vv. 9,15,17). Not only does this distance underscore the horror of the destruction, but it also suggests that they are attempting to distance themselves from a judgment which they also deserve.[188] The sea traders add a similar lament to that of the other two groups.

Each of the three groups laments, 'Alas, alas, that great city!' This is repeated three times, almost verbatim (vv. 10,16,19). Their amazement is at least partially because the destruction takes place with such speed. 'In one hour' is usually interpreted metaphorically to mean an extremely short period of time.[189] For such an enterprise to fall so fast was devastating. From the perspective of modern-day technology, this horror and its speed of destruction evoke thoughts of the damage brought about by weapons of mass destruction.

Although the laments of the groups are remarkably similar, there are some distinctive features. Each group mourns in terms of its own interests: the kings marvel at the fall of such a 'strong city' (v. 10) and the merchants lament that she (the city) will no longer be adorned with gold and lavish garments (v. 16). The sea captains throw dust on their heads and weep for their loss of wealth (v. 19). (The significance of the throwing of dust on one's head as a sign of mourning is evident from Josh. 7:6; Job 2:12; Lam. 2:10; 1 Macc. 11:71-2.) The common denominator of all of these mourners is concern for the loss of their own status and/or fortune, not necessarily for the loss of a great city.

Verse 20, with its enthusiastic call to rejoice over the fall and destruction of Babylon, is an abrupt change of tone from the laments of the kings, merchants and seamen. Again, it is unclear whose voice is speaking. Probably it is a return to the voice of either the angel (vv. 2,3) or the heavenly voice (v. 4). Whichever it is, it is directly addressed to 'you saints and apostles and prophets'. Perhaps these are the souls under the altar (ch. 6), those who have suffered martyrdom. The qualifying comment, 'because God has pronounced judgment for you

---

[187] These terms are not entirely clear; see Mounce, pp. 331-32, and Aune, pp. 1004f. for details.

[188] H. Preisker, 'μακράν, μακρόθεν', *TDNT* IV (1967), p. 373.

[189] For example, in Josephus, *War* III 227f., the Jews burn up the Roman siege machines 'in one hour' (cf. also II 457, for a similar use).

against her', seems to support this perspective. The translation 'God has imposed on her the sentence she passed on you' also underscores this option and echoes v. 6 about God's retribution for her deeds (in this case, the killing of the saints).

In the final verses of ch. 18 (vv. 21-24), the author describes the devastation of the city from within. A dirge is introduced by a prophetic action performed by a 'strong angel'. This final angel violently throws a millstone into the sea (v. 21). This is a clear reflection of the prophetic action of Jeremiah (51:63-64; LXX 28:63-64), in which God says, 'When you finish reading this book, bind a stone to it, and cast it into the midst of the Euphrates and say, "Thus shall Babylon sink, to rise no more, because of the evil I am bringing upon her."'[190] It is interesting to note the three appearances of this 'strong angel'. He appears first in Rev. 5:2, where he guards the scroll with seven seals and then again in 10:1, where he appears with the little scroll and announces the seven peals of thunder which cannot be revealed. Here (ch. 18), he appears for the final time to pronounce the final destruction of Babylon/Rome. Could this third appearance also represent the consummation or completion of the contents of both scrolls?[191] The word used to describe the 'mighty fall' of the stone into the sea is βληθήσεται, from the same root used to describe the violent plunge of the swine into the sea in Jesus' miracle at Gadara (cf. Mk 5:13), and it is used in Acts 19:29 to describe the rush of the crowd into the Ephesian theatre. In denoting a violent plunge it indicates the violent and sudden destruction of Babylon/Rome.

The dirge in vv. 21-24 captures the sense of complete and utter desolation and devastation. Several times the phrase 'no more at all' heralds the reign of total silence. It is instructive to compare the 'no mores' of this desolation with the 'no mores' of the new heaven and new earth (21:1-7; 22:3-5). There will be no more music, no more craftmaking, no more mill-grinding, no more light, no more rejoicing over weddings. In contrast, in the new heaven and earth, there will be no more crying, no more pain or dying (21:4), no more night (23-25), and no more curse. It is worth looking more closely at the 'no mores' of Babylon: the sound of music will be heard no more (18:22). Various instruments were associated with various celebratory and festive events: timbrels, harps and flutes were associated with carousing (Isa. 5:12; cf. also Ezek. 26:13; Isa. 24:8) and rejoicing before the Lord (2 Sam. 6:5), at various festivals (Isa. 30:29) and even funerals (Mt. 9:23). Trumpets were used at the games and theatres (Juvenal IV, 249).

---

[190] Cf. also Neh. 9:11; *Sib.Or.* 5:155-61; Pliny, *Hist. Nat.* II 25.
[191] Cf. Caird, pp. 230-31.

In addition to music, the sounds of craftspeople are stilled (Rev. 18:22). Many crafts were essential features of ancient Rome including bricklaying, glassmaking, pottery, carving, sculpture, masonry, spinning, weaving, etc. With the fall of the economy (v. 22) comes the collapse of the crafts. The sound of the mills ceases. Wheat was ground by everyone almost every day so that every household would have owned and operated a mill of some kind. The stilling of the mills would imply the ceasing of everyday activity. Not only is there silence in the city, there is also darkness. The sequence here echoes Jer. 25:10, suggesting John's familiarity with prophetic literature. The joy of weddings has ceased as well. The implication here is that the city has no future, no hope of survival.

The translation of the final verses (23-24) is rough, but the imagery is vivid. The dirge is completed with the first phrase in v. 23a: 'The light of the lamp will not shine in you any longer; and the voice of the bridegroom and the bride will not be heard in you any longer...' The remainder of vv. 23 and 24 cite three clear reasons for this utter desolation and devastation: (1) The merchants had become proud and arrogant. (2) The city had deceived the nations with its religious apostasy (see anticipation in 17:2; 18:3). The word used here (v. 23) is sorcery or witchcraft, implying the religious character of the deception. This appears to correspond to the religious aspects of the false prophet (13:12-14), who apparently is in charge of causing the people to worship the beast by performing signs and wonders.[192] (3) The city is charged as responsible for the martyrdom of the prophets, saints and 'all who have been slain on the earth'. The persecution of the saints is now being avenged. Perhaps this is the time anticipated in ch. 6, where the souls under the altar (the martyrs) are told to await God's vengeance and vindication, which would eventually take place.

In summary, ch. 18 addresses the fall and destruction of Babylon/Rome, anticipated in 14:18; 17:16-18. Three reasons are given in v. 3 for her divine judgment from God: (1) The nations of the earth have participated in her immoralities (her religious apostasy). (2) The kings of the earth have become corrupt through their alliances with her. (3) The merchants of the earth have become arrogant and excessively wealthy through commercial interactions with her. However, God has had the 'last word' and Babylon, symbolic of the kingdoms of all time who have rejected God, is now laid desolate, inhabited only by birds of prey and disease.

---

[192] See Gause, p. 236.

Chapter 19

The first section of ch. 19 (19:1-5) includes *three responses* to the fall of Babylon (ch. 18): (1) a great multitude sings a hallelujah chorus (vv. 1-2); (2) the 24 elders and four creatures echo this worship (vv. 3-4); (3) a heavenly voice from the throne praises God (v. 5). The great multitude in vv. 1-2 is praising God for salvation, for God's righteous and true judgment of Babylon and for God's vengeance for the blood of the martyrs. The term 'hallelujah' is a Greek transliteration of a Hebrew liturgical formula (הללויה). It means 'praise the Lord' and was often used in Christian liturgy.[193] *Hallelu* is the plural imperative, 'Praise!' and *jah* is an abbreviated form of God's name, Yahweh. The form is often used in the Old Testament to introduce psalms (e.g. 106, 111-13, 117, 135, 146-50). It is also found in Hellenistic literature as a conclusion; for example, 'Hallelujah, holy, holy is the Lord, to the glory of God the Father, Amen' concludes *Apoc. Moses* (43:4; cf. Tob. 13:18; *3 Macc.* 7:13-14). It can also be used to conclude psalms (cf. Pss. 104:35; 105:45; 106:48).

Within this context, salvation is probably not so much personal individual salvation, as the triumphal culmination of God's entire redemptive plan. In particular, this group is praising God for his just judgments on Babylon. There is a parallel in 15:3 (the song of Moses sung by the 144,000 about God's victory over the beast), and an almost word-for-word verbatim parallel in 16:7b when the voice from the altar says '... true and righteous are thy judgments!' There is also a parallel in *Apoc. Moses* 27:5: 'Then the angels fell on the ground and worshiped the Lord saying, "You are just, O Lord, and you judge rightly."' In all of these parallels, the group or speaker is in heaven before the throne. In ch. 19, the praises become more explicit. The multitude praises God for his judgment on the 'great harlot' (Babylon/Rome, ch. 18) and his avenging of the blood of the martyrs (v. 2). The sins of the harlot (Babylon) have been referred to several times in earlier passages: Babylon has corrupted the kings of the earth (14:8; 17:2; 18:3); she has spilled the blood of the righteous martyrs (cf. allusions in 17:16; 18:24). Now the group in heaven is rejoicing over her destruction. All in all, the praise is for the righteousness and justice of God's judgment.[194]

The crowd resounds with a second 'Hallelujah! And the woman's smoke rises up forever and ever' (v. 3). Probably this is a reflection of Isa. 34:10 'Its smoke shall go up forever', referring to the enemies of

---

[193] Cf. J. Hempel, 'Hallelujah', *IDB* II (1962), pp. 514-15.
[194] See Gause, p. 238, who considers this a major theme of Revelation.

Zion. An additional reason for praise is supplied: the city is destroyed *forever*. The allusion to Babylon's burning echoes 18:9,18, where the kings, merchants and seamen lament the burning of the city. The emphasis is on the finality and totality of the devastation. Again, correctly and justifiably, the theme of God's righteous judgment predominates: God has punished the wicked; he has avenged the righteous who have been harmed; he has vindicated their righteousness – they were killed because of their righteousness, not because of criminal deeds.[195]

The 24 elders and four creatures who praise God around the throne join in the rejoicing over the destruction of Babylon (v. 4). They have appeared elsewhere in Revelation, responding to God's actions on earth (4:10; 5:8,14; 7:11; 11:16; 19:4). It is noteworthy that this is the final appearance of the elders and creatures in Revelation. Their 'Amen, hallelujah!' is similar to the conclusions in the Psalter (Ps. 106:48; cf. also 1 Chron. 16:36; Neh. 5:13). The elders and creatures first appear in the throne-room scene in ch. 4 and again in ch. 5, when the Lamb takes the scroll from God. They appear again in ch. 7 with the white-robed multitude (the redeemed, 7:11), at the opening of the seventh seal (11:17) and with the harpists in 14:3. In each of these appearances, the elders and creatures are around the throne, responding to God's actions with praise and worship. Their reappearance in ch. 19 is an appropriate final response to the conclusion of God's judgments.

A voice from the throne adds to the praise (v. 5). It is unclear whose voice this is, but most likely it is that of one of the heavenly beings around the throne. The voice invites another group to join the praises. A similar pattern is found in Psalm 148, where vv. 1-6 focus on the praise of God in heaven. Then, vv. 7-14 call for praise from the earth. In ch. 19, the heavenly voice functions like a worship leader, first leading the heavenly beings in praise (v. 4) and then inviting an even larger group to join (vv. 5-7). This larger group consists of 'all you bondservants, you who fear him, both small and great'. It is interesting that in 11:17-19, the elders and living creatures are worshiping God with a more expanded version of the same praise: 'We give thanks, O Lord God Almighty ... thou hast taken thy great power and hast reigned ... and the time has come ... to give their reward to thy bondservants the prophets, and to the saints and to those who fear thy name, the small and great.'

Perhaps the multitude of 19:4-6 is the same group referred to in 11:17. These are evidently *all* of God's servants, not just a select group. The phrase 'small and great' probably refers to socio-economic status as well as spiritual maturity. Everyone joins in the praises of God. This

---

[195] See Gause, p. 239.

textual event serves both as the glorious conclusion to the praise for the victory over Babylon (ch. 18) and as the introduction to the marriage supper of the Lamb (19:6-10). Everyone is praising God because the Lord, the Almighty, reigns (v. 6). The title 'God Almighty' suggests that God is the one who holds all things in his control. With the overthrow of Babylon and the outpouring of the final bowls of God's wrath, God's redemptive plan is consummated and the time of rejoicing has arrived. At the same time, the multitude are rejoicing because this Almighty God is the 'Lord, *our* God', perhaps suggesting the individual personal aspect of the relationship of God with each of his servants. God is not only in control of the universe; he is also Lord of each life.

Great sounds accompany the rejoicing of the multitude and introduce the supper (v. 6). This is an appropriate accompaniment to the establishment of God's reign on earth (cf. similar dramatic accompaniments of God's actions in Ezek. 1:24; 43:2; Dan. 10:6; Rev. 1:15). Three metaphors describe the powerful loudness of the singing and rejoicing: (1) the roaring of a huge crowd (cf. 19:1; *Ps. Sol.* 8:2); (2) the crashing of the sea (cf. 1:15; 14:2; Isa. 17:12; Ezek. 1:24); and (3) the crash of thunder (Rev. 6:1; 14:2; *3 Bar.* 11:3-6; 14:1-2).

Verse 7 shifts to an introduction of the marriage supper of the Lamb (vv. 6-10): 'Let us rejoice and be glad and give glory to him, for the marriage of the Lamb has come and his bride has made herself ready.'

The metaphor of marriage to represent the relationship between God and his people has its roots in the Old Testament. For example, God says to Israel, 'I will betroth you to me forever.'[196] This same idea is found in the New Testament. Jesus compares the kingdom of heaven to a marriage feast given by a king for his son (Mt. 22:2ff.). Paul also uses marriage imagery to explain the bond between Christ and his Church. As a man leaves his parents to commit his life to his wife, thus creating a single unit, the Church separate from the world to commit themselves to Christ. This enables Christ to present the righteous 'holy and blameless' (Eph. 5.27) to God.[197] This multitude, then (v. 6), is comprised of the righteous of all time.

In biblical times two major events were involved in a marriage: betrothal and the wedding itself. The betrothal involved a commitment of faithfulness almost as binding as the wedding vows. It should be

---

[196] Hos. 2:19; cf. Isa. 54:6-7 for a similar passage. For an extensive discussion see J. Jeremias, 'γαμέω νυμφίος', *TDNT* IV (1967), pp. 1099-1106; Halle Ethelbert Stauffer 'γάμος,' *TDOT* I (1964), pp. 657-58.

[197] Eph. 5:32; 2 Cor. 11:2; cf. also early Christian literature: *2 Clem.* 14.3; Tertullian, *Adversus Marcionem* 5.18; Clement of Alexandria, *Stromata* 3.6; Methodius, *Symposium* 7.7; Augustine, *Sermons* 40.6.

understood that the Church is espoused currently to Christ and is waiting for his return for his bride (19:6-10). Faith enables the Church to maintain her commitment and to trust in his promise to return. In this passage, the bride (the righteous of all time) is present to meet her bridegroom (Christ).

The bride is pictured arrayed in special bridal clothes, fine linen, bright and pure. These undoubtedly represent faithfulness and purity. The grammar used (the passive voice) to describe her clothes suggests that they were given to her by another.[198] It is notable that the bride is clothed in linen, which according to the text, symbolizes 'the righteous deeds of the saints' (v. 8). The term 'deeds' (τὰ δικαῶματα) or 'acts' is plural, suggesting that these are the many deeds of obedience and faithfulness that comprise the life of the one who is committed to God, rather than the one act of salvation. The deeds function as adornments to the Church's already pure and transformed state. The beauty and purity of the bride is in marked contrast to the ugliness and sensuality of the harlot in ch. 18, who is dressed in purple and scarlet (carnality) and adorned with a gaudy assortment of jewelry indicative of her status as a prostitute.

The marriage supper itself appears to be introduced by the interpretive angel seen in ch. 17: 'Blessed are those who are invited to the marriage supper of the Lamb' (v. 9). This is the fourth of the seven beatitudes in Revelation (1:3; 14:13; 16:15; 19:9; 20:6; 22:7,14). The introductory command to John to write indicates that what follows is especially significant. The confirmatory statement following the beatitude, 'These are true words of God', further underscores the importance of this blessing. The nature of the blessing is the invitation to the marriage supper. This call assures the invited ones that they will indeed be included in the feast.[199] Curiously, John mistakes the interpreting angel for the Lord and falls down before him (v. 10). This event is repeated in 22:8-9. It is not clear why John mistakes the angel's identity. Perhaps his response is actually to the immediately preceding words rather than to the angel himself: in both cases (in the event in ch. 19 and when he refers back to it in ch. 22), God affirms the reliability of his words. In 19:9, the marriage-supper scene has unfolded and the interpreter says, 'These are the true words of God.' In 22:8-9, the Lord says, 'Behold, I am coming quickly. Blessed is he who heeds the words of the prophecy of this book' (22:7). John affirms his own witness, that he has heard and seen 'these things' (22:8). In 19:10, the

---

[198] Gause, p. 242.
[199] *Ibid.*

angel interprets John's action as a response to himself and refuses to be worshiped.

Revelation 19:10 is especially significant because the angel interprets the meaning of 'the testimony (or witness) of Jesus'. The interpreter states that the testimony of Jesus is the 'spirit of prophecy', which equates the testimony with the content of the prophetic message delivered by Jesus. An interpretive issue here revolves around whether the testimony is *about* Jesus or *by* him. The grammatical construction is ambiguous, and there are many possible interpretations.[200] As explained above, it should probably be interpreted as the testimony *by* Jesus. This is summarized in Mk 1:15: 'The kingdom of God is at hand; repent and believe in the gospel.' Jesus' message, then, is the essence of the prophetic one, the coming of God's Kingdom. In fact, this statement is particularly significant in that it identifies New Testament prophecy as in the same category as Old Testament prophecy; indeed it unifies Old Testament and New Testament saints and prophets in the same relation to the witness of Jesus – all are co-worshipers and fellow servants of God. The reason for this unity is clear: all have the same testimony or witness of Jesus,[201] namely 'to distinguish the one true God and his righteousness from idolatry and its evils'.[202] Indeed, this is the key point of Revelation itself as prophecy, to describe the triumph of the true God over the forces of evil. The interpreting angel underscores this: 'I am a fellow servant with you and your brothers and sisters the prophets, and with those who keep the words of this book. Worship God' (19:10, 22:9). According to the angel, he also belongs to the category of prophet.

The pertinent question is, What is prophecy for the seer? Clearly, the author views the text of Revelation itself as prophecy (1:3; 22:6-7, 18-19). Moreover, the book is composed of the three primary elements of prophecy.[203] (1) It includes *discernment* of the situation of the time in which it was written. A major emphasis of Revelation is the exposition of deception by the truth, which brings all hidden things into the light of God's perspective. In this way, the author calls the churches to be aware of their surroundings, in which they are called to witness. (2) The text certainly includes *prediction*. The author clearly distinguishes 'what is' from 'what must take place after this', namely, the coming of God's kingdom (cf. 1:1,19; 4:1). (3) Finally, prophecy elicits or demands a *response* to its presentation of the truth. In Revela-

---

[200] See Aune, pp. 1038-39, for discussion.
[201] See Gause, p. 243; Bauckham, pp. 118-19.
[202] Bauckham, p. 121.
[203] *Ibid.*, pp. 148-49.

tion, the reader is aware that there is the possibility of repentance, although people reject it and instead blaspheme. This hope for repentance, however, comes to an end with their final rejection, and God's judgment is carried out in the remainder of the text (see particularly chs. 17-19). Whereas the Ninevites repented and were spared (see Jonah), the people of the beast's kingdom merely respond with more blasphemy and are thus judged and condemned to their final fate, the Lake of Fire (Rev. 20:11-15).

There are two additional relevant features of prophecy which Revelation as prophecy fulfills.[204] First, the biblical tradition understands God to be consistent in his acts of salvation and judgment. Therefore, these can and should be considered as models for what he will do in the future. The author of Revelation clearly follows this tradition, echoing and reflecting Old Testament prophecies and using Old Testament imagery, such as the Exodus, to highlight his own prophecy. For example, John echoes God's judgment on Tyre when he addresses the doom of Babylon. His readers would further understand his words to refer to their current situation under the power and suppression of Rome. There is always an element in this kind of prophecy that allows the prophecy to transcend the example from the past. The prophecy, then, allows for the prophetic principle to apply to a later situation which surpasses the wickedness or circumstance of the current situation. In this way, the author of Revelation reflects similar past situations (e.g. the Exodus or the captivity by Babylon) but allows the reader to apply the principle to the current situation, which usually transcends the original reference in terms of wickedness, destruction, etc.

Second, prophetic promise often goes beyond the historic fulfillment.[205] For example, the restoration of Israel after the Babylonian captivity did not completely fulfill the prophetic expectation. Certainly, Israel was restored and vindicated, but there is still a sense that the ultimate fulfillment is yet to come. Here the hope in an ultimate eschatological event continues as in most of apocalyptic eschatology.[206] In this way, prophecies are taken to be partially fulfilled by the current situation while encouraging hope in the future ultimate arrival of the reign of God at the end of time.

Revelation, in its peculiar relation to the ultimate fulfillment of all prophecy, draws many of the strands of prophecy together to create a 'kind of eschatological hyperbole that intrinsically transcends [its] con-

---

[204] Cf. Bauckham, pp. 152-56, for a complete discussion of this concept.
[205] *Ibid.*, p. 153.
[206] *Ibid.*, p. 154.

text'.[207] The author of Revelation accomplishes this by using universalist language. So the 'multitude' in 5:9 and 7:9 is from 'every tribe, and tongue, and people, and nation'; the eternal gospel is announced to all nations (14:6); the trial during the reign of the beast is on the 'whole world' (3:10); the beast's reign encompasses 'all the inhabitants of the earth' (13:7-8); the whole world is represented at the battle of Armageddon (16:14); Babylon deceives 'all nations' (14:8; 18:3,23). The coming of God's kingdom is eschatologically universal and transcends both the past situation (e.g. the Exodus) and the historic situation of the readers. At the same time, the readers can relate to the message of the apocalypse because while having a universal hope, it still is relevant to their particular specific historic situation: e.g. Babylon may represent the universal and final confrontation between God and evil, but it also reflects the readers' situation with the battle between the power of Rome and the Church.

In summary, Revelation itself is prophecy that unites Old Testament and New Testament prophecy, as well as the words and witness of all saints and prophets: all those who are righteous hold to the 'testimony or witness of Jesus' in that all prophecy anticipates the coming kingdom of God.

From the text of Revelation 19, one expects a description of the marriage feast to follow, but as often in Revelation the details are revealed later (see chs. 21-22 for the details of the supper). Perhaps this great feast is anticipated in Isa. 25:6-8, which states that the Lord prepares a great banquet on Mount Zion and 'swallows up death forever'. Jesus himself refers to such a meal when he says that people from all points of the compass will 'recline at the table in the kingdom of God' (Lk. 13:29; see also Mt. 26:29). The rejoicing of the righteous at the meal provides a marked contrast to the horrifying supper of God described in the following passage (19:17-18), where the birds of prey are summoned to a supper to eat the flesh of God's conquered enemies.

In vv. 7-9, the righteous are portrayed as both the bride and the guests. Again, the flexible nature of apocalyptic writing must be taken into account. The main point is that the bride (the righteous of all time) is now prepared to meet Christ. It was assumed and accepted in ancient times that whoever was invited to a wedding would also be staying for the following celebrations. Although this passage does not directly address the identification of the guests, it probably can be inferred from the great multitude, 'his servants, small and great' (v. 5), that this group includes the righteous saints from all time.

---

[207] *Ibid.*, p. 155.

This scene of worship and praise for God's victory, judgment and the arrival of the marriage feast of the Lamb concludes the larger unit, 17:1-19:10. There follows an abrupt shift to the entrance of the Bridegroom, the white horse warrior who rides forth to make war and to bring the present age to a close.

The motif of heaven opening is associated directly with divine revelation. The throne-room scene (ch. 4) is introduced by 'a door standing open' (4:1): again in 15:5 the 'Temple of the tabernacle of testimony in heaven' opens to introduce the seven angels with bowls of God's wrath. Luke 3:21,22 describes the heavens opening at Jesus' baptism when the Holy Spirit descends on him; they open also at Stephen's martyrdom (Acts 7:56) and at the revelation to Peter about Cornelius (Acts 10:11). This association also reflects Ezek. 1:1, where the heavens open to enable Ezekiel to receive the 'visions of God'.[208] The readers would understand that something particularly special is about to be revealed.

The warrior figure on a white horse emerges from the open heavens. This is certainly Christ returning with the armies of his saints (v. 4) to confront the beast with his armies of the wicked. The description here echoes in many respects the description of the glorified Christ in Rev. 1:13. First, he is faithful and true. 'Faithful witness' is the first description of him in Rev. 1:5; he is again characterized in his appearance to the Laodicean church as the 'faithful and true witness' (3:14). It is notable that these characteristics are mentioned first here. Christ has been faithful, trustworthy, and reliable as to his promises. He is now riding forth to carry out the next stage of his faithful promise, to fulfill the covenant relationship promised by God. This ultimately involves confrontation with the forces of wickedness themselves.

Another descriptive phrase is 'in righteousness (or justice) he judges and wages war'. The use of the present tense suggests customary or usual actions. Hence, not only are his immediate actions of destroying his enemies just actions, but these terms and tenses suggest that his past actions have also been just.[209] His title 'faithful and true' should be understood in relation to the previous texts, where he is called faithful and true Witness (1:5; 3:14). Just as he has been faithful and true in carrying out God's promises in the past, he is now faithful in carrying

---

[208] This association is also found in apocalyptic literature such as *2 Bar.* 22:1 (cf. also *Test. Levi* 2:6).

[209] See T. Holtz, *Die Christologie der Apokalypse des Johannes*, 2 vols., 2nd ed. (Berlin: Akademie Verlag, 1971), pp. 169-70; Mathias Rissi, *The Future of the World: An Exegetical Study of Revelation 19:11–22:15*, SBT 23 [2nd series] (Naperville, IL: Allenson, n.d.), p. 22; see also Mounce, p. 345, and Aune, pp. 1053-54, for the relation to the Old Testament concept of God as judge.

out the remainder of God's plan. A further understanding of truth in relation to witness is important here: the truth, symbolized by the two-edged sword, is indeed two-edged as witness; only the witness to the truth can expose lies and deception and lead people from the worship of the beast to the worship of God. On the other hand, when this witness is rejected, it becomes the means by which such lies and deception are judged and condemned.[210]

The imagery here is not only military; it is also judicial:[211] the sword in his mouth is his word of judgment (cf. 1:16; 2:12,16). His eyes as a flame reveal hidden lies and judge these by the truth (cf. 1:14; 2:18,23). His faithfulness to the truth ultimately qualifies him to judge and condemn the lies and deception which bind the nations to the beast (cf. Jn 12:46-50, where the Word which comes to save the lost becomes the means of condemnation when rejected).

The third descriptive passage includes two parts: (1) 'his eyes are as a flame of fire' directly reflects the vision of Christ in 1:14 and suggests that nothing can be hidden from him; (2) he is also wearing 'many diadems'. These are royal tiaras worn in bands like a turban, symbolizing rulership. Each band represents an area of the person's governance.[212] His many diadems contrast sharply with the mere seven crowns of the dragon (one on each of the seven heads, 12:3), and the ten crowns of the beast (one on each of the ten horns, 13:1). In the ancient world, kings wore appropriate numbers of crowns symbolizing the extent of their rule. For example, Ptolemy VI entered Antioch (c. 169 BCE) wearing two crowns representing his rule over Egypt and Asia.[213] Christ as the 'King of Kings and Lord of Lords' appropriately wears 'many diadems' (v. 16). His sovereignty is unlimited.

The white horse rider's name is unknown to everyone but himself (v. 12). Evidently, the name is observable to others, but the meaning is not apparent.[214] There are many interpretations of what it means: the reason for the secret and where the name is inscribed.[215] Perhaps it is relevant to recall the secrecy motif in apocalyptic literature in this context. Probably, the best interpretation at this point is that the mystery underscores his divine status: the divine always involves some aspect of the unknown.

Christ's robe is dipped in blood (v. 13), which is the basis for the metaphor of blood and wine. This metaphor is also found in Isa. 63:1-6,

---

[210] Bauckham, p. 105; see also Rev. 15:3; 16:7; 19:2, which connect justice and truth.
[211] Bauckham, p. 105.
[212] Gause, p. 244.
[213] 1 Macc. 11:13; Josephus, *War*, XIII 113.
[214] Gause, p. 244.
[215] See Aune, pp. 1055-57; Mounce, pp. 344-45, for discussion of these theories.

where the prophet cites God as answering the prophet's inquiry about why his garments are stained red like blood and spilled wine. God answers, 'I trod them (his enemies) in my anger and trampled them in my wrath; their life-blood is sprinkled upon my garments.' This metaphor is particularly relevant since wine and blood have been linked earlier in the description of the harlot (ch. 17): she is 'drunk with the blood of the saints' (17:6). In this passage, Christ's robe is stained not by blood from his own injuries, but from the blood of his enemies. A similar association can be seen in a passage of the Palestinian Targum on Gen. 49:11, which reads: 'How beauteous is the King Messiah! Binding his loins and going forth to war against them that hate him, he will slay kings with princes, and make the rivers red with the blood of their slain... His garments will be dipped in blood, and he himself, like the juice of the winepress' (cf. Rev. 14:14-20). The bloodstained divine warrior coming to conquer his enemies is a common theme in the Old Testament as well.[216] Certainly, in Revelation Christ's bloodstained garments symbolize the victory that is about to take place.

In seeming contrast to v. 12 (his name is unknown), the rider is identified in v. 13 as 'The Word of God' (v. 13). In v. 13 the name 'The Word' is linked with the description in v. 15 of the two-edged sword in Christ's mouth (see Heb. 4:12). In Hebrew thought a word is not a static thing, but an active agent that enables the intention of the speaker to be achieved.[217] In this sense, the Word of God fulfills his divine purpose, which is to 'smite the nations' (v. 15). It is significant that as the world was created by 'the Word' (Jn 1:3), it will now be destroyed by that same 'Word'. The very same Word which came bringing truth and salvation (Jn 1:1-14; 12:46-50) now will judge and condemn the world.

Christ is not alone; he is accompanied by armies from heaven (v. 14). They are dressed in pure white linen and are riding on white horses. Although it would seem that this army could be comprised of heavenly beings and/or angels, their description (wearing white, pure linen) suggests that they are more likely the 'called, chosen and faithful' mentioned in 17:14. Probably, then, this army is composed of the righteous saints. In any case, there is no evidence that they participate in the battle.

Christ attacks in three ways. (1) He smites with the sword (cf. also Dan. 11:4), his Word of judgment, as mentioned above. The Word brings salvation, but when rejected becomes the means of condemna-

---

[216] E.g. Exod. 15; Deut. 33; Judg. 5; Heb. 3; Isa. 26:16–27:6; 59:15-20; Zech. 14:1-21. See also T. Hiebert, 'Divine Warrior', in *ABD* VI (1992), pp. 876-80.

[217] Mounce, p. 346.

tion and judgment. The point that John is making by the use of the figure of the two-edged sword in Christ's mouth is that the Word itself is the instrument which brings about the judgment. (2) He will rule with a rod of iron. Psalm 2:9 sheds light on the meaning of ruling with a rod of iron. The term 'rule' (ποιμάνει) can have the sense of gentle care as in Rev. 7:17, where it explains that the Lamb will guide the redeemed to springs of water. In the other citations in Revelation (2:27; 12:5; 19:15) the term is accompanied by the phrase 'with a rod of iron' connoting a sense of punishment. The imagery of the rod indicates two implements: a shepherd's crook can be used in gentle guidance of the sheep, but it can also be used as a weapon to protect the sheep from external danger, such as from wild animals. This destructive connotation is clearly meant here: Christ is riding forth to destroy his enemies, not only with the sword, but also with the rod of iron (see also Zech. 9:11-14). The dual nature of the rod of Christ provides vivid imagery of his rule: he rules with justice as well as with mercy. As severe as his judgments are, they are tempered by mercy. Here, however, the world has had the chance to repent. Instead they have rejected God, even blasphemed during the final plagues (see ch. 16). Hence, Christ is coming with severe and total judgment and destruction. (3) Finally, he will tread the winepress of the fierce wrath of God the Almighty (v. 15). The winepress as a metaphor for divine judgment is often found in the Old Testament (cf. e.g. Isa. 63:2-3). It was also used in Rev. 14:19-20 as a symbol of God's wrath. Perhaps that reference (ch. 14) is being elaborated upon here (ch. 19).

The final description of Christ is the title 'King of Kings and Lord of Lords' (v. 16). It is unclear how this mention of his name relates to the secret name mentioned in v. 12, except that whereas the secret name is unintelligible, this one is understandable. There are many interpretations of its meaning and significance. In fact, one scholar has even computed the name to equal the number 777 in vivid contrast to the beast's number 666. However, in order to arrive at the figure, he translated the name into Aramaic and omitted the 'and'.[218] In any case, the main point of the name is to emphasize the universality of Christ's sovereignty and power over his enemies. He is ruler of the entire universe.

The seer is not shown the actual battle. The scene immediately shifts to the results, the great supper of God (vv. 17-21). The scene opens with the announcement by the angel in the sun, a location which (1) indicates a position of splendor appropriate to the messenger of victory;

---

[218] See Patrick Skehan, 'King of Kings, Lord of Lords (*Apoc.* 19:16)', *CBQ* 10 (1948), p. 398.

(2) provides the best position from which to deliver his message effectively. The message itself is horrific and is addressed to the birds of prey: 'Come to the great supper to gorge on the flesh of the fallen!' (vv. 17-18). This invitation reflects several passages in the Old Testament. Ezekiel 39:17 includes a summons to the birds to come to God's feast to eat of the flesh and blood of the mighty princes. This supper of God presents a startling contrast to the rejoicing at the marriage supper of the Lamb (19:7). God has provided the means for humans to choose which 'supper' to attend. Revelation gives no indication that the choice is still available at the eschatological time. Quite clearly, the time to choose is *now* – the time of the author as well as the time of every reader.[219]

Verse 18 lists the kinds of people who will be involved. They include all classes and levels of status: kings (government), commanders (military), mighty men and their horses, *all people,* free and slave, small and great. God's judgment makes no distinction – all of God's enemies will be destroyed.

Verses 18 and 19 add a few details to the battle that were merely alluded to in 16:13-16 and 17:14. Chapter 16 sets the scene in a 'place called in Hebrew Har-Magedon' (16:16). The armies of the world are gathered together by the demonic spirits that emerge from the mouth of the dragon, the beast and the false prophet. Revelation 17:14 specifies Christ's name as 'King of Kings and Lord of Lords'. The armies of the 'called, chosen and faithful' are with him. Both of these references (16:13-16 and 17:14) clearly refer to this same event because both specify that God or Christ is waging war with the beast and his armies (16:14; 17:14; 19:19). The war itself is not described, so it is uncertain what form this confrontation will take. The main point is that although the beast and his followers gather to confront Christ, it is indeed God who is in control (see 17:17, 'God has put it in their hearts to execute his purpose').

The beast and false prophet are both 'seized', a term which usually means 'to lay hold of with hostile intent'. The false prophet is again characterized by his two main objectives: (1) deception of humans by working great signs (cf. 13:13-15) and (2) branding of the worshipers of the beast with the mark (cf. 13:16-17). Both of these functions suggest a relation to religion. It can probably be inferred that the false prophet represents the religious component of the beast's reign. Both of them are thrown *alive* into the Lake of Fire (19:20).

---

[219] Cf. Bauckham, pp. 101-102, who discusses the issue of the response to God's final plagues as blasphemy rather than repentance.

Although the 'Lake of Fire' is not found in Old Testament tradition, divine punishment by fire is frequent. The Psalmist declares, 'May our God come and not keep silence; fire devours before him' (Ps. 50:3; cf. also Lev. 10:2; Num. 16:35). Apocalyptic literature also refers to divine punishment by fire. For example, 1 En. 54:1 speaks of 'a deep valley with burning fire' as the location of divine judgment. 2 Enoch 10 describes it as a place of terror with a variety of tortures, including a fiery river. Gehenna (an abbreviation of 'valley of the son of Hinnom'), the modern Wadi or Rababi, is located to the south and west of Jerusalem. It was often associated with fire and the wicked dead in New Testament times because of its reputation as an ancient cultic site where human sacrifices were offered (Mt. 5:22; Mk 9:43). Because of this extreme wickedness it was denounced by Old Testament prophets (Jer. 7:32; 19:6) and was equated with the place of final judgment in apocalyptic literature.[220] Revelation 19:20 is the first reference to the Lake of Fire in Revelation, and the term appears nowhere else in the New Testament. A general description, however, can be obtained from Revelation itself: it is the final punishment for the beast, the false prophet (19:20), and the Devil himself (20:10). Death and Hell are also cast there (20:14) along with all those whose names are not found in the Book of Life, after the Great White Throne Judgment (20:15). This includes all evil doers (21:8). The torment there is constant (day and night, 20:10); it is called the second death (20:14,15; 21:8); it is like burning sulfur (brimstone) and reflects the punishment wrought upon Sodom and Gomorrah (Lk. 17:29). In short, the punishment there is everlasting (20:10), and is for spiritual beings (19:20; 20:10) as well as for all the wicked (20:14,15; 21:8).

The remainder of the wicked armies are destroyed by the sword 'projecting from the mouth of Christ' (v. 21). Several metaphors are linked here, as discussed earlier. The word of divine judgment is linked with the sword as the means of killing the wicked. Indeed, God's wrath destroys them all and the birds of prey eat their remains. The ancients were haunted by the idea of remaining unburied. The Old Testament has numerous references to this effect; for example, Deut. 28:26 says, 'And your dead body shall be the food for all birds of the air and for the beasts of the earth, and there shall be no one to frighten them away' (see also 19:17-18). The destruction by Christ, the Word, is comprehensive.

---

[220] See Jeremias, 'γέεννα', *TDNT* I (1964), pp. 657-58.

Reflection and Response (Part 6)

Reflection
This section of Revelation (chs. 6-19) is actually a coherent unit in which the message is repeated over and over: the righteous, those who are faithful to God and acknowledge his Lordship of their lives, will triumph with God at the end. Even if they suffer martyrdom during their earthly existence like the souls under the altar (ch. 6), they will still celebrate with the great multitude at the marriage supper of the Lamb (ch. 19). In contrast, the wicked, those who do not repent of their idolatry and immorality (chs. 6; 9; 13; 17-18), will experience the outpouring of God's wrath (the seals, the trumpets, and finally the bowls). The metaphorical section (chs. 11-13) echoes this same theme: God will triumph over evil and will ultimately vindicate the righteous and destroy the wicked. Again and again the author draws the vivid contrast between the righteous who are saved by the blood of the Lamb and the wicked who are destroyed by the wrath of the Lamb.

This text of Revelation is so vast and describes such devastation, beyond human experience, that one is tempted to appreciate it only for its literary awesomeness and to fail to allow it to challenge one's own heart. Yet it is important to hear the message of this text and allow the Holy Spirit to search our hearts. With this in mind, the following questions are suggested: Are there individuals or groups known to you who are not being faithful to the Lordship of God? What are the signs which suggest this identification to you? To what extent do these people resemble the descriptions of the wicked who refuse to acknowledge God as Lord (see especially chs. 6 and 9)? Is there some way to bring the fact of God's coming judgment to their attention?

It is not enough to reflect on others only. It is important to consider one's own state before God. These questions might be helpful. Are there areas in my life which indicate unfaithfulness to God as described in the text of Revelation? What is my attitude about behavior that might indicate a lack of adherence to the Lordship of God? How often do I reflect on what his Lordship means in terms of how I live my life? Are there opportunities in my church for me to repent and change my attitude? Have I made use of these opportunities so that God's Lordship would be reflected more effectively? How often do I allow the Spirit to search my life to reaffirm the Lordship of God over my behavior?

Response
These are extremely serious issues to consider; yet the consequences of not considering them are even more serious. The following suggestions might be helpful by way of response:

1. Prayerfully examine your life, reflecting carefully on the questions suggested above. Ask the Holy Spirit to indicate areas that are especially problematic in relation to the Lordship of God.
2. As you identify each area, describe each in a personal journal. Be as specific as possible.
3. Consult with a brother or sister, confessing the problems you have discovered.
4. Join a prayer group and/or Bible study group to which you can be accountable and which can add support and spiritual strength. Particularly emphasize relevant passages of Scripture.
5. Periodically review your progress. Have any of the areas regressed? Are some of them progressing? What supports or verifies your answer? You should include a trusted friend in this evaluative process.

Revelation 20:1-22:21

Chapter 20

Chapter 19, as noted, concludes with the great supper of God (vv. 17-21) where the enemies of God are completely destroyed and the birds eat the remains. The beast and false prophet are cast into the Lake of Fire (v. 20). The next vision (of Satan bound, 20:1-2) follows, with the typical introduction of a new vision, 'And I saw' (see also 19:11,17,19; 20:1,4,12; 21:1). An angel comes from heaven with the key to the abyss and a great chain to bind Satan (v. 1). In other apocalyptic literature, the abyss was thought to be a 'bottomless' subterranean cavern used to imprison those waiting to be judged by God. For example, Jude 6 explains that the fallen angels are kept in eternal bonds waiting for the great day of judgment. Similarly, *1 En.* 88:1 describes the place as 'narrow and deep, horrible and dark' (cf. also Jude 5; Lk. 8:31). The angel with the key is not identified but he could be the one given the key to open the abyss to release the plague of locusts (9:1-11). In any case, the angel 'seizes' Satan and binds him. The term 'seizes', as noted, has the connotation of the exercise of power ('to lay hold of with hostile intent').[1] All four titles of Satan in Revelation are mentioned in v. 2: Satan, dragon (Rev. 12:7-8); serpent (12:15); and devil (12:12). It is significant that one angel is able to bind him and that his demons are conspicuously absent. Apparently they are powerless while Satan is being bound.

There is debate about when the binding of Satan takes place. Some scholars suggest it refers to the present age: Satan is unable to destroy or deter the spread of the Church in the current era.[2] In contrast, others argue that this event indicates that Satan is *completely powerless* during the millennial period, an eschatological era.[3] A careful consideration of

---

[1] Mounce, p. 352 n. 5.
[2] Hendricksen, p. 226.
[3] Cf. Walvoord, p. 291.

this passage appears to support more strongly the second interpretation, but this is the subject of much debate among scholars. Verses 2-3 explicitly state that Satan is bound for a thousand years in the abyss which is *shut* and *sealed*. The purpose is also stated: 'So that he should not deceive the nations any longer, until the thousand years are completed; after these things he must be released for a short time' (v. 3). 'Shut' and 'sealed' are fairly strong terms, indicating that Satan's power is at least temporarily cut off. The figure of sealing the pit recalls the actions of the Romans: when they imprisoned someone they sealed the door with the imperial seal. Similarly, God 'seals' the pit where Satan is bound: he is powerless to escape until God allows him to do so.[4] The language describing Satan's release further supports the conclusion that Satan's release is in God's control – Satan is released so that the remainder of God's plan will be accomplished. This imprisonment is not necessarily for punishment. It is specifically to shut down Satan's activity temporarily (v. 3).

The nations mentioned in v. 3 could be the remnants of the nations who survived the Battle of Armageddon or could be those which did not oppose the Messiah. They are most likely the survivors from the Battle of Armageddon (see chs. 19–21). God completely destroys the armies (18:19-21), but not necessarily all the *people of the world*.

The scene shifts to the thousand-year reign itself (vv. 4-6). Thrones are seen. It is not exactly clear who is sitting on them. Whoever they are, the seer also sees the souls of the martyrs, 'those who had been beheaded because of the testimony of Jesus' and 'the righteous Jews of the Tribulation' (those who had not worshiped the beast and had not received the mark of the beast). Whether these are sitting on the thrones or whether the seated ones are a heavenly group is not certain. Other references in the New Testament suggest several options: (1) in Mt. 19:28, the Twelve Apostles expect to reign with Christ; (2) in 1 Cor. 6:2-3, the Church is reminded that they will judge both the world and angels; (3) in Rev. 3:21, all who remain faithful are promised to reign; (4) Dan. 4:26 suggests that the judges will be a heavenly court. The text is disturbingly ambiguous on this issue. Two groups in Rev. 20:4 are particularly named: (1) 'those who had been beheaded because of the testimony of Jesus and because of the Word of God', and (2) 'those who had not received the mark of the beast'. The term for 'beheaded' is probably a general term representing all those who have wholly committed themselves to Christ. In ancient Rome, there were various methods of execution. The term used here is decapitation by an axe. It seems strange that the group would be so selective. Also,

---

[4] See Gause, pp. 251-52.

there are such remarkable similarities between the souls under the altar (6:9; 20:4) and this group that it is most probable that they are the same group – the righteous who have given their lives for God. The second group is somewhat more easily identifiable. Those who refused to receive the mark would have to be the righteous Jews who survived (or were killed) in the Tribulation (the offspring of the sun-clothed woman, 12:1-8). Hence, v. 4 seems to indicate that all the righteous will be included with Christ in the millennium even if they are not the ones sitting on the thrones of v. 4.

Another ambiguity has to do with the thousand-year reign: Is this a literal thousand years or is it merely symbolic of a long but indefinite time? Behind this issue lies the even more complex issue about the nature of the millennial reign and when it will take place.[5] The text of Revelation is decidedly vague on many of the theological issues about the millennium. The important point here is that there is a lengthy period of time during which Christ reigns with the saints.[6] Bauckham suggests that there is mainly one point, that the author has only one purpose for the millennium in Revelation: 'the theological point of the millennium is solely to demonstrate the triumph of the martyrs'; it serves mainly to vindicate the martyrs whose witness resulted in death. These martyrs will triumph in the kingdom of Christ while Satan and his cohorts will be bound. Although Satan is released to deceive the nations one final time, God and Christ, along with the martyrs, are ultimately triumphant. This interpretation of Revelation suggests, however, that John is not concerned with the concept of a temporary earthly messianic kingdom as portrayed in Jewish apocalyptic.[7] Also during this time, Satan is bound (v. 3). Unfortunately, this passage (ch. 20) does not describe the details about Christ's reign. Old Testament prophets like Isaiah (cf. especially 11:1-16; 65:20-25; Dan. 7:14-27) give some details, for example, that people will live considerably longer than during our present time ('a child will be 100 years old ...' Isa. 65:20), and there will be total harmony in nature (the lion will lie down with the lamb, Isa. 11:6-9, etc.). In any case, Revelation does not address the nature of the reign. The seer focuses primarily on the fact that there is a lengthy event during which Christ reigns with the righteous and Satan is bound (vv. 3-4).

---

[5] See Mounce, pp. 356-58; Aune, pp. 1089-90; Ladd, p. 265, etc. (For the position that the millennium should not be viewed literally, see Bauckham, p. 108.)

[6] See Bauckham, pp. 106-108, for an explanation for Revelation's ambiguity on so many issues.

[7] See *2 Bar.* 40:3; *4 Ezra* 7:28-29.

The seer's concern turns to the two resurrections. The most challenging issues revolve around whether there are actually one or two resurrections, who is involved and how the resurrections relate to the first and second deaths. According to ch. 20 there are two resurrections and two deaths. They can be differentiated and explained as follows.

The first resurrection is identified in vv. 4-6 as immediately preceding the thousand-year reign of Christ. It includes the martyrs who died because of the testimony of Jesus and the Word of God, and those who did not take the mark of the beast during the Tribulation (v. 4). It is difficult to identify these groups with certainty, but probably the martyrs who died because of the testimony of Jesus and the Word of God should be associated with the 'saints under the altar' (7:13). Although it is not entirely clear who these represent, they are certainly people who have lost their lives because of their belief in God. The second group (those who did not take the mark of the beast) should probably be identified as the 144,000 who did not take the mark and were sealed by God during the Tribulation (see 7:4-8; 14:1-5; 15:2-4). A third group is most likely also included in the 1000-year reign, but not mentioned here: the righteous who come with the white horse rider to fight the Battle of Armageddon (19:14). They are referred to briefly as with Christ in this battle (17:14). The seer describes them in 20:6 as 'Blessed and holy'. He also says that the second death has 'no power over them', and that they will be 'priests of God and of Christ and will reign with him for a thousand years' (20:6). This is another of the seven beatitudes in Revelation. These people are blessed because they do not participate in the second death, and because they are priests of God and Christ. As priests, they are privileged to have direct access to the presence of God.

There is no reason to interpret the above text as suggesting that the Old Testament sacrificial system will be reinstated; indeed, Revelation is quite clear that there is no Temple in the Holy City (21:22). As priests of God and Christ, the righteous will abide in his presence directly. Perhaps one can see a fulfillment of the promise of priesthood in Exod. 19:6, where God promises: 'You shall be called the priests of the Lord, the ministers of the Holy One.'[8] In any case, these are the ones who will reign with Christ for a thousand years (Rev. 20:6). The first resurrection, then, is that of the righteous who died before and during the Tribulation. This resurrection is distinct from the second resurrection, when all the wicked dead will be raised to stand before God's White Throne Judgment (vv. 11-13).

---

[8] Cf. E. Schüssler Fiorenza, *Priester für Gott* (Münster: Aschendorff, 1972), pp. 336-38.

In contrast to the first resurrection stands the 'second death' (vv. 6,14), which is reserved for the wicked. The text implies a first death, most likely death in human existence. The wicked dead, both small and great from all time, appear from everywhere, even the sea (vv. 12-13), to stand before the Great White Throne of God (v. 11). They are judged according to their deeds recorded in the books of God (v. 12). They are also judged by the fact that their names are *not* written in the Book of Life, which is also present before the throne (v. 12). The judgment concludes with the wicked, along with Death and Hades, being thrown into the Lake of Fire (vv. 14-15). The seer concludes, 'This is the second death, the lake of fire' (v. 14). The second death is mentioned two additional times in Revelation. In 2:11, the church of Smyrna is promised that the ones who overcome will not be hurt by the second death. In 21:8, the wicked are described as the 'cowardly, unbelieving, abominable, murderers, immoral persons, sorcerers, idolaters, liars: their part will be in the lake that burns with fire and brimstone, which is the second death.' Clearly, then, the second death refers to the ultimate fate of the wicked.

When the thousand years are complete, Satan will be released and will deceive the nations of the world again (vv. 7-8). The grammatical construction here indicates that he deceives the nations 'in order to gather them for war (v. 8) against God'. He gathers them from the whole world. 'The four corners' (v. 8) suggests the universality of the gathering. It must be understood that this war is different from that described in 7:14 and 19:19 (the Battle of Armageddon). The primary difference is that this war follows the millennium, when Satan is released, whereas the war in chs. 17 and 19 precedes Satan's capture and imprisonment.

Gog and Magog

Revelation 20:7-9 identifies Gog and Magog as those who oppose God in this last war. Scholars are not agreed as to whom Gog and Magog represent. They are cited in Ezek. 38-39 as a Prince (Gog) of the land of Magog, which is somehow associated with Meshech and Tubal. Ezekiel 38:5 also discusses Persia, Cush, and Put, as well as Gomer and Togarmah. Ezekiel states that these people (or countries) will join together from the north (of Israel) to attack Israel in the last days. The description of the battle that ensues shows marked similarities to the battle against God in Rev. 10:7-9. The question who these people are continues to occupy scholars.

One of the earliest mentions of them is in Gen. 20:2-4, where Gomer, Magog (listed here as a person), Madai, Javan, Tubal, Meshech, and Tirac are listed as the sons of Japheth, the son of Noah.

Cush, Mizraiai, Put, and Canaan are identified as the sons of Ham, the son of Noah (Gen. 10:3). Togarmah is a son of Gomer (v. 6).

There are a variety of theories which identify these people with actual historical nations, although scholars are divided as to which ones are meant. The broader problem is whether they should be considered as historical realities at all, or whether they should be interpreted as figurative concepts representing evil, the ultimate force of the wicked which opposes God throughout history and finally culminates in the great conflict in the end time.

In apocalyptic literature, Gog and Magog function as representatives of all heathen opponents.[9]

On the other hand, some of these names can be associated 'with some degree of certainty' as historical realities,[10] with the following countries (or peoples):

> Meshech in Phrygia
> Tubal in Cilicia
> Gomer in the Armenian mountains, eastern Europe
> Togarmah in the territory east of Cilicia

Herodotus (I, 103, 107; IV, 1) states that the Greeks identify (in his day) Magog as the Scythians. Josephus agrees with this and associates Thobel (Tubal?) with the Thoebelites and the Moschevi with Meshech. He comments, 'now they are called Cappadocians' (Josephus, *Ant.* I 6.1). Josephus also identifies Phut (Put) as the founder of Libya and Cush as the people of Ethiopia (Josephus, *Ant.* I 6.2-3).

In summary, there appears to be support for both alternatives, that Gog and Magog should be considered as historical realities and they should also be interpreted as figurative representatives of the forces of evil which oppose God throughout history and ultimately in the end times. Although some scholars (mostly in earlier scholarship), have associated them with particular countries which will be expected to attack Israel (like in Ezek. 38:9), it is probably wisest also to interpret them figuratively.

The exact location of 'the broad plain of the earth', the site of this battle (v. 9), is uncertain. This verse can also be translated 'they marched up across the breadth of the earth and surrounded the encampment of the people of God'.[11] This translation would seem to emphasize the main point, which is that armies come from all over the

---

[9] E.g. *Jub.* 7:19; 9:8. See R.H. Charles, *Commentary on Revelation*, ICC 2 (1920), pp. 188f.; D.S. Russell, *The Message of Jewish Apocalyptic*.
[10] Otzen, *TDOT* II, 419-25.
[11] Cf. Aune, p. 1026.

world in great numbers. The term 'marched up' (ἀνέβησαν) is an idiom usually used in reference to Jerusalem.[12]

The 'Beloved City' most certainly refers to Jerusalem. The phrase is often used in the Old Testament to refer to the earthly Jerusalem: e.g. Jer. 11:15; 12:7. Both of these references include accounts of God's calling Jerusalem 'My Beloved' (see similar references to Mount Zion in Pss. 78:68; 87:2; Sir. 24:11). There is some debate about whether this city is the earthly or heavenly Jerusalem. Since the new Jerusalem does not appear in Revelation until 21:10, perhaps this should be interpreted as the earthly site.[13] The battle scene itself is not described except to imply that God fights for Israel and fire devours his enemies (20:9). Fire, as divine judgment, is familiar from Old Testament examples, such as Elijah calling down fire on the series of soldiers (2 Kgs 1; for a similar story cf. *4 Ezra* 13:1-12, where fire destroys the enemy of the Messiah).

The devil is now cast into the Lake of Fire, where he joins the fate of the beast and the false prophet (19:20). This will also be the fate of Hades, Death and all the unrighteous whose names are not found in the Book of Life (20:14-15; cf. 14:10). The torment will be continuous: 'day and night forever and ever'.

The final scene in ch. 20 is the White Throne Judgment Seat of God (vv. 11-15). Several points are noteworthy. This throne is pictured differently from any of the other thrones. However, the reader is left with little doubt whose throne it is: 'The one who sits on the throne' has been used throughout Revelation to refer to God himself (4:2,3,9; 5:1,7,13; 6:16; 7:10,15; 19:4; 21:5). The size of the throne is noteworthy as well as its color. The word 'white' means 'bright, shining' and is the same word used to describe Jesus' clothing at the Transfiguration (cf. Mk 9:3). The connotation is of a shining, shimmering translucence. The absence of Christ at the Judgment is also striking. This is not the Mercy Seat (cf. 2 Cor. 5:10). This is the throne of God 'from whose presence earth and heaven fled away...' (v. 11).

As explained above, all the wicked dead stand before the throne, even from the sea and from Hades (v. 12). These are most likely 'the rest of the dead' referred to in v. 5. These were not included in the first resurrection (of the righteous, vv. 4-6). All of the wicked are included here, the 'great and small' (v. 12), denoting the 'important and unimportant'. It is interesting that there are no wicked survivors; the living are not mentioned. Evidently all of the wicked are destroyed by God's devouring fire (v. 9). The reference to judgment according to

---

[12] Aune, pp. 1096-97.
[13] Aune, p. 1098.

one's deeds (v. 12) echoes Babylon's judgment, which was appropriate because of her wickedness against God. God pays her back 'double according to her deeds' (18:6). Likewise, 'the wicked will pay according to their deeds' (20:13).

Book*s* (plural) are opened. The passive voice suggests that they are opened by God himself, or an angel for God's use. The plural (book*s*) is also found in Dan. 7:10, where this judgment scene is anticipated. 'Another book was opened, which is the Book of Life' (v. 12). The Book of Life is mentioned a number of times in Revelation (3:5; 13:8; 17:8; 20:12,15). Particularly in 3:5 and 13:8, it appears to belong to the Lamb and apparently includes the names of those who have committed their lives to him.

The idea of a divine register of names can also be found in ancient texts. In the Old Testament (Exod. 32:32), Moses asks God to blot out his name from the book if God withholds forgiveness from the people who had sinned (cf. Dan. 12:1; Mal. 3:6). Apocalyptic literature also refers to books that contain records of deeds to be considered as evidence for judgment.[14] It is interesting that several books are said to be present at the Great White Throne (Rev. 20:12). Perhaps the books provide a sort of 'double checking' of the wicked: their deeds are recorded as evidence of their wickedness in one book, while the absence of their names from the Book of Life provides further evidence for their condemnation to the Lake of Fire (vv. 14-15). The judicial imagery is again evident (see Rev. 20:13, where the Word becomes the means of condemnation and judgment when its message of salvation is rejected). The Book of Life, which carries salvation to those within it, becomes evidence to condemn those who are not included. The point is clearly made that God's judgment is based on recorded evidence.

Finally, Death and Hades are cast into the Lake of Fire, where Satan, the beast and the false prophet are already in torment (19:20; 20:10). As discussed earlier, this is the second death. Alford comments, 'As there is a second and higher life, so there is a second and deeper death. And as after that life, there is no more death (20:4), so after that death, there is no more life.'[15]

The seer concludes this scene with a warning to his readers, the simple statement that anyone whose name is not found in the Book of Life will suffer the same fate (v. 15).

---

[14] E.g. *1 En.* 90:20; *2 Bar.* 24:1; *4 Ezra* 6:20.

[15] Henry Alford, 'Apocalypse of John', in *The Greek Testament*, IV (1958), pp. 735-36.

Chapter 21

The old order of the earth is formally finished. Chapter 21 begins the vision of the transformation of the new order. As with previous visions, this new vision is introduced by the words, 'And I saw'. A 'new heaven and new earth' emerge: the first heaven and the first earth have passed away, and there is no longer any sea (21:1). This imagery would most certainly remind the reader of the words of Isa. 65:17, that God would 'create new heavens and a new earth'. A new order is also a common theme in apocalyptic literature. For example, in *1 En.* 45:4-5 the heaven and earth are to be transformed as a place for the elect. *4 Ezra* 7:75 also mentions a future time when God will 'renew the creation' (cf. also *2 Bar.* 32:6). 2 Pet. 3:10-13 tells of a future conflagration when the world will melt with fire and a new heaven will emerge, where the righteous will live forever. Paul implies a new order in Rom. 8:19-22, where he speaks about creation groaning, longing for its freedom from decay.

Two major interpretive challenges are found in this passage: (1) whether this new order is a physical one or is merely symbolic; and (2) whether the old earth is simply transformed or is something totally new. Neither Old Testament nor apocalyptic sources are definitive on either issue.[16] From the text of Revelation, it appears that there will be at least a partial, if not complete, destruction of the existing earth, because Revelation 16 describes the pouring out of the seven bowls that brings considerable physical destruction to the earth. At least, extensive renovation will be needed. Since the thousand-year reign occurs after God's display of wrath, however, evidently the earth is not completely destroyed. Whether or not the earth is completely new or merely restored, the main point of importance is that this is now a new order. Beasley-Murray says, 'We cannot be sure how he (the seer) viewed the new heaven and new earth, but the context of this statement suggests that his real concern is not with physical geography, but with description of a context of life for God's people which ascends with the great and glorious purpose God has in mind for them.'[17] The term used for 'new' heaven and earth (v. 1, καινήν) sheds some light in that it 'suggests fresh life rising from the decay and wreck of the old world'.[18] It is curious that there will no longer be any sea. There are varied explanations for this. Perhaps one of the best is that the sea is a negative symbol for chaos in Revelation. For example, in Rev. 13:1, the beast

---

[16] See Aune, pp. 1118-20, for an extensive discussion of sources and alternatives.
[17] Beasley-Murray, p. 308.
[18] Swete, p. 275.

214 *Pentecostal Commentary on Revelation*

emerges from the sea.[19] In the Old Testament the sea is an especially negative place (Isa. 57:20). It is also possible that the sea, together with day and night and the seasons are no longer needed because all of them have to do with time. The sea is affected physically by the moon and the tides have to do with time. In the new order, time no longer exists.

Verse 2 introduces the new vision: 'And I saw' (see 6:1; 8:2; 10:1; 13:1; 14:1; 15:1; 19:11; 20:1; 21:1). Here 'the Holy City' is clearly identified as the heavenly Jerusalem. Whether the entire heaven and earth are completely new or merely transformed, the seer clearly states that 'Jerusalem, the Holy City' is new. It descends from heaven as 'a bride adorned for her husband' (v. 2).[20]

The New Jerusalem stands in marked contrast to the great whore, Babylon, presenting a hope for the hidden and suffering, earthly holy city, which was destroyed by Rome in 70 and again in 134 CE. The reader of Revelation has seen the devastation of the earthly Jerusalem and so, Revelation provides a new alternative – the New Jerusalem from heaven. In its radiance and invincibility, it resides on top of a mountain. It towers over Satan's throne in Pergamum (2:13) and shimmers above even Babylon with all its wickedness (17:9). Although this still lies in the future, the anticipation of it provides comfort and hope to the readers of Revelation, who are suffering in despair.[21]

Throughout Revelation, the phrase 'descending from heaven' associates a particular event directly with God. For example, in 10:1, an angel 'descends from heaven' and announces the seven peals of thunder which are so awesome that God does not allow the seer to describe

---

[19] Cf. Aune, pp. 119-20, for a discussion of Old Testament Judaic, Hellenistic and apocalyptic sources regarding God and the sea.

[20] Bauckham, *The Theology of the Book of Revelation* (pp. 126-28), interprets the entire imagery of the New Jerusalem as symbolic: the people of the ancient world were directly related to and dependent on cities. Moreover, cities were often symbolized in literature as women (e.g. the goddess Roma). Revelation picks up on this imagery, but portrays Rome as 'the great whore' (17:1), built on seven hills (17:9), and represented with all the corrupting influences of ancient Rome. All the other cities are dependent on her, so when she falls, so do they (16:19). Bauckham shifts this interpretation somewhat in addressing Jerusalem: there are two Jerusalems in Revelation (p. 126): the New Jerusalem from heaven is a new creation; like Babylon, she is both a woman and a city, and presents a sharp contrast with the woman/city/Babylon, the whore. In addition, there is the 'Holy City' of 11:2; this is not the earthly Jerusalem (p. 127) since the actual earthly Jerusalem was destroyed by Rome in 70 CE. Rather, the author represents the earthly Jerusalem as the faithful Church being persecuted and martyred by the beast. Like the two witnesses in 11:1-3 and the heavenly woman in 12:5, 13-16, who are spiritually protected while being hunted and attacked by the beast, the Church is protected by God while being persecuted by the dragon.

[21] See Bauckham, *Theology*, pp. 131-32, for an extensive list of the contrasts of the New Jerusalem, Christ's bride, and Babylon the harlot.

them. In Rev. 18:1, 'another angel coming down from heaven ... bright with his splendor' announces the fall of Babylon. Finally, in 21:1-2, the New Jerusalem 'descends from heaven' adorned as a bride (v. 2). The beauty and purity of Jerusalem stands in marked antithesis to the debauchery of the harlot Babylon.[22] In the Epistles, the city is from 'above' (Gal. 4:26); its builder and maker is God (Heb. 11:10; cf. also similar references to it in Heb. 12:22; 13:14; Phil. 3:20).

A challenging interpretive problem here has to do with the symbolic meaning of the new Jerusalem. Does it represent the saints? Does it symbolize the Church?[23] A careful consideration of the text suggests that the city is the place where the righteous reside. The metaphor of the city as a bride would not imply that the city *itself* is the bride of Christ. Rather, the city is adorned 'like a bride'... The Bride of the Lamb has already been identified as the righteous (19:1-7). The seer is contrasting the beauty and purity of the bride (Jerusalem) with the wickedness and apostasy of the harlot (Babylon).

A loud voice 'from the throne' announces, 'Behold the tabernacle of God is among men, and he shall dwell among them and they shall be his people, and God himself shall be among them' (v. 3). It is not clear whose voice this is. Since God is mentioned in the third person, it is not God's voice. Unidentified voices from heaven have announced events before (cf. e.g. Rev. 10:4,10; 18:4). In most of the references, they can simply be identified as a voice of one of the heavenly beings around the throne of God. They underscore the significance of what is about to occur.

The message of the voice echoes the Old Testament. Leviticus 26:11-12 says: 'I will make my abode with you ... I will be your God, and you shall be my people' (cf. also Jer. 31:33; Ezek. 37:27; Zech. 8:8 for similar passages). Interestingly, the Greek word for 'tabernacle' (σκηνή) is closely related to the Hebrew word *Shekinah*, which denotes the presence and glory of God.[24] The tabernacle in the wilderness during the Exodus was a symbol of the abiding presence of God. The language also reflects the covenant language of Exod. 29:45: 'And I will dwell among the people of Israel, and will be their God' (cf. also Jer. 31:33). It is significant here that this Old Testament covenant lan-

---

[22] Cf. 17:4-6: the 'adornments of a bride' are probably her jewels (see Isa. 49:18); also Jacques van Ruiten, 'Isaiah 65:17-20 and Revelation 21:1-5b', *EB* LI (1993), pp. 488-93; see also Blumner, pp. 138-39, for a discussion of a bride's clothing and jewels in the Greek world.

[23] McKelvey, pp. 167-76; Holtz, pp. 191-95; R.H. Gundry, *The Church and the Tribulation* (Grand Rapids, MI: Zondervan, 1973); Schüssler Fiorenza, *Priester für Gott*, pp. 348-50.

[24] Mounce, p. 371.

guage is applied in Revelation to all righteous people, not only to the select group of Israel (note the plural 'peoples', λαοί). Several literary aspects clarify and emphasize the point that the New Jerusalem incorporates the hope of both Israel and the Church:

1. The names of the twelve tribes of Israel are on its gates (21:12), reflecting Ezekiel's vision (Ezek. 48:30-5), while the names of the twelve apostles are on its foundations (21:14).
2. The very dimensions are laid out with the number 12, which is symbolic of the people of God (21:12-14,16,19-21; cf. 22:2 and multiples of 12; e.g. [144]; 21:17; cf. 7:4, 14:1).
3. The covenant formula: 'I will be their God and they will be my people' is adapted to apply to all nations (21:3) as well as to the Christian martyrs and witnesses (21:7).
4. Similarly, the promise of becoming a 'kingdom and priests to one God' (5:10; cf. 1:5,9) is related to both Israel and Christians. As priests, they will all worship God in his immediate presence (22:3b-4) and as kings, they will participate in his reign (22:5).[25]

The phrase 'God is with' (someone) appears throughout the Old Testament to refer to God's presence, sometimes in battle (see Deut. 7:21,20) or to refer to other spiritual blessings (see Gen. 21:20; 31:5). In the new Jerusalem, the announcement is that the presence of God will now be with them in eschatological reality forever. Erdman comments, 'It is the presence of God, and fellowship with him, which forms the essential feature of the age to come.'[26] The significance of God dwelling with the righteous is further described in the remainder of chs. 21 and 22.

The voice proceeds to list what will cease as a result of God's presence: no longer will there be weeping, death, mourning, or pain. It is noteworthy that this voice reiterates the message of 7:17, 'and God shall wipe every tear from their eyes'. Echoed here is the passage in Isa. 35:10, 'and sorrow and sighing will flee away', and Isa. 25:8, 'and he will swallow up death forever'. The comment 'the previous things have passed away' repeats Rev. 21:1 and emphasizes the significance of the end of these things in the new order. There will be no more death, weeping, mourning, or pain. During the thousand-year reign these things temporarily ceased. The new earth will bring complete annihila-

---

[25] Bauckham, pp. 137-38.
[26] Charles R. Erdman, *The Revelation of John* (Philadelphia: Westminster [1936], c1966, 1977), p. 167.

tion of pain, sorrow, and death forever.[27] This is a complete reversal of the nature of human existence; the cycle of birth, growth, death and decay will no longer exist.

There follows a short proclamation by God himself, which emphasizes the significance of this entire section. The words of God himself supply the basis for the trustworthiness of the message: 'And he who sits on the throne said, "Behold, I am making all things new". And he [the heavenly voice] said, "Write, for these words are faithful and true"' (v. 5). This is the final command to write in the book (cf. 1:11,19; 10:4; 21:5). So God's words should be taken as an affirmation not only of the immediately preceding message, but also of the entire message of Revelation. The paired words 'trustworthy and true' are actually one idea expressed in two words, a hendiadys.[28] The repetition serves to emphasize the meaning of the message: these words are trustworthy and can therefore be relied upon.

Section 21:1-8 is God's final statement: 'It is done' (γένοναν, v. 6). This word can be translated 'these things have taken place; it is finished'. The use of the perfect tense denotes absolute certainty that the events referred to (probably the entire book of Revelation) will indeed come about. A similar idea of completion can be found in 16:17, where a voice from the throne announces the completion of the outpouring of God's wrath. Perhaps also reflected here, although in different words, is Jesus' final utterance from the cross: 'It is finished' (τετέλεσται) (Jn 19:30). The meaning is the same: God's plan has been completed.

God underlines the proclamation of Revelation with the guarantee based on who he is: he is the Alpha and the Omega, the Beginning and the End (v. 6). This title was used earlier in Revelation with reference to Christ as well as God (1:8; 21:6; 22:13). In each case, it appears along with other titles, emphasizing the absolute power and sovereignty of Christ (or God). In the old order, God was the Alpha and Omega. He participated in the Creation, in the development and maintenance of the complex organization of the universe. He ruled it and guided it through history until its end. Now he also stands in the new order as Alpha and Omega.[29] He initiated the new order by sending his Son in the fullness of time (Acts 1:7). Now God seals his promise with the guarantee of this title – Alpha and Omega. The title 'Beginning and End' has a similar meaning to Alpha/Omega except

---

[27] Ruiten, pp. 504-505.
[28] See Aune, p. 1126.
[29] Gause, pp. 267-68.

that it also includes a cosmological connotation,[30] rather than a temporal one: God encompasses all things; he is the beginning, middle (implied) and end of all things; he is creator, or source, the origin of all things; he is sustainer; and finally, he is the culmination and/or goal of all things. Upon this nature of God rests the guarantee that the events of Revelation will take place.

The promise of living water follows. A similar promise is cited again in 22:17 (cf. also Jn 7:37-38; *Odes Sol.* 30:1-2). 'Living water' refers to flowing water or an active spring (e.g. *Didache* 7:1,2). It is used as a metaphor in Jn 4:4-15 where Jesus promises a quality of life which forever quenches thirst (the Samaritan woman's thirst in Jn 4). Significant concepts to be noted are: (1) that the water will 'be given' by God; (2) it will be given without cost; and (3) it is available to anyone who thirsts. The promise of eternal water is available to 'those who overcome' (v. 7). Again, the reliability of the promise is grounded in the nature of God himself: 'for I will be their God and they will be my children'. This promise reflects ancient adoption language, which underscores God's relation to us as adopted children.[31] The idea also reflects God's promise to Abraham, 'I will be God to you and to your descendants after you' (Gen. 17:7; cf. also the promise to David in 2 Sam. 7:14). Paul explains that people of faith are heirs to Abraham's covenant (cf. Gal. 3:29). God himself affirms this relationship in Revelation.

It should be noted that the overcomer is the one who inherits the promise of the blessings of the new order: Overcomers, in the particular seven churches of Revelation, are also mentioned and given promises in chs. 2 and 3: (1) they will eat of the tree of life (2:7); (2) they will not be hurt by the second death (2:11); (3) they will be given hidden manna and a white stone (2:17); (4) they will receive power over the nations (2:26); (5) they will not have their name blotted from the Book of Life (3:5); (6) they will be a pillar in the Temple of God (3:12); (7) and they will sit with Christ on his throne (3:21). In the new order, 'these things' are available to all 'overcomers' (21:7).

In contrast to the overcomers stand those who do not commit themselves to God (v. 8). It is noteworthy that the list of sins in v. 8 reflects that of the Ten Commandments and parallels other early Christian lists of vices.[32] It is interesting that the 'cowardly' are listed first.

---

[30] See W.C. van Unnik, *Het godspredikaat 'Het begin en het einde' bij Flavius Josephus en in de openbaring van Johannes* (Amsterdam: Noord-Hollandsche Uitgevers Maatschappij, 1976), cited in Aune.

[31] See Aune, pp. 1129-30, for an extensive discussion of adoption language.

[32] *Ibid.*, p. 1131.

The word literally means 'fearful' (δειλοῖς) and most likely refers to those who took the mark of the beast out of fear of persecution. This fear is probably not a natural timidity, but rather shows a lack of the commitment needed to carry one through persecution.[33] This word may be related to Jesus' words to the disciples 'Why are you acting like cowards, you of little faith?' (Mt. 8:26). Cowardice in the Greek world was regarded in an even broader sense, as a general term for moral degradation.[34]

In a sense, then, this first term summarizes the rest of the vices. They all refer to a general immoral state, a state of being uncommitted to God. 'Unbelieving' is second in the list and probably also refers to those who have apostatized their faith. The 'abominable' are likely those associated with the cult of emperor worship. The term has connotations of sexual immorality usually associated with the lifestyles of ancient Rome. 'Murderers' are those who kill other human beings, but may also refer to those who killed others because of the tyranny of the beast (13:15). 'Immoral persons' probably includes all the sins of sexual immorality. The practice of sorcery involves the magic arts (cf. Acts 19:19) and was fairly common in ancient Roman times. 'Idolatry' was a key component of pagan worship, which flourished in ancient times. The final sin is listed as lying. 'Liars' are particularly appropriate to this list, as they stand in striking contrast to the emphasis on truth in Revelation. Lying as an antithesis to truth is also a major theme in the Gospel of John and 1 John. For example, anyone who sins, or who says he walks in the light but sins, is a liar and does not do the truth (1 Jn 1:7-10). In the Gospel of John, Jesus stands as the true light (1:9); the true witness (8:14); the bearer of truth (8:31-40); the way, the truth, and the life (14:6); the true vine (15:1), etc. In Revelation, God and Christ, as truth and the true witness, stand in marked contrast to the deception of the beast and those who follow him (Rev. 13:14); indeed, Satan is characterized by his work of deceiving the nations (Rev. 20:3,8,10; Jn 8:44-45).

All of these vices (Rev. 21:8), then, were common factors in the pagan life of Rome and are portrayed vividly as part of the lifestyle and character of the harlot (symbolic of Rome, ch. 17). They are all antithetical to the life committed to God. The seer clearly states that those participating in these sins will be cast into the lake that burns with fire

---

[33] Mounce, p. 375.
[34] See Plato, *Republic* 395E-396A, 486B; Dio Chrysostom, *Orationes* 23,8. For additional references, cf. Christopher R. Hutson, 'Was Timothy Timid? On the Rhetoric of Fearlessness [1 Corinthians 16:10-11] and Cowardice [2 Timothy 1:7]', *BR* 42 (1997), pp. 59-70 n. 55.

and brimstone, which is the 'second death' (21:8). The 'second death' refers to the fact that these have died, were resurrected to be judged (20:12-13) and now are to experience the death which is forever in the Lake of Fire (21:8).

One of the seven angels, 'who had the seven bowls with the seven last plagues', now approaches John to invite him to come and view the holy city (21:9). Possibly this is the same angel as in 17:1, who announces the vision of the harlot. If so, this literary connection enhances the sharp contrast between the harlot (Babylon/Rome) and the bride of the Lamb (the holy city/new Jerusalem): the harlot is dressed in gaudy clothes and jewels and is surrounded by wicked deeds of immorality in which she participates, while the bride is beautiful, clothed in purity (white linen). She is adorned with jewels symbolizing her faithfulness and honor before God. There is no problem with her being referred to as the 'bride' as well as 'wife' of the Lamb (v. 9). As the 'bride' she is pure, faithful and lovely; as 'wife' she enjoys the intimacy of the relationship with the Lamb.[35] By using both images the author emphasizes both aspects of the relationship of the believer and Christ.

The angel transports the seer to a 'great and high mountain' to show him the city (v. 10) descending from heaven. To attempt to determine whether this is a literal or symbolic mountain is to misunderstand the nature of visionary expression and apocalypticism in particular. The mountain is part of the vision of the holy city in the same way as the wilderness functions as part of the vision of the harlot (17:3). Both of these locations are accompanied by the phrase 'in the Spirit' (see also 1:10; 4:2; 17:3). This phrase indicates the state in which John views the eternal things. In addition, mountains are significant in Jewish and apocalyptic thought: Moses encounters God on Mount Sinai (Exod. 19ff.); Ezekiel receives the vision of the restored Temple on a 'high mountain' (Ezek. 40:1-2). Enoch describes one of the highest and most beautiful mountains as the throne of God (*1 En.* 24-25). Jesus takes his disciples to a 'high mountain' to witness his transfiguration (Mk 9:2).[36]

The city shimmers with the glory of God (v. 11). This brilliance is symbolized as a glittering jewel, appropriately the 'crystal-clear jasper' (v. 11). The designation 'jasper' was used in ancient times to designate any opaque stone, but the adjectives 'crystal-clear' would underscore the shimmering quality of what the seer is attempting to describe. Probably, this particular 'jasper' would be most similar to the modern diamond. The jasper usually denotes purity and value.

---

[35] Mounce, p. 377.
[36] For additional references, see Aune, p. 1152.

The city has a 'great and high wall' with twelve gates guarded by twelve angels. The names of the twelve tribes of Israel are inscribed on the gates (v. 12). In Ezekiel's vision (Ezek. 48:30-34), the gates which have the names of each of the tribes are for use only by the appropriate tribe. In Revelation, however, the gates are for everyone's use, for everyone 'whose names are written in the Lamb's Book of Life' (21:24-27). The number twelve is evidently important since not only are there twelve gates with twelve angels, but the measurements of the city are also in multiples of twelve (vv. 16,17). The number twelve multiples of twelve occur significantly in Revelation: the 144,000 (12,000 from each tribe, 7:5-8); and 24 elders (4:4). In the final chapter, the tree of life bears 'twelve crops of fruit and yields her fruit every month' (22:2). Possibly the number twelve is symbolic of completeness and perfection.[37] As such, it is entirely appropriate and relevant that twelve is a key feature of the holy city.

The inscription of the names of the twelve tribes of Israel on the gates of the new Jerusalem is especially significant, since it implies the realization of one of the concerns of Jewish eschatology, the restoration of the twelve tribes.[38] Three gates are located on each side of the city. The main point of the twelve gates equally available in all directions is that entrance is available in abundance to the inhabitants of the city.

The wall of the city is built on twelve foundation stones, upon which are inscribed the names of the twelve apostles. Perhaps this reflects Paul's idea that the Church is built 'on the foundation of the apostles and prophets'.[39] In any case, it is appropriate that 'the juxtaposition of the twelve tribes and the twelve apostles shows the unity of ancient Israel and the New Testament Church'.[40] There is no longer a distinction between Jew and Gentile, Israel and the Church: all are united in the bride of Christ. It should be noted, however, that each group, the twelve tribes and the twelve apostles, appears to have a distinct role – one group makes up the foundations, the other comprises the gates; together, in their own distinctive ways, they complete the unified whole of the City.

In v. 15 an angel tells John to measure the city with a gold measuring rod. In ch. 11 an angel tells John to measure the city, its altar and those that worship there (11:1; see notes on ch. 11 for elaboration). In both instances (11:1 and 21:15) the action reflects the symbolic activity

---

[37] Johnson, p. 481.
[38] Aune, p. 1155.
[39] Eph. 2:20; cf. Mt. 16:18; see also Eduard Lohse, *Die Offenbarung des Johannes*, Das Neue Testament Deutsch, 11 (Göttingen: Vandenhoeck & Ruprecht, 1960), pp. 109-110.
[40] Mounce, p. 379.

in the Old Testament.[41] In ch. 21, the *angel* does the measuring and only measures the city, its gates, and its wall (vv. 15-17). In ch. 11 no actual measurements are given, perhaps symbolizing the metaphorical nature of the procedure. The measuring in ch. 11 most likely symbolizes the part of the Temple to be protected by God during the coming events. In ch. 21, the measurements are given and are made with a golden rod or staff. It is not certain what this device is; but it is gold, an appropriate material to measure a heavenly city.[42]

Although it is uncertain which measuring device is being used as well as what the resulting measurements are, the point that God intends is clear: the city is enormous. Apparently the city is in the shape of a cube. A great many solutions have been suggested to the problem of the size of the city. The problem has to do with the nature of the measuring rod and the method used to measure. The most common feature among the interpretations is that the city is fantastic in size and shape, surpassing anyone's understanding. For example, one interpretation suggests the size of the city is approximately 2,400 miles in each direction, east/west, north/south, and up! Whatever the actual dimensions, the measurements are in multiples of twelve and symbolize the greatness of God.

The material of the wall is jasper, the brilliant diamond-like crystal mentioned earlier in v. 11. The city itself, however, is 'pure gold, like clear glass' (v. 18). This is usually interpreted as having a transparent quality. This transparency would reflect the brilliance of the glory of God.[43] Perhaps John, as well as his readers, would be reminded of Herod's Temple, which had a solid golden front that reflected the morning sunlight so brilliantly that according to Josephus, people had to look away from its 'fiery splendor'.[44]

In addition, each of the twelve foundations is adorned with precious stones, a different one for each foundation (vv. 19-20). It is noteworthy that these stones are similar to those on the breastplate of the high priests (Exod. 28:17-20). Although there are several differences of opinion as to the nature of these ancient stones, the descriptions which follow are the most widely accepted.[45]

---

[41] Cf. 1 Kgs 22:11; Isa. 8:1-4, 20:1-6; Jer. 13:3-11, 27:1–28:16; Ezek. 24:3; Acts 1:11.

[42] See Aune, pp. 1159-60, for a discussion about the description of a recently published fragment from Qumran of an apocalypse which supports this description of the heavenly Jerusalem.

[43] See Walvoord, p. 325.

[44] Josephus, *War* V 5.6.

[45] Cf. I. Howard Marshall, 'Jewels and Precious Stones', *NBD*, 2nd ed. (1982), pp. 631-34. Although there is some speculation as to how these stones relate to the stones

1. *Jasper* – a diamond-like, opaque stone. Used to describe God's glory in 4:3 and is also the material of the wall (21:18).
2. *Sapphire* – a deep blue stone
3. *Chalcedony* – a green silicate of copper found near Chalcedon in Asia Minor
4. *Emerald* – a brilliant green stone
5. *Sardonyx* – a layered red and white stone
6. *Sardius* – a blood red stone, often used for engraving. The city of Sardius was named after it because of the red earth found there.
7. *Chrysolite* – probably a yellow topaz or golden jasper. Pliny refers to its particularly 'tawny luster' (Pliny, *Orig.* 16.15.2; *Hist. nat.* 36.126).
8. *Beryl* – a green stone used often for magical amulets. It was occasionally called the "stone of Zeus" (*Cyranides*, 1.2.20-26).
9. *Topaz* – a greenish gold or yellow stone
10. *Chrysoprase* – an apple-green color
11. *Jacinth* – a bluish-purple similar to the modern sapphire
12. *Amethyst* – a purple quartz

The author has sketched a picture of brilliance, iridescence and splendor that stretches human imagination. Mounce expresses it well: 'it [the city] is described in language which continually attempts to break free from its own limitations in order to do justice to the reality it so imperfectly describes'.[46]

The twelve gates bearing the names of the twelve tribes are each made of one pearl (v. 21). Evidently, these are giant single pearls rather than inlaid mother of pearl. Several rabbinic traditions support this in speaking of the gates of the new Jerusalem as being giant pearls. For example, R. Johanan[47] writes, 'The Holy One, blessed be He, will in the time to come bring precious stones and pearls which are thirty (cubits) by twenty, and will set them up in the gates of Jerusalem.' In ancient times, the pearl was a mark of affluence (cf. 1 Tim. 2:9). Jesus told a parable of a man who sold all that he had to purchase a certain special one (Mt. 13:45-46).

The street of the city is 'pure gold, like transparent glass' (v. 21). There is a question whether the term for street (ἡ πλατεῖα) refers to the one main street of the city (most ancient cities at this time had one

---

of the Zodiac, it is highly unlikely that John had that intention since the mythology of the Zodiac was repudiated by John's theology (cf. Gause, p. 272).

[46] Mounce, p. 383.

[47] Although late, R. Johanan's remarks are relevant to the context of Revelation (*b. Baba Bathra* 75a).

main street through the center of the city),[48] or whether all of the streets are gold since the entire city is gold.[49] A third option is that the 'street of gold' could refer to a central plaza or square.[50] The main idea is that the people of God will walk upon pure gold. It is interesting to note that the Old Testament priests who ministered in the Temple sanctuaries also walked on golden floors (1 Kgs 6:30).

Verses 23-27 describe a series of 'no mores', that is, common features of the natural earth that will not be present in the new Jerusalem.

The seer begins this section with the fact that there is no Temple (v. 22). This may seem surprising in view of two things: (1) the restored Temple is described in some detail in Ezekiel's vision (Ezek. 40-46), which parallels John's vision of the new Jerusalem in many ways; and (2) the Temple was *the* central focus of Judaism. Some scholars go so far as to suggest that the inclusion of this detail (no Temple) reflects an anti-Temple polemic within early Christianity.[51] However, the Scripture itself (v. 22) tells why there is no Temple: 'for the Lord God, the Almighty, and the Lamb, are its Temple'. Perhaps the title of God used here gives a clue as well. This title for God (Lord God Almighty) is used several times in Revelation: in 4:8 by the living creatures; in 11:17 by the 24 elders; in 15:3 by the martyrs; in 16:7 by the altar; in 19:6 by the great multitude. Each time the title underscores the sovereignty, power, and majesty of God. The link with the title 'the Lamb', for Christ, sets the context for the quality of life within the new Jerusalem: God and his Son, the Lamb (which emphasizes his sacrificial nature), are the central focus of eschatological existence.

A consideration of the purpose of the Temple will perhaps be helpful. The purpose of the Temple in the Old Testament was to provide the means by which humanity could approach God. In the New Jerusalem, God will relate directly to his people (v. 3). Jesus himself anticipated this when he told the Samaritan woman that the time would come 'when the true worshipers shall worship the Father in spirit and truth' rather than in a geographical location (Jn 4:24). The imagery is

---

[48] Cf. D.W. Hadorn, *Die Offenbarung des Johannes*. THKNT 18 (Leipzig: Deichert, 1928), pp. 208-10; A. Wikenhauser, *Die Offenbarung Johannis*, 3rd ed., Das Neue Testament 9 (Regensburg: Pustet, 1959), p. 159; Jan Fekkes III, *Isaiah and Prophetic Traditions in the Book of Revelation*, JSNTSup 93 (Sheffield: Sheffield Academic Press, 1994), pp. 244 n. 48.

[49] Cf. Bousset, p. 450; Charles, II, p. 170; cf. also *Tob.* 13:17, which particularly refers to the street*s* (plural) of the eschatological Jerusalem.

[50] Cf. Adolf von Schlatter, *Das Alte Testament in der johanneischen Apokalypse* (London: SPCK, 1955), p. 335; J.B. Sickenberger, *Erklärung der Johannesapokalypse* (Bonn: Hanstein, 1940), p. 194; W.W. Reader, 'Die Stadt Gottes in der Johannesapokalypse' (diss., Göttingen, 1971), pp. 147-48.

[51] See Aune, pp. 1166-67.

clear, then. The presence of God himself is the Temple, providing immediate access to his presence.

There will be no more sun, moon (v. 23), nor night (v. 25) because the Lamb will be the light (v. 23). Isaiah foresaw this (cf. 60:19-20). John also called Jesus 'the light of the world' (Jn 8:12; cf. also 3:19; 12:35) and 'the true light which enlightens every man' (Jn 1:9; cf. also 4 *Ezra* 7:39-42). It is also possible that the sun and moon are not necessary because of the absence of time itself. Part of the quality of eternality is its timelessness. The sun and moon are markers of time. In Gen. 1:14, God creates the sun and moon as 'lights in the expanse of the heavens to separate the day from the night ... for signs, and for seasons, and for days and years'. In the new Jerusalem, there is no need for the markers of time. Neither is there need for the 'lights in the heavens'. There is no darkness (Rev. 21:25), because Christ provides continual light by his presence. 'The glory of God has illumined it (the city) and its lamp is the Lamb' (vv. 23-25). The light not only illuminates the new Jerusalem, it is also visible to others outside the city: 'The nations shall walk by its light and the kings of the earth shall bring their glory into it' (v. 24). Isaiah 60 provides a clue to help one understand what this passage could mean: in Isa. 60:1-3 the glory of the Lord is so radiant upon Jerusalem that other 'nations will come to your light and kings to the brightness of your rising'.

The interpretive challenge here is the identity of the 'nations' and 'kings of the earth' in v. 24. The problem is that the nations and kings of the earth with their armies have been completely destroyed (19:17-21; 20:7-9). Scholars have suggested a number of interesting solutions to this problem.[52] One possibility is that the people outside Jerusalem are redeemed saints who do not belong to the twelve tribes; these are righteous people who belong spiritually, but not racially, to the twelve tribes.[53] Others suggest that this is a description of the earthly Jerusalem during the millennium rather than at the end of time.[54] Most likely, this is simply a description of activities carried on in the new Jerusalem. Although the reference to nations and kings (v. 24) is curious, several points are certainly clear:[55] (1) Since the term used for nations (τὰ ἔθνη) refers to people other than Jews, the people of the new Jerusalem represent many ethnic groups. (2) These are certainly people of God since v. 27 clearly indicates that no wicked are in the city. (3) Finally,

---

[52] *Ibid.*, pp. 1171-72.
[53] Cf. R.C.H. Lenski, *The Interpretation of St. John's Revelation* (Minneapolis: Augsburg, 1943), p. 644; cf. also Kiddle, p. 439.
[54] Cf. Aune, pp. 1170-72.
[55] See Gause, p. 274.

the new Jerusalem is the center of existence of the new earth: people are coming and going, interacting with the city. The people are 'bringing the glory and honor of the nations into it' (v. 26). Glory and honor are paired in v. 26 as being the purpose of the interactions of the people. The two words together can indicate material wealth, but more likely in this context, they indicate gifts of worship and adoration,[56] particularly the worship of God, which is the central focus of existence. Could this description, then, be descriptive in some way of the activities of the righteous in the eschatological future?

The main point of vv. 25-26 is linked with v. 23: there is no need for natural light (sun, moon) because the Lamb provides continuous light. The reader is, no doubt, struck with the continuity and reliability of the Lamb's presence. As natural light sustains life on the first earth, so the Lamb sustains life in the new Jerusalem. In any case, the glory and splendor of God is so great that it is visible even outside the city. Verse 25 notes that the gates will never be closed, primarily because 'there shall be no night there' (v. 25). The reader is, no doubt, reminded here of Zech. 14:6-7: 'in that day there will be no light; the luminaries will dwindle, for it will be a unique day which is known to the Lord, neither day nor night ... at evening time there will be light'.

Finally, v. 27 reiterates that nothing unclean and no one who practices abomination and lying shall ever enter the city. Only those whose names are written in the Lamb's Book of Life are allowed. The term 'unclean' (κοινόν, synonym of ἀκαθάρτος, unclean, defiled) denotes impurity.[57] This sanctity of the city was anticipated by Old Testament prophets (cf. Isa. 52:1; Ezek. 44:9) as well as New Testament writers (cf. 1 Cor. 6:9-10; 2 Pet. 3:13). The terms 'abomination and lying' probably refer to sexual immorality and idolatry,[58] all of which would separate a person from God's holiness and purity. Although this verse appears to be implying that wicked people are outside of the city, it is probable that John is exhorting his readers that anyone who practices wickedness now will not be allowed into the city at the end time.

---

[56] Cf. Aune, p. 1173.
[57] Friedrich Hauck, 'κοινός', *TDNT* III (1965), pp. 797.
[58] Aune, p. 1175.

Chapter 22

Chapter 22:1-9

This section should immediately follow ch. 21 with only a slight pause since the topic of the holy city continues. In 21:10-27, the seer describes his vision of the new Jerusalem, its measurements (vv. 15-17), its materials (vv. 18-21) and the nature of life there (vv. 22-27). There is a slight break between 21:27 and 22:1 since v. 1 repeats 'And he showed me ...' The following text includes special details within the city itself.

John sees a 'river of the water of life, clear as crystal' (v. 1) coming from God's throne. The imagery is of clear water gushing from its abundant source. 'Rivers of water' or 'fountains of waters of life' are a recurring theme in Revelation (cf. 7:17; 21:6; 22:17). Perhaps one can see a metaphorical reference to the Holy Spirit,[59] who makes possible the abundant life available in God.[60] The main point in ch. 22 is that in this transformed world of the new Jerusalem, the righteous are living with the very source of life, which proceeds directly from the throne of God.

The description of the physical layout is not clear (vv. 1-2). Evidently, the physical geography is not the main point. The meaning must then be found in the symbolic imagery.

The abundantly clear water certainly represents the life-sustaining quality of eternal life. Jesus himself referred to divine water as thirst-quenching water. He tells the Samaritan woman in the Gospel of John, 'Whoever drinks of the water that I shall give him shall never thirst; but the water that I shall give him shall become in him a well of water springing up to eternal life' (Jn 4:14). The water in the new Jerusalem flows 'in the middle of the street' (22:1-2). How this fits with the description of the trees on either side of the river is not entirely clear. In any case, the 'middle of the street' would seem to indicate the water's central focus.

The tree of life is 'on either side of the river'. Most likely this means that the tree is spread along the entire main street of the city. In Ezekiel's vision (47:12), there are multiple trees which bear fruit mostly for food and whose leaves are for healing. Probably John's singular word tree (ξύλον) is a collective noun for Ezekiel's multiple trees. The imagery of abundance conveys the message of the abundant life available from God. There is a sharp contrast between the luxuriant plenty in the New Jerusalem and the one tree that was not to be touched or

---

[59] Cf. Swete, p. 298.
[60] Barclay, *The Revelation of John*, II, p. 283.

eaten in the Garden of Eden (Gen. 3:22). The significant point is that the tree of life is directly related to the river of life flowing directly from God's throne. In the creation of the first earth, Adam and Eve were banished from the Garden of Eden lest they disobey God and eat of this tree of life and attain immortality (Gen. 2:9; 3:22). In the *new* Jerusalem, the tree of life is available to all. In fact, its two main purposes are (1) to provide fruit every month, and (2) to provide healing for the nations (v. 2). This raises the question of who needs to be healed in 'this eternal state where there is no pain nor death' (Rev. 21:4). Probably this should be interpreted symbolically. The tree itself with its abundant fruit and healing leaves stands as indication of the nature of the abundant life, free from want, physical or spiritual disease or pain. Verse 3 underscores this: 'There shall no longer be any curse.' The curse involved disease, decay, and death (Gen. 3:14-19).

The nature of the New Jerusalem is summed up in vv. 3 and 4, 'And the throne of God and of the Lamb shall be in it, and his bond servants shall serve him; and they shall see his face, and his name shall be on their foreheads.' Several things are noteworthy here. The word 'serve' denotes the service of worship. The reader should be reminded of the beings around the throne whose main function is to worship God. In the new order, the righteous will join the heavenly beings in worship. The righteous will 'see his face'. In Judaism and early Christianity, to see the face of God is a metaphor for the full awareness of the presence and power of God.[61] Here, at last, the transformation begun at conversion (2 Cor. 3:18), will be complete. The followers of God will see God's face; they will have his name on their foreheads (v. 4). The 144,000 (14:1) are also described as having the name of the Father on their foreheads. The metaphor of bearing a name on one's forehead is taken from slave imagery. The name indicates ownership and likeness. The righteous will not only bear the sign of belonging to God, they will reflect him. As John writes in 1 Jn 3:2, at the return of Christ 'we shall be like him, for we shall see him as he is'. The special aspect of God's greatness and transcendence is that it is impossible for any human being to see him. Moses came the closest, but could not observe the complete presence of God (cf. Exod. 33:20,23). He was allowed only to see the back of God.

It is notable to consider the interesting link between the presence of God and worship. To see the face of God is 'the height of worship ... the face of God is the revelation of himself ... to see his nature and his

---

[61] Cf. Job 33:26; Pss. 10:10-11, 17:15; 3 Jn 11; see also Wilhelm Michaelis, 'ὁράω, εἰδόν, βλέπω, ὀπτάνομαι, θεάομαι θεωρέω', *TDNT* V (1967), pp. 329-30.

glory... Worship is the response of those in whom the image of God has been fully renewed'.[62]

The seer concludes this section with a reiteration that there will be no night, nor need of lamp or sun because 'God will illumine them' (v. 5). As light sustains nature in the earth as we know it, so God himself will sustain everything in the new order.

Finally, the righteous shall 'reign forever and ever' (v. 5). The subject of the verb ('they') refers to the servants of God (v. 3). Most likely, the reigning involves participation in the worship and praise of God. Revelation 5:10 provides the most detail and associates the reigning with worship: 'And hast made them (the righteous) to be a kingdom and priests to our God and they will reign forever and ever.' Whatever the reigning entails, it has to do with sharing and participating in Christ's rule. Certainly it is not ruling as we understand it. Christ himself rejects dominating one another as the Gentiles do (Lk. 22:24-30).[63] 'Reign' probably refers to the participation of the righteous in God's reign by worshiping him. This participation suggests the perfect reconciliation of God's sovereignty and human freedom. Bauckham expresses it: 'Because God's will is the moral truth of our own being as his creatures, we shall find our fulfillment only when, through our full obedience, his will becomes also the spontaneous desire of our hearts.' In God's kingdom there will be perfect harmony between God's theonomy and human autonomy.[64]

Verse 6 reiterates 21:5-6: the promises in chs. 21-22 are guaranteed on the basis of the faithfulness and trustworthiness of God himself. There follows (vv. 7-21) an epilogue of loosely related comments concluding the entire book of Revelation. There are three major themes throughout this section; (1) the authenticity of the book as divine revelation; (2) the nearness of the end times and (3) the blessings promised to those who obey the message. The similarity of this section to the prologue provides a frame for the entire book.[65]

Rev. 1:1-3	Rev. 22:6-10,18
¹to show his servants	⁶to show his servants
(δεῖξαι τοῖς δούλοις αὐτοῦ)	(δεῖξαι τοῖς δούλοις αὐτοῦ)
what must soon happen...	what must soon happen...
(ἃ δεῖ γενέσθαι ἐν τάχει...)	(ἃ δεῖ γενέσθαι ἐν τάχει...)
³blessed ... those who hear	⁷blessed [is] the one who obeys

---

[62] Gause, p. 277.
[63] Ibid., p. 278.
[64] Bauckham, pp. 142-43.
[65] Aune, pp. 1205-1206.

(μακάριος ... οἱ ἀκονόντες)
the prophetic words
(τοὺς λόγους τῆς προφητείας)
and obey the things (καὶ τηροῦντες
τά) written in it (ἐν αὐτῃ
γεγραμμένα)

(μακάριος ὁ τηρῶν)
the prophetic words
(τοὺς λόγους τῆς προφητείας)
of this book...
(τοῦ βιβλίου τούτου...)
[9] the words (τοὺς λόγους) of this book ... (τοῦ βιβλίου τούτου)
[10] the words of this (τοὺς λόγους τῆς) prophetic book... (προφητείας τοῦ βιβλίου τούτου...)

[18] the prophetic words (τοὺς λόγους τῆς προφητείας) of this book ... (τοῦ βιβλίου τούτου ...)

for the time is near.
(ὁ γὰρ καιρὸς ἐγγύς.)

[10] for the time is near...
(ὁ καιρὸς γὰρ ἐγγύς ἐστιν.)

The authenticity of the book is grounded first in the interpreting angel himself as faithful and true witness (22:6; the angel is identified in 21:9 as one of the seven angels who had the seven bowls). The seer introduces the theme of the authenticity of Revelation by confirming the chain of prophecy: *God* sent his *angel* to reveal to *John* the message to the *seven churches*, which is also passed to *us*. The angel strongly emphasizes that God is the origin and source of the prophecy. He uses an unusual title for God here: 'the God of the spirits of the prophets' (22:6). Certainly, the reader should interpret this reference to the Spirit within the context of John's theme of the seven spirits. As discussed earlier, the Spirit in Revelation is not only the means of conveying the prophecy, but is the means by which God has brought about the victory of the Lamb. Further, the Spirit will continue working through his prophets and bond-servants to bring about God's plan for the future of the world. The use of the plural for 'spirits' most likely also indicates that he is referring to the natural faculties of the prophets moved by the Holy Spirit.[66] John is very clear that God controls the utterances of the prophets, thus ensuring the reliability and truth of their message. Peter echoes a similar idea: 'for no prophecy was ever made by an act of human will, but men moved by the Holy Spirit spoke from God' (2 Pet. 1:21). The chain of prophecy is evident again: God himself, as the source of the prophecy, moves upon the faculties of humans to speak or write his message. Christ also affirms the authenticity of the prophecy (22:7): 'Blessed is the one who keeps the words of the

---

[66] Cf. Swete, p. 303.

prophecy of this book.' The confirmation serves as witness to the words of the entire book, but also to the words of the verse which follows immediately: 'See, I am coming soon.'

The Lord concludes his affirmation of the prophecy with a promise: 'Blessed is he who heeds the words of the prophecy of this book' (v. 7). The promise would be especially encouraging to the readers of John's day who were about to undergo persecution.

The Lord's announcement of his imminent return (v. 7) echoes several other passages in Revelation: 2:16; 3:11; 22:7,12,20. Paul held to this idea also (see 1 Cor. 7:29-31; 1 Thess. 4:15). It is interesting that Jesus himself is the one who announces his imminent coming, not John, nor even the interpreting angel. Yet one is struck by the fact that indeed he has not come. Explanations continue to be problematic as the temporal distance between these statements and the present time grows. Again, Peter sheds some light on the issue. His assurance is that, indeed, the Lord is not slow; rather, he is being patient so that more souls have time to come to repentance (2 Pet. 3:9).

The third witness to the truth and reliability of the prophecy is stated in Rev. 22:8: John himself. In ancient times, a witness was considered to be most reliable and trustworthy if he actually *saw* and *heard* the event.[67] John clearly states that he *heard* and *saw* what he had written.

The identity of the angel referred to in vv. 8-9 is problematic. Most likely he is the interpreting angel first mentioned in 1:1 and is again the speaker in 22:6,8-11. This angel is important in the revelatory chain since he is mentioned in both 1:1 and here in 22:8. Probably John is referring to the event in 19:10 when he falls down to worship the angel, rather than this being a second occurrence. This interpretation of this verse (22:8) suggests that the particular events he is referring to are those in 19:1-10, the worship of God before the throne. This immediately precedes the description of the marriage supper of the Lamb. The important point of the angel and the seer is 'to worship God' (v. 9).

The section vv. 6-9 serves two functions. It concludes the large textual unit (17–19:10) and now provides a transition to the epilogue (22:10-20).[68]

---

[67] See David E. Aune, *The New Testament in Its Literary Environment* (Philadelphia: Westminster Press, 1987), pp. 91-92.

[68] See Paul Gaechter, 'The Original Sequence of Apocalypse 20-22', *TS* 10 (1949), pp. 508-13; Schüssler Fiorenza, 'Composition and Structure of the Book of Revelation', *CBQ* 39 (1977), p. 364; J.R. Michaels, *Interpreting the Book of Revelation* (Grand Rapids, MI: Baker Book House, 1992), p. 71.

Chapter 22:10-21
The Epilogue

The epilogue is made up of a number of fragmented sayings which appear to comment on the entire text of Revelation. The seer begins by contrasting the righteous with the wicked (vv. 11, 15), but the main theme continues to be the witness and affirmation to the authenticity and reliability of the prophecy. A number of things are noteworthy.

First, the angel (probably the interpreting angel, v. 10) commands John: 'Do *not* seal up the words of the prophecy of this book...' The reason the angel gives is that the time for the recorded event is 'near' (v. 10). This is markedly different from the vision of Daniel (Dan. 12): which appears to anticipate the context of Revelation 22: the angel commands Daniel to 'shut up the words and seal the book, until the time of the end' (Dan. 12:4). The imminence of the end is striking in Revelation.

In fact, for the seer in Revelation the end is so near that there is no time to alter the behavior of people on earth (v. 11): 'Let the evildoer still do evil ... and the righteous still do right ...' This can be interpreted in several ways, but most likely it emphasizes the fact that there comes a time when the character of people will be fixed. At the end the possibility of change ceases and one is locked into the state produced by habitual living: 'the deliberate choice of each man has fixed his unalterable fate'.[69]

It appears that Christ himself interprets the narrative to underscore the imminence of his coming. Verse 12 is very similar in construction and context to 16:15, where Christ interrupts the textual topic with a comment which closely echoes his words to his disciples (Mk 9:1; cf. also 1 Thess. 5:2). The term 'behold' (ἰδού) functions as a marker underscoring the truth and reliability of the saying.

Christ reiterates his promise to come quickly. His coming is clearly as a judge: to reward everyone according to what they have done (v. 12). The concept of the distribution of rewards on the basis of deeds is found throughout Scripture. For example, Jer. 17:10 states: 'I the Lord, search the mind and try the heart, to give to everyone according to their ways, according to the fruit of their doings.' Paul echoes the same idea, that God 'will render to every man according to his works' (Rom. 2:6). Peter agrees that God 'judges each one impartially according to his deeds' (1 Pet. 1:17).[70] This should not be interpreted as a contradiction of salvation by faith. The seer is emphasizing that the

---

[69] Erdman, p. 178.
[70] See similar passages in Prov. 24:12; Isa. 59:18; 2 Cor. 11:15; 2 Tim. 4:14; Rev. 2:23; 18:6; 20:13.

wicked have sealed their own fate by their deeds. This is further underscored by the judging of the wicked by the book detailing their wicked deeds at the White Throne Judgment (20:12).

Christ now applies the title 'Alpha and Omega, the first and the last, the beginning and the end' to himself. Previously the Alpha/Omega title was applied to God (1:8; 21:6). The other two titles have already been used to refer to Christ (1:17; 2:8). The significance of the titles being applied to both Christ and God underlines that their essential natures are the same. Whatever is said of one can be said of the other (see Jn 8:12-20, where Jesus explains his relation to the Father; that they are one in nature: 'if you knew me, you would know my Father also', 8:19; but they are distinct in mission and function: 'I am he who bears witness of myself, and the Father who sent me bears witness of me', v. 18). All these titles in Rev. 22:13 set Christ apart from creation and indicate his limitlessness. The terms (beginning and end; first and last) can be classified as antithetical: two terms are used 'to express a divine characteristic by implying that, since he is both extremes, he encompasses the continuance defined by the antithetical terms'.[71] The point is that Christ encompasses all time and experience (see comments on 21:6).

The seventh of the beatitudes occurs here: 'Blessed are those who wash their robes' (v. 14). The metaphor of washed robes can be interpreted in at least three ways: (1) these people have been baptized; (2) they have made the decision to lead a morally upright life; or (3) they have been martyred. The example of the white-robed multitude in Rev. 7:14 enlightens interpretation. In 7:14, they have 'come out of the Tribulation and have washed their robes and made them white in the blood of the Lamb'. Quite clearly, these people 'washed their robes' through salvation. The use of the verb tenses is significant. In 7:14, the verb 'washed' (ἔπλυναν) is aorist, a past tense which indicates an action which occurred once at a specific time. In contrast, the verb 'washed' (πλύνοντες) in Rev. 22:14 is in the present tense, which indicates a continuous or repeated action ('they kept washing'). Perhaps, then, one can conclude that washing can occur at one special time such as martyrdom or conversion, but must also be a constant activity, showing consistent faithfulness to God. The metaphor can also be viewed within the context of the purification ritual of the Levitical law.[72] The purification rites are especially appropriate since those who have washed their robes are now able to enter the gates into the Holy City (v. 14). In the Old Testament tradition, the Israelites were com-

---

[71] Aune, p. 1219.
[72] Cf. Louw-Nida, p. 478.

manded to wash their clothes before entering the presence of God (Exod. 19:10,14), and Levites were required to wash their garments at the ritual of consecration (Num. 8:7,21). The metaphor in this passage, then, probably refers to the act of conversion, but also implies the continual activity of spiritual and moral cleansing (see Titus 3:5; Heb. 10:22). The continuity probably also implies the habitual daily life lived in commitment and obedient faithfulness to God. These people are the ones who are given the right to the tree of life and may enter the gates of the city (Rev. 22:14). Adam and Eve were cast out of Eden lest they disobey God and eat of this tree, which would cause them to live forever (Gen. 3:22). In the end time, the righteous, those who have 'washed their robes in the blood of the Lamb', will be given the right to this tree, i.e. to eternal existence.

In contrast, the wicked are 'outside'. The list of vices enumerated here (Rev. 22:15) is similar to the list in 21:8. Both lists include sorcerers, immoral persons, idolaters, and liars. 'Dogs' and 'murderers' are unique to the list in ch. 22. It can be argued that the terms in both lists are general enough to cover various kinds of wickedness so that the differences in the lists are not noteworthy. The added term "dogs" (κύνες) in ch. 22, however, is interesting. It is often used in the New Testament to denote impurity and viciousness.[73] In Deut. 23:17-18 the term is also used in reference to male cult prostitutes.[74] Verse 15 probably does not intend to imply that evildoers are living just outside the city. In fact, Rev. 20:15 condemns everyone whose name is not in the Book of Life to the Lake of Fire. Verse 15 merely makes a sharp distinction between the blessed state of the righteous and the alienation of the wicked. In fact, it should be noted that generally throughout Revelation, parallel statements contrast the states of the righteous and the wicked. This chapter describes in some detail the blessed state of the righteous. It is appropriate for the contrast to be drawn with the alienation of the wicked. Indeed, for John, God is just because he not only rewards the righteous, but condemns the wicked.[75]

It is also clear from v. 16 that the message of Revelation is not for the seer alone. The object 'you' (ὑμῖν) is plural: 'I sent my angel to you [plural] with this testimony for the churches ...' The 'you' obviously refers to more than just John. There are several options, but it is probably best simply to interpret the plural 'you' to refer to all who would read Revelation through the ages. Jesus himself again adds his affirmation to the book (v. 16). Here he uses two unusual titles of him-

---

[73] Gause, p. 282.
[74] Charles, II, 178.
[75] Gause, p. 282.

self: 'the root and descendant of David', and 'the bright morning star'. Verse 16 is also notable as one of the five ἐγώ εἰμι ("I am") sayings (1:8, 17; 2:23; 21:6; 22:16). The title 'root of David' is found in 5:5 where Jesus is introduced as the only one worthy to open the book and the seals. It is the traditional messianic title 'root of David' (see Isa. 11:1,10; Rom. 1:3) combined with the title 'offspring of David'. Both titles underscore that Jesus is worthy to be Messiah because he fulfills the messianic criterion that the Messiah would be related to David (cf. Isa. 11:10).

In Rev. 2:28, 'the morning star' is something received by Jesus from the Father that he will then pass on to anyone who overcomes. There are several possible interpretations. This title should definitely be linked with the coming Messiah. The prophecy in Num. 24:17 predicts that 'a star will come forth from Jacob'. This was usually interpreted messianically within Judaism. The Qumran texts (cf. Num. 14:17) include a 'recurring *testimonium* of the messianic warrior of the end time'.[76] It is also possible to interpret the 'morning star' in a broader sense: as the promise of the end of the tribulation and the dawn of the eschatological day. In any case, both titles (Root of David and Morning Star) refer to the messiahship of Jesus.

Verse 17 includes four invitations: two of them can be interpreted as specific requests for Christ to return. The last two invite participation in what Jesus has to offer: the 'water of life'. Probably the first two should be interpreted in light of the last two.[77] This means that all four invitations are addressed to the entire world, summoning everyone to partake of the available water of life. The 'Spirit' is undoubtedly the Holy Spirit and the Bride is probably the resurrected Church (see 21:2,9): the Holy Spirit, through the Church, is summoning everyone to come and partake of the gifts Christ is offering. The four invitations function in this passage as responses to Jesus in v. 12, where he promises to come quickly with his rewards. The reader is called to join the Spirit and the Bride in responding to Jesus' words to summon others to come and partake of Christ.

Verses 18-19 add a severe warning to anyone who would add to or take away from the words of the prophecy. Several things are noteworthy. Here, John re-identifies the book as 'prophecy' (see also 1:3). It is not clear who the speaker is. Verse 20 implies that the speaker is

---

[76] Bruce, p. 666.
[77] Cf. Ladd, p. 294.

Jesus ('The one who testifies to these things says, "Surely I am coming soon"').[78]

This kind of affirmation of the authenticity of a text (vv. 18-19) is called an *integrity formula*. John testifies to his work as a divine revelation that is both complete and sacred. His concern that a future reader might add or subtract from the text is a valid concern. The textual history of other Jewish and Christian apocalypses indicates that texts were often modified by those who transmitted them.[79] The severity of warning is enhanced by the punishment to be carried out: the plagues will come upon the one who adds to the text; the Tree of Life and the Holy City will be taken from the one who subtracts from it (vv. 18-19). In short, the one who alters the text will lose eternal life and his/her place in the new Jerusalem.

Verse 20 reiterates both Christ's witness to his imminent return and the seer's response: 'Amen, come Lord Jesus'. 'Amen' and 'yes' (ναί) function as synonyms meaning 'surely, with certainty'. They emphasize the solemn affirmation that indeed the previous statements are true. Whether the phrase 'Come, Lord Jesus' functions as a liturgical formula is not a significant issue here. It is noteworthy, however, that the phrase probably functions in two ways: (1) as an eschatological request for the future coming of Jesus; (2) in a broader sense, perhaps, it also calls for his immediate presence in the churches in which it was to be read and heard.

The apocalypse closes with a benediction: 'The grace of the Lord Jesus be with you all. Amen' (v. 21). This is unusual, but is appropriate here since the book began as an epistle (cf. 1:4a); it now closes as an epistle. The form of this particular benediction is closely related to the one used by Paul at the end of his epistles,[80] consisting of three elements: (1) the term 'grace' (χάρις); (2) the specification of the source of grace (the Lord Jesus) and (3) the specification of those who were to benefit from the grace (all).[81] As a typical formulation of epistles, the

---

[78] See Swete, p. 311; Charles, II, p. 218; Mounce, p. 396; Ernest B. Allo, *Saint Jean L'Apocalypse du Saint Jean* (Paris: Gabalda, 1933), p. 333. For other possibilities, see Theodor Zahn, *Die Offenbarung des Johannes*, II (2 vols.) (Leipzig: Deichert, 1924), pp. 628-29; Lohmeyer, p. 181; Caird, p. 287, who says the speaker is John; Heinrich Kraft, *Die Offenbarung des Johannes*, HNT 16a (Tübingen: J.C.B. Mohr, 1974), pp. 281-82, ascribes these 'interpolated curses' to Jesus.

[79] See Gerhard Dautzenberg, *Unchristliche Prophetie. Ihre Voraussetzungen im Judentum und ihre Struktur im ersten Korintherbrief*, BWANT (Stuttgart: W. Kohlhammer, c1975), pp. 122-48; David E. Aune, *Prophecy in Early Christianity and the Ancient Mediterranean World* (Grand Rapids, MI: Eerdmans, 1983), pp. 217-29.

[80] See Rom. 1:16-20; 1 Cor. 16:23; 2 Cor. 13:14; Gal. 6:18; Phil. 4:23; 1 Thess. 5:28; 2 Thess. 3:18; Phlm. 25.

[81] See Aune, pp. 1239-40.

benediction effectively conveys the basic component of the Christian faith that the grace only available by Jesus Christ is available to everyone who desires it. The book closes, as Mounce puts it, with the assurance that the world is in the hands of a God who controls the course of human destiny.[82]

In the conclusion (vv. 18-21), then, John reconfirms the many purposes of the text: (1) he refers to it as a 'book of prophecy'; (2) he closes with a typical formulation of a letter; (3) he places it within an apocalyptic context with the seriousness of retribution to anyone who modifies the text and with the final concept that ultimately God is in control of human destiny. The text is guaranteed by the One who stands at the beginning and end of history and of existence, the Alpha and Omega.

Reflection and Response (Part 7)

Reflection

A significant theme which weaves throughout the text of Revelation and is finally defined in ch. 19 is the testimony of Jesus. In 19:10 it is finally defined as the 'Spirit of prophecy', thereby equating the testimony of Jesus' message with prophetic content. Indeed, Jesus' message is linked with that of the prophets, that is, the coming of God's Kingdom. This suggests the unity of the prophetic message through the ages, emphasizing that Old Testament and New Testament saints alike, along with Jesus himself, are co-worshipers and servants of God, and, each in their own era, are heralding the triumph of the true God over all the forces of evil. The core of the message is plainly stated by the interpreting angel, 'Worship God'. The text concludes with the description of the final state of the righteous in the Holy City (chs. 21; 22), and the wicked in the Lake of Fire (ch. 20). Chapters 21 and 22 both include descriptions of those who are included in and those who are excluded from the Holy City. In short, those who lived their lives acknowledging God as Lord will participate in the place where God himself is at the center of existence. In contrast, those who have lived their lives rejecting the Lordship of God will be eternally excluded from the city (21:8; 22:11,15).

In order to facilitate our reflection on this text, the following questions might be considered. Do you know any individuals who consider themselves to be Christian, yet their behavior more closely reflects the description of those who reject God's Lordship? What leads you to this identification? Do these people still participate in your church com-

[82] Mounce, p. 396.

munity? What situations are available to them in which the Holy Spirit could convict them of their state?

A consideration of others is not enough, one must also allow the Holy Spirit to search one's own heart. The following questions might prove helpful. Is my life characterized by the Lordship of God? What is my attitude toward the vices described in Revelation as characteristic of those who are not faithful to God? How do I understand the life governed by God's Lordship? How seriously do I take the issue that there may be actions in my life that do not reflect his Lordship as described in Revelation? Is it easier for me to detect unfaithfulness in my brothers' and sisters' lives rather than in my own? To what extent do I believe and act on Christ's power to enable me to live a life free from sinful vices and reflective of God's Lordship? When was the last time I asked the Holy Spirit to search my life in regard to this kind of sinful activity? How long has it been since I responded to such ministries in my church community?

Response
Some suggestions may be helpful to guide your response to these questions.

1. Prayerfully examine your life in light of the above issues.
2. Identify and acknowledge specific areas which correspond to the descriptions of those who will be excluded from the Holy City.
3. Confess these areas to the Lord and then to a brother or sister in Christ. Identify the areas which may require long-range attention.
4. Pray together, not only confessing your repentance, but also receiving the healing of the Holy Spirit and his guidance for restoration.
5. Join a Bible study or prayer group through which you can receive the strength of corporate worship.
6. Consistently review your progress with a trusted friend. Focus on living a victorious life, reflecting the forgiveness and love of the Lord.

Conclusion

Filled with symbols, visions, dreams, angels, beasts, earthly devastation, and heavenly rejoicing, Revelation is an enigmatic and intriguing text which constantly challenges the reader and scholar to continue searching for the meaning of the message. Certainly, the author is grappling with the timeless issues of the nature of human destiny and whether there is Someone who is ultimately in control. For the author of Revelation, however, this is not an issue which has alternative solutions: God, the Almighty, the Alpha and Omega, the first and last, the beginning and end, is, was, and always will be in control (Rev. 1:8; 22:12,13). Indeed, the righteous will be rewarded with eternal existence with God (chs. 21; 22), while the wicked along with evil itself (symbolized by Satan, ch. 20) will be doomed to eternal existence in the Lake of Fire. The author wraps the entire scenario in apocalyptic language and imagery so that the message appears illusory at times (e.g. the sun-clothed woman, ch. 12), yet devastatingly clear at others (e.g. the destruction of Babylon, ch. 18). Even when the message appears to be straightforward, however, the imagery urges the reader to look beyond the symbols and see that there is more to be found (e.g. although it is quite clear that Babylon will be destroyed, the reader is not sure what Babylon actually represents). Certainly, some of the most intriguing issues will continue to be shrouded in mystery (e.g. 666, the number of the Beast, ch. 13).

The reader is also struck by the tension between the imminence of Christ's coming on the one hand and the eschatological delay on the other (see Reflection, Part 4). Every generation of readers continues to be challenged to live each moment to the fullest, in the understanding and context of the imminent coming of Christ. Indeed, the readers (whether the intended readers of the original seven churches or the current readers of today) find courage and hope for whatever situation he or she is facing; those struggling with hostile environments as well as those undergoing more serious persecution are encouraged that, ultimately, God is in control, even of the wicked, and will eventually vindicate the righteous by judging the wicked and exalting the righteous to an existence of eternal rejoicing.

Revelation is significant for the study of the history of the early church since it closes the New Testament canon and the history of the New Testament.[83] Even if chronologically it is not the latest to be written, it appropriately closes the canon as the final book of the New

---

[83] M.C. Tenney, *Survey of the New Testament*, ed. W.M. Duane (Leicester, UK: Eerdmans, Intervarsity Press, 1990), p. 381.

Testament, since it shows a church fully developed and functioning in the world. It shows the conflicts and struggles which challenge the Church of this time, but concludes with the promise and hope of final vindication of the righteous, and destruction of the wicked. The Church in the late first century, as seen in Revelation, is persecuted by the government, is struggling with how to live as Christians without being influenced by pagan society, and is attempting to refine its understanding of Christology. Some, like the church at Ephesus, have lost their first enthusiasm for the Gospel while others are being killed because of their faith (Smyrna and Pergamum). More than any of the other New Testament books, Revelation reflects the prophetic tone of the Old Testament prophets, which serves as a warning and as hope for the future. In essence, Revelation gives 'the divine perspective on history'[84] that distinguishes between the righteous and the wicked through the past, the present and the future, reflecting the past time of the author himself; the fourth chapter opens with an introduction to 'the things which must come to pass hereafter' (4:1), indicating the period from the author's time to the present and concludes with the last two visions which have not yet occurred (the new heaven and new earth, chs. 21, 22). Clearly, God appears as Lord of the past, the present and the future.[85] The reader is struck by the fact that the message of Revelation is not a message locked into the context of the first century CE, rather it covers the centuries in between and speaks anew to each generation: God is in control – worship him!

---

[84] *Ibid.*, p. 394.
[85] *Ibid.*

Bibliography

Alexander, P., '3 (Hebrew Apocalypse of) Enoch, Fifth-Sixth Century A.D.' in *Old Testament Pseudepigrapha*, ed. J.H. Charlesworth, vol. I (London: Darton, Longman & Todd, 1983).
Alford, Henry, 'Apocalypse of John', in *The Greek Testament*, IV (Chicago: Moody Press, 1958), 544-750.
Allegro, John M., ed., *Qumran Cave 4*, Discoveries in the Judaean Desert 5 (Oxford: Clarendon Press, 1968).
Allo, Ernest Bernard, *Saint Jean: l'Apocalypse*, Etudes Bibliques (3rd ed.; Paris: J. Gabalda, 1933).
Archer, Gleason L., Jr. 'Daniel' in *The Expositor's Bible Commentary* VII, ed. F.E. Gaebelein (Grand Rapids, MI: Regency Reference Library/Zondervan, 1985).
Aune, David E., *Revelation*, 3 vols., 52a,b,c (Dallas, TX: Word Books, 1997, Nashville, TN: T. Nelson, c1998).
—, *The New Testament and Its Environment* (Philadelphia, PA: Westminster Press, 1987).
—, *Prophecy in Early Christianity and the Ancient Mediterranean World* (Grand Rapids, MI: Eerdmans, 1983).
Barclay, William, *The Revelation of John*, The Daily Study Bible Series, 2 (Philadelphia: Westminster Press, 1960).
—, *Letters to the Seven Churches* (New York: Abingdon, 1957).
Barr, David, ed., *The Reality of the Apocalypse: Rhetoric and Politics in the Book of Revelation* (Atlanta: SBL Sym 39, 2006).
Bauckham, Richard J., *The Theology of the Book of Revelation*, New Testament Theology Series (New York: Cambridge University Press, 1993).
—, *The Climax of Prophecy: Studies in the Book of Revelation* (Edinburgh: T. & T. Clark, 1993).
—, *Scripture, Tradition, and Reason. Essays in Honour of Richard P.C. Hanson*, ed. Richard Bauckham and Benjamin Drewery (Edinburgh: T & T Clark, 1988).
Bauer W. and B. Aland, *The Text of the New Testament*, trans. E.F. Rhodes (Leiden: Brill; Grand Rapids, MI: Eerdmans, 1987)
Beagley, Alan James, *The 'Sitz im Leben' of the Apocalypse, with particular reference to the Role of the Church's Enemies*, BZNW 50 (New York: W. de Gruyter, 1987).

Beasley-Murray, George R., *The Book of Revelation*, New Century Bible Commentary Series, 66 (London: Marshall, Morgan & Scott, 1978).
Beck, D.M., 'Nicolaitans', *Interpreter's Dictionary of the Bible* (Nashville: Abingdon, 1976).
Beckwith, Isbon Thaddeus, *The Apocalypse of John* (New York: Macmillan, 1919).
Bell, Albert A., 'The Date of John's Apocalypse. The Evidence of Some Roman Historians Reconsidered', *New Testament Studies* 25 (1978), 93-102.
Benware, Paul N., *Understanding End Times Prophecy* (Chicago: Moody Press, 1995).
Berger, Klaus, *Die Amen-Worte Jesu. Eine Untersuchung zum Problem der Legitimation in apokalyptischer Rede,* BZNW 39 (Berlin: W. de Gruyter, 1970).
Blaiklock, E.M., *Cities of the New Testament*, London: Pickering & Inglis, 1965.
Blenkinsopp, Joseph, *A History of Prophecy in Israel* (Philadelphia: Westminster Press, 1983).
Blumner, Hugo, *The Home Life of the Ancient Greeks*, trans. Alice Zimmern (New York: Cooper Square Publishers, 1966).
Boesak, Allan A., *Comfort and Protest: Reflections on the Apocalypse of John of Patmos* (Philadelphia: Westminster Press, 1987).
Boice, James M., *The Minor Prophets*: an Expositional Commentary, II (Grand Rapids, MI: Zondervan, 1986).
Boismard, M.E., 'Notes sur l'Apocalypse', *Revue Biblique* 59 (1952), 161-81.
Bomer, Franz, *Untersuchungen über die Religion der Sklaven in Griechenland und Rom* (Wiesbaden: Steiner, 1981-1990).
Bornkamm, Günther, 'Die Komposition der apokalyptischen Visionen in der Offenbarung Johannis', *ZNW* 36 (1937), 132-49.
——, 'ληνός, ὑπολήνιον', *TDNT* IV (1977), 254-57.
Bousset, Wilhelm, *Die Offenbarung Johannis* (Göttingen: Vandenhoeck & Ruprecht, 1956).
Brettler, Marc Zvi, *God is King: Understanding an Israelite Metaphor,* JSOTS 76 (Sheffield: Sheffield Academic Press, 1989).
Bruce, F.F., 'The Revelation to John', in *A New Testament Commentary,* ed. G.C.D. Howley (London: Pickering & Inglis, 1979).
Buchanan, George Wesley, *The Book of Revelation: Its Introduction and Prophecy*, MBCNT Series, 22 (Lewiston, NY: E. Mellen Press, 1993).
Bullock, C. Hassell, *An Introduction to the Old Testament Prophetic Books* (Chicago: Moody Press, 1986).
Caird, G.B., *A Commentary on the Revelation of St. John the Divine*, Harper's New Testament Commentaries 17 (New York: Harper & Row, 1966).
Carrington, P., *The Meaning of Revelation* (London, New York, Toronto: Macmillan, 1931).
Cashdon, E., 'Zechariah' in *The Twelve Prophets*, ed. A. Cohen (London: Soncino Press, 1957).
Charles, Robert H., *The Apocrypha and Pseudepigrapha of the Old Testament in English* (2 vols.; Oxford: Clarendon Press [c1913], 1973).
——, *A Critical and Exegetical Commentary on the Revelation of St. John*, ICC 45 (2 vols.; New York: Charles Scribner's Sons, 1920).

Charlesworth, James H., ed., *The Old Testament Pseudepigrapha*, 2 vols. (Garden City: Doubleday, 1983).
Collins, John J., *Daniel with an Introduction to Apocalyptic Literature*, Forms of the Old Testament Literature Series, 20 (Grand Rapids, MI: Eerdmans, 1984),
Craigie Peter C., *Psalms 1-50* (Waco, TX: Word Books, 1983).
Culley, Robert C., *Oral Formulaic Language in the Biblical Psalms*, Near and Middle East Series 4 (Toronto: University of Toronto Press, 1967).
Dautzenberg, Gerhard, *Urchristliche Prophetie. Ihre Erforschung, ihre Voraussetzungen im Judentum und ihre Struktur im ersten Korintherbrief* (Stuttgart: W. Kohlhammer, 1975).
Davies, W.D., *The Gospel and the Land* (Berkeley: University of California Press, 1974).
Davis, R.D., 'The Relationship Between the Seals, Trumpets and Bowls in the Book of Revelation' *JETS* 16 (1973), 150f.
Delling, Gerhard, 'καιρός, ἄκαρος', *TDNT* III (1965), 455-64.
Diels, Hermann, 'Empedocles frags. B96, B98, B107, B115' in *Die Fragmente der Vorsokratiker: griechisch und deutsch*, 6th ed., ed. Walther Kranz (Berlin: Weidmann, 1952, 1960).
Durbeck, H., *Zur Charakteristik der griechischen Farbenbezeichnungen* (Bonn: Habelt, 1977).
Erdman, Charles R., *The Revelation of John* (Philadelphia: Westminster [1936] c1966, 1977).
Erlandsson, Seth, '(זנה) *zanah*; (זנונים) *z^{e}nunim*; (זנות) *z^{e}nuth*; (תזנות) *taznuth*, *TDOT* IV (1980), 99-104.
Fekkes, Jan, *Isaiah and Prophetic Traditions in the Book of Revelation*, JSOTS 93 (Sheffield: Sheffield Academic Press, 1994).
Fitzer, Gottfried, 'σφραγίς, σφραγίζω, κατασφραγίζω', *TDNT* VII (1964-76), 939-53.
Fitzgerald, John T. and L. Michael White, eds., *The Tabula of Cebes* (Chico, CA: Scholars Press, 1983).
Foerster, Werner, 'βδελύσσομαι, βδέλυγμα, βδελυκτός', *TDNT* I (1964).
——, 'σῴζω, σωτηρία', *TDNT* VII (1971), 598-600.
Ford, J. Massyngberde, *Revelation*. The Anchor Bible, Garden City, NY: Doubleday (1975).
Friedrich, G., 'σαλπίζω, σαλπιστής', *TDNT* VII (1971), 71-88.
Gaebelein, Frank E., ed., *The Expositor's Bible Commentary: with the New International Version of the Holy Bible*, XII (Grand Rapids: Zondervan, c1976-1993).
Gaechter, Paul, 'The Original Sequence of Apocalypse 20-22', *TS* 10 (1949).
——, *Faith, Hope, and Worship*, ed. H.S. Versnel (Leiden: Brill, 1981).
Galling, Kurt, ed., *Biblisches Reallexikon*, Handbuch zum Alten Testament, 1st series, 1 (Tübingen: J.C.B. Mohr [Paul Siebeck], 1937).
Gause, R. Hollis, *Revelation* (Cleveland, TN: Pathway Press, 1983).
Grozinger, Karl-Erich, 'Engel III', *Theologische Realenzyklopädie*, IX (Berlin: de Gruyter, 1977).
Gundry, R.H., *The Church and the Tribulation* (Grand Rapids, MI: Zondervan, 1973).

Guthrie, Donald, *New Testament Introduction, Hebrews to Revelation* (Chicago, IL: InterVarsity Press, 1962).
Hadorn, D.W., *Die Offenbarung des Johannes*, Theologischer Handkommentar zum Neuen Testament 18 (Leipzig: Deichert, 1928).
Hailey, Homer, *Revelation: An Introduction and Commentary* (Grand Rapids, MI: Baker Book House, 1979).
Hanson, Paul D., *The Dawn of Apocalyptic* (Philadelphia: Fortress Press, 1975).
Harrington, Hannah, 'Zechariah', *The Twelve*, II (forthcoming).
Harrison, Everett F., *Introduction to the New Testament* (Grand Rapids, MI: Eerdmans, 1964).
Hartman, Lars, *Prophecy Interpreted* (Lund: CWK Gleerup, 1966).
Hauck, Friedrich, 'κοινός,' *TDNT* III (1965).
Hellholm, David, *Apocalypticism in the Mediterranean World and the Near East* (Tübingen: Mohr, 1989).
Hemer, Colin J., *The Letters to the Seven Churches of Asia in Their Local Setting*, JSNTSup 11 (Sheffield: JSOT Press, 1986).
Hempel, Johannes, 'Hallelujah', *Interpreter's Bible Dictionary*, II (Nashville: Abingdon, 1962), 415-16.
Hendricksen, William, *More Than Conquerors* (Grand Rapids, MI: Baker Book House, 1944).
Hiebert, Theodore, 'Divine Warrior', *Anchor Bible Dictionary*, VI (New York: Doubleday, 1992).
Hill, D., 'Prophecy and Prophets in the Revelation of Saint John', *New Testament Studies* 18 (1971-72), 401-18.
Holtz, Traugott, *Die Christologie der Apokalypse des Johannes*, Texte und Untersuchungen, 2 (2nd ed.; Berlin: Akademie-Verlag, 1962).
Hutson, Christopher R., 'Was Timothy Timid? On the Rhetoric of Fearlessness (1 Corinthians 16:10-11) and Cowardice (2 Timothy 1:7)', *Biblical Research* 42 (1997), 69-70.
Jeremias, Joachim, 'γέεννα', *TDNT* I (1964), 657-58.
——, 'νύμφη, νυμφίος', *TDNT* IV (1967), 1099-1106.
——, *Jesus' Promise to the Nations*, Studies in Biblical Theology, 24 (London: SCM Press, 1967).
Johnson, Alan F., *Revelation*, Expositor's Bible Commentary Series, 12 (Grand Rapids: Zondervan, 1981).
Jones, C.P., 'Stigma: Tattooing and Branding in Graeco-Roman Antiquity', *Journal of Religious Studies* 77 (1987), 139-55.
Kiddle, Martin, *The Revelation of St. John*, The Moffatt New Testament Commentary (London: Harper, 1940).
Koch, Klaus, *The Rediscovery of Apocalyptic*, trans. Margaret Kohl, Studies in Biblical Theology, 2nd series, 22 (London: SCM Press, 1972).
Kraft, Heinrich, *Die Offenbarung des Johannes*, Handbuch zum Neuen Testament, 16a (Tübingen: J.C.B. Mohr, 1974).
Kümmel, W.G., *The New Testament: The History of the Investigation of Its Problems* (London: SCM Press, 1973).
Kuhn, Georg, 'βαβυλών', *TDNT* I (1964).
Ladd, George E., *A Commentary on the Revelation of John* (Grand Rapids, MI: Eerdmans, 1972).

—, 'Why Not Prophetic-Apocalyptic?', *JBL* 76 (1957), 192-200.
Lenski, R.C.H., *The Interpretation of Saint John's Revelation* (Minneapolis: Augsburg, 1963).
Lilje, Hanns, *The Last Book of the Bible: The Meaning of the Revelation of St. John*, trans. Olive Wyon (Philadelphia: Muhlenberg Press, 1957).
Lohmeyer, Ernst, *Die Offenbarung des Johannes*, 3rd ed., Handbuch zum Neuen Testament, 16 (Tübingen: Mohr-Siebeck, 1953).
Lohse, Eduard, *Die Offenbarung des Johannes*, Texte zum Neuen Testament, 11 (Göttingen: Vandenhoeck & Ruprecht, 1960).
Louw, J.P. and E.A. Nida, eds., *Greek-English Lexicon of the New Testament Based on Semantic Domains* I (2 vols.; NY: United Bible Societies, 1988).
McKelvey, R.J., *The New Temple: The Church in the New Testament* (London: Oxford University Press, 1969).
Malina, Bruce J., *On the Genre and Message of Revelation: Star Visions and Sky Journeys* (Peabody, MA: Hendrickson, 1995).
Marshall, I. Howard, 'Jewels and Precious Stones', *The New Bible Dictionary* (2nd ed.; Leicester, UK and Downer's Grove, IL: InterVarsity Press, 1996), 593-96.
Mellor, M. ΘΕΑ ΡΩΜΗ: *The Worship of the Goddess Roma in the Greek World* (Göttingen: Vandenhoeck & Ruprecht, 1975).
Michaelis, Wilhelm, 'ὁράω, εἶδον, βλέπω, ὀπτάνομαν, θεάομαι, θεωρέω', *TDNT* V (1967), 313-82.
Michaels, J.R., *Interpreting the Book of Revelation* (Grand Rapids, MI: Baker Book House, 1992).
Michel, O., 'μιμνήσκομαι, μνεία, μνήμη, μνῆμα μνημεῖον, μνημονεύω', *TDNT* IV (1967), 675-83.
Michl, Johann, 'Engel II', *Reallexikon für Antike und Christentum* V (1962).
Moore, R.D., 'Personification of the Seduction of Evil: "The Wiles of the Wicked Woman"' *Revue de Qumran* 10 (1979-81), 505-19.
Morris, Leon, *The Book of Revelation*, rev. ed. Tyndale New Testament Commentary, 20 (Downers Grove, IL: InterVarsity Press, 1987).
Mounce, Robert H., *The Book of Revelation*, NICNT, 17 (Grand Rapids, MI: Eerdmans, 1977).
Muller, U.B., 'Literarische und formgeschichtliche Bestimmung der Apokalypse des Johannes als ein Zeugnis frühchristlicher Apokalyptik', *Apocalypticism in the Mediterranean World and the Near East*, ed. D. Hellholm (Tübingen: Mohr, 1989).
Mussies, G., *The Morphology of Koine Greek as Used in the Apocalypse of St. John: A Study in Bilingualism* (Leiden: Brill, 1971).
Nock-Festugiere, A.D. and A.J. Festugiere, Corpus Hermeticum (Paris: Société d'édition "Les Belles Lettres", 1945-54).
Parker, Robert, *Miasma: Pollution and Purification in Early Greek Religion* (Oxford: Clarendon, 1983).
Pentecost, Dwight J., *Things to Come* (Grand Rapids, MI: Zondervan, 1964).
Preston, Ronald H. and Anthony T. Hanson, *The Revelation of St. John the Divine*, Torch Bible Commentaries (London: SCM, 1962).
Preisker, H., 'μακράν, μακρόθεν', *TDNT* IV (1967), 372-74.

Provan, Iain, 'Foul Spirits, Fornication and Finance: Revelation 18 from an Old Testament Perspective', *JSNT* 64 (1996), 81-100.

Ramsay, William M., *The Letters to the Seven Churches of Asia and Their Place in the Plan of the Apocalypse* (Grand Rapids, MI: Baker Book House, [1904] 1963).

—, *The Cities and Bishoprics of Phrygia*, II (Oxford: Clarendon Press, 1895-1897).

Reader, W.W., 'Die Stadt Gottes in der Johannesapokalypse' (diss., Göttingen, 1971).

Reinhold, M., *The History of Purple as a Status Symbol in Antiquity* (Brussels: Latomus, 1970).

Rengstorf, Karl H., 'δεσπότης, οἰκοδεσπότης, οἰκοδεσποτέω', *TDNT* II (1964), 44-49.

Richardson, Cyril C., *Early Christian Fathers*, Library of Christian Classics, 1 (Philadelphia: Westminster, 1953).

Rissi, Mathias, *The Future of the World: An Exegetical Study of Revelation 19:11-22, 15*, Studies in Biblical Theology, 2nd series, 23 (Naperville, IL: Allenson, 1972).

—, 'The Rider on the White Horse: A Study of Revelation 6:1-8'. *Interpretation* 18 (1964), 407-18.

Rowley, Harold H., *The Relevance of Apocalyptic* (London: Lutterworth, 1947).

Ruiten, Jacques van, 'The Intertextual Relation between Isaiah 65,17-20 and Revelation 21,1-5b', *Estudios Biblios* 51 (1993), 473-510.

Russell, D.S., *Prophecy and the Apocalyptic Dream: Protest and Promise* (Peabody, MA: Hendrickson, 1994).

—, *The Method and Message of Jewish Apocalyptic, 200 BC-AD 100* (Philadelphia: Westminster, 1964).

Schlatter, Adolf von, *Das Alte Testament in der Johanneischen Apokalypse*, trans. Paul P. Levertoff (Gütersloh: Bertelsmann, 1912).

Schüssler Fiorenza, Elisabeth, *The Book of Revelation – Justice and Judgment* (Minneapolis: Fortress Press, 1998).

—, 'Composition and Structure of the Revelation of John', *CBQ* 39 (1977), 344-66.

—, *The Book of Revelation* (Chicago: Franciscan Herald Press, 1976).

—, 'Apocalyptic and Gnosis in the Book of Revelation', *JBL* 92 (1973), 565-81.

—, *Priester für Gott: Studien zum Herrschafts- und Priestermotiv in der Apokalypse* (Münster: Aschendorff, 1972).

Schneider, J., 'τιμή, τιμάω', *TDNT* VIII, 169-80.

Schrenk, Gottlob, 'βίβλος, βιβλίον', *TDNT* I (1964), 615-20.

Sherk, Robert K., *Roman Documents from the Greek East; Senatus Consulta and Epistulae to the Age of Augustus* (Baltimore: Johns Hopkins University Press, 1969).

Sickenberger, J.B., *Erklärung der Johannesapokalypse* (Bonn: Hanstein, 1940).

Skehan, Patrick W., 'King of Kings, Lord of Lords (Apoc. 19:16)', *CBQ* 10 (1948), 398.

Souza Nagueira, P.A. de, 'Der Widerstand gegen Rom in der Apokalypse des Johannes: Eine Untersuchung zur Tradition des Falls von Babylon in Apokalypse 18' (diss., Heidelberg, 1991).
Stauffer, Halle Ethelbert, 'γαμέω, γάμος', *TDNT* I (1964), 648-57.
Stengel, P., 'ἀπάρχαι', Pauly-Wissowa *Real-Encyclopädie der classischen Altertumswissenschaft*, I (Stuttgart: J.B. Metzler, 1978), 26-27.
Stonehouse, Ned Bernard, *The Apocalypse in the Ancient Church* (Goes, Netherlands: Oosterbann & Le Cointre, 1929).
Strobel, A. 'Abfassung und Geschichts-Theologie der Apokalypse nach Kap. XVII.9-12', *NTS* 10 (1963-64), 433-45.
Stuhlmacher, Peter, *Evangelium – Schriftauslegung – Kirche: Festschrift für Peter Stuhlmacher, zum 65. Geburtstag* (Göttingen: Vandenhoeck & Ruprecht, 1997).
Sturm, R., 'Defining the Word Apocalyptic' in *Apocalyptic and the New Testament: Essays in Honor of J. Louis Martyn*, ed. Joel Marcus and Marion L. Soards (Sheffield: JSOT Press, c1989).
Swete. Henry B., *The Apocalypse of St. John* (Grand Rapids, MI: Eerdmans, [1906] 1951).
Tenney, Merrill C. *Interpreting Revelation* (Grand Rapids, MI: Eerdmans, 1980).
—, *New Testament Times* (Grand Rapids, MI: Eerdmans, 1957).
—, *Survey of the New Testament*, rev. W.M. Dunne (Leicester, UK: Eerdmans; Intervarsity Press), 1990.
Thomas, John Christopher, *1 John, 2 John, 3 John* (Sheffield: Sheffield Academic Press), 2004.
Unnik, W.C. van, *Het godspredikaat 'Het begin en het einde' bij Flavius Josephus en in de openbaring van Johannes* (Amsterdam: Noord-Hollandsche Uitgevers Maatschappij, 1976)
Versnel, H.S., 'Religious Mentality in Ancient Prayer', in *Faith, Hope and Worship: Aspects of Religious Mentality in the Ancient World*, ed. H.S. Versnel (Leiden: Brill, 1981).
Vos, Louis Arthur, *The Synoptic Traditions in the Apocalypse* (Kampen: J.H. Kok, 1965).
Wainwright, Arthur W. *Mysterious Apocalypse: Interpreting the Book of Revelation* (Nashville, TN: Abingdon Press, 1993).
Wall, Robert W., *Revelation*, NIBC (Carlisle: Paternoster, 1991; Peabody, MA: Hendrickson, 1995).
Walvoord, John F., *The Revelation of Jesus Christ; A Commentary* (Chicago: Moody Press, 1966).
Weiss, Johannes, *Die Offenbarung des Johannes: Ein Beitrag zur Literatur- und Religionsgeschichte* (Göttingen: Vandenhoeck & Ruprecht, 1904).
Wettstein, J.J., *Novum Testamentum Graecum*, II (repr. Graz: Akademische Druck- und Verlagsanstalt, 1962).
Wikenhauser, A., *Die Offenbarung Johannes*, Das Neue Testament, 9 (3rd ed.; Regensburg: Pustet, 1959).
Winston, David, *The Wisdom of Solomon. A New Translation with Introduction and Commentary* (Garden City, NY: Doubleday, 1979).
Wright, William, *The Chronicle of Joshua the Stylite* (Amsterdam: Philo Press, 1968).

Yamauchi, Edwin M., *The Archaeology of New Testament Cities in Western Asia Minor* (Grand Rapids, MI: Baker Book House, 1980).

Yarbro Collins, A., *The Combat Myth in the Book of Revelation* (Missoula, MT: Scholars, 1976).

Zahn, Theodor, *Die Offenbarung des Johannes* (2 vols.; Leipzig: Deichert, 1924-26).

Index of Names

Alexander, P.S. 152
Alford, H. 210
Allegro, J. 171
Allo, E.B. 236
Archer, G. 127
Aune, D. 8, 52, 53, 58, 59, 53, 65, 67, 68, 69, 70, 71, 78, 79, 85, 87, 90, 91, 93, 96, 98, 100, 102, 103, 107, 109, 110, 111, 112, 116, 117, 118, 119, 123, 124, 125, 127, 128, 130, 131, 134, 137, 142, 144, 147, 151, 153. 164, 165, 169, 173, 174, 175, 183, 186, 194, 197, 198, 207, 210, 211, 213, 214, 217, 218, 219, 220, 221, 222, 224, 225, 226, 229, 231, 233, 236

Barclay, W. 129, 227
Bauckham, R. 1, 4, 17, 63, 86, 87, 104, 107, 117, 125, 143, 153, 156, 158, 178, 194, 195, 196, 201, 207, 214, 229
Bauer, W. & B. Aland 89
Beagley, A.J. 182
Beasley-Murray, G.R. 13, 18, 60, 67, 110, 118, 213
Beck, D.M. 34
Beckwith, I.T. 43, 157
Bell, A.A. 9
Benware, P. 84
Blaiklock, E.N. 52
Blount, B.K. 68
Blummer, H. 150, 215
Boice, J. 135
Boismard, M.E. 144
Bomer, F. 146

Bornkamm, G. 110, 154
Bousset, W. 182, 224
Brettler, M.Z. 71
Bruce, F.F. 165, 235
Buchanan, G.W. 3, 7, 9

Caird, G.B. 77, 89, 130, 145, 188, 236
Carrington, P. 145
Cashdon, E. 135
Charles, R.H. 5, 8, 9, 36, 53, 90, 99, 110, 124, 182, 210, 224, 234, 236
Charlesworth, J. 160, 185
Collins, A.Y. 127, 154
Collins, J.J. 114
Craigie, P.C. 157
Cully, R.C. 70

Dauzenberg, G. 236
Davies, W.D. 87
Delling, G. 119
Diels, H. 166
Durbeck, H. 171

Erdman, C. 216, 232
Erlandsson, S. 170

Fekkes, J. 224
Fitzer, G. 67
Fitzgerald, J.T. 171
Foerster, W. 89, 171
Ford, J.M. 7, 10, 144, 145, 147, 157, 158, 182
Friedrich, G. 93

Gaechter, P. 231
Galling, K. 152

Gause, H. 22, 36, 60, 69, 71, 72, 73, 78, 118, 119, 120, 127, 131, 133, 142, 146, 156, 157, 158, 165, 172, 173, 175, 177, 178, 181, 182, 186, 189, 190, 191, 194, 197, 198, 206, 217, 223, 225, 229, 234
Grozinger, K.E. 152, 185
Gundry, R.H. 215
Guthrie, D. 8

Hadorn, D.W. 224
Hailey, H. 41, 44
Hanson, P. 3
Harrington, H. 135
Harrison, E.F. 8
Hartmann, L. 119
Hauck, F. 226
Hellholm, D. 2
Hempel, J. 190
Hendricksen, W. 102, 205
Hill, D. 173
Holtz, T. 197
Hutson, C. 219

Jeremias, J. 50, 109, 192, 202
Johnson, A. 13, 17, 20, 27, 29, 30, 39, 34, 39, 42, 43, 44, 45, 47, 50, 53, 58, 59, 60, 63, 64, 75, 76, 113, 117, 127, 137, 176, 180, 221
Jones, C.P. 171

Kiddle, M. 111, 125, 145, 225
Kraft, H. 236
Kranz, W. 166
Kuhn, G. 170
Kümmel, W.G. 11

Ladd, G. 4, 49, 50, 101, 102, 107, 110, 117, 122, 125, 143, 207, 235
Lenski, R.C.H. 225
Lilje, H. 119, 161, 177
Lohmeyer, E. 110, 153, 156, 174, 236
Lohse, E. 221
Louw, J.P. & E.A. Nida 70, 78, 233

Marcus, J. & M. Soards 3
Marshall, I. 223

McCartney, E.S. 167
McKelvey, R.J. 89, 215
Mellor, M. 178
Michaelis, W. 228
Michaels, J.R. 231
Michel, O. 184
Michl, J. 152, 185
Moore, R.D. 171
Morris, L. 12
Mounce, R.H. 13, 20, 23, 37, 39, 40, 43, 44, 45, 47, 48, 49, 50, 53, 58, 59, 60, 63, 65, 66, 67, 68, 73, 75, 80, 86, 96, 97, 99, 101, 102, 107, 110, 111, 113, 116, 118, 119, 120, 124, 125, 127, 129, 131, 146, 147, 149, 150, 151, 154, 158, 162, 163, 164, 165, 170, 173, 186, 197, 198, 205, 207, 215, 219, 220, 221, 223, 236, 237
Muller, U.B. 182
Mussies, G. 149, 181

Nock, A.D. & A.J. Festugiere 82
Nogueira, S. 184

Otzen, B. 210

Parker, R. 161
Pentecost, D.W. 12, 14
Preston, R. & A.T. Hanson 70, 89
Priesker, H. 187
Provan, I. 182

Rad, G. von 72
Ramsay, W.M. 108
Reader, W.W. 224
Reinhold, M. 171
Rengstorf, K. 80
Rissi, M. 78, 197
Rowley, H.H. 3
Ruiten, J. 215, 217
Russell, D.S. 2, 3, 210

Schlatter, A. 224
Schneider, J. 72
Schüssler-Fiorenza, E. 34, 108, 110, 215, 231
Sherk, R.K. 51

Shrenk, G. 110
Sickenberger, J.B. 224
Skaggs, R. & T. Doyle 68, 84, 85, 86, 90
Skehen, P. 200
Stengel, P.W. 146
Stonehouse, N.B. 6
Strobel, A. 174
Stuhlmacher, P. 109
Sturm, R. 3
Swete, H. 62, 116, 213, 227, 230, 236

Tenney, M.C. 8, 14, 239, 240
Thomas, J.C. 7

Unnik, W.C. van 218

Versnel, H.S. 184

Wall, R.W. 50, 63, 99, 103, 109
Walvoord, J. 49, 50, 58, 102, 164, 205, 222
Weiss, J. 147
Wettstein, J.J. 167, 178
Wikenhauser, A. 224
Winston, D. 120
Wright, W. 100

Yamauchi, E.M. 10, 38, 39, 41, 42, 45, 51, 52

Zahn, T. 236

Index of Biblical and Other References

OLD TESTAMENT
Genesis
1:14-19 97
1:21 134
2:9 227
3:1-19 129
3:14-19 227
3:22 227, 234
4:1-15 146
8:1 184
10:3 209
11:4 184
17:7 218
19:24 94, 102
19:28 150
19:29 184
20:2-4 209
21:20 216
22:12 148
30:22 184
31:5 216
37:9 125, 126
41:42 54
49:9-10 69
49:11 153

Exodus
1:22 131
3:14 64
7:12 97
7:14 94
7:20-21 96
7:20 161
9:13-35 95
9:31-32 96
10:1-20 99

10:22 161
13:2-16 146
13:21-22 90
13:21 160
14:8 131
15 157, 199
15:1-19 157
15:1-18 156
15:11-13 157
15:13 157
15:14-16 157
15:15 158
15:17 157
15:18 158
16:33-36 40
19:4 131
19:5-6 70
19:10 233
19:14 233
19:16 61, 160
19:18 81
19ff 220
25:22 159
27:3 94
28:17-20 220
28:17 59
29:12 80
29:45 215
30 93
30:1-10 93
32:15 159
32:32-33 47
32:47 47
33:20 228
33:23 228
38:21 159
40:34 159, 160

Leviticus
2:1 94
4:7 80
6:8 94
10:1-3 94
10:2 202
14:52 94
16:11-14 94
17:11 80, 94
23:40 88
24:16 163
24:19-20 185
26 90
26:11-12 215
27:26-27 146

Numbers
3:13 70
3:44-51 146
7:89 108
8:7 233
8:12 233
10:5-6:10 93
10:9 93
16:6-17 94
16:31-33 130
16:35 202
16:40 93
24:17 235
24:25 40
25:31 40
29:1 93
31:8 40
31:16f 40

Deuteronomy
1:28 184

Index of Biblical and Other References

7:21-20 216
9:1 184
10:5 159
10:17 177
13:1 140
14:22-26 146
18:15 118
18:18 114
19:21 185
20 144
23:9-10 144
23:17-18 234
28:42 99
29:23 102
31:29 103
31:30-32 156
32:10-11 131
32:14 53, 153
32:17 103
33 199

Joshua
3:10 84
7:6 187

Judges
4:6-16 165
5 199
5:4 94
5:19 165
5:20 98
7 165
8:26 172
16:28 184
18:30-31 86

1 Samuel
1:27 174
2:10 71
3:38 174
4:10 175
17:43-44 181
18:1-4 54
21:5 145
21:22 174
29:1 165
31:1-7 165

2 Samuel
1:19 174
3:31 115
6:5 188
7:14 218
11:11 145

1 Kings
1:14 64
1:16 64
1:34 93
3:9 93
6:30 224
7:50 94
8:10-11 160
8:37 99
12:25-33 86
16:7 103
17:1 115
17:2-3 126
18:4 42
18:19 42
18:38 140
19:3-4 126
19:4 170
19:11 94, 111
22:11 222
22:19 58, 129
22:20 68

2 Kings
1 211
1:10 94, 115, 140
9:13 93
9:22 42, 170
12:14 94
19:4 84
19:16 84
20:3 184
22:17 103

1 Chronicles
5:10 175
20:8 175
24:4-5 60
25:9-31 60
28:18 93
28:19 120

2 Chronicles
5:13-14 160
7:13 100
34:25 103

Ezra
7:27 176
9:6 184
11:43 184

Nehemiah
8:15 88
9:1 115
9:11 188
10:35 146
11:1 112

Esther
6:6-11 54
8:15 172
11:5-6 164

Job
1:6-9 128
1:6-11 129
1:6 93
1:20 129
2:6 100
4:16 92
33:26 228
38:7 98
40:15-24 134
40:15 126
41:1-34 134

Psalms
2 44
2:1-2 119, 164
2:6 143
2:9 200
18:3 115
18:6 79
18:10 61
18:12-16 61
19:10 110
23:1 91
28:8 71
29:10 63
33:2-3 70

33:3 70
33:3 70, 144
40:3 144
43:4 70
46:6 119
50:3 202
57:7-9 70
62:1 92
65:7 119
68:8 94
69:28 47
71:20 99
71:22 70
74:2 184
74:14 126
75:8 150
77:18 61
78:44 161
78:46 99
79:10 80
81:1-3 70
82:1 129
89:5-7 129
89:10 126
90 157
92:1-3 70
94:3 80
94:10-12 55
96:1 63, 70, 144
97:5 167
98:1 70, 119
98:4-6 70
104:2 59, 80
104:3 63
104:25-26 134
104:35 190
105:29 161
105:37 03
105:45 190
106 190
106:48 191
108:1-3 70
110:1 151
110:5-6 44
111:10 148
111-113 190
115:4 103
115:13 120
118:25 88

136:2-3 176
139:16 67
141:1 70
141:2 92
144:7 170
144:9 70, 144
146-50 190
147:7 70
148:1-6 191
148:7-14 191
149:1 144
150:3-5 70

Proverbs
3:11-12 55
5:3-4 96
8:13 148
8:22 53
24:12 232

Ecclesiastes
9:8 88

Isaiah
1:18 45
2:2 179
2:8 103
4:3 47
5:1 188
6 65
6:1-2 61, 64
6:1-4 160
6:2-3 61
6:3 64, 65
6:6 64, 94
6:8 68
11:1-16 207
11:1-10 69
11:1 235
11:6-9 207
11:10 235
11:14 44
13:9-10 95
13:10 97
14:12 98, 128
14:13-14 136
15:3 115
17:1 126
17:8 103

17:12 192
20:1-6 111, 222
20:2 115
21:3 125
21:9 181
22:10 115
22:15-25 48
23-24 181
23:1 182
23:15-16 181
23:16-17 168
23:47 181
24:8 188
24:18-20 95
24:21-22 126
24:23 143
25:6-8 196
25:8 91, 216
26:16–27:6 199
26:17-18 125
27:1 123, 126, 174
27:13 93
29:11 67
30:29 188
30:33 102
31:4 95, 143
34:5 172
34:9 102
35:10 216
37:3 125
37:36 128
40:2 185
40:4 167
40:9-10 148
40:11 91
40:25 48
40:31 131
42–53 69
42:10 70, 144
42:15 167
45:2 167
48:2 112
48:20 183
50:3 115
51:9 126
51:17-23 168
51:17 150
51:21 172
52:1 112

Index of Biblical and Other References

52:11 183
53:7 69
54:1 125
54:6-7 192
54:10 167
57:20 214
58:1 93
59:15-20 199
59:18 232
60:19-20 225
63:1-6 198
63:2-3 200
63:3 94, 153
65:16 52
65:17 213
65:20-25 207
65:20 207
66:6 161, 165
66:7-10 132
66:7-9 125
66:7 125, 132

Jeremiah
1:11 89
1:13 89
1:16 103
2:3 146
2:20-37 169
4:8 115
4:26-27 182
4:28 78, 81
6:24 125
7:20 161
7:32 202
9:10-12 182
9:15 96, 211
12:7 211
13:3-11 111, 222
13:21 125
13:27 169
14:31 125
15:2 137
16:18 185
17:10 232
19:6 202
22:5-6 182
22:14-5 181
22:23 125
23:18-22 129

24:13 89
25:6-7 103
25:10 189
25:15-38 150
25:30 107
27:1–28:16 222
28:7 148
28:27 182
28:63-64 188
30:6 125
31:16 91
31:33 215
32:30 103
32:40 148
36:2 67
47:2 170
48:25 69
49:36 84
50:8 183
50:29b 185
50-51 181
51:6 183
51:8 181
51:9 184
51:25 174, 179
51:37 181
51:45 183
51:63-64 188

Lamentations
1:15 153
2:10 187
3:19 96
4:5 172

Ezekiel
1 64
1:1 197
1:5-25 61
1:5-10 61
1:10 61
1:14, 16 64
1:16 64
1:20-21 65
1:22 63
1:24 144, 192
1:26 59
1:28 108
2:9 67

2:9-10 107, 110
2:10 67
3:17 136
6:9 170
6:14 182
7:8 161
8:10-11 94
9 84
9:2 159
9:3 181
9:8 161
9:9 161
10:1-22 61
10:2-3 94
10:4 181
10:8 181
10:9 94
10:16 62
10:19 181
14:19 161
14:21 79
16:15ff 169
16:23 170
16:37-39 54
20:8 161
20:13 161
20:21 161
20:25-27 146
21:31 161
22:22 161
23:25-26 179
24:3 111, 222
26–27 181
26:13 188
28:2 136
28:13 59
30:15 161
32:3 126
32:7 82
32:7-8 81, 95
34:23 91
37f. 116
37:3 89
37:27-28 90
37:27 215
38:5 209
38:19-20 116
38:20, 22 167
38:22 102

38–39 164, 209, 210
39:3 77
39:17 201
39:29 161
40–46 225
40:1-2 220
40:3–48:35 112
40:5 111
43:2 192
43:7 170
43:9 170
44:9 226
47:12 227
48:30-35 216
48:30-34 221

Daniel
2 182
2:31-45 119
2:35 179
2:45 119
2:47 176
3:4-6 141
4:26 206
4:31-32 108
5:7 172
5:16 172
5:29 172
7–9 139
7 123, 135
7:2 84
7:7-8 176
7:7 134
7:8 134
7:10 71
7:13 151, 152
7:20 69, 134, 176
7:21 136
7:22 69
7:23-27 78
7:23-28 138
7:24-26 139
7:24 138, 176
7:25 134, 136, 138
7:26-28 131
7:24 134
8:9-14 136, 138
8:10 98, 113
8:10-12 136

8:23-25 78, 138, 139
8:24 139
8:26 67
9 127
9:3 115
9:25-27 127, 138
9:26 127
9:27 113, 126, 128, 131, 132, 136, 139
10:5 159
10:6 192
10:16 136
11:4 199
11:36 134, 136
11:36-39 139
12 232
12:1 47, 49, 90, 109, 165, 212
12:2 47, 49
12:3 44
12:4 232
12:5-7 107
12:7 107, 109
12:9 107
12:10 46, 141
12:11 107, 114
12:12 87

Hosea
1:2 170
2:3 182
2:5 169
2:14 127
2:19 192
10:8 82
11:10 108
12:9 53

Joel
1:2–2:11 100
2:1-3 93
2:2 97
2:10 82
2:31 81, 95, 163
2:32 87, 143
3:2 164
3:2-17 153
3:12-14 154
3:3 152, 3

3:15 81, 82
3:16 108
3:19 182

Amos
1:2 108
3:7 59
3 108
5:18 97
7:8 89
8:2 89
9:3 126

Jonah
1:2 184
3:5-8 115

Micah
1:7 170
4:6-8 87
4:9 12
5:13 103
7:19 64

Nahum
1:6 82
3:4 169, 170

Habakkuk
1:2 80
1:8 97
2:20 79, 92

Zephaniah
1:7 92
1:14-16 81, 93, 95
2:13 182

Haggai
2:6-7 167
2:17 167
2:21 167

Zechariah
1:8-17 76
2:10 90
2:13 92
4:1-14 63
4:5 89

Index of Biblical and Other References 257

8:8 215
9:14 95
11:5 53
14:6-7 226
14:13 78

Malachi
1:2-3 182
3:6 212
3:2 82
4:5-6 118
4:5 114

APOCRYPHA AND
PSEUDEPIGRAPHA

1 Enoch
1:8 71
1:9 71
1:66 185
9:4 171
10:3 153
10:11-16 129
10:12 78
12:38 177
14:6 174
14:22 71
18:14 89, 126
18:15 89
19:1 103
21:3-6 126
21:6 89
21:10 89
22:7 89
22:3 89
22:9 89
23:4 89
24:25 220
25:3 89
34:3 84
34:23 91
38:5 177
38:96 177
39:4-9 151
39:11-14 64
40:1 71
40:2 109
40:7 129

45:4-5 213
45:55 58
47:3 67
53:1 54
53:3-5 151
53:3 101, 185
54:1 202
56:1 101, 151, 185
56:5-8 164
60:1-11 126
60:1 71
60:11-21 153
60:12-22 161
60:7-11,24 134
61:1 147
61:10 161
62:3-5 58
62:11 101, 151, 185
62:12 171
62:14 55
62:16 80
63:1 151, 185
66:1 101
71:3 109
71:6-8 59
71:8 71
71:9 71
76 84
81:1-2 67
86:1-3 126
88:1 205
88:3 126
89:71 67
90:2 212
90:9 69
90:12-19 164
90:35 69
90:37 69
91:12 177
97:8 53
97:9 53
98:12 177
99:4 119
99:7 103
106:19 67
107:1 67

2 Enoch
3:3 63

4:6 162
10 202
18:8-9 64
19:3-6 64
21:1-2 64
22:8 80
29:4-5 128
42:3-4 64

2 Esdras (4 Ezra)
2:42-47 143
8:25 176

2 Maccabees
2:4-7 40
2:7 120
2:29 141
3:24 116
5:14 29
7:13-14 190
11:8 61
12:34-5 174
13:4 177
13:17 224
14:4 88

Sirach
24:11 211
49:8 181

Tobit
3:17 101
12:7 19
12:11 19
13:18 190

Wisdom
2:22 109
4:7 151
18:3 109

NEW TESTAMENT

Matthew
2 126
3:11-12 152
4:1-11 170
4:4-10 135

4:5 112
4:8-9 119
4:15 112
5:2 135
5:6 90
5:22 202
7:15 140
8:11 71
8:12 97
8:26 218
9:23 188
10:5 112
10:18 110
11:2-6 109
11:13-19 109
11:14 114
13:45-46 223
16:12 40
17:17-19 100
19:28 55-56
21:31 161
22:2 192
22:16 48
24 75
24:3 75
24:9 112
24:12-13 75
24:14 78
24:15-16 128
24:15 131
24:24 76
24:29 75, 81, 82
24:30 75
24:31 75, 93, 95
24:42-44 165
25:13 46
25:41 129
26:29 196
27:51 95
27:53 112
28:3 61
28:18 73
29:28 206

Mark
1:14-15 109, 148
1:15 194
1:24 48
2:14 48

5:13 188
7:21-22 103
9:1 232
9:2 220
9:11 114
9:43 202
13:7-13 90
13:9 10
13:9 9
13:21-23 140
13:25 82
15:33 97
16:5 60

Luke
1:9 93
1:12 116
1:19 93
3:21-22 197
4:1-13 134
8:31 99, 205
10:18 98, 129
10:20 47
11:49 89
12:6 100
12:15-24 54
12:52 100
13:29 196
14:16-30 109
17:29 102, 202
18:23 109
22:24-30 229
22:28-30 71
22:30 55
22:31 129
24:47 112

John
1 1-14 199
1:3 199
1:9 225
2:18 233
2:23 140
3:2 140
3:19 225
3:32 120
4:4 91
4:4-15 218
4:14 91, 227

4:24 225
4:54 140
6:2 140
6:14 114
6:35 90
7:16-17 40
7:18 48
7:31 140
7:37-38 218
7:38 91
7:40 114
8:12-20 233
8:12 225
8:19 233
8:44-45 218
9:16 140
10:1-30 91
12:13 88
12:35 225
12:46-50 198
13:2 129
14 140
14:62 151
18:37 120
19:30 217
20:12 61
21:15-17 91

Acts
1:8 71
1:10 61
1:11 111, 222
2:19 95
7:41 103
7:44 120
7:56 197
8:35 135
10:11 197
16:14 41
16:40 41
19:17 116
20:6 100
21:9 42
24:1 100

Romans
1:1-2 103
1:3 235
1:14-17 71

Index of Biblical and Other References 259

1:16-20 236
1:18-32 103
1:21-25 103
1:28 103
2:6 232
3:9-18 119
8:19-22 213
10:7 99
12:19 80
13:9 103

1 Corinthians
1:8 44
1:24 89
2:7 89
3:8 119
6:2-3 206
6:9-10 226
6:20 146
7:23 146
7:29-31 231
8:9-11 43
1:14 103
1:16 88
1:18 175
11:3 129
11:27-29 43
11:32 55
12:28 41
14:7 70
14:19 100
15:24-25 90
15:52 93, 95
16:9 48
16:10-11 219
16:23 236

2 Corinthians
1:13 44
2:12 48
3:18 227
5:10 211
6:14-15 97
6:17 184
11:2 192
11:15 232
12:4 108, 144
13:14 236

Galatians
3:7 114
3:8 109
3:29 218
4:26 215
6:18 236

Ephesians
1:19-20 72
1:7 72, 88
2:2 129
2:6 136
2:13 88
2:13-17 71
3:10 89
4:11 42
5:27 192
5:32 192
6:10 72

Philippians
2:9-10 73
2:10 68
2:17 161
3:20 215
4:3 47
4:23 236

Colossians
1:13 97
1:15 53
1:18 53
2:1 53
2:3 72
2:4 53
2:15 53
2:16 53
3:1 136
4:3 48

1 Thessalonians
1:8 94
4:15 231
4:15-17 49,
4:16 93, 95
5:2 232
5:8 136

2 Thessalonians
2:1-12 49
2:3-9 139
2:3-4 139
2:3 109
2:4 135, 138
2:6 78
2:9-12 139
2:9 135, 138
3:18 136

1 Timothy
2:9 223
2:14 129
6:16 59

2 Timothy
1:7 219
2:19 84
4:6 161
4:14 232

Titus
3:5 233

Philemon
25 236

Hebrews
3:3 48
8:1-5 120
8:1-2 60
8:5 60
8:12 79
8:23-25 79
9:4 93
9:5 181
9:7 120
9:14 88, 146
9:23-24 60
9:24 120
10:19 88
10:22 233
11:10 215
12:5-6 55
12:22 215
12:23 47
12:26 93
13:14 215

James
1:27 46

1 Peter
1:17 54, 232
1:19 88, 146
3:9 102
7:9 54

2 Peter
1:21 230
3:9 231
3:10-13 213
3:13 226

1 John
1:2-3 53
1:7-10 218
1:7 88
2:18 139
2:22 138, 139

3:2 227
3:12 48
3:18 48
4:3 139
4:6 228
8:14 228
8:31-40 228

2 John
7 139

3 John
11 228

Jude
5 205
13 98
23 46

www.ingramcontent.com/pod-product-compliance
Lightning Source LLC
Chambersburg PA
CBHW022011300426
44117CB00005B/124